T0176693

**Intelligent Pervasive Computing Systems
for Smarter Healthcare**

Intelligent Pervasive Computing Systems for Smarter Healthcare

Arun Kumar Sangaiah and S. P. Shantharajah
VIT University
Vellore, India

Padma Theagarajan
Sona College of Technology
Salem, India

Registered Office(s)
John Wiley & Sons, Inc., 111 River Street, Hoboken, NJ 07030, USA

Editorial Office
111 River Street, Hoboken, NJ 07030, USA

For details of our global editorial offices, customer services, and more information about Wiley products visit us at www.wiley.com.

Wiley also publishes its books in a variety of electronic formats and by print-on-demand. Some content that appears in standard print versions of this book may not be available in other formats.

Library of Congress Cataloging-in-Publication Data

Names: Sangaiah, Arun Kumar, 1981- editor. | Shantharajah, S. P., 1972- editor. | Theagarajan, Padma, 1968- editor.
Title: Intelligent pervasive computing systems for smarter healthcare / Arun Kumar Sangaiah, VIT University, Vellore, India, S.P. Shantharajah, VIT University, Vellore, India, Padma Theagarajan, Sona College of Technology, Salem, India.
Description: First edition. | Hoboken, NJ : John Wiley & Sons, Inc., [2019] | Includes bibliographical references and index. |
Identifiers: LCCN 2019009752 (print) | LCCN 2019012900 (ebook) | ISBN 9781119438991 (Adobe PDF) | ISBN 9781119439011 (ePub) | ISBN 9781119438960 (hardcover)
Subjects: LCSH: Medical care–Data processing. | Ubiquitous computing. | Medical electronics.
Classification: LCC R859.7.U27 (ebook) | LCC R859.7.U27 I58 2019 (print) | DDC 610.285–dc23
LC record available at https://lccn.loc.gov/2019009752

Cover design by Wiley
Cover image: © ktsimage/Getty Images

Set in 10/12pt WarnockPro by SPi Global, Chennai, India

Printed in the United States of America

V10012479_080219

v

Contents

List of Contributors

Amudha Thangavel
Department of Computer
Applications
Bharathiar University
Coimbatore
India

Ponnuraman Balakrishnan
Department of Analytics, SCOPE
VIT Deemed University
Vellore
India

Angelo Brayner
Computing Science Department
Federal University of Ceará
Fortaleza
Brazil

Chandrasekaran Vellankoil Marappan
School of Advanced Sciences
VIT University
Vellore
India

Habiba Chaoui
Systems Engineering Laboratory
National School of Applied Sciences
Ibn Tofail University
Kenitra
Morocco

Ashraf Darwish
Faculty of Science
Helwan University
Cairo
Egypt

Deepa Ganesan
School of Advanced Sciences
VIT University
Vellore
India

Dinakaran Karunakaran
Department of Information
Technology
Saveetha Engineering College
Chennai
India

Sumathi Doraikannan
CSE
Malla Reddy Engineering College
JNTUH
Hyderabad
India

Younès El Bouzekri El Idrissi
Systems Engineering Laboratory
National School of Applied Sciences
Ibn Tofail University
Kenitra
Morocco

Fatna Elmendili
Systems Engineering Laboratory
National School of Applied Sciences
Ibn Tofail University
Kenitra
Morocco

Gowthambabu Karthikeyan
School of Computer Science and
Engineering
VIT University
Vellore
India

Aboul Ella Hassanien
Faculty of Computers and
Information
Cairo University
Cairo
Egypt

Jothilakshmi Rajendiran
Department of Physics
Veltech University
Chennai
India

Ramanathan Lakshmanan
School of Computer Science and
Engineering
Vellore Institute of Technology
Vellore
India

João Paulo Madeiro
Institute for Engineering and
Sustainable Development
University for the International
Integration of the Afro-Brazilian
Lusophony
Redenção
Brazil

Mary Mekala
School of Information Technology
and Engineering
VIT University
Vellore
India

José Maria Monteiro
Computing Science Department
Federal University of Ceará
Fortaleza
Brazil

Rui Silva Moreira
ISUS unit at FCT
University Fernando Pessoa
Porto, Portugal
INESC TEC and LIACC at FEUP
University of Porto
Porto
Portugal

Jayashree Nair
AIMS Institutes
Bangalore
India

Patitha Parameswaran
Department of Computer
Technology
MIT Campus, Anna University
Chennai
India

Padma T.
Sona College of Technology
Salem
India

Ricky Parmar
Dell EMC
Bangaluru
India

Deepalakshmi Perumalsamy
Department of CSE
Kalasalingam Academy of Research
and Education
Krishnankoil
India

Praba Bashyam
Department of Mathematics
SSN College of Engineering
Affiliated to Anna University
Chennai
India

Swarnalatha Purushotham
School of Computer Science and
Engineering
Vellore Institute of Technology
Vellore
India

Pethru Raj
Site Reliability Engineering (SRE)
Division
Reliance Jio Infocomm. Ltd. (RJIL)
Bangalore
India

Rajakumar Krishnan
School of Computer Science and
Engineering
VIT
Vellore
India

Rajeswari Rajendran
Department of Computer
Applications
Bharathiar University
Coimbatore
India

Nersisson Ruban
School of Electrical Engineering
VIT University
Vellore
India

Stela Vitorino Sampaio
Department of Computer Science
and Engineering
Heart Hospital Dr. Carlos Alberto
Studart
Fortaleza
Brazil

Sangeetha Archunan
Department of Computer
Applications
Bharathiar University
Coimbatore
India

Sasikala Ramasamy
School of Computer Science and
Engineering
VIT University
Vellore
India

Gehad Ismail Sayed
Faculty of Computers and
Information
Cairo University
Cairo
Egypt

Prabha Selvaraj
CSE
Malla Reddy Institute of Engineering
and Technology
JNTUH
Secunderabad
India

Kannan Shanmugam
Department of Computer Science
and Engineering
Malla Reddy Engineering College
Hyderabad
India

Rajalakshmi Shenbaga Moorthy
Department of Computer Science
and Engineering
St. Joseph's Institute of Technology
Anna University
Chennai
India

Christophe Soares
ISUS unit at FCT
University Fernando Pessoa
Porto
Portugal

Pedro Sobral
ISUS unit at FCT
University Fernando Pessoa
Porto
Portugal

Rajkumar Soundrapandiyan
School of Computer Science and
Engineering
Vellore Institute of Technology
Vellore
India

Karthik Subburathinam
Department of Computer Science
and Engineering
SNS College of Technology
Chennai
India

Suresh Kumar Nagarajan
School of Computer Science and
Engineering
VIT University
Vellore
India

José Torres
ISUS unit at FCT
University Fernando Pessoa
Porto
Portugal

Valarmathie Palanisamy
Department of Computer Science
and Engineering
Saveetha Engineering College
Anna University
Chennai
India

Navya Venkatamari
Department of ECE
Kalasalingam Academy of Research
and Education
Krishnankoil
India

Krishnamoorthy Venkatesan
Department of Mathematics
College of Natural Sciences
Arba Minch University
Arba Minch
Ethiopia

Veeramuthu Venkatesh
School of Computing
SASTRA Deemed University
Thanjavur
India

Vishnu Priya
Department of Computer Science
and Engineering
P.M.R. Engineering College
Anna University
Chennai
India

1

Intelligent Sensing and Ubiquitous Systems (ISUS) for Smarter and Safer Home Healthcare

Rui Silva Moreira[1,2], José Torres[1], Pedro Sobral[1], and Christophe Soares[1]

[1] *ISUS unit at FCT, University Fernando Pessoa, Porto, Portugal*
[2] *INESC TEC and LIACC at FEUP, University of Porto, Porto, Portugal*

1.1 Introduction to Ubicomp for Home Healthcare

The concept of ubiquitous computing (ubicomp), coined by Mark Weiser in 1991, focused on having computation in any regular "smart" object (Weiser, 1991). The key idea of ubicomp (aka pervasive computing (Satyanarayanan, 2001)) is the use of embedded technology everywhere and disappearing in background, i.e. not requiring any extra cognitive effort to use such "augmented" objects. Later, in 1999, Kevin Ashton devised the term Internet of things (IoT), which envisioned the interconnection of any physical object through the Internet (Ashton, 2009). Such concept opens the door for sensing massive amounts of data into cloud databases (cf. big data) and exposing general environment contexts to a multitude of analytic and automation tools. The ability to reasoning about human context environments allows also the orchestration of such environments by pushing back actuation over physical objects. Both ubicomp and IoT propose basically similar seminal ideas and are considered synonyms of physical computing.

It is clear that ubicomp or IoT technologies can tackle the growing need for ambient assisted living (AAL) environments, which are mainly driven by the aging of the world population. This phenomenon is usually associated with chronic or disabling diseases, such as memory loss, disorientation and loss hazards, polymedication coping, difficulties in adhering to clinical treatments, unintended erroneous medication intake, adherence to therapeutic exercises, etc. These problems pose several difficulties on executing even simple daily life tasks. However, some of these issues may be addressed and mitigated by the integration of ubicomp home support systems specially developed and tailored for the elderly or those with special needs, thus promoting and allowing outpatient and home healthcare. Therefore, this work advocates that there are

Intelligent Pervasive Computing Systems for Smarter Healthcare, First Edition.
Arun Kumar Sangaiah, S.P. Shantharajah, and Padma Theagarajan.

several key capabilities that must be provided so that AAL environments may be automated from independently developed commercial off-the-shelf (COTS) systems. These key capabilities are as follows:

Processing and sensing issues: Ubicomp systems sense and explore any knowledge about the context they operate in. The context refers to information that may be used to characterize the situation of an entity (Abowd et al., 1999) and may refer to user, physical, computational, and time context (Chen and Kotz, 2000). Sensors are fundamental to collect data from any environment; however, raw sensor data most of the times is not enough to provide useful high level context information. Therefore, raw data must be processed into more high level information constructs. For example, use the signal of Bluetooth Low Energy (BLE) beacons to estimate distances and calculate the location of devices; use a three-axis accelerometer data time series to estimate the posture of a person (e.g. fall, run, walk, stand, lay, sit).

Integration and management issues: The deployment of COTS systems in the same AAL household has two fundamental concerns: (i) The standard interconnection and orchestration of devices for enabling seamless interactions and automation. The integration of COTS systems could be achieved through the use of local or edge middleware frameworks such as openHAB or Simple Network Management Protocol (SNMP)-like tools. Another important trend is the integration through cloud services that glue together heterogeneous deployed systems. (ii) The secure or safe integration of COTS systems that are developed by independent vendors without integration concerns, thus not planned to be deployed together. These systems must coexist in the same ecosystem without causing crossed malfunctions. For example, a drug dispenser (DD) periodically issuing a sound alarm until the user takes a prescribed medicine could suffer a functional interference from an entertainment system that simultaneously could be playing a movie or TV series. When two or more systems compete for a shared medium (e.g. user attention), that may cause a behavior interference (e.g. prevent user from taking medication).

Communication and coordination issues: Home healthcare COTS systems play an important role in the deployment of AAL smart spaces. However, it is important to guarantee agile and affordable deployment mechanisms without preinstalled communication infrastructures. Wireless mesh technologies are therefore fundamental to enable the growth and widespread of such ubiquitous systems. Most of smart spaces use body and environmental sensor motes deployed together without the need for fixed infrastructures. These modules communicate through heterogeneous wireless technologies, thus typically requiring bridging gateways equipped with multiple shields [e.g. ZigBee, Bluetooth (BT), Wi-Fi, General Packet Radio Service (GPRS)], thus enabling simple and adaptable wireless topologies. These agile solutions allow easy data collection and storage for further analytical treatment and consultation by healthcare providers and also control interactions and trigger real-time alerts in dangerous situations.

Intelligence and reasoning issues: The representation of context information is fundamental in AAL systems. It is necessary to use knowledge representation models and tools that enable to reason about the premises and conditions about the user and its surroundings. Such tools may use typically deductive or inductive processes. This section proposes the use and combination of both types of reasoning. The former, deductive reasoning, uses the Semantic Web Rule Language (SWRL) that combines OWL and Rule Markup Language (RuleML) to allow the definition of Horn-like rules. These rules specify a set of state conditions related by boolean operators that will allow the inference of other states or terms. The latter, inductive reasoning, uses machine learning (ML) algorithms that typically capture/learn patterns on sets of observations (training sets) and then generalize those patterns to classify new observations.

The remaining sections will revisit each of these key research issues on separate sections. For every topic, the respective section details one or two example project outcomes related with the research solutions typically applied to home healthcare use cases. Section 1.2 addresses the aspects related with processing raw data sensor signals to filter noise and build higher level useful information about the context of home healthcare scenarios and users profiles (e.g. activity, location). Section 1.3 focuses on the safe integration and management of heterogeneous ubicomp systems deployed together on the same household without interfering with each other. Section 1.4 is concerned with the communication and networking aspects that are faced when deploying ubicomp systems on premises without available connection infrastructures. Section 1.5 centers the analysis on different approaches for addressing reasoning in AAL scenarios. Each of these sections presents real use case solutions and examples applied to home healthcare scenarios. Finally, Section 1.6 summarizes the major contributions of this chapter by highlighting the main results of each section.

1.2   Processing and Sensing Issues

Working with hardware sensors and in general with physical computing is not an easy task. Most of the time sensors require careful calibration to the environment in order to adjust their readings to the reality. All sensor readings are also subject to noise. In many cases they require intensive signal processing techniques and statistical treatment in order to accurately represent the environment. In the following sections two application scenarios in the context of IoT are presented. The first application, presented in Section 1.2.1, deals with ambient monitoring and user activity detection for AAL scenarios (Goncalves et al., 2009). The second application, presented in Section 1.2.2, takes advantage of BLE beacons to enable indoor location and tracking scenarios in smart spaces (Gomes et al., 2018). Both examples deal with the sensing issues stated before. Moreover, the algorithms used to gather and process useful information from raw sensor data are crucial for the performance of both applications.

1.2.1   Remote Patient Monitoring in Home Environments

As the average span of life increases, people at the age of 65 or older are the fastest-growing population in the world. According to the projections of a Eurostat report (Giannakouris, 2008), the median age of the European population will rise from 40.4 years in 2008 to 47.9 years in 2060. The share of people aged 65 years or over in the total population is projected to increase from 17.1% to 30.0%, and the number is projected to rise from 84.6 million in 2008 to 151.5 million in 2060. The healthcare system in the developed countries is growing under pressure and will not be efficient enough to provide a reliable service on the health treatment for this aging population (Venkatasubramanian et al., 2005).

A smart home-care system can hold the essential elements of diagnostic used in medical facilities. It extends healthcare from traditional clinic or hospital settings to the patient's home. A smart home-care system benefits the healthcare providers and their patients, allowing 24/7 physical monitoring, reducing labor costs, and increasing efficiency. Wearable sensors can notice even small changes in vital signs that humans might overlook (Stankovic et al., 2005).

There are some projects for remote medical monitoring (Jurik and Weaver, 2008). The following are some of the most relevant ones:

- *CodeBlue*: It is a wireless sensor network intended to assist the triage process for monitoring victims in emergencies and disaster scenarios (Welsh et al., 2004).
- *AMON*: It encapsulates many sensors into one wrist-worn device that is connected directly to a telemedicine center via a GSM network, allowing direct contact with the patient (Anliker et al., 2004).
- *AlarmNet*: It continuously monitors assisted-living and independent-living residents. The system integrates information from sensors in the living areas as well as body sensors (Wood et al., 2006).

The main goal of this project is to develop an activity monitoring system with the following requirements such as design simplicity, reliability, and low cost and with the less possible user interaction as possible. The system has two elements: a corporal device and a wireless gateway. The corporal device detects the patient's vital signs as well as its activity. All the data gathered from the sensors is sent over a wireless point-to-point link to the gateway. The data can then be sent to a local WEB service or to the cloud.

1.2.1.1 Hardware Device

All system components are built using low-cost hardware. Size and shape of the corporal device were considered to improve the device usability. Sensor raw data is processed in the device and then transmitted to the gateway. For the device data processing and control, an Arduino Wee was used. The wireless link between the device and the gateway is established using a point-to-point wireless link configured on MaxStream XBee pro radios. Temperature sensing is done using a DALLAS DS18B20-PAR 1-wire Parasite-Power digital thermometer. For patient activity monitoring the system uses a Freescale Semiconductor MMA7260QT ±1.5g-6g Three Axis Low-g Micromachined Accelerometer.

The corporal device should be placed above the patient's right hip, pointing up, because this is the location in the human body with less position changes during activity. The accelerometer measures the acceleration on a 3D axis of that given point. The digital temperature sensor measures skin temperature, so for a more reliable body temperature, the sensor must be placed in the patient's armpit. The corporal device transmits the current patient activity and body temperature (Figure 1.1).

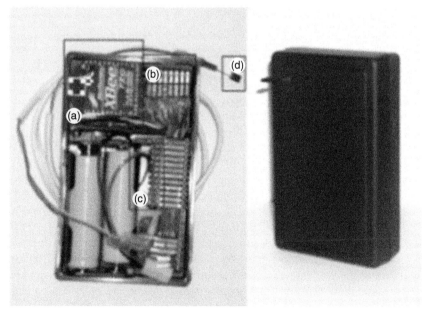

Figure 1.1 Corporal device. (a) XBee pro radio, (b) accelerometer, (c) microcontroller, and (d) digital temperature sensor.

1.2.1.2 Sensed Data Processing and Analysis

After a series of tests, where the volunteered subjects performed their daily routine activities, the following main activities can be identified by the accelerometer: standing, sitting, walking, running, laying down (sleeping), and falling.

It is possible to determine if the patient is sleeping in the back position, side position, or stomach position. Although this is not a particular important distinction for monitoring elderly patients, it can be important for monitoring infant's sleeping position. For example, an infant sleeping on his stomach has up to 12.9 times more probability to die from sudden infant death syndrome (SIDS); hence, forcing children to sleep on their backs reduces the incidence of SIDS by 40% (Baker et al., 2007).

Detecting a fall is a two-class decision problem; there may be positive samples for a fall and negative data for non-fall. While the positive samples have a lot of commonness, negative samples are extremely diversified. So, for training a classifier correctly, a lot of negative samples are required, and even so a real fall could be classified into a doubtful dataset (Zhang et al., 2006). Processing all this data takes a lot of processing power and wastes a lot of battery power. These requirements are not suitable for this system. So, the goal was to find an algorithm to accurately classify activities in real time without heavy hardware demands. In Section 1.5 a different approach to this system is presented in which several ML techniques were tested in order to detect user activity from the accelerometer data.

For determining the activity pattern values, the volunteered subjects performed their activities, and we recorded the raw accelerometer data into the database. One value for each axis was reported by the accelerometer every 100 ms. After several runs, 200 values for each activity were selected. The analysis of the graphics generated by the stored data shows that single values have no meaning; sets of values, however, could be used to determine pattern activities. Nevertheless, different activities may sometimes produce similar sets of values, so it was important to find another characteristic that, combined with the set of values, could identify, without any doubt, a given activity. Further graphical analysis shows that the value of each axis could also determine an activity. Combining both parameters the current activity can be accurately determined.

The next challenge was to decide how large should be the set of values; if it is too small, it will not allow to identify a pattern, but if it is too large, the risk of overlapping different activity patterns increases. So a set of values cannot be longer than the fastest occurrence of an activity. In fact, the activity that takes less time to occur is a fall (about one second). Based on this, we selected a set of 10 values. Figures 1.2 and 1.3 show a sample of the graphics for walking and falling; the fall occurs only between readings 33 and 43; after that the volunteer subject lies down on his stomach.

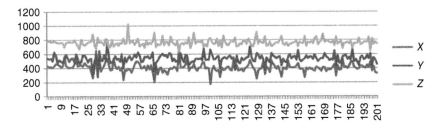

Figure 1.2 Walking accelerometer raw data.

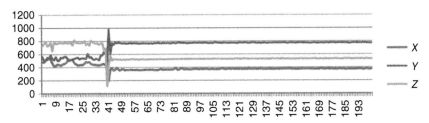

Figure 1.3 Fall accelerometer raw data.

A formula was needed for transforming each set of values into a single value without losing its meaning. The statistical variance was the best way to do it, but calculating the variance for the set of values of each axis would give us three distinct values. Hence, the average between these values would give us a value for activity indicator (VAI). The variance and VAI formula are shown in Eqs. (1.1) and (1.2):

$$S^2 = \frac{1}{n-1} \sum_{i=1}^{n} (x_i - \bar{x})^2 \tag{1.1}$$

$$\text{VAI} = \frac{(Sx^2 + Sy^2 + Sz^2)}{3} \tag{1.2}$$

The accelerometer values vary from subject to subject, and it is impossible, for example, to walk exactly the same way all the time. A list of range values for each activity was needed. Therefore using the VAI formula and the raw data previously acquired, Table 1.1 was built.

Table 1.1 shows that sit and laying down activities have the same VAI range. In these cases the axis values are used to classify the activity. With this definition most activities can be well identified. Fall detection requires a different approach. Sometimes running is misidentified as fall, and a fall may be misidentified as running. To solve this problem we added to the algorithm an activity matrix that incorporates known situations in which a fall occurs, e.g. if someone is running and in the next second is lying in his stomach, it is feasible to say

Table 1.1 Max and min VAI values for each activity.

	Stand, sit, laying down	Walk	Run	Fall
Min	0	450	50 000	15 000
Max	120	5 000	—	48 000

he suffered a fall. In order to correlate the past and present activities, a matrix was defined. The matrix is composed by two past activities, the activity to analyze, two future activities, and the activity we wish to identify. In real time an array is filled with the activities identified by the accelerometer readings. This array has two past activities, the "present" activity to analyze, and two "future" activities. The array is then compared with the matrix. If we have a match with a sequence of events in the matrix, then the algorithm outputs the corresponding activity. If we do not have a match, the algorithm decides based on the single window of data for the "present" activity. In reality, the detection has a delay of three seconds, because we need to wait for two more future readings before making a decision. After the use of the known scenario matrix, the fall detection improved from 30% to 60%, and adding more known cases to the matrix will improve even more the detection. However, it can cause some false positive detection. Running activity detection has a rate of 70% accuracy, and this number can be improved by adding known case for running to the matrix. All the other activities have 95% detection accuracy. However, when tested on an elderly subject, and being that our main objective, due to their degraded motor skills, the activity detection improves for near 100%.

1.2.2 Indoor Location Using Bluetooth Low Energy Beacons

Localization systems currently have a high accuracy and suppress various needs in our daily lives. When it comes to location systems, the best known is the global positioning system (GPS). This system uses signals sent by satellites, and with the appropriate number of signals, the device with a GPS receiver can with high precision estimate the current location coordinate (Kaplan and Hegarty, 2006). A different challenge is trying to estimate the location inside closed spaces where systems that rely on satellite reception are unable to operate due to the lack of coverage. For this purpose there is the need to take advantage of other technologies (Namiot, 2015; Becvarik and Devetsikiotis, 2016). One example is the BT technology that, after version 4.0, includes a low power version called Bluetooth Low Energy that can be used for indoor location systems. In this section we present an approach to indoor location estimation using BLE beacons. These are small and energy-efficient devices that transmit small data packets that can be interpreted by intelligent devices whenever they are within reach. BLE beacons are used in different contexts. A very common scenario is their use in advertising where they present detailed information about a product on client's mobile devices when they are nearby. These devices are also used to search for lost objects. Once a beacon is attached to an object, it is possible through a mobile application to hear the BLE signals and thus to know if the object is in the vicinity of the user.

1.2.2.1 Bluetooth Low Energy

BLE technology is specified in Gupta (2016). The advertising mode on the BLE standard allows a very short message transmission in order to save energy. Those messages can be used for a device to detect the proximity of a specific location based on the received signal strength indicator (RSSI). The lightweight protocol stack allows integration with existing BT technology; long battery life, easy maintenance, and good signal coverage are very important factors to take into account. It is a recent technology whose characteristics make it very attractive for indoor location projects (Faragher and Harle, 2014, 2015).

BLE beacons are small portable devices that consist of a combination of electronic components inserted into a small circuit board. These devices use BLE technology to transmit data in the form of BT frames at predefined intervals. These signals include information about the beacon, allowing device identification, and can trigger certain predefined actions on the client device. Communication is unidirectional, from beacon to the receiving equipment. When a communication between the beacon and the mobile device is established, one of two possible actions can happen.

- *Passive*: The information that the communication has been established is simply stored on the mobile device.
- *Active*: Communication causes a particular application to be started on the mobile device or acts on an activity in an application prepared to deal with the events and signals of the beacons.

1.2.2.2 Distance Estimation

The distance estimation layered architecture is shown in Figure 1.4. The data collection process is responsible for capturing the frames emitted by the beacon device. It is necessary to perform the calibration process for the client device because the RSSI readings are affected by its hardware and software configuration. In the RSSI signal processing layer, several algorithms and statistical methods are applied to the raw data values in order to improve the accuracy of the distance estimation. Finally, the distance calculation process is responsible for calculating the distance between the beacon device and the mobile equipment.

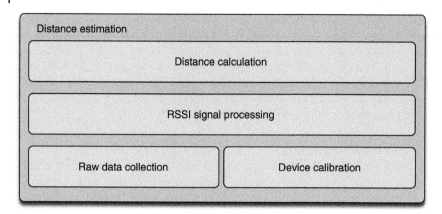

Figure 1.4 Distance estimation layered architecture.

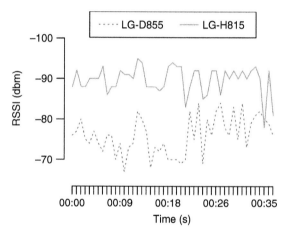

Figure 1.5 RSSI readings for two LG phones on the same conditions.

The distance calculation layer receives real-time RSSI values affected by signal reflections, obstacles, and even interference from other radio communication signals (Seybold, 2005). However, it was expected that mobile devices, subject to the same conditions, would capture the same number of beacon frames with close RSSI values. This is not true as shown in Figure 1.5. The RSSI readings for the BLE beacon frames on the mobile device are influenced by the radio chipset and its configuration. For example, some vendors reduce the BLE beacon receiving rate in order to save battery. In this context, it was necessary to create a calibration process in order to adapt the distance estimation to each equipment.

Each time a frame is captured by the mobile device, the BT chipset measures the strength of the received signal returning an RSSI value. One of the other fields present in all captured frames is the txPower, which indicates the power

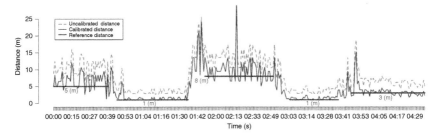

Figure 1.6 Calibrated vs. uncalibrated distance calculation.

used in the transmission of the beacon. The propagation of the radio-frequency (RF) signal varies considerably depending on the distance, building materials, interference sources, etc.

The equipment calibration is performed as follows:

- Calculate the mode of the RSSI values received for n known distances: 0.5, 1, 2, 3, 4, 5, 6, 7, 8, 9, 10, 12 m from the beacon. For each of the n distances, m samples are received. During the calibration process we used fifty samples for each distance ($m = 50$).
- For each of the n distances, calculate

$$\text{ratio}[i] = \frac{\text{mode}[i]}{\text{txPower}} \tag{1.3}$$

- Calculate the potential regression where independent values (x) are given by n ratios and dependent values (y) are given by the (n) distances.

The results of applying the calibration process on a mobile phone (LG D855) is presented in Figure 1.6. We can see that the calibrated line shows much better accuracy on estimating the distance than the uncalibrated raw RSSI values.

One way of calculating the distance estimation based on the RSSI of the received signal is to calculate a power regression taking into account parameters fitted during the calibration process. The calculation is done through a nonlinear model represented by a power function:

$$\text{distance} = a * \frac{\text{RSSI}^b}{\text{txPower}} \tag{1.4}$$

The regression algorithm returns the appropriate constants a and b to be used in Eq. (1.4) for the equipment used in the calibration process. In order to filter the noise from the samples received in real time by the mobile device while the user moves around the smart space, an algorithm was developed that takes into account the maximum movement speed for a person (walking or running) and the time interval between consecutive beacons. Considering that a person can reach a maximum of 2 m/s in the movement, we can discard values that determine a distance greater than possible for that speed in a certain period of time.

Equation (1.5) is used to determine the acceptable distance for the movement of a person inside a building:

$$\text{Distance}_{\text{max}} = \Delta t * 2 \text{ m/s}$$
$$\Delta t = t_{\text{rssi}} - t_{\text{rssi}-1} \tag{1.5}$$

where t_{rssi} is the instant of time when the device received the beacon and $t_{\text{rssi}-1}$ is the time instant of the previously received beacon. If the difference between the distance determined by the RSSI value read at the instant t_{rssi} and the distance determined by the RSSI value read at the instant $t_{\text{rssi}-1}$ is greater than the acceptable distance, that value is discarded, since it would indicate that the person would have moved faster than 2 m/s, which is considered to be unlikely. In case the value is discarded, the $t_{\text{rssi}-1}$ time instant is not updated and is used in the following calculations. If the algorithm discards consecutive signals, the time window Δt increases because $t_{\text{rssi}-1}$ is not updated. This allows the algorithm to adapt to unforeseen circumstances very quickly and has very satisfactory results in mobility scenarios. The ignored RSSI values are stored in a data structure, and a moving average with these values is calculated. The distance is calculated with the average of the last three filtered values. The algorithm is presented in Figure 1.7.

The comparison of moving average algorithm with the raw data RSSI values is presented in Figure 1.8 where it is clear that the distance estimation becomes much more accurate and stable. Another important feature of the moving average algorithm is its adaptability to motion. In Figure 1.8 four reference distances (1, 3, 5, 8 m) are represented, and the mobile equipment is at the same distance during the reference lines and moves in the interval between them. As can be seen, the graph shows the smoothing of the received signal that is reflected in the calculated distance as well as the adaptation of the algorithm to the movement.

The smoothing of the received values aims to reduce the distance estimation error. As shown in Figure 1.9, the application of the moving average algorithm decreases the variance of the calculated distances. As we move away from the beacon, the instability of the received signal increases as does the error of the distance. Smoothing the signal improves the calculation behavior as shown in the graph.

Having a good distance prediction algorithm using BLE beacons will enable the development of many interesting applications on a smart space. There is ongoing work to apply this results in two areas: (i) developing an indoor navigation system where the user using a mobile application installed in the smartphone can navigate inside a complex building (our test bed is the University Hospital where we can navigate patients to their medical appointment place) and (ii) developing a high value asset tracking system where the location of important equipment is always known (our test bed is also in University Hospital tracking some portable expensive medical equipment).

Figure 1.7 Moving average algorithm.

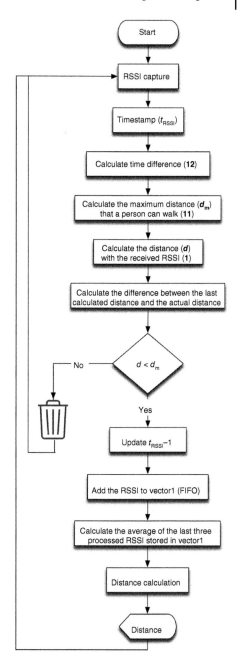

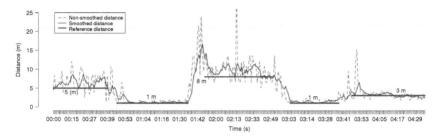

Figure 1.8 Moving average algorithm results.

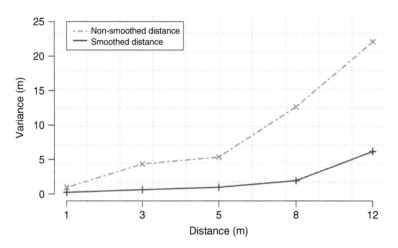

Figure 1.9 Improving error variance with moving average algorithm.

1.3 Integration and Management Issues

In the context of AAL systems and particularly safe home healthcare environments (Chen and Kotz, 2000; Chen, 2005), the integration of heterogeneous
ubiquitous systems is fundamental for being able to easily monitor and orches-
trate deployed COTS systems. This work advocates two forms of integration:
(i) via local or edge open hubs (e.g. openHAB or SNMP based) offering middleware frameworks for the automation of home environments (such solutions
are agnostic in terms of supported COTS system's vendors and technologies)
and (ii) via the use of cloud services that require connections between the home
premises and the cloud infrastructure. This section reports our experiences
on implementing home-care scenarios based on both types of approaches.
Section 1.3.1 reports the use of several cloud services to manage the integration
of a DD system together with a mobile application, both developed for improving the autonomy of outpatient users. Section 1.3.2 reports an SNMP-based

integration of COTS systems for dealing with behavior interferences among such systems. Both projects are clear demonstrators of the deployment and integration of smart and secure home healthcare environments.

1.3.1 Cloud-Based Integration of Personal Healthcare Systems

The integration of ubiquitous and mobile systems through the cloud will be fundamental in a multiparty response to outpatient users. This section reports the use of two systems that have been developed and integrated through the cloud to improve and mitigate the problems of lack of memory and disorientation associated with aging: (i) DD, specially developed to be integrated into a service cloud-based architecture, and (ii) PerUbiAssis Android app, integrating on the smartphone the management of the DD together with other monitoring features, by taking advantage of a panoply of cloud services [cf. calendar, maps, time sync, mail, and Voice over IP (VoIP)]. There are several projects and products involving the use of ubiquitous technologies for home-care support (Murtaza et al., 2006; Chaudhry et al., 2011; Lim et al., 2008; Fischer, 2008; Soares et al., 2012). These solutions focus on improving people's daily quality of life (e.g. cognitive stimulation, support alerts and task organization, mnemonics for management of daily routines, etc.). In addition, there are market solutions (Choi et al., 2006; Henricksen et al., 2005) typically addressing drug dispensary and treatment adherence problems. However, most focus on the specific functional aspects rather than on higher levels of integration with other systems and services. Hence, it is important to address the integration concerns in the genesis of COTS systems to facilitate future interoperation and coordination. For example, the medication dispensary prototype operation, scheduling, and alerts are coordinated through Google Calendar and SMS services; the PerUbiAssis Android app uses the smartphone communication interfaces (cf. Wi-Fi and BT) to interact with various cloud services (cf. Maps, Calendar, Contacts) and the DD to coordinate the user's medicine intake and other daily activities and alerts (Figure 1.10).

The DD prototype was built on the Arduino Mega platform and uses a set of hardware modules (cf. GSM/GPRS and BT BlueSMiRF shields, LCD, etc.). The initialization of the dispensary lasts about twenty seconds, time required for GSM/GPRS registration and sync with smartphone, via BT or SMS. In the latter case, the DD sends an SMS to the smartphone and waits for the automatic response, syncing date/time with the operator's messaging service. Calendar sync between Arduino and Android app may also use BT. The schedule information is stored in the Arduino EEPROM, and the current medicine intake info is placed on LCD. Reaching the next dose time, it rotates the medicine cup and triggers a series of beeps. The user must press the button to confirm the dose and stop the warning sound. For missed intakes, the DD rotates back to a rest position and an alert SMS is sent to caregiver.

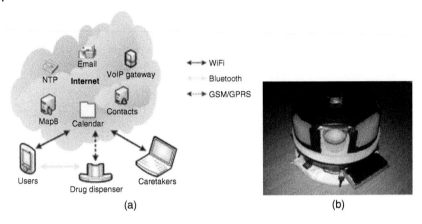

Figure 1.10 (a) Cloud services for integration of COTS systems (b) DD prototype.

The PerUbiAssis app uses the Amarino API [4] for BT linking with the DD Arduino that uses the MeetAndroid library. The main functionalities focuses on monitoring the elderly's location and the interaction with the DD: visualize current and relative location of elderly and caregivers; show return path to home or caregiver's address, in manual or automatic mode; manage daily activities and send SMS alerts when the security perimeter is exceeded or a missed task is detected; keep a history of elderly's locations; and configure the application, namely, the refresh rate of the map, the selection of caregivers, the definition of security perimeter, the activation of alerts by SMS, etc.

During initialization the operating conditions are checked (cf. status of data links and GPS state). An SMS is then sent to contacts marked as caregivers to check their availability to follow the elderly. Each caregiver will have to respond with a predefined SMS to be considered in the list of available caregivers. One of the main functionalities of the application is the visualization of the elderly location in relation to available caregiver.

The application maintains the elderly location history, and whenever surpassing the secure perimeter, an SMS alert is triggered for the nearest available caregiver. The application also allows the elderly to return to comfort zone, by routing him/her to the nearest available caregiver. The app also allows managing daily activities scheduled in the agenda, i.e. prescribed medicines and tasks. These tasks are considered accomplished when the elderly confirms its execution. Any unconfirmed and out-of-date task will result in an SMS alert to warn the caretaker.

Regarding evaluation, a set of predefined tasks was planned in order to assess the integration and health support provided by the DD and PerUbiAssis app. The application was set up in automatic mode and medication (placeholder placebos) was loaded according to a schedule with two tasks. Tests were performed by users not involved in the development and focusing on the fulfillment of tasks.

1.3.2 SNMP-Based Integration and Interference Free Approach to Personal Healthcare

The SNMP is the standard protocol for managing network devices. This section proposes to generalize the use of SNMP for getting/setting the functional state of COTS systems deployed in the same physical environment. Such systems are developed by independent vendors and, without integration concerns, thus may lead to unplanned interactions between them. This motivates the need for exposing the functional behavior of COTS systems to enable open integration and management. Knowing the expected behavior of devices allows to check if they perform correctly or any have malfunctions due to functional interferences from other systems.

The proposed approach use of graphs for representing all known state transitions of COTS systems, i.e. graph of expected states (GoES) (see Figures 1.11 and 1.12). Interestingly, previous work by Moreira et al. (2016) demonstrates that the GoES may be automatically built using unsupervised learning algorithms. In addition, the graph representation allows also identifying which media are affected by each state and vice versa (see Figure 1.12). Thus, whenever a given state does not occur as expected, it is possible to identify which states from other COTS systems may be interfering through a shared medium. For example, if both a DD and a VoIP phone are competing for the user attention (awareness), then a functional interference occurs, and the user may miss the medicine intake because it was dealing with the VoIP call. Hence, observing the occurring states enable us to identify the causes of interferences and trigger planned corrective actions (e.g. alarms/warning).

The runtime behavior introspection of COTS systems is possible through the use of an SNMP-based reflective architecture (Figure 1.13) (Moreira et al., 2012). COTS systems (user included) must have an associated SNMP agent

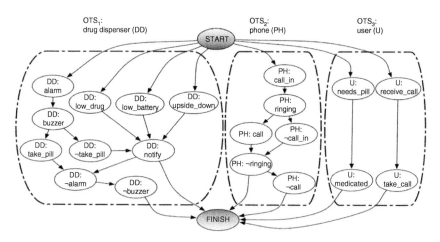

Figure 1.11 Graphs and media: SHC test graphs.

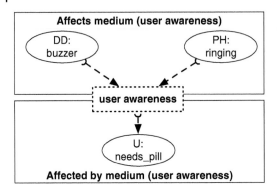

Figure 1.12 Graphs and media: shared medium user awareness.

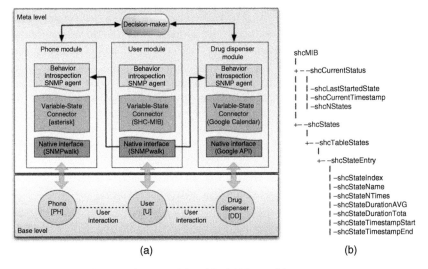

Figure 1.13 SHC SNMP architecture (a) and SHC-MIB tree (b).

responsible for storing system state information and making it available through the SNMP protocol. The Variable-State Connector is responsible for processing data from the Native Interface and the current state from the SNMP agent, associating/triggering a new state. The Variable-State Connector is COTS system specific and knows which variables are associated with possible states exposed by the SNMP agent. The connector offers a common set of information for state behavior introspection regardless of COTS system. This info is composed of current and historic data. The former data holds ongoing state and timestamp information; the later historic data comprises the following: (i) the number of times each state was active, (ii) the total time spent on each state, (iii) the timestamp of the last time each state started, and (iv) the timestamp of the last time each state ended. This info is stored on a management information base (MIB) – see Figure 1.13. The shcMIB object is the root of SHC-MIB. Inside, it has two other objects: shcCurrentStatus and shcStates. These objects are groups of variables that define the current status and the statistics of every state, respectively. The object shcCurrentStatus contains (i) shcLastStartedState, which is an index of the last started state in the shcTableStates table; (ii) shcCurrentTimestamp, which is the timestamp of the last state transition stored; and (iii) shcNStates, which gives the number of states of the COTS system.

The SNMP agent was developed under Debian GNU/Linux with the C NetSNMP agent development libraries (cf. netsnmpagent, netsnmphelpers, netsnmpmibs, and netsnmp). When the agent starts, it calls the initData function that initiates all the objects in the SHC-MIB, specially the shcTableStates, whose size depends on the number states. The Variable-State Connector communicates with the SNMP agent through the getData and setData functions. The getData function has two arguments, the object identifier (OID) and the OID length, and returns a pointer to a shcRetrievedData structure that contains a pointer to a netsnmp vardata structure, the data type, and length, making it easy to operate with SNMP libraries. The setData function receives three arguments: a pointer to a shcRetrievedData structure, the OID, and the OID length. This function stores the data in the corresponding OID and returns an integer, indicating whether it was successful or not. The MIBs for the SNMP agents use the Abstract Syntax Notation One (ASN.1) (ITU-T Recommendation, 2008), and so does the SHC-MIB.

The evaluation of this SNMP-based reflective approach was performed on a few home healthcare scenarios (Moreira et al., 2016; Soares et al., 2012). One scenario has a DD, VoIP phone, and a user (i.e. all graphs from Figure 1.11). At runtime, the decision maker used the SNMP agents for introspecting ongoing states and built the graph of observed states (GoOS). This graph was then compared against the expected states (cf. GoES). This enabled to detect the causes of interference whenever a given state did not occur as expected (i.e. a mismatch between the GoOS and GoES). For example, it was possible to detect the interference between the DD and VoIP phone when competing for the user awareness and trigger a warning for the user not to forget to take the medicine.

1.4 Communication and Networking Issues

The exponential growth of the IoT has been fueled by low-cost, highly integrated, and powerful embedded computing devices interconnected by wireless networks. An important feature of IoT systems is its easy deployment in places without any available infrastructure. These systems can be designed to work in the bottom of the sea, on the top of a mountain, under the polar ice, inside volcanoes, etc., places where no power grid is available (so the system has to rely on energy harvesting or batteries) and where no communication infrastructure is available (so the system has to be built around wireless networking protocols). It becomes clear that communication and networking technologies on IoT scenarios should cope with a high number of design challenges:

- *Wireless communication*: In many situations there are no wired infrastructure available, and due to the mobility of the end devices, it is not even an option. RF propagation issues like attenuation and interference have to be considered.
- *Low power*: In power-constrained devices whose batteries sometimes have to last years and cannot be replaced, the use of the radios has to be carefully tailored. Network protocols have to deal with intermittent connections where, most of the time, radios are shut down to save power and wake up at certain time slots to send and receive data.
- *Bandwidth*: IoT systems usually do not require high bit rate communication. For the end device, a periodic low bandwidth communication channel is enough to receive requests and report sensor data.
- *Routing*: IoT systems can cover very large areas with end device mobility. This means that a dynamic network topology, called a mesh network, has to be managed. Efficient routing in mesh networks where end nodes enter and leave communication range of each other dynamically requires the use of special routing protocols.

There are a number of network technologies that were developed to meet the needs of IoT scenarios. Some are "native" communication protocols that were born to support communication in wireless personal area networks (WPAN) like ZigBee (Kim and Moon, 2014) and 6LoWPAN (Mulligan, 2007), both based on the IEEE 802.15.4 standard, and also BT (Gupta, 2016) based on IEEE 802.15.1 that was recently updated to version 5 where it has received mesh network routing capabilities. Others are "newcomers" to the IoT arena such as the IEEE 802.11ah (Sun et al., 2013), a standard extending the most used wireless local area network (WLAN) protocol IEEE 802.11, also known as Wi-Fi. Other protocols were developed to be used in low power wide area networks (LPWANs) like the LoRaWAN (Bo et al., 2017). All these networking protocols were thought to meet the design challenges stated before with different approaches in physical layer (e.g. network range and topology, channel frequency and bandwidth, modulation, output power), data link layer (e.g. frame format, MAC protocol, error and flow control), network layer (e.g. routing protocols, IPv6 compatibility), and application layer (e.g. application profiles).

The next section presents an application of the ZigBee protocol stack. This application basically extends the project presented in Section 1.2 adding the appropriate network communication infrastructure to allow a large number of modules to work together in a mesh network topology. A two-way gateway module collects alerts and vital or context data from the sensor network and transmits that information to a server. This server monitors the data in real time and can interact with the end devices or trigger alerts in dangerous situations; it also stores data for further statistical treatment and consultation by healthcare providers or caregivers.

1.4.1 Wireless Sensor Network for Home Healthcare

Wireless sensor networks represent the hardware infrastructure that together with the intelligence component and ubiquitous computing enable the deployment of intelligent spaces. Certain characteristics such as flexibility, fault tolerance, reliability, low cost, and speed of implementation of wireless sensor networks open up a wide range of application areas for this type of network, for example, environmental and corporal monitoring, industrial control, military applications, and home automation, among others (Tang et al., 2007).

In healthcare, the creation of smart spaces allowing the remote monitoring of health parameters can help to maintain a high level of care with controlled costs. This is because the use of remote monitoring systems avoids the presence of specialized and permanent teams at supervised sites. It also allows the automatic collection and transmission of the environmental and corporal context of several individuals to a central server, where data can be stored, compared, correlated, and analyzed by different specialists. In this way, it will be possible to optimize the work of health professionals and to improve the efficiency of healthcare teams and to adopt health promotion programs, based on the data collected, that would otherwise hardly reach a wide range of the population.

This project proposes a vital and environmental monitoring system using wireless sensor networks. It is a low-cost system, with a simple installation and maintenance. It does not require the existence of any network infrastructure preinstalled at the place of use. It is a scalable system both from the point of view of the number of individuals and the geographic scope covered. Due to the characteristics of the mesh network topology used, the system also has high reliability and redundancy. The developed prototype is based on microcontroller-based end devices and sensors that allow monitoring of various physiological parameters (e.g. temperature, heart rate, etc.) and ambient (e.g. brightness, temperature, etc.). All data collected is transmitted (using ZigBee technology) to a gateway that routes data, in this case via GPRS, to a central server. This system facilitates the installation of environmental motes and the mobility of the users, offering a dynamic and adaptable architecture to various conditions, spaces, and application scenarios.

1.4.1.1 Home Healthcare System Architecture

In the design of the system, the use of low-cost hardware and open-source software tools was privileged. The system presented here extends the work developed in Goncalves et al. (2009) in order to create a decentralized, agile, and noninvasive tool for monitoring the vital signs of multiple patients.

Data collection and processing modules use Arduino systems. In the environmental module the Arduino Diecimila that has an ATmega168 micro-controller with 16 KB of flash memory for code storage. 1 KB of SRAM, and 512 bytes of EEPROM is used; several analog and digital inputs/outputs allow the acquisition of data from different types of sensors, as well as the control of various types of actuators. Diecimila also has a USB connection through which the serial connection is made to the programming environment, very convenient in the development phase of the initial prototype. This system will later be replaced by the Arduino Nano that has equivalent capabilities but with a fraction of the size. Its miniaturization made possible its use in the body module described in Goncalves et al. (2009). Finally, the gateway module uses an Arduino Mega with a microcontroller that offers more processing power (ATmega1280), more memory (128KB flash, 8KB SDRAM and 4KB EEPROM), and four serial ports that may be used for connecting several shields and provide interconnection with the Internet. The architecture of the system is presented in Figure 1.14

The body module (already presented in Figure 1.1) is carried by each individual and has the ability to monitor the physical activity developed (lying down, sitting, walking, and running) and to detect falls that may occur (Goncalves et al., 2009). A temperature sensor is used to periodically report the individual's

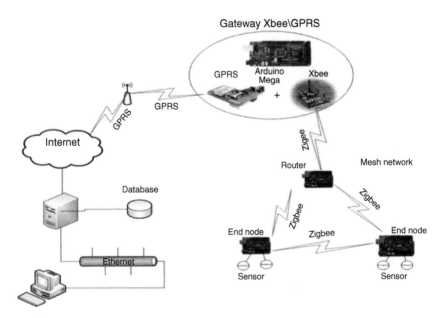

Figure 1.14 Wireless sensor network architecture.

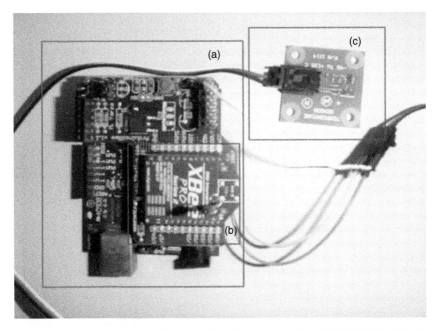

Figure 1.15 Environmental module: (a) Arduino Diecimila + XBee shield, (b) Rádio XBee Pro 2, and (c) analog temperature sensor.

body temperature. The environmental module (see Figure 1.15) has a dual function: to be used as a repeater to increase the reach of the wireless network where this function is imposed by the topology of the space to be covered by the system (this need is verified during site survey at the installation site) and to be used to report environmental parameters of the monitored site (e.g. temperature, humidity, lightness, barometric pressure, etc.) that can be correlated with the information obtained from the body modules in decision making of health professionals.

The XBee/GPRS gateway (see Figure 1.16) has the function of bridging the sensor network with the Internet using the GPRS module. This module is responsible for initiating the ZigBee network, of which it is the coordinator, and for maintaining a TCP/IP connection with the server through which the data obtained by the physical and environmental modules present in the topology is periodically reported. This TCP/IP connection is bidirectional and allows the interrogation of physical and environmental units through the Web server interface by health professionals or family members.

The server is a computer running the Linux operating system and a Web application written in PHP that launches a dedicated process to each gateway in the system (the server can track N gateways in parallel). The received data is processed and the information is later stored in a MySQL database. The data

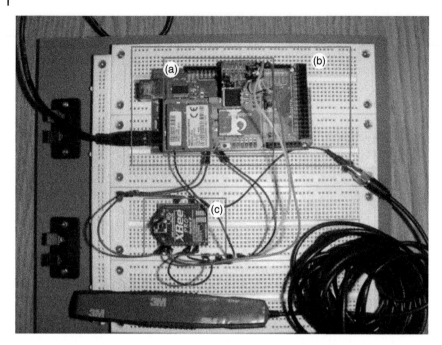

Figure 1.16 XBee-GPRS gateway: (a) GPRS Hilo SAGEM module, (b) Arduino Mega, and (c) XBee Pro 2 radio.

obtained can be treated statistically in order to guarantee an integrated view to the health professional or familiar and to trigger alarms automatically when the information obtained requires immediate action.

In order to ensure the best possible network coverage at the installation site, a mesh network topology is used. In this network topology it is not necessary that all the devices are within reach of the coordinator of the network to be able to communicate with it. Intermediate nodes (as routers) can be used to replicate the information so that it can reach its destination. Each node of the network, in addition to performing its specific job of acquiring and processing data from its own sensors, is also a potential repeater for messages to and from other nodes of the network.

The modules implementation is structured in three overlapping layers: the lower level addresses the communications module; at the central level there is the message processing module; and the top level has the sensor management module. In the communications layer, the process of sending and receiving information from the network nodes in the mesh is programmed via ZigBee. At the gateway node this layer also deals with configuring, establishing, and maintaining the TCP/IP connection to the server via GPRS. In the message processing layer, the message construction is programmed, where the sensor data and the syntactic verification of the received messages are reported. In the management layer of the sensors, the data of each sensor is periodically collected. All information collected by the mesh and sent to the server is available on a Web page that will serve to consult the data of each patient. This data is only available to users with appropriate permission.

1.4.1.2 Wireless Sensor Network Evaluation

In order to assess the reliability of the system proposed here, some preliminary tests were performed on the functionalities of the different modules. The data collected by the body module show good reliability as demonstrated in Goncalves et al. (2009). The tests carried out essentially aim to ensure the reliability and scalability of the communications within the sensor network and between this and the Internet using the ZigBee/GPRS gateway. One of the conclusions of the tests carried out was that reliable communication within the mesh network is strongly dependent on the location of the system. Although the radios announced range is appreciable (1500 m to 60 mW at 2.4 GHz) in practice, the topology of buildings, the materials used in their construction, and the thickness of the walls, for example, considerably influence the propagation capacity of the radio signals in the band used by ZigBee (industrial, scientific, and medical (ISM)). For this reason, and to ensure that the data of all patients arrive at the gateway regardless of their locations in the buildings, it was necessary to place repeaters (routers) at predetermined key places. In these places, environmental modules have been installed that perform the repetition of the frames and, at the same time, provide data on the environmental parameters of the installation sites. In the case of communications between the gateway and the server via GPRS, no problems were detected. This module has been in operation for long periods of time without losing contact with the server and periodically reporting the data collected by the network.

Given its nature, the system offers good scalability capabilities both in terms of the extent of covered areas and the number of users monitored. This is because the periodic frequency of sampling of the sensors need not be very high. A period between one and five minutes is perfectly acceptable for situations of normality. Alarm situations such as falls or abnormal values of heart rate can be immediately reported (these situations are, of course, uncommon). Under these circumstances the mesh network can support hundreds of devices (XBee, 2008). The data aggregation point, therefore the gateway, can also support a large number of devices even at a 56 kbps rate. Considering 100 devices in the mesh with three sensors each and a sending frequency of one minute, we have 2700 bytes per minute at the application level (a little more at the physical level considering the protocol overhead), which is perfectly compatible with the minimum transfer rate of the GPRS module.

1.5   Intelligence and Reasoning Issues

The area of application of the IoT has decisively contributed to the triggering, nowadays, of the big data era, in which there is a tremendous increase in the amount of information produced, stored, and processed in digital form.

In this section we describe some information processing techniques in order to extract knowledge from data in IoT context. The solutions offered, for instance, by artificial intelligence, ML, and knowledge representation are fundamental to apply inference in IoT systems.

In the context of smart home healthcare, the problem of activity detection, in particular, is described. Two systems are described, integrating each other, offering architectural solutions, application scenarios, and validated results that point to directions in a rapid developing area.

1.5.1   Intelligent Monitoring and Automation in Home Healthcare

The IoT area, in the context of smart spaces and home healthcare, poses some challenges that have been tackled in various research efforts. One is the amount and diversity of existing devices, from different manufacturers, and the difficulty of interconnecting them in the same system. This raises questions, also, of the architectural nature of the system itself. In Moreira (2017) an ongoing project is described that establishes a reference architecture using, as an integrating element, openHAB (OpenHAB Foundation, 2017b), an open-source and agnostic software platform that, thanks to its modular organization, allows this component to function as the integrator element, the system orchestrator, responsible for simple automation tasks and decision and for communication with additional inference modules that may be placed locally or in the cloud. In Figure 1.17 it is possible to verify the integration of an inductive inference module using the Weka (Frank et al., 2016) data mining software framework with an OWL and SWRL rule reasoner implemented using the software frameworks Protégé Stanford University School of Medicine (2017) and Jena Apache Software Foundation (2017a).

One of the goals of the (Moreira, 2017) project is to propose an intelligent system for automation and monitoring of senior citizens living in their homes. The knowledge representation module uses ontologies, expressed in OWL, and rules, in SWRL, to represent semantics of the application domain. In the mentioned project, this module was used to infer complex activities from simple activities based on information acquired from the sensors and passed through the integrating component. For example, the identification of the simple activity is performed by a device affixed to the user's waist that is able to recognize from among five activities or postures, namely, sitting, standing, walking, running, and lying down. A complex activity can be considered as the occurrence, according to a sequence pattern, of a certain number of events, among which stand out simple activities.

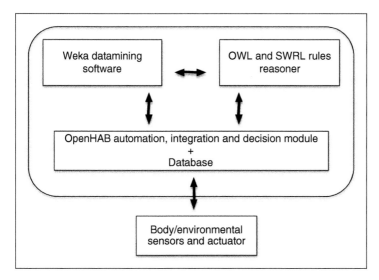

Figure 1.17 System architecture.

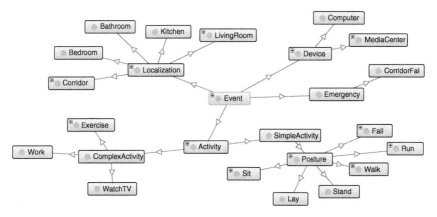

Figure 1.18 Taxonomy expressed in OWL.

The ontological data model created in the project is represented in Figure 1.18. The model has a root class called Event whose purpose is to represent any event. An Event has a start time (hasBeginning property) and an end time (hasEnd property). Both properties belong to the OWL-Time Ontology (see http://www.w3.org/TR/owl-time/). The Event class has four subclasses – Localization, Device, Activity, and Emergency.

The Localization class is used to represent the presence of the user in a particular division of its home. One of the advantages of this approach is to combine the temporal and the spatial dimension. From the point of view of the model, every event is contained in the temporal dimension, and any event occurring in the spatial dimension is also represented in terms of its occurrence in the temporal dimension. Thus, it is possible to represent that the presence of a person in the living room takes place between two temporal instants, in this case, when it enters and when it leaves the division.

The Device class represents the use of any device within the environment. Examples of relevant devices are represented by the MediaCenter, TV, and Computer subclasses. The Activity class represents the activities performed by the user, be they simple postures or even complex activities. Information about the user's postures is given by a sensor that is positioned at his or her waist, being considered standing, sitting, walking, running, or lying down. This sensor also detects the fall of the user, but, for purposes of the model, this is not represented as a posture. Activities and postures are considered together as simple or atomic activities in the sense that they are indivisible. The model also considers the existence of complex activities, that is, activities composed of more than one event. For example, WatchTV can be considered as the composition of some events, such as the fact that the user is in the living room (LivingRoom), sitting (Sit), and having the television on (TV). The granularity of the description of a complex activity can be complemented by the existence of more data sources, that is, the information that the user is sitting on the couch where he usually watches television can be included.

Regardless of the granularity or level of detail that one wishes to confer on a complex activity, it should be noted that a complex activity can be represented as events, related between them in a specified way, from a temporal point of view. This work assumes that there is more than one event and that, in a given time interval, they occur simultaneously. For instance, when certain events occur simultaneously, or when they occur during others, and considering the algebra described by Allen (1983), the existence of a complex activity is considered. Taking the example above, WatchTV activity may be considered to occur when the user enters the living room, sits, and turns on the television. From the standpoint of the model, this sequence of events is translated as follows: the beginning of LivingRoom is previous to that of Sit and that of the previous one to that of TV and the end of this being before the end of Sit and, likewise, the end of this one being earlier than LivingRoom.

In this way, SWRL rules are used to identify complex activities. For the above example, the SWRL rule could be decomposed into three parts as follows.

The WatchTV rule occurs when Sit, LivingRoom, and MediaCenter occur simultaneously. As can be seen, temporal verification is done by the eventDuring rule:

$$
\begin{aligned}
&\text{LivingRoom } (?x) \wedge && \text{Sit } (?y) \wedge && \text{MediaCenter } (?z) \wedge \\
&\text{eventDuring } (?x, ?y) \wedge && \text{eventDuring } (?y, ?z) && \Rightarrow \text{WatchTV } (?z)
\end{aligned}
$$

$$(1.6)$$

The rule eventDuring occurs when, given two events, the first has the beginning before the beginning of the second and the end of the second is before the end of the first:

$$\text{Event } (?x) \wedge \text{ Event } (?y) \wedge$$
$$\text{hasBeginning } (?x, ?startX) \wedge \text{ hasBeginning } (?y, ?startY) \wedge$$
$$\text{hasEnd } (?x, ?endX) \wedge \text{ hasEnd } (?y, ?endY) \wedge \quad (1.7)$$
$$\text{before } (?startX, ?startY) \wedge \text{ before } (?endY, ?endX)$$
$$\Rightarrow \text{eventDuring } (?x, ?y)$$

The *before* rule allows you to compare two instants x and y from the time point of view:

$$\text{Instant } (?x) \wedge \text{ Instant } (?y) \wedge$$
$$\text{inXSDDateTime } (?x, ?z) \wedge \text{ inXSDDateTime } (?y, ?w) \wedge \quad (1.8)$$
$$\text{swrlb : lessThanOrEqual } (?w, ?z) \Rightarrow \text{before } (?y, ?x)$$

In summary, the example described above allows us to deduce, based on an OWL and SWRL reasoner, whether a person is watching television based on temporal relationships between the person's presence in the room (LivingRoom), the television being connected (MediaCenter), and the person sitting (Sit).

The learning module, implemented using Weka (Frank et al., 2016), is aimed at the tasks of inductive learning using several classification, grouping, and other algorithms. An example of using this module is precisely the detection and classification of the user's posture (sitting, lying down, walking, running, falling). In the workflow of the system, this information is later passed to the module of knowledge representation to detect and infer the type of complex activity to be performed.

Throughout this system, the orchestration, whose responsibility is of the integrator component (framework based on openHAB), plays a fundamental role. This component links the things, sensor devices and actuators, the inductive learning component, knowledge representation, and the system data repository.

A simpler use case, but one that belongs to the set of evaluated use cases in this project, used only simple condition-type rules, implemented using the rules system of the openHAB itself. In this use case the system worked as an automation framework for controlling the temperature and lighting of the living room when the television was switched on.

The system described in this section represents a proposal to integrate three forms of inference used in artificial intelligence: condition–action rules system, inductive learning, and knowledge representation and deductive reasoning. It also represents a solution for integrating these types of reasoning with a diversity of multi-vendor systems using an agnostic orchestrating element from a manufacturer and protocol point of view.

1.5.2   Personal Activity Detection During Daily Living

The adoption of several sources of information and even multiple sources of inference raises the need to use, at the time of the final decision, the fusion of information. The personal activity detection system (PADS), described in Vale (2013), uses Bayesian inference for this purpose.

The PADS was developed with the purpose of detecting and monitoring the activity of people in smart spaces, typically households, using multiple sources of sensory information that are aggregated in a data fusion module.

An important argument to justify the PADS approach is to consider that each source of information, when used isolated, has a margin of error associated with the determination of activity greater than the conjugation of several sources and several sensors in an intelligent way. By aggregating all the available information through a probabilistic network, the likelihood of obtaining more reliable results is increased, i.e. to obtain classifications of activities with less errors.

The specified hardware architecture makes use of a smartphone, webcams, cloud, and a local or cloud computing framework used to store collected data and process it through data fusion, as illustrated in Figure 1.19.

In the figure the following modules are considered:

- The Activity Detection Module, which refers to a mobile device, is responsible for the classification of the physical activity that the user is currently performing – standing, walking, running, lying, or falling – that is, the variable consists of a numerical value between 1 and 5 (Torres et al., 2012) (PhysicalActivity).

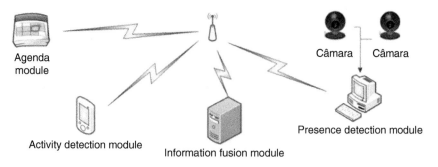

Figure 1.19 Deployment architecture.

- The Presence Detection Module is responsible for identifying the presence of people in predefined locations, through the recognition of the user's predefined face in the system, using one or several video cameras and computer vision. In the scenario tested, three video cameras aligned with "TV," "drug dispenser," and "telephone" were considered. In this way it would be possible to recognize the user in front of each of these devices or, as the "other" class, if none of the cameras detected the face of the user. Therefore, four classes to be considered in total (Presence).
- The Agenda Module, consults Google Calendar where the medication is scheduled for the patient to be monitored. The medication is stored and organized in a DD. For each instant of time, the module indicates whether or not the user has to take the medication: "yes," "no" (AgendaMedication).
- The Information Fusion Module is a software module where the information collected and generated by PADS is stored, and it is also in this element that the information fusion is executed. In the case of the study carried out, the six outputs considered were "In front of TV," "Taking medication," "Exercising in front of TV," "On the phone," "Fall," and "Other" (UserActivity).

The algorithmic technique used in the data fusion was the adoption of a dynamic Bayesian network (DBN) (Russel et al., 2010). A DBN divides the model into time slices. Each time slice consists of random variables whose conditional dependencies are expressed using a directed acyclic graphical (DAG) model. Between adjacent time slices, conditional dependencies can be represented. In Figure 1.20 a dependency between random variables "Activity" in consecutive time slices, $t - 1$ and t, is represented.

In this model, for each time slice, t, three observed nodes (PhysicalActivity, AgendaMedication, Presence) and a hidden node (UserActivity) were considered. The inference algorithm uses Gibbs sampling, and learning is done using expectation maximization (EM) (Paluszewski and Hamelryck, 2010), based on a training set organized in order to be meaningful of the user's activities that are to be detected. The tests performed confirmed that, for example, even in a momentary failure scenario of the presence system, the time dependence tends to compensate for this and the fusion system correctly interprets the activity to be performed.

Information fusion is an almost mandatory task in a home healthcare and AAL system. Naturally, this need arises from the quantity and variety of sources of information collected from both the user and the environment. The project described above adopts a probabilistic approach so that from a model point of view, each source of information or a combination of information sources is associated with the respective random variable with the appropriate probability distribution. In the work described, all random variables followed a categorical distribution (discrete node).

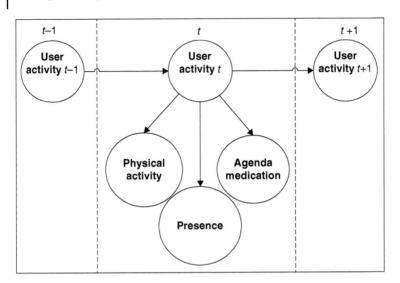

Figure 1.20 Bayesian network model.

The two systems presented Moreira (2017) and Vale (2013) point to the importance of intelligence and reasoning issues. They point out paths at the appropriate architecture level to incorporate reasoning into AAL systems and what the main components are and how they can integrate with each other. In an area where there is much to do, these works intend to represent a contribution to its development.

1.6 Conclusion

There is an escalating need for home and ambulatory healthcare solutions due to the limits of health systems that are unable to cope with the ever-rising needy population. In addition, people's preferences are predominantly for living and being cared for at home. As such, next-generation ubicomp solutions will need to provide multimodal and safe support for home healthcare (e.g. daily life activity assistance and security, treatment adherence, etc.).

On the other hand, everyone witnesses a progressive increase in the diversity of COTS devices related to AAL and home healthcare available in the market. Nevertheless, several challenges need to be solved in this area. Some of the problems, lines of research, and application scenarios have been addressed throughout this chapter. Key capabilities were identified and described for the development of AAL environments along with the presentation of some works that best illustrate them.

It is predictable that in the very near future, sensor devices applied to AAL and healthcare will be increasingly accurate and easier to use on day-to-day scenarios. The problems of security, usability, reliability and accuracy, communication, and integration of all the components of the home healthcare ecosystem are some of those that will continue to be studied. AAL systems will tend to produce increasingly large amounts, streams, of data. The storage and, fundamentally, the processing of these data are key areas. Providing these, big data, systems with algorithmic abilities to infer relevant information to improve people's lives, with emphasis to the elderly population, will perhaps be the area that will require greater research and development effort in the times that follow.

Bibliography

Abowd, G.D., Dey, A.K., Brown, P.J. et al. (1999). Towards a better understanding of context and context-awareness. In: *Handheld and Ubiquitous Computing. HUC 1999*, Lecture Notes in Computer Science, vol. **1707** (ed. H.W. Gellersen), 304–307. Berlin, Heidelberg: Springer-Verlag.

Allen, J.F. (1983). Maintaining knowledge about temporal intervals. *Communications of the ACM* **26** (11): 832–843.

Anliker, U., Ward, J.A., Lukowicz, P. et al. (2004). AMON: a wearable multiparameter medical monitoring and alert system. *IEEE Transactions on Information Technology in Biomedicine.* **8** (4): 415–427.

Apache Software Foundation (2017a). Apache Jena. https://jena.apache.org/index.html (accessed February 2019).

Ashton, K. (2009). That 'internet of things' thing: electronic resources. *RFiD Journal* **22**: 97–114.

Baker, C.R., Armijo, K., Belka, S. et al. (2007). Wireless sensor networks for home health care. AINA Workshops.

Becvarik, M. and Devetsikiotis, M. (2016). Modeling of user quality of experience in location aware smart spaces. In: 2016 Digital Media Industry & Academic Forum (DMIAF), 207–212. IEEE. https://doi.org/10.1109/DMIAF.2016.7574934. ISBN: 978-1-5090-1000-4; http://ieeexplore.ieee.org/document/7574934/.

Bo, C., Gaoming, Z., and Haiping, L. (2017). LoRaWAN Ad-Hoc Network Equipment. Chinese Patent Office.

Chaudhry, S.A., Song, W., Vulla, M.H., and Sreenan, C.J. (2011). EMP: a protocol for IP-based wireless sensor networks management. *JUSPN - Journal of Ubiquitous Systems and Pervasive Networks* **2** (1): 15–22.

Chen, G. (2005). Solar: building a context fusion network for pervasive computing. Hanover, NH: Dartmouth College. ISBN: 0-496-95707-4.

Chen, G. and Kotz, D. (2000). A Survey of Context-Aware Mobile Computing Research. Technical report. Hanover, NH: Dartmouth College Hanover. http://www.ncstrl.org:8900/ncstrl/servlet/search?formname=detail&id=oai %3Ancstrlh%3Adartmouthcs%3Ancstrl.dartmouthcs%2F%2FTR2000-381.

Choi, D., Jang, H., Jeong, K. et al. (2006). Delivery and storage architecture for sensed information using SNMP. In: *Management of Convergence Networks and Services. APNOMS 2006*, Lecture Notes in Computer Science, vol. **4238** (ed. Y.T. Kim and M. Takano), 582–585. Berlin, Heidelberg: Springer-Verlag.

Digi XBee (2008). Wireless Mesh Networking: ZigBee vs. Digi Mesh.

Faragher, R. and Harle, R. (2014). An analysis of the accuracy of bluetooth low energy for indoor positioning applications. In: Proceedings of the 27th International Technical Meeting of the Satellite Division of the Institute of Navigation (ION GNSS+ 2014), 201–210. http://www.cl.cam.ac.uk/rmf25/papers/BLE.pdf.

Faragher, R. and Harle, R. (2015). Location fingerprinting with bluetooth low energy beacons. *IEEE Journal on Selected Areas in Communications* **33** (11): 2418–2428. https://doi.org/10.1109/JSAC.2015.2430281.

Fischer, M. (2008). Enhancing the ReMoteCare prototype by adding an SNMP proxy and video surveillance. Institut für Wirtschafts- und Verwaltungsinformatik, XVIII, 75.

Frank, E., Hall, M.A., and Witten, I.H. (2016). *The WEKA Workbench. Online Appendix for "Data Mining: Practical Machine Learning Tools and Techniques"*, 4e. Elsevier.

Giannakouris, K. (2008). Ageing characterises the demographic perspectives of the European societies. Statistics in focus.

Gomes, A., Pinto, A., Soares, C. et al. (2018). Indoor location using bluetooth low energy beacons. In: *Trends and Advances in Information Systems and Technologies* (ed. Á. Rocha, H. Adeli, L.P. Reis, and S. Costanzo), 565–580. Cham: Springer International Publishing. ISBN: 978-3-319-77712-2.

Goncalves, P., Torres, J., and Sobral, P. (2009). Remote patient monitoring in home environments. 1st International Workshop on Mobilizing Health Information to Support Healthcare - MobiHealthInf 2009.

Gupta, N.K. (2016). *Inside Bluetooth Low Energy*, 2e. Artech House.

Henricksen, K., Indulska, J., McFadden, T., and Balasubramaniam, S. (2005). Middleware for distributed context-aware systems. OTM Conferences.

ITU-T Recommendation (2008). X.680 Abstract Syntax Notation One (ASN. 1): Specification of Basic Notation.

Jurik, A.D. and Weaver, A.C. (2008). Remote medical monitoring. *Computer* **41** (4): 96–99.

Kaplan, E. and Hegarty, C. (2006). *Understanding GPS Principles and Applications*, 2e. Artech House.

Kim, Y.-D. and Moon, I.-Y. (2014). ZigBee and IEEE 802.15.4 Standards.

Lim, Y.Y., Messina, M., Kargl, F. et al. (2008). SNMP proxy for wireless sensor network. In: 5th International Conference on Information Technology: New Generations (ITNG 2008), 738–743. https://doi.org/10.1109/ITNG.2008.121.

Moreira, A. (2017). Assistência à autonomia no domicílio com integração de Automação e Inteligência Artificial.

Moreira, L., Soares, C., and Moreira, R.S. (2012). A decentralized SNMP-based approach for behavior introspection and awareness in ubiquitous computing. 3rd International Conference on Wireless Mobile Communication and Healthcare (MOBIHEALTH 2012).

Moreira, R.S., Morla, R.S., Moreira, L.P.C., and Soares, C. (2016). A behavioral reflective architecture for managing the integration of personal ubicomp systems: automatic SNMP-based discovery and management of behavior context in smart-spaces. *Personal and Ubiquitous Computing* **20** (2): 229–243.

Mulligan, G. (2007). The 6LoWPAN architecture. In: Proceedings of the 4th Workshop on Embedded Networked Sensors, EmNets '07, 78–82. New York: ACM. http://doi.acm.org/10.1145/1278972.1278992; ISBN: 978-1-59593-694-3.

Murtaza, S.S., Amin, S.O., and Hong, C.S. (2006). Applications of SNMP in ubiquitous environment. *KNOM Review* **8** (2): 14.

Namiot, D. (2015). On indoor positioning. *International Journal of Open Information Technologies* **3** (3): 23–26.

OpenHAB Foundation (2017b). openHAB - Empowering the smart home. http://www.openhab.org (accessed February 2019).

Paluszewski, M. and Hamelryck, T. (2010). Mocapy++–a toolkit for inference and learning in dynamic Bayesian networks. *BMC Bioinformatics* **11** (1): 126. https://doi.org/10.1186/1471-2105-11-126.

Russel S., Norvig P., Russell, S.J., and Norvig, P. (2010). *Artificial Intelligence - A Modern Approach*, 3e. Pearson Education. ISBN: 978-0-13-207148-2.

Satyanarayanan, M. (2001). Pervasive computing: vision and challenges. *IEEE Personal Communications* **8** (4): 10–17.

Seybold, J.S. (2005). *Introduction to Propagation*. Hoboken, NJ: Wiley. http://twanclik.free.fr/electricity/electronic/pdfdone8/Introduction.to.RF.Propagation.Wiley.Interscience.Sep.2005.eBook-DDU.pdf.

Soares, C., Moreira, R.S., Morla, R. et al. (2012). Interference free integration of pervasive applications. 2012 IEEE 11th International Conference on Trust, Security and Privacy in Computing and Communications.

Stanford University School of Medicine (2017). Protege. http://protege.stanford.edu (accessed February 2019).

Stankovic, J.A., Cao, Q., Doan, T., and Fang, L. (2005). Wireless sensor networks for in-home healthcare: potential and challenges. Wireless Sensor Networks for In-Home Healthcare: Potential and Challenges. Workshop on High Confidence Medical Devices Software and Systems (HCMDSS).

Sun, W., Choi, M., and Choi, S. (2013). IEEE 802.11ah: a long range 802.11 WLAN at sub 1 GHz. *Journal of ICT Standardization* **1**: 83–108.

Tang, F., Guo, M., Li, M. et al. (2007). Wireless mesh sensor networks in pervasive environment: a reliable architecture and routing protocol. 2007 International Conference on Parallel Processing Workshops (ICPPW 2007).

Torres, J.M., Sobral, P., Moreira, R.S., and Morla, R. (2012). An adaptive embedded system for physical activity recognition. Proceedings of CISTI 2012 - 7ª Conferência Ibérica de Sistemas e Tecnologias de Informaç ao.

Vale, S. (2013). PADS personal activity detection system. PhD thesis. University Fernando Pessoa.

Venkatasubramanian, K.K., Deng, G., Mukherjee, T. et al. (2005). Ayushman - a wireless sensor network based health monitoring infrastructure and testbed. In: *Distributed Computing in Sensor Systems. DCOSS 2005*, Lecture Notes in Computer Science, vol. **3560** (ed. V.K. Prasanna, S.S. Iyengar, P.G. Spirakis, and M. Welsh), 406–407. Berlin, Heidelberg: Springer-Verlag.

Weiser, M. (1991). The computer for the 21st century. *Scientific American* **265**: 94–104.

Welsh, M., Moulton, S., Fulford-Jones, T., and Malan, D.J. (2004). CodeBlue: An Ad Hoc sensor network infrastructure for emergency medical care. Paper presented at the International Workshop on Wearable and Implantable Body Sensor Networks, April, London, UK.

Wood, A., Virone, G., Doan, T. et al. (2006). *ALARM-NET: Wireless Sensor Networks for Assisted-Living and Residential Monitoring*. University of Virginia.

Zhang, T., Wang, J., Liu, P., and Hou, J. (2006). Fall detection by embedding an accelerometer in cellphone and using KFD algorithm. *IJCSNS International Journal of Computer Science and Network Security* **6** (10): 277–284.

2

PeMo-EC: An Intelligent, Pervasive and Mobile Platform for ECG Signal Acquisition, Processing, and Pre-Diagnostic Extraction

Angelo Brayner[1], José Maria Monteiro[1], and João Paulo Madeiro[2]

[1]*Computing Science Department, Federal University of Ceará, Fortaleza, Ceará, Brazil*
[2]*Institute for Engineering and Sustainable Development, University for the International Integration of the Afro-Brazilian Lusophony, Redenção, Ceará, Brazil*

2.1 Electrical System of the Heart

The heart, or the cardiac muscle, has the function of pumping blood to the organs and specifically to the lungs, aiming at the exchange of gases, absorbing oxygen and eliminating carbon dioxide. It is divided into upper (atriums) and lower (ventricles) chambers, and it may also be considered to be composed of two separate pumping systems: a right heart that pumps blood through the lungs and a left heart that pumps blood through the peripheral organs. Each atrium helps to move blood into the ventricle, and the ventricles supply the main pump force needed to push blood through the pulmonary and peripheral circulation systems (Hall, 2015).

In addition to the atrial and ventricular muscles, myocardial tissue consists of excitable and contractile fibers capable of developing self-regenerative electrical activity, presenting specific functions of generation, conduction, and contraction, depending on its anatomical location. There are two primary groups of cells in the myocardium that are important for cardiac function.

The contractile apparatus of cardiac fibers consists of a complex of contractile proteins, composed of actin, myosin, tropomyosin, and troponin, which, in the presence of calcium and adenosine triphosphate, interact with each other, causing contraction. Such cells possess the property of contractility, i.e. the ability to shorten and then return to their original length. For a myocardial cell to contract, the cell membrane must be discharged electrically (a process called depolarization), causing a change in electrical charge across the membrane, resulting in the flow or movement of certain ions (especially sodium). The depolarization process also allows the entry of calcium into the cell, where it is responsible for the binding part between actin and myosin of the sarcomere (basic contractile unit of myocardial fibers), resulting in contraction.

Intelligent Pervasive Computing Systems for Smarter Healthcare, First Edition.
Arun Kumar Sangaiah, S.P. Shantharajah, and Padma Theagarajan.
© 2019 John Wiley & Sons, Inc. Published 2019 by John Wiley & Sons, Inc.

The cells that make up the electrical system of the heart are responsible for the formation of the electric current and the conduction of this impulse to the contractile cells of the myocardium, where the depolarization activates the contraction. Certain cells in the electrical system have the ability to generate an electrical impulse (a property referred to as spontaneous automaticity or depolarization). Cells possessing this property are known as "pacemaker" cells. These cells are found in the sinus node, in the cells responsible for atrial conduction, in the area immediately above the atrioventricular (AV) node, in the low portion of the AV node, in the His bundle, and in the Purkinje ventricular system.

2.2 The Electrocardiogram Signal: A Gold Standard for Monitoring People Suffering from Heart Diseases

The electrocardiogram (ECG) signal is a record of the potential differences produced by the electrical activity of the heart cells. The body by itself acts as a giant conductor of electrical current, and any two points in the body can be connected by electrodes to record an ECG or monitor the heart's rhythm.

The trace recorded from the electrical activity of the heart forms a series of waves and complexes that have been arbitrarily called P-wave, conglomerate of the characteristic waves Q, R and S of the electrocardiogram (QRS) complex, T-wave, and U-wave. The waves or deflections are separated by regular intervals (see Figure 2.1).

The depolarization of the atrium produces the P-wave; depolarization of the ventricles produces the QRS complex. Ventricular repolarization causes the T-wave. The significance of the U-wave is uncertain, but may be due to

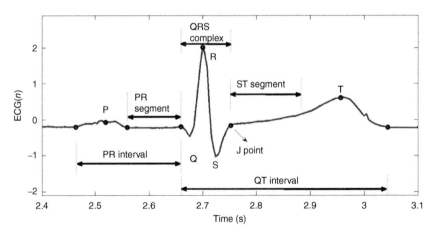

Figure 2.1 ECG signal. Characteristic waves and some basic parameters for ECG.

repolarization of the Purkinje system. The PR interval (iPR) extends from the beginning of the P-wave to the beginning of the QRS complex. This should not exceed 0.20 seconds measured on ECG paper where each small square represents 0.04 seconds. The upper limit of the normal duration of the QRS complex is <0.12 seconds. A duration less than 0.12 seconds means that the impulse was initiated at or above the AV node (supraventricular). A duration of QRS >0.12 seconds may mean an impulse originating from the ventricle or originating from the supraventricular tissue but with prolonged conduction through the ventricle. The T-wave is the ventricular recovery or repolarization of the ventricles.

The key to the interpretation of cardiac arrhythmia is the analysis of the interrelationship of the P-wave, the iPR, and the QRS complex, including its duration and configuration. The ECG should be analyzed with respect to the frequency, rhythm, locus of the dominant pacemaker, and the configuration of the P-wave and the QRS complex. The relationship between ECG and cardiac anatomy is shown in Figure 2.2.

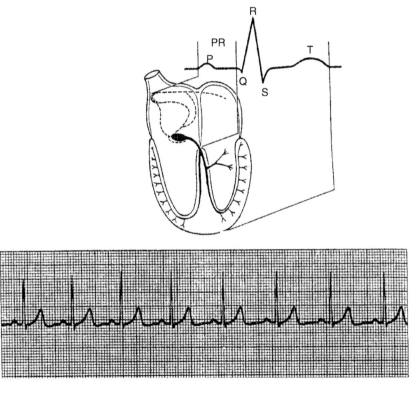

Figure 2.2 Electrocardiogram vs. anatomy of the conduction system. Relationship between the electrocardiogram and the anatomy of the conduction system.

The middle line of the diagram presented in Figure 2.2 is the His bundle dividing into the two branches of the conduction system. Any dysfunction above this point affects the P-wave and the iPR, while below this level it will affect the QRS complex. Some important events that can be observed from the morphology or time duration of P-wave, iPR, and QRS complex are emphasized below:

- *P-wave*: If for some reason the sinus node fails as a normal pacemaker cell, another atrial focus may take over and then P-wave may have changes in its morphology. Alternatively, a second focus may assume the main rhythm, i.e. a secondary focus of the pacemaker (for example, the AV node) such that we will have an escape rhythm.
- *iPR*: When conduction through the atrium, AV node, or His bundle is slow, the iPR becomes increased. Changes in AV node conduction are the most common causes of increased iPR.
- *QRS complex*: If there is a delay or interruption in conduction within the branches, the QRS complex will typically widen, i.e. right bundle branch block (RBBB) or left bundle branch block (LBBB). An ectopic focus that initiates a pulse in the ventricle may also alter the shape of the QRS complex. When the ectopic focus originates above the bundle of His or not, but not in the branches, the ventricles are activated normally, and the QRS complex will remain the same, assuming that there is no delay in conduction in the branches. If the focus originates below, the QRS complex will widen due to different driving sequences.

2.3 Pervasive and Mobile Computing: Basic Concepts

Advances in portable computing devices and wireless network technology have boosted the development of a new computing paradigm, denoted ubiquitous computing. This new paradigm makes possible on-demand access to services provided through a wireless communication infrastructure, regardless of their physical location or movement patterns. Thus, users carrying smartphones or tablets, for instance, may identify services provided in a given physical location (e.g. a hospital) and access them.

Although several authors consider that ubiquitous computing and pervasive computing represent a single unique paradigm, we claim that, in fact, the ubiquitous computing paradigm involves properties of two different paradigms, namely, mobile and pervasive computing (Brayner et al., 2009). In a mobile computing environment, network nodes do not have a fixed physical location. For that reason, people using a portable computing device may access services (e.g. patient medical records) and resources (e.g. a printer) regardless of where they are located or if they are moving across different physical locations and geographical regions. From a mobile computing perspective, mobility may be categorized into two different types:

- *Physical mobility*: This type of mobility copes with the spatial mobility of computing devices through different space regions. Applications supporting physical mobility provide full access to computing services to users regardless of their movements in different geographical areas.
- *Logical mobility*: This kind of mobility occurs in the logical space. In this sense, it is related to application migration among several mobile devices. Thus, applications may be started in a given computing device, more specifically in a portable device, and part of its code has to travel to different platforms to execute specific tasks. When migrating from one device to another, mobile applications should carry data and execution context. For instance, an application executing on a biosensor may migrate to a smartphone for running a more complex task.

To implement full features of mobile computing, mobile applications should present support for the aforementioned mobility types.

Pervasive computing provides applications the capability of obtaining information from the computational environment in which they are inserted. By doing this, applications may dynamically build computational models. Such a property is denoted context awareness. Thus, applications implementing a pervasive computing paradigm are able to discover services and resources and make them available to users. In other words, a pervasive computing paradigm requires that part of the pervasive applications' code should be embedded in the computing devices' hardware, e.g. a printer or a wireless sensor.

It is worthwhile to mention that pervasive computing does not require any type of mobility. Nevertheless, pervasive computing may be used to implement support for logical mobility.

To illustrate pervasiveness, consider the following scenario. Several hospitals employ an application A, which may run on smartphones or tablets, capable of reading basic information from pacemakers. This way, in an emergency, a patient with a pacemaker may go to any hospital (using A), and the application A, running on a physician's tablet, may get vital information on the patient's pacemaker.

Therefore, the ubiquitous paradigm takes profit from both pervasive and mobile computing features (Friedewald and Raabe, 2011). In this sense, we advocate that ubiquitous applications should present the following features:

- *Support for physical and logical mobility*: The goal of this feature is of a twofold nature. First, it guarantees access to services, regardless of physical location or movement of mobile devices. Second, it ensures mobile applications' migration among different devices, for instance, from a biosensor to a smartphone and from the latter to a server in a cloud computing service.

- *Context awareness*: Applications should automatically react to modifications in the computational environment in which they are inserted by adapting their behavior, without human interference.
- *Anytime and anywhere availability*: Applications may provide vertical and horizontal handoff (Sgora and Vergados, 2009).

2.4 Ubiquitous Computing and Healthcare Applications: State of the Art

As healthcare costs are continuously increasing, chronic noncommunicable diseases (NCD), including heart disease, stroke, cancer, diabetes, and chronic lung disease, are collectively responsible for almost 70% of all deaths worldwide, according to the World Health Organization (WHO) (Daar et al., 2007), and also considering that world population is aging, there has been a significant need to monitor a patient's health status while he is in his personal environment. In this context, a variety of developed system prototypes aim at providing real-time feedback information about an individual's health condition, either to the user himself, to a medical center, or directly to a professional physician.

Wearable systems for health monitoring comprise various types of miniature sensors, wearable or even implantable, which are capable of measuring from one to three ECG leads, among other physiological signals, and sending the obtained parameters either via a wireless or a wired link to a microcontroller board. The latter may then in turn transmit the conditioned and digitized signal to a smartphone, a computer, or a collaborative medical database center. Once the raw signal is conditioned and digitized, algorithms for digital signal processing, wave segmentation, and cardiac disease recognition can be performed on a variety of microprocessed platforms. Therefore, a whole wearable medical system encompasses a wide variety of components: sensors, wearable materials, smart textiles, actuators, power supplies, wireless communication, control and processing units, interface for the user, software, and advanced algorithms for data extracting and decision making (Pantelopoulos and Bourbakis, 2010).

Ubiquitous computing has gained critical importance for implementing healthcare applications. By doing this, it is possible to make healthcare services available for anyone at anytime and anywhere. For example, patient data stored in wearable radio-frequency identification (RFIDs) may be read by a physician's smartphone or tablet by means of a wireless communication infrastructure, or data sensed by a pacemaker may be analyzed by the patient's mobile device, and, depending on that analysis, an alert may be sent her/his physician. Furthermore, ubiquity provides the necessary support for monitoring organs (e.g. heart activity) and even patient physical activity by means of biosensors. A mobile application may execute data analytic techniques on collected data.

Thereafter, the application may forward collected data and analytic data to physician's or clinic's computers.

In order to increase the scalability of ubiquitous medical and healthcare applications, one may implement them on an Internet of things (IoT) infrastructure (Islam et al., 2015). It is a matter of fact that IoT provides support for a plethora of applications in healthcare, from remote monitoring to smart sensors and medical device integration. Therefore, integrating ubiquitous medical and healthcare systems with an IoT backbone makes it possible to develop applications for monitoring, for instance, which citizens in a city are in the imminence of having a heart attack.

In da Silva et al. (2015), the authors describe a biosensor for sensing ECG signals, with minimal electrical contact points with users. By doing this, it is possible to avoid the use of gel or conductive paste in the interface with the skin. The authors denoted such an approach as off-person ECG. The key goal of off-person ECG is to support ECG signal acquisition at the palms or fingers. Thus, the proposed biosensor can be embedded in any object with which the user interacts.

CardioNet (2017) provides a mobile cardiac outpatient telemetry (MCOT) service in the United States. MCOT requires the use of proprietary devices, a biosensor, and monitor (Mcot S3) (Kumar et al., 2008). ECG signals are acquired by the biosensor and sent to the monitor. The monitor in turn is in charge of transmitting the ECG signal to a server located in the monitoring center, where certified cardiac technicians analyze the signals. Besides relying on the use of proprietary equipment, making the solution device dependent, ECG signals are analyzed by humans, reducing, in this way, the scalability of the MCOT approach.

A literature review on pervasive healthcare systems is presented in Orwat et al. (2008). According to the authors, 60% of investigated systems provide analytical and diagnostic functionality. Nevertheless, only 46% implement automatic alerting, and from this set of systems, only 14% support an alerting function generated by a mobile device.

As the whole pervasive healthcare system encompasses a wide variety of components, behaving as a multidisciplinary project, one can divide it into a more detailed state of the art for each specific area of study: ECG data acquisition systems (Gari et al. (2006); Yoo et al. (2009); Venkatachalam et al. (2011)), real-time ECG digital signal processing (Pan and Tompkins (1985); Bahoura et al. (1997); Madeiro et al. (2012, 2013); do Vale Madeiro et al. (2017)), feature extraction (Exarchos et al. (2005); Martis et al. (2014); Elhaj et al. (2016)), ECG remote monitoring systems (Pandian et al. (2008); Wen et al. (2008); Worringham et al. (2011)), collaborative databases (Kokkinaki et al. (2006); Gonçalves et al. (2007, 2011)), and machine learning techniques (Faezipour et al. (2010); Yeh et al. (2012); Luz et al. (2016); Elhaj et al. (2016); Shadmand and Mashoufi (2016)). In the next section, the authors will present the modules that compose the proposed framework for PeMo-EC – an intelligent, pervasive, and mobile platform for ECG signal processing and pre-diagnostic extraction – and also provide a detailed literature review related to each specific process.

2.5 PeMo-EC: Description of the Proposed Framework

The proposed framework for the pervasive and mobile platform for ECG signal acquisition, processing, and pre-diagnostic extraction encompasses the following modules: acquisition module, patient's smartphone application and ECG signal processing module, physician's smartphone application and query/alarm module, and collaborative database and data integration module. Figure 2.3 synthesizes the adopted methodology, emphasizing the physiological data flow, from the patient to the physician and to the collaborative database, and also the main actors involved in the process.

2.5.1 Acquisition Module: Biosensors and ECG Data Conditioning

With respect to PeMo-EC, the proposed architecture for the acquisition stage, containing the unidirectional route of the physiological data from the signal acquisition itself until the signal conditioning and local storage of the data

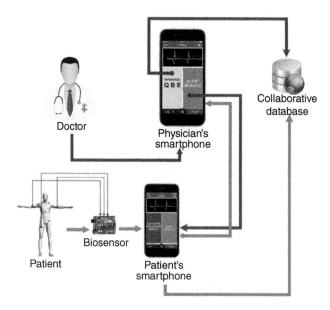

Figure 2.3 Proposed framework. Framework for the pervasive and mobile platform for ECG signal acquisition, processing, and pre-diagnostic extraction.

Figure 2.4 General architecture. General architecture for acquisition stage.

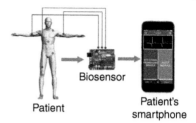

Biosensor

Patient

Patient's smartphone

resulting from ECG processing and feature extraction, beyond the signal itself, in a smartphone environment, is illustrated in Figure 2.4.

ECG recording is classically performed using a so-called electrocardiograph, which measures and registers the electric potentials derived from heart electrical activity. It works as a galvanometer sensitive to minimal current intensities that run in a circuit closed by electrodes placed on body surfaces at predetermined locations. The limb connections (right arm (RA), left arm (LA), and left leg (LL)) are connected as input signals to a switching network through transient protection circuits. Bipolar leads are obtained by referencing each of the limb connections to one of the other two (RA to LA is lead I, RA to LL is lead II, and LA to LL is lead III) (Gari et al. (2006); Hall (2015)).

A block diagram of a typical ECG data recording system is shown in Figure 2.5. The individual ECG wires are connected to the terminal block, and, then, they are routed to various input amplifiers. Before the first stage of amplifying, the transient protection circuits include devices that prevent high voltages at the input of the biosensor from reaching internal circuits, as voltage limiter diodes and Zener diodes. The potential difference of each wire pair (lead) is amplified by an instrumentation amplifier with satisfactory noise

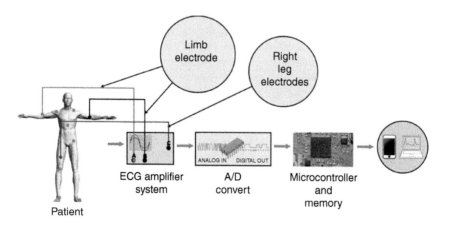

Figure 2.5 Block diagram. Block diagram of a typical ECG data recording system.

and common-mode rejection characteristics (Venkatachalam et al., 2011). Concerning the right leg driver, because the output of the instrumentation amplifier has some noise at line-related frequencies, the outputs of each wire pair are also summed, inverted, and fed back to the patient through a right leg electrode. In practice, this configuration cancels out the original interference components present on the patient's body.

A preamplification stage consists of the first amplification of the raw ECG signal, performed by a differential operational amplifier, which may be directly coupled to the electrodes. Some requirements must be considered so that an operational amplifier can be applied for medical instrumentation: a well-known high input impedance and common-mode rejection, stability for low gain values, low amplitude for bias current, and low values for offset and drift (Prutchi and Norris, 2005). After the preamplifier stage, the raw signal achieves relatively high gain values of up to a few tens. A second amplifier stage is configured to provide gain values to amplify the signal amplitude to higher levels such that the ECG signal can be processed by the further system components (A/D converter and microprocessor). The operational amplifiers at this stage also work as active filters providing analog filtering and a specific frequency response needed for achieving a coherent digitizing process of the ECG signal.

Once provided with the amplifying and filtering processes, the biopotential signal is finally digitized by the A/D converter. The sampling frequencies commonly range from 100 to 500 Hz for conventional electrocardiographs, reaching 2 kHz on high resolution electrocardiographs. For digitizing, the A/D converter must provide a satisfactory resolution, that is, a measure of the ability to distinguish minimum differences in signal amplitude. A 12-bit A/D converter has 4096 levels that can be assigned to an input instantaneous voltage. The MIT-BIH Arrhythmia Database, a well-known database containing digitized ECG signals for validating QRS complex detectors, adopted the 11-bit resolution standard (Goldberger et al. (2000); Venkatachalam et al. (2011)).

For the proposed framework, an arrangement of three electrodes is adopted: one at each arm and one at right leg. The latter (the right leg) is used as a reference for attenuating external interference (Winter and Webster, 1983).

The proposed framework adopts a methodology for ECG recording hardware including the biosensor and the signal conditioning for subsequent transmission of buffers of digitized data to a smartphone (see Figure 2.4). The biosensor (portable electrocardiograph) has one lead and is integrated to a smartphone or other mobile device through Bluetooth protocol. Regarding acquisition itself, one defines the class of electrodes deployed and the placement configuration over the body surface. We consider using three disposable adhesive and conductive electrodes, from Meditrace: Electrode Meditrace 200 Adult, Ag/AgCl, Solid Gel (Hydrogel). They are placed as standardized by leads I, that is, one electrode for the left arm, another electrode for the right arm, and the third one for the right leg, the right leg drive circuit.

The electrodes arranged on the upper extremities provide the input signals for the instrumentation amplifiers containing an alternating current (AC) and a direct current (DC) component (preamplifier). DC potential can reach ±300 mV. The proposed architecture deploys an AC-coupled instrumentation amplifier, which uses a feedback amplifier for restoration of baseline, that is, for canceling the DC component. If the DC component in the input signal increases, the output of the instrumentation amplifier tends to increase. However, an integrator circuit receives, as input signal, the instantaneous output of the instrumentation amplifier and provides an equivalent voltage value, but with inverted polarity, to the reference point of that amplifier, causing the cancelation of the electrode's offset. Thus the original DC coupling for the input signal transforms into AC coupling. Furthermore, the subsequent amplifying stages may enhance the AC component of the ECG signal with a low probability for saturation.

The deployment of a protection circuit is very useful in order to avoid high levels of input voltage reaching other internal electronic circuits causing damage to equipment devices. A practical solution, adopted by Lebedev (2004), consists of inserting a resistor in series with each input line (left arm, right arm, and right leg) such that we can achieve a secure limitation for the input current. Additionally, fast-commuting diodes such as 1N4148 can limit input voltage to 600 mV. Therefore, 390K resistors are inserted in series with each electrode.

The amplifying stage is subdivided into two complementary steps. The first one provides an initial and low-gain amplifying and consists of an instrumental operational amplifier with a high input impedance, and the gain amplitude is of order 10 (INA326, electronic manufacturer Texas Instruments). The input signal of this first step is the potential difference related to lines originating from the left arm and the right arm. Subsequent to the first step of amplifying, the output signal behaves as input signal for a second amplifying circuit, based on an integrator circuit (OPA2335, electronic manufacturer Texas Instruments). This integrator circuit works as a low-pass filter and performs anti-aliasing. The cut frequency is located around 106 Hz and the resultant gain is around 46 dB. The whole amplifying process for the ECG raw signal consists of an instrumental differential amplifier and an integrator circuit, providing a resultant differential gain around 60 dB.

A notch filter is deployed aiming to eliminate the 60 Hz noise component. For this, the instrumental amplifier is combined with the notch twin-T filter and also an operational amplifier on voltage follower configuration (Prutchi and Norris, 2005).

Once filtered and amplified, the analog ECG signal is digitized by an A/D converter provided as a module of the microcontroller PIC16F687 (electronic manufacturer Microchip), which is able to generate a binary code with a resolution of 10 bits, to represent discrete samples of the original signal. Sampling frequency is configurable through the firmware, and the optional values are 250 Hz, 360 Hz, or 1 kHz.

As a bridge for carrying the ECG physiologic signal from the analog world to the digital processing world, a microcontroller is deployed: PIC16F687. Beyond applying the A/D conversion, this processing platform manages data transmission to a smartphone. The microcontroller PIC16F687 is recommended for embedded applications, operating on a wide range of voltages (2–5.5 V), having internal EEPROM memory, low power consumption, 12-channel A/D converter and 10-bit resolution, and EUSART interface, which supports RS-232, RS-485, and LIN 2.0 communication.

For data transmission to computing mobile devices, a Bluetooth interface via a serial port profile is adopted. In order to support data transmission via Bluetooth protocol, the present approach uses an RN41 Class 1 Bluetooth Module from Roving Networks. The RN41 module is a small platform and has a low power class 1 Bluetooth radio that is available for developers who want to add wireless capability to their systems. It supports multiple interface protocols, having an on-chip antenna and support for Bluetooth Enhanced Data Rate (EDR), delivering up to a 3 Mbps data rate for distances up to 100 m. The developed platform is parameterized to use slave and self-discovering pairing mode so that, after the first pairing, it automatically recognizes the PIN of the mobile phone to which the microcontroller should send data, preventing other devices from connecting to the ECG acquisition module and, therefore, accessing the physiological information.

Finally, the firmware, which is a set of programmable instructions recorded in the internal memory EEPROM of the microcontroller, is responsible for managing all the hardware peripherals, parameterizing the sampling frequency for a given acquisition process, controlling the process of the A/D converter (defining a buffer size), and synchronizing the communication with the smartphone to send ECG signal data.

Once the equipment is powered on, the system performs hardware peripheral setup, the Bluetooth radio is activated, and the pairing process between the biosensor (microcontroller) and the smartphone is established. A message in the smartphone app indicates that the pairing process is finished. Then, according to firmware instructions, the microcontroller remains waiting for a request command from the patient's smartphone application.

There are five specific commands that are supported by the firmware concerning communication with patient's smartphone application: parameterizing sampling frequency, testing electrodes, defining buffer size, start exam, and finish exam. The first command allows the definition of the sampling frequency to be applied in the acquisition process, from three possible values: 250 Hz, 360 Hz, or 1 kHz. The second command is to verify if the electrodes are properly adhered to the patient's skin by measuring the impedance of the electrode–tissue interface. Through the third command, one can adjust the

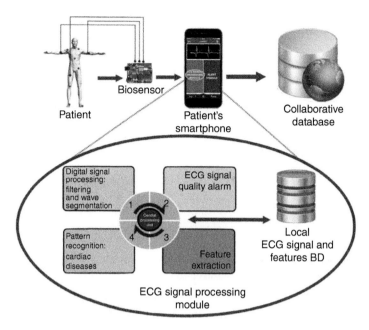

Figure 2.6 ECG signal processing module. ECG signal processing module: processes performed over the digitized ECG signal in the smartphone environment.

temporal size of the buffer of ECG digitized samples that are sent periodically to the patient's smartphone. The default value for buffer size is eight seconds, but a range of values from the interval (7.5–10 seconds) is permissible. Finally, the command start exam is to begin the acquisition process itself, and the last one finishes the acquisition process. All the set of instructions for the firmware is developed in the C language.

Although the capturing of ECG data by a single lead can be considered a limitation of the present approach, the project incorporates a signal quality analysis technique into the ECG signal processing module (Section 2.5.2). Such solution provides for alarms of low signal quality occurrences.

2.5.2 Patient's Smartphone Application: ECG Signal Processing Module

In Figure 2.6, the fundamental processes performed in the smartphone environment needed for achieving feature extraction and recognition of patterns of cardiac diseases and for sending data to a collaborative database are presented.

According to Figure 2.6, an ordered set of signal processing tasks is performed over the buffered and digitized ECG signal, composed of filtering and wave segmentation, signal quality analysis, feature extraction, and recognition of patterns of cardiac diseases. All the algorithms explained in this section need to be implemented using the Java programming language and the code embedded in the Android operating system.

Concerning ECG segmentation, from the automatic processing of the ECG signal through specific algorithms, metrics are extracted from each cardiac cycle and, then, used for the descriptive report of the ECG, namely, duration and amplitude of the P-wave, duration of the iPR (from the beginning of the P-wave until the beginning of the QRS complex) and QT interval (ranging from the beginning of the QRS complex to the end of the T-wave), QRS complex duration and amplitude, and ST-T interval changes.

In spite of the several research studies already developed and published in the literature, the noise removal or attenuation from the ECG signal remains an important object of study. The purpose of the noise filtering process is to reduce the level of interference over the signal while avoiding the occurrence of distortions of the waveforms. The prevention of distortion, as a characteristic of an efficient filtering process, is of vital importance for an accurate analysis or diagnosis of the ECG signal (Agante and De Sá (1999); Luo and Johnston (2010)). Among the most common sources of noise are power network interference, external electromagnetic fields, electrode contact noise, patient movement artifacts, chest wall activity noise, instrumentation noise, and the respiratory activity itself (Nayak (2012); AlMahamdy and Riley (2014); Martis et al. (2014)).

Removal of baseline wandering was one of the first challenges in the area of biomedical signal processing. The two main techniques classically employed are the high-pass linear filtering and the polynomial approximation (Romero, 2008).

The design of a linear and time-invariant high-pass filter requires parameterization of the cutoff frequency and phase response characteristic. One should select the cutoff frequency in such a way that the clinical information present on the ECG signal waves does not distort, i.e. it must be below the lowest ECG signal frequency component (approximately 0.5 Hz). Finite impulse response (FIR) filters provide phase linear response, which is necessary to avoid phase distortions, but depending on the specifications required for the filtering process, such as attenuation in the rejection band and ripple level in the passband, may contain an excessive number of coefficients. The use of infinite impulse response (IIR) filters is more computationally efficient than FIR filters but introduces signal distortion due to nonlinear phase response. As a solution, one use the forward–backward filtering, whose final result corresponds to a zero-phase transfer function (Romero, 2008). In spite of its simplified computational implementation, IIR and FIR filters have limited application and are not capable of eliminating oscillations and interferences of a nonlinear nature, or even abrupt baseline variations present. A simple alternative, which can provide greater robustness and adaptation of the filter to the baseline oscillations, is the polynomial approximation (Lemay et al., 2007). The main disadvantage of this methodology is that the QRS detection and segmentation process, whose accuracy and performance depends on the degree of interference in the signal, must be performed in advance to locate the "anchors" samples.

The elimination of muscle activity noise (EMG noise) remains a challenge not sufficiently overcome in the literature. The bandwidth of its frequency components is significant, overlapping the spectral content of all ECG characteristic waves. Linear bandpass filters do not remove interference caused by EMG noise without causing considerable distortion in the clinical information. On the other hand, the techniques based on wavelet transform (TW) and empirical mode decomposition (EMD) are more effective in attenuating this type of noise (Singh and Tiwari (2006); Tang and Qin (2008)).

The QRS complex is the most expressive waveform of the ECG signal, considering the aspects of amplitude and period of oscillation. The high amplitude of its fiducial point, usually associated with the R-wave, makes the task of its detection easier than for other characteristic waves, thus constituting the first step for complete segmentation of the ECG signal. The correct detection of the QRS complex and its precise delineation are fundamental conditions for efficient detection and segmentation of the other waves, as well as being the basis for the algorithms of recognition of patterns of cardiac arrhythmias (Kohler et al. (2002); Addison (2005)).

The algorithms for signal processing described here are applied over eight second ECG signal buffers. Considering the arrangement of consecutive buffers and that a given QRS complex can start on a given segment and terminate on the subsequent segment, it is defined that each buffer has 0.5 seconds of overlap with the previous segment and 0.5 second overlap with the posterior segment.

The structure of the algorithms is divided into two stages: preprocessing and analysis. The preprocessing step is composed of two filtering processes: elimination of noise components and enhancement of QRS complexes. Considering the use of wavelet transform, the process for denoising requires the accomplishment of the following stages: decomposition, thresholding, and reconstruction (Addison, 2005). For this task, the choice of the base function and the decomposition level is critically important. Considering the spectral content of the ECG signal and the 360 Hz sampling frequency of the analyzed signals, the present approach proposes deploying the Daubechies wavelet of order 4 as the base function and the eighth level of decomposition for eliminating low-frequency noise. For high-frequency noise suppression, the detail coefficients related to the outputs of high-pass filters from the second and third levels of decomposition are eliminated.

After applying wavelet transform for the denoising process, a sequence of filtering routines is established for enhancing the QRS complex and attenuating artifacts and other physiologic waves. As illustrated in Figure 2.7, the

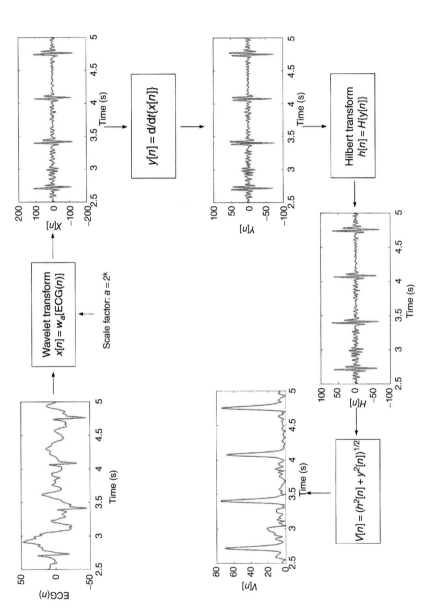

Figure 2.7 QRS detection. Enhancement and detection of QRS complexes.

wavelet transform, the first-derivative function, and the Hilbert transform are sequentially computed, and the module of the resultant analytical signal $V[n]$ is used at a decision stage. An adaptive threshold algorithm is applied over the signal $V[n]$ for individual detection of each QRS (Madeiro et al., 2012).

If the number of detected beats (or QRS complexes) is less than 70% of the analyzed buffer duration (in seconds) or greater than 3.5 times the same duration, an alarm concerning ECG signal quality is activated, which suggests the need for adjustment or repositioning of the electrodes.

Considering a regular number of detected QRS complexes, obeying the conditional limits given above, the computation of an indicator related to the area covered by the QRS complex provides the detection of QRS onset and offset (Madeiro et al., 2012). The envelope is defined as the modulus of the complex signal formed by the filtered ECG signal (the real part) and the Hilbert transform of the filtered ECG signal (the imaginary part) (Sornmo and Laguna, 2005). The detection of QRS onset and offset provides the computing of QRS duration, which is an important feature for recognition of patterns of cardiac diseases.

Concerning the methodology for P-wave and T-wave detection and segmentation, a recently published approach for mathematical modeling of P and T waveforms is applied (Madeiro et al. (2013); do Vale Madeiro et al. (2017)). Firstly, wavelet transform is applied over signal windows established between segmented QRS complexes for estimating T-wave and P-wave peak locations (Martínez et al., 2004). Then, a synthetic function computed as a composition of two Gaussian functions is fitted to each waveform (T-wave and P-wave) by computing the normalized root mean square (RMS) error. This approach provides the delineation of each waveform (by detecting onsets and ends) and the computing of parameters related to the wave width and to a distortion factor of the Gaussian functions that also characterize their morphologies.

After proceeding with the segmentation of the characteristic waves, the proposed system achieves a diversified set of features that may be properly used by machine learning techniques aiming at recognition of patterns of cardiac diseases. It is well known that arrhythmia is a cardiac condition caused by abnormal electrical activity of the heart. The Association for the Advancement of Medical Instrumentation (AAMI) proposes combining all different types of beats into five classes: non-ectopic beats (N), fusion beats (F), supraventricular ectopic beats (S), ventricular ectopic beats (V), and unknown beats (U). Here, it is proposed combining nonlinear features, such as high-order statistics, with linear features, concerning principal component analysis of discrete wavelet transform coefficients, for building heartbeat classification methods (Elhaj et al., 2016).

Finally, built as an Android or iOS app, a graphical interface is provided by the patient's smartphone application. Beyond the specific commands to control processes for starting and finishing ECG acquisition and saving ECG data in a collaborative database, the app allows the patient to receive alerts from his/her physician, who can access the ECG signal data through the collaborative database. Also some input information is asked to an individual patient. Thus, considering any complaints about his/her state of health, the system categorizes the following events: chest pain, shortness of breath, headache, dizziness, palpitations, and accelerated heartbeat, among others.

2.5.3 Physician's Smartphone Application: Query/Alarm Module

The physician's smartphone application aims to provide a graphical interface, also built as an Android or iOS app, for presenting parameters extracted from an ECG signal collected from a given patient and synthesized reports. As illustrated in Figure 2.8, this app also allows a physician to query the collaborative database concerning a set of patient data (signals and extracted features), to write medical reports, and also to trigger alerts, which can be classified as emergency conditions, suspicious conditions, or regular conditions. Each triggered alert is forwarded to the corresponding patient's smartphone application.

As we can observe from the literature review, there are other approaches similar to the proposed framework, with some limitations and drawbacks, not comprehending all the functionalities delineated in this chapter.

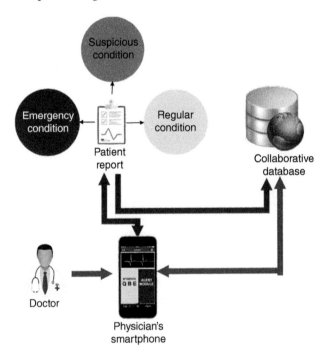

Figure 2.8 Physician's smartphone application. Physician's smartphone application: queries and alert triggering.

In Wen et al. (2008), the authors propose an ECG telemonitoring system. According to their approach, the Holter records the ECG signal of the patient continuously up to 48 hours. The monitored data is transmitted to the server through the Internet when a wired network is available. The Holter also contains a software program performing real-time ECG classification. When specific abnormal heartbeats are detected, the Holter transmits them with the global positioning system (GPS) information to the server via multimedia messaging service (MMS) in real time. The physician at the server side can communicate with the patient also by using MMS if necessary. In the server, a geographic information system (GIS) is resided for locating the patient in an emergency case by using the GPS information packaged in the MMS message.

In Pandian et al. (2008), the authors describe a prototype Smart Vest system used for remote monitoring of physiological parameters and present the clinical validation of the data. The Smart Vest consists of a vest with sensors integrated for monitoring physiological parameters, wearable data acquisition and processing hardware, and remote monitoring station. The wearable data acquisition system is designed using microcontroller and interfaced with wireless communication and GPS modules. The physiological signals monitored are ECG, photoplethysmogram (PPG), body temperature, blood pressure, galvanic skin response (GSR), and heart rate. The acquired physiological signals are sampled at 250 samples/s, digitized at 12-bit resolution and transmitted wireless to a remote physiological monitoring station along with the geo-location of the wearer.

In Worringham et al. (2011), the authors propose a system to enable walking-based cardiac rehabilitation in which the patient's single-lead ECG, heart rate, GPS-based speed, and location are transmitted by a programmed smartphone to a secure server for real-time monitoring by physicians. According to the authors, the feasibility of this approach was evaluated in 134 remotely monitored exercise assessment and exercise sessions in cardiac patients unable to undertake hospital-based rehabilitation. Completion rates, rates of technical problems, detection of ECG changes, pre- and post-intervention six minute walk test (6 MWT), cardiac depression, and quality of life (QOL) were key measures. Several exercise and post-exercise ECG changes were detected.

2.5.4 The Collaborative Database: Data Integration Module

2.5.4.1 Motivation

Innovation in heart disease research has been severely hampered in part by the fragmented gathering and storing of data. In general, data about patients, treatments, drugs, and ECGs are housed in isolated silos. Since the 1970s, the storage of ECG data has been the object of standardization initiatives. Among the major ECG standards, we can highlight (i) AHA/MIT-BIH (PhysioNet) (Goldberger et al., 2000), an ECG data format extensively used in cardiac physiology research; (ii) SCP-ECG (Mandellos et al., 2010), which is an ECG

European standard that specifies a data format and a transmission protocol for ECG records; and (iii) HL7 aECG (Bond et al. (2011)), which is an ECG data American standard adopted by the Food and Drug Administration (FDA), from the United States, for clinical research.

Nevertheless, the concepts underlying these ECG standards are heterogeneous in spite of the fact that all of them address the same domain. This heterogeneity, even with respect to the core ECG concepts, could be partially justified by their different purposes. The focus of these ECG standards is mostly on how data should be represented in computer and messaging systems. In this way, such standards are to encompass headers, IDs, and sections. Thus, they do not favor a possible consensual model of ECG, which is essential to data integration (Gonçalves et al., 2011).

This knowledge needs to be integrated. To make matters worse, typically heart disease knowledge is expressed in ambiguous terminology. Without the aid of a well-defined knowledge representation, the ad hoc data integration is a hard work. In addition to the challenge of ad hoc data integration, an equal challenge to heart research is querying complex heart data.

In this context, we propose a collaborative and integrated database whose purpose is:

- To integrate data in heterogeneous ECG standards, that is, stores ECG data coming from various sources with different data standards (AHA/MIT-BIH, SCP-ECG, and HL7 aECG).
- To integrate data about patients, treatments, drugs, and ECG.
- To store ECG data coming from patient's smartphones.
- To make possible querying complex heart data.
- To answer SPARQL queries coming from physician's smartphones.
- To support the collaboration among teams of physicians, which can access the same ECG data and share diagnostic information and second opinion, according to their expertise.
- To enable running data mining algorithms over integrated data.
- To store historical records about the alerts generated by both the patient's and the physician's apps.

In order to design and build this integrated database, it is essential:

- To build a consensual model of ECG data.
- To build an integrated model encompassing concepts about ECG, patients, treatments, and drugs.
- To wrap data described in heterogeneous ECG standards into the integrated mode.
- To store the integrated data.
- To build a Query by Example (QBE) interface to query and export the integrated data.

Thus, to support the design of the collaborative database, we give up the Semantic Web technologies, such as RDF, OWL, SKOS, and SPARQL. These technologies enable the explicit representation of knowledge and its processing to deduce new knowledge from implicitly hidden knowledge. Besides, they provide an environment where heterogeneous data can be combined based on a common knowledge representation, the schemata can be extended in an easily and dynamic way, applications can query that integrated data and draw inferences using vocabularies, etc. Next, we will discuss how some Semantic Web technologies were used to design the proposed database.

2.5.4.2 The Design of the Collaborative Database

The Semantic Web technology, and its various standards, seeks to promote common data formats and exchange protocols on the Web. Thus, Semantic Web technology provides a common framework that enables people to share and reuse data across application, enterprise, and community boundaries. It combines a highly distributable addressing and naming mechanism (Uniform Resource Identifiers (URIs)) with a formal knowledge representation (RDF and OWL) and a common query language (SPARQL).

Therefore, the key Semantic Web provides the following advantages:

- Use of a standard terminology.
- Support for unanticipated modeling extensions.
- Support for data integration and mapping with external sources and terminologies.
- Support for accurate answering of expressive queries.

According to W3C, "vocabularies" define the concepts and relationships (also referred to as "terms") used to describe and represent an area of concern. So, vocabularies are used to classify the terms that can be used in a particular domain, characterize relationships between terms, and define constraints on using those terms. In practice, vocabularies can be very simple (describing few concepts) or very complex (with thousands of terms).

Unfortunately, there is not a clear division between what is referred to as "vocabularies" and "ontologies." In general, the trend is to use the word "ontology" for a more complex and quite formal collection of terms, whereas "vocabulary" is used when such formalism is not necessary.

It is important to highlight that vocabularies are the basic building blocks for inference techniques on the Semantic Web. Vocabularies are used to help data integration when, for example, ambiguities may exist in the terms used in the different datasets or to support the discovery of new relationships. Consider, for example, the application of ontologies in the field of heart disease. Medical professionals use them to represent knowledge about symptoms, treatments, and ECG signals. Pharmaceutical companies use them to represent information about drugs, dosages, and allergies. Combining the patient data with pharmaceutical companies' knowledge enables a whole range of intelligent applications such as decision support tools that search for possible causes or treatments, monitor drug efficacy and possible side effects, and support heart disease research.

In Gonçalves et al. (2011), the authors proposed an ECG reference ontology, that is, an ontology resulting from an application-independent representation of the ECG domain. This reference ontology can be used to support the design of interoperable versions of ECG data formats like AHA/MIT-BIH, SCP-ECG, and HL7 aECG. So, the elements that are present in these data formats could be semantically mirrored with the entities in the ECG reference ontology. Thus, it can be employed in an effective manner to achieve semantic data integration between ECG standards.

The ECG reference ontology proposed in Gonçalves et al. (2011) is composed of three sub-ontologies: the anatomy sub-ontology [based on the FMA (Rosse and Mejino, 2003)], the heart electrophysiology sub-ontology [based on the OF (Burek et al., 2006)], and the ECG sub-ontology. The ECG sub-ontology comprises two main models. The first one covers the ECG representation on the side of the patient, i.e. the ECG as it is acquired from a patient. The second one covers ECG representation on the side of the physician, i.e. the waveform resulting from the process of ECG acquisition.

Besides, the work presented in Gonçalves et al. (2011) discusses the semantic integration between the proposed reference ontology and three different ECG data formats: AHA/MIT-BIH, SCP-ECG, and HL7 aECG. This was conducted as follows. Firstly, each element of each ECG data format has been analyzed in order to match a corresponding entity in the ECG reference ontology. These correspondences are relationships that give to the ECG data standards' symbolic elements a real-world semantics according to the ECG reference ontology.

This ECG reference ontology can be used to support the redesign and the possible unification of existing ECG data standards. In this sense, it can be used to support the design of an interoperable and collaborative ECG data repository, which can store ECG signals from various data sources with different ECG data standards. However, in order to build a wide ECG repository that makes it possible to answer complex queries, it is necessary to extend the reference ontology proposed in Gonçalves et al. (2011), adding concepts related to drugs, treatments, and disease causes, among others, which is one of the goals of the proposed framework for PeMo-EC.

With this in mind, we designed a collaborative and integrated database that is based in the Semantic Web technologies. Figure 2.9 illustrates the architecture of the proposed database. The main components of this database are discussed next:

- *Extended reference ontology*: An ontology integrating concepts related to ECG, drugs, treatments, and disease causes.

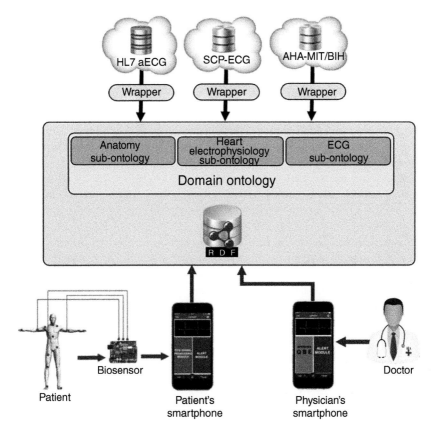

Figure 2.9 Collaborative database. Proposed collaborative and integrated database for ECG Data.

- *RDF repository*: An open-source repository for heart research. It makes possible the identification of data cohorts (including patients, medicines, treatments, and ECGs) for study and the export of data for statistical analysis. Besides, the RDF repository will make it possible to infer new knowledge through the use of machine learning algorithms.
- *Wrappers*: Encapsulate sources, converting the underlying ECG data to a common data model.

2.5.4.3 Data Mining and Pattern Recognition

It is a consensus that ECG data contain valuable knowledge and can reveal information about several diseases. Over the years, ECG data has been used in order to diagnose cardiovascular diseases and to analyze the prognoses for upcoming abnormalities. On the other hand, in the last two decades, machine learning algorithms have been used for heartbeat classification and arrhythmia disease diagnostics.

Recent trends in medical applications highly demand automation in ECG signal processing and heartbeat classification. In the last few years, several works have been produced in the area of automatic ECG beat detection. In Faezipour et al. (2010), the authors proposed a patient-adaptive cardiac profiling scheme using the repetition-detection concept. They introduced a technique for profiling the normal ECG waveform for any person by first detecting the beats accurately. The proposed beat detection scheme was a hybrid of Pan and Tompkins' algorithm (Pan and Tompkins, 1985) and wavelet analysis approach. Then, it classified the detected features of the beats by means of repetition-based packet-processing techniques. The outcome is a profiling curve specific to any person, representing a graphical view of the existence of abnormal beats.

In Shadmand and Mashoufi (2016), the authors proposed an approach to classify ECG signals in five classes according to the AAMI recommendations (N, VEB, SVEB, F, and Q). The features that are extracted from ECG signals have been used as block-based neural network (BBNN) inputs. Hermite function coefficients and RR interval have been used as feature vector parameters. The particle swarm optimization method was used as a BBNN training algorithm and also to optimize the BBNN structure and the weights.

In Elhaj et al. (2016), the authors investigated the representation ability of linear and nonlinear features and proposed a combination of such features in order to improve the classification of ECG data. In this study, five types of beat classes of arrhythmia, as recommended by the AAMI, are analyzed: non-ectopic beats (N), supraventricular ectopic beats (S), ventricular ectopic beats (V), fusion beats (F), and unclassifiable and paced beats (U). The proposed method for ECG arrhythmia classification consists of a combination of PCA with DWT, ICA, and HOS feature extraction methods and two different classifiers (SVM-RBF and NN).

In Yeh et al. (2012), the authors proposed an approach of analyzing an ECG signal in order to diagnose cardiac arrhythmias utilizing the cluster analysis (CA) method. The proposed approach can classify and distinguish the difference between normal heartbeats (NORM) and abnormal heartbeats. Abnormal heartbeats may include the following classes: LBBB, RBBB, ventricular premature contractions (VPC), and atrial premature contractions (APC). In the proposed approach, the analysis of an ECG signal consists of three major stages: (i) detecting the QRS waveform, (ii) selecting qualitative features, and (iii) determining heartbeat case. CA was used to determine the patient heartbeat case.

It is important to highlight that these works focus on the heartbeat classification and on the arrhythmia disease diagnostics. However, using the proposed collaborative database that includes information about patients, symptoms, diseases, diseases causes, treatments, and drugs will make it possible to build more intelligent systems, answer more complex queries, and discover new patterns. For example, given an ECG signal, besides classifying this signal and indicating a possible arrhythmia disease, it will be possible to evince, with some probability, what are the possible causes of the disease.

2.6 Conclusions

In this chapter, we presented a ubiquitous platform, called PeMo-EC, for prevention, follow-up, and aid to cardiological urgency. PeMo-EC is composed of (i) a hardware component, responsible for acquiring an ECG signal and sending it to a mobile computing device, and (ii) a software layer, running on portable devices and servers, which is in charge of providing visualization, automatic analysis, and pre-diagnostic data, based on the collected ECG signals. Additionally, a collaborative database for ECG signal data, diagnostic, and tracing interpretation information is available to researchers and physicians.

PeMo-EC supports full ubiquitous computing properties. By doing this, it is available to patient or health professionals anywhere and anytime.

The following innovation points can be highlighted for the proposed platform: an ECG acquisition system based on open code and open structure; algorithms for ECG signal analysis, segmentation, and feature extraction running on different mobile platforms, including Android and iOS operating systems; methodology for automatic alarms and signaling of events to the physician, based on the extracted parameters; design of a collaborative database with a reference ontology for ECG data, aiming at storage of patient data and signals; support for SPARQL queries; and communication and integration of data between the collaborative database and other public databases of physiological signals.

Currently, the biosensor and the ECG signal acquisition module are in test phase, and the patient's smartphone application and the physician's smartphone application are in development, as are the collaborative database and the ECG reference ontology.

Acknowledgements

The authors acknowledge the support of the Brazilian Research Council, CNPq (Grants n. 426002/2016-4 and n. 446090/2014-0).

Bibliography

Addison, P.S. (2005). Wavelet transforms and the ECG: a review. *Physiological Measurement* **26** (5): R155.

Agante, P.M. and De Sá, J.P.M. (1999). ECG noise filtering using wavelets with soft-thresholding methods. In: Computers in Cardiology, 535–538. IEEE.

AlMahamdy, M. and Riley, H.B. (2014). Performance study of different denoising methods for ECG signals. *Procedia Computer Science* **37**: 325–332.

Bahoura, M., Hassani, M., and Hubin, M. (1997). DSP implementation of wavelet transform for real time ECG wave forms detection and heart rate analysis. *Computer Methods and Programs in Biomedicine* **52** (1): 35–44.

Bond, R.R., Finlay, D.D., Nugent, C.D., and Moore, G. (2011). A review of ECG storage formats. *International Journal of Medical Informatics* **80** (10): 681–697.

Brayner, A., Aguiar, J., Filho, M. et al. (2009). Ensuring mobile databases interoperability in ad hoc configurable environments: a plug-and-play approach. In: *Methods and Supporting Technologies for Data Analysis* (ed. D. Zakrzewska, E. Menasalvas, and L. Byczkowska-Lipinska), Studies in Computational Intelligence, vol. **225**, 187–217. Springer-Verlag.

Burek, P., Hoehndorf, R., Loebe, F. et al. (2006). A top-level ontology of functions and its application in the open biomedical ontologies. *Bioinformatics* **22** (14): e66–e73.

CardioNet (2017). MS Windows NT kernel description. http://www.cardionet .com (accessed 01 August 2017).

Daar, A.S., Singer, P.A., Persad, D.L. et al. (2007). Grand challenges in chronic non-communicable diseases. *Nature* **450** (7169): 494–496.

Elhaj, F.A., Salim, N., Harris, A.R. et al. (2016). Arrhythmia recognition and classification using combined linear and nonlinear features of ECG signals. *Computer Methods and Programs in Biomedicine* **127**: 52–63.

Exarchos, T.P., Tsipouras, M.G., Nanou, D. et al. (2005). A platform for wide scale integration and visual representation of medical intelligence in cardiology: the decision support framework. In: *Computers in Cardiology*, 167–170. IEEE.

Faezipour, M., Saeed, A., Bulusu, S.C. et al. (2010). A patient-adaptive profiling scheme for ECG beat classification. *IEEE Transactions on Information Technology in Biomedicine* **14** (5): 1153–1165.

Friedewald, M. and Raabe, O. (2011). Ubiquitous computing: an overview of technology impacts. *Telematics and Informatics* **28** (2): 55–65.

Gari, D.C., Francisco, A., and Patrick, E.M. (2006). *Advanced Methods and Tools for ECG Data Analysis*. Artech House, Inc.

Goldberger, A.L., Amaral, L.A.N., Glass, L. et al. (2000). Physiobank, physiotoolkit, and physionet. *Circulation* **101** (23): e215–e220.

Gonçalves, B., Guizzardi, G., Gonçalves, J., and Pereira Filho, J.G. (2007). An electrocardiogram (ECG) domain ontology. In: *Workshop on Ontologies and Metamodels for Software and Data Engineering*, 2e, 68–81. Brazil: Jo ao Pessoa.

Gonçalves, B., Guizzardi, G., and Pereira Filho, J.G. (2011). Using an ECG reference ontology for semantic interoperability of ECG data. *Journal of Biomedical Informatics* **44** (1): 126–136.

Hall, J.E. (2015). *Guyton and Hall Textbook of Medical Physiology E-Book*. Elsevier Health Sciences.

Islam, S.M.R., Kwak, D., Kabir, M.D.H. et al. (2015). The internet of things for health care: a comprehensive survey. *IEEE Access* **3**: 678–708.

Kohler, B.-U., Hennig, C., and Orglmeister, R. (2002). The principles of software QRS detection. *IEEE Engineering in Medicine and Biology Magazine* **21** (1): 42–57.

Kokkinaki, A., Chouvarda, I., and Maglaveras, N. (2006). Integrating SCP-ECG files and patient records: an ontology based approach. Information Technology Applications in Biomedicine.

Kumar, S., Kambhatla, K., Hu, F. et al. (2008). Ubiquitous computing for remote cardiac patient monitoring: a survey. *International Journal of Telemedicine and Applications* **2008**: 19. https://doi.org/10.1155/2008/459185.

Lebedev, V.V. (2004). Comparison of two circuits for protection of an electrocardiograph against defibrillator pulses. *Biomedical Engineering* **38** (1): 32–33.

Lemay, M., Vesin, J.-M., Van Oosterom, A. et al. (2007). Cancellation of ventricular activity in the ECG: evaluation of novel and existing methods. *IEEE Transactions on Biomedical Engineering* **54** (3): 542–546.

Luo, S. and Johnston, P. (2010). A review of electrocardiogram filtering. *Journal of Electrocardiology* **43** (6): 486–496.

Luz, E.J.S., Schwartz, W.R., Cámara-Chávez, G., and Menotti, D. (2016). ECG-based heartbeat classification for arrhythmia detection: a survey. *Computer Methods and Programs in Biomedicine* **127**: 144–164.

Madeiro, J.P.V., Cortez, P.C., Marques, J.A.L. et al. (2012). An innovative approach of QRS segmentation based on first-derivative, Hilbert and Wavelet transforms. *Medical Engineering & Physics* **34** (9): 1236–1246.

Madeiro, J.P.V., Nicolson, W.B., Cortez, P.C. et al. (2013). New approach for T-wave peak detection and T-wave end location in 12-lead paced ECG signals based on a mathematical model. *Medical Engineering & Physics* **35** (8): 1105–1115.

Mandellos, G.J., Koukias, M.N., Styliadis, I.St., and Lymberopoulos, D.K. (2010). e-SCP-ECG+ protocol: an expansion on SCP-ECG protocol for health telemonitoring–pilot implementation. *International Journal of Telemedicine and Applications* **2010**: 1.

Martínez, J.P., Almeida, R., Olmos, S., Rocha, A.P., and Laguna, P. (2004). A wavelet-based ECG delineator: evaluation on standard databases. *IEEE Transactions on Biomedical Engineering* **51** (4): 570–581.

Martis, R.J., Acharya, U.R., and Adeli, H. (2014). Current methods in electrocardiogram characterization. *Computers in Biology and Medicine* **48**: 133–149.

Nayak, S. (2012). Filtering techniques for ECG signal processing.

Orwat, C., Graefe, A., and Faulwasser, T. (2008). Towards pervasive computing in health care – a literature review. *BMC Medical Informatics and Decision Making* **8** (1). https://doi.org/10.1186/1472-6947-8-26.

Pan, J. and Tompkins, W.J. (1985). A real-time QRS detection algorithm. *IEEE Transactions on Biomedical Engineering* 3: 230–236.

Pandian, P.S., Mohanavelu, K., Safeer, K.P. et al. (2008). Smart vest: wearable multi-parameter remote physiological monitoring system. *Medical Engineering & Physics* **30** (4): 466–477.

Pantelopoulos, A. and Bourbakis, N.G. (2010). A survey on wearable sensor-based systems for health monitoring and prognosis. *IEEE Transactions on Systems, Man, and Cybernetics Part C: Applications and Reviews* **40** (1): 1–12.

Prutchi, D. and Norris, M. (2005). *Design and Development of Medical Electronic Instrumentation: A Practical Perspective of the Design, Construction, and Test of Medical Devices*. Wiley.

Romero, V.B. (2008). ECG baseline wander removal and noise suppression analysis in an embedded platform. Proyecto Fin de Master en Ingeniería de Computadores, Master en Investigacion en Informatica, Facultad de Informatica, Universidad Complutense de Madrid.

Rosse, C. and Mejino, J.L.V. (2003). A reference ontology for biomedical informatics: the foundational model of anatomy. *Journal of Biomedical Informatics* **36** (6): 478–500.

da Silva, H.P., Carreiras, C., Lourenço, A. et al. (2015). Off-the-person electrocardiography: performance assessment and clinical correlation. *Health and Technology* **4** (4): 309–318. https://doi.org/10.1007/s12553-015-0098-y.

Sgora, A. and Vergados, D.D. (2009). Handoff prioritization and decision schemes in wireless cellular networks: a survey. *IEEE Communications Surveys & Tutorials* **11** (4): 57–77.

Shadmand, S. and Mashoufi, B. (2016). A new personalized ECG signal classification algorithm using block-based neural network and particle swarm optimization. *Biomedical Signal Processing and Control* **25**: 12–23.

Singh, B.N. and Tiwari, A.K. (2006). Optimal selection of wavelet basis function applied to ECG signal denoising. *Digital Signal Processing* **16** (3): 275–287.

Sornmo, L. and Laguna, P. (2005). Biomedical signal processing in cardiac and neurological applications. In: *Biomedical Engineering*. New York: Academic Press.

Tang, G. and Qin, A. (2008). ECG de-noising based on empirical mode decomposition. In: The 9th International Conference for Young Computer Scientists, 2008. ICYCS 2008, 903–906. IEEE.

do Vale Madeiro, J.P., dos Santos, E.M.B.E., Cortez, P.C. et al. (2017). Evaluating Gaussian and Rayleigh-based mathematical models for T and P-waves in ECG. *IEEE Latin America Transactions* **15** (5): 843–853.

Venkatachalam, K.L., Herbrandson, J.E., and Asirvatham, S.J. (2011). Signals and signal processing for the electrophysiologist. *Circulation: Arrhythmia and Electrophysiology* **4** (6): 965–973.

Wen, C., Yeh, M.-F., Chang, K.-C., and Lee, R.-G. (2008). Real-time ECG telemonitoring system design with mobile phone platform. *Measurement* **41** (4): 463–470.

Winter, B.B. and Webster, J.G. (1983). Driven-right-leg circuit design. *IEEE Transactions on Biomedical Engineering* **1**: 62–66.

Worringham, C., Rojek, A., and Stewart, I. (2011). Development and feasibility of a smartphone, ECG and GPS based system for remotely monitoring exercise in cardiac rehabilitation. *PLoS ONE* **6** (2): e14669.

Yeh, Y.-C., Chiou, C.W., and Lin, H.-J. (2012). Analyzing ECG for cardiac arrhythmia using cluster analysis. *Expert Systems with Applications* **39** (1): 1000–1010.

Yoo, J., Yan, L., Lee, S. et al. (2009). A wearable ECG acquisition system with compact planar-fashionable circuit board-based shirt. *IEEE Transactions on Information Technology in Biomedicine* **13** (6): 897–902.

3

The Impact of Implantable Sensors in Biomedical Technology on the Future of Healthcare Systems

Ashraf Darwish [1], Gehad Ismail Sayed [2], and Aboul Ella Hassanien [2]

[1] *Faculty of Science, Helwan University, Cairo, Egypt*
[2] *Faculty of Computers and Information, Cairo University, Cairo, Egypt*

3.1   Introduction

Wireless sensor network (WSN) technology has the ability to change the style of life in different areas of the real-world applications such as healthcare monitoring, industry management of emergency situations, environment, and other applications (Darwish and Hassanien 2011). Body sensor network can be divided into wearable body area network (WBAN) (where sensors are worn on the body) and implantable body area network (IBAN) (sensors are placed at an accessible location). The structure of body sensor network includes different kinds of networks, wearable and implantable sensors, and other wireless devices that are capable of monitoring elderly and people with chronic diseases by transmitting information over a short/long distance. In existing IBANs, sensor nodes are implanted either by invasive surgery or under the skin of patients and connected to a base station using a wireless link. A patient's physiological data such as heart rate and blood pressure can be monitored in this way to increase the chances of early detection of diseases.

In the last decade, researchers in fields such as information technology, nanotechnology, and medical sciences have focused on working together to ensure a broad vision for the future of IBANs. There are a number of the developments of monitoring systems developed and used in medical applications as in Yuce (2010), Yuce et al. (2009), and Espina et al. (2008) based on biomedical technology.

In WBANs there are multiple sensors that are involved and wires are used to connect the sensors to a wearable wireless transmitter of data. In addition, WBANs restrict the movement of patient's level, especially during sleep studies and they can cause skin infections. On the other hand, IBANs have showed a great success and significant advantages over the traditional WBANs where patients are continuously being monitored in real time with different diseases. Furthermore, IBANs have the possibility of reducing the cost of healthcare monitoring (Mohseni and Najafi 2005; Yuce 2010). The implementation of medical monitoring systems uses sensor nodes and has no standard for WSNs of medical applications. Most of wireless technologies that are used in healthcare monitoring are described in Table 3.1.

Table 3.1 contains medical bands such as Medical Implant Communication Service (MICS) and Wireless Medical Telemetry Service (WMTS) that are used for healthcare monitoring by most of communication commissions around the world as in Hanna (2009). In addition, there are classes of implantable devices such as sensors for nerve stimulation that can ease acute pain, sensors for detection of electric signals in the brain, and sensors for monitoring the biological analysis in the brain with implanted drug delivery systems. The range of implantable biomedical devices such as neural stimulators, pacemakers, and drug delivery systems will increase significantly over the next few years, thanks to improved technology in Micro Systems Technologies achieved during the last years. ISs category represents an important class of biosensors according to their ability to measure metabolite levels without the need for the intervention of patient, regardless of the patient's physiological position (sleep, rest, etc.) (Clark and Lyons 1962; Shults et al. 1994). For example, ISs represent a desirable solution for diabetes management, which currently relies on the data obtained using blood test via finger pricking, which is not only painful but also is incapable of reflecting the overall direction, trends, and patterns associated with the habits of everyday life (Reach and Wilson 1992; Vaddiraju et al., 2010). In another example, IBANs can assist blind people to improve their vision as in Khan et al. (2009). Patients with no vision or who are visually impaired can see at a reasonable level by using retina prosthesis chips implanted within a human eye, as shown in Figure 3.1. There are a large number of researches of IBANs with different applications in the healthcare field as in Schwiebert et al. (2001) and Aziz et al. (2006).

This chapter explores IBANs to provide rich contextual information and alerting mechanisms for continuous monitoring of patients under abnormal conditions at large. In addition, this chapter provides the state-of-the-art research activities and presents the issues to be addressed to improve the quality of life through the IBANs. Research problems, recent trends, and the future work from the perspective of ISs for healthcare monitoring have been addressed in the end of this chapter. Inspired by well-known indications in literature surveys, we adopt the research methodology schematically depicted in Figure 3.2.

This chapter is organized as follows: Previous and related works have been presented in Section 3.2 and the purpose of this work in Section 3.3. In Section 3.4 some fundamental of IBANs are discussed with emphasis on

Table 3.1 Wireless technologies used in healthcare applications as described in (Espina et al. 2008; Clark and Lyons 1962).

Item	MICS	WMTS	UWB IEEE (802.15.6)	IEEE 802.15.4 (ZigBee)	IEEE 802.15.1 (Bluetooth)	WLAN (802.11b/g)
Frequency band	402–405 MHz	608–614, 1395–1400, 1429–1432 MHz	3–10 GHz	2.4 GHz (868/915 MHz Eur./US)	2.4 GHz	2.4 GHz
Bandwidth data rate	3 MHz, 19 or 76 MHz	6 MHz, 76 kbps	>500 MHz, 850 kbps, 20 Mbps	5 MHz, 250 kbps (2.4 GHz)	1 MHz, 721 kbps	720 MHz, > 11 Mbps
Multiple access	CSMA/CA, polling	CSMA/CA, polling	Not defined	CSMA/CA	FHSS/GFSK	OFDMA, CSMA/CA
Trans. power	−16 dbm (25 μW)	≥10 dbm and<1.8 db	−41 dbm	0 dbm	4, 20 dbm	250 mW
Range	0–10 m	>100 m	1, 2 m	0–10 m	10, 100 m	0–100 m

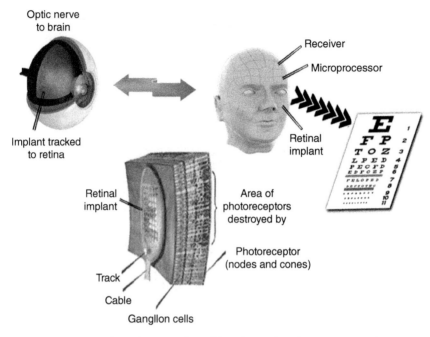

Figure 3.1 Retina implants. Source: Adapted from (Darwish and Hassanien 2011).

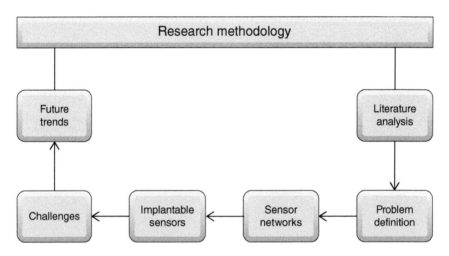

Figure 3.2 Research methodology.

ISs, applications, and security issues. Challenges and future work have been presented in Section 3.5, and conclusion and recommendation of the chapter Section 3.6.

3.2 Related Work

IBANs for healthcare applications have been presented in research papers covering a survey and analyze this kind of networks in wireless communication environment. Authors in Vaddiraju et al. (2010) presented a comprehensive review of ISs, highlighting the synergy between nanotechnology and sensor performance. This chapter focuses on the electrochemical method of detection in light of its wide use of considerable improvements in nanotechnology in various performance aspects of electrochemical sensors. Issues concerning toxicity and biocompatibility of nanomaterials, along with future prospects for the application of nanotechnology in ISs are also discussed in this chapter. A review of the activities of the smart sensor for medical applications is presented in Ponmozhi et al. (2012). The development for smart implants such as hip and knee arthroplasty caused a revolution in the field of medicine with less work for the doctors and worry for the patients. The implantable enzyme amperometric sensors is still the dominant in vivo format for the detection, monitoring, and reporting of biochemical analytes related to a wide range of pathologies. An implantable enzyme amperometric sensor is a bioanalytical technology system that is intended to measure and remotely transmit a specific record of molecular level of a biological analyte within the human body. In Kotanen et al. (2012), there are some challenges to successful deployment of chronically implantable amperometric enzyme sensors, which emphasizes the emerging technological approaches in their continued development as outlined. Although the research and development for body area networks has gained maturity in recent years, IBANs built from nanomachines represent a new and important direction of research. In-body nanocommunication, which is based on molecular and acoustic supports, is the exchange of messages between these in-body devices. The control and communication with external units are not fully understood. In Dressler (2015), the authors investigated the challenges and opportunities of connecting body area networks and other external gateways with in-body nanodevices, paving the way toward more efficient Internet of Nano Things systems, which represent a new direction of research in healthcare applications. ISs in the cardiac resynchronization therapy device play an important role and provide a unique opportunity for continuous monitoring of the patient's clinical heart failure status by measuring the cardiac rhythm, intracardiac pressures, cardiac events, and physical activities, as well as detecting any device malfunction. Therefore, detecting signs of deteriorating clinical cases provides a quick preemptive medical intervention to improve the heart failure management. Therefore, authors in Liu and Tse (2013) introduced the latest available device-based remote monitoring systems and the most up-to-date evidence for the use of remote monitoring in cardiac resynchronization therapy. To overcome the high power demand of wireless communication in IBAN, the concept of wake-up radio and some Medium Access Control (MAC) protocols with the wake-up feature that are suitable for IBAN have been presented in Ramachandran et al. (2014). Wireless power transfer concept offers users the freedom from annoying wires and allows seamless powering and charging of portable devices in an unburdened mode. Basic radio-frequency-based wireless technologies, such as wireless communication, wireless sensing, and wireless powering, are nowadays playing a critical role in social and economic activities of our daily life. As the usage of portable electronic devices (e.g. cell phones, laptops, tablets, and PDAs), high power electric vehicles and biomedical implant sensors equipped with rechargeable batteries become pervasive, and regular charging of these devices has become a critical problem despite their portability and ability to communicate wirelessly. Most of these devices still require manual plugging with the wired charging system when the charge is depleted. From such nuisance, the need for cordless charging or powering has resurfaced in order to offer feasible connector-free portable devices. Authors in Barman et al. (2015) highlight the recent research activities on wireless power technology that cover history, basic concepts, and principles of magnetic resonant coupling, and early researches on resonant coupled wireless power transfer and the two fundamental concepts of power transmission, the maximum power transfer and maximum energy efficiency principles, are resummarized in this chapter in terms of their energy efficiency and transmission distance capabilities. A wireless programmable electronic platform for implantable monitoring of blood glucose level was developed and preliminary tested on bench in Valdastri et al. (2009) .The authors in this chapter proposed a new system that allows extremely low power bidirectional telemetry, based on the IEEE802.15.4-2003 protocol, thus enabling typical battery lifetime up to six months and wireless networking of multiple sensors. An implantable encapsulated structure that can deliver localized heating (hyperthermia) and controlled concentrations of prodigiosin (a cancer drug) synthesized by bacteria has been presented in Danyuo et al. (2014). Even though blood pressure is one of the most important physiological parameters, there is at present no means available for continuously monitoring this quantity without limiting a patient's movement. Continuous long-term monitoring of blood pressure over a day would provide considerably more physiological insights than isolated clinical measurements. But there are efforts in this direction. One of these investigations is presented in Theodor et al. (2014), where a sensor system for the continuous monitoring of blood pressure using an acceleration sensor implanted in an artery using minimally invasive techniques. The sensor depends on the measurements of the reflected wave transit time. In addition, this implantable system is fabricated on a flexible substrate using 2 mm × 2 mm acceleration sensors and a telemetric unit for transmission of the data. The proposed system in this work was implanted in an animal and was able to telemetrically transmit acceleration plethysmographs with high quality output of the awake animal. Diabetes has become a global pandemic. The World Health Organization declared that about 350 million people in the world suffer from diabetes, and on the basis of current projections, diabetes will be one of the 7 diseases that cause the death in 2030 (Danaei et al. 2011). Clark and Lyons (1962) is the "The Father of Biosensors," and the modern-day glucose sensor used daily by millions of diabetics is based on his research. The application of a simple model is considered in determining the glucose concentrations on the use of an immobilized glucose oxidase membrane, which was the first amperometric biosensor found in the literature by Clark and Lyons (1962). Diabetes is characterized by hyperglycemia, an elevated level of glucose (sugar) in the blood, which can be caused by either the lack of production of insulin in the body or by the body's inability to use its produced insulin. Insulin is the hormone that may help the glucose in blood to be absorbed by the body's cells. Both types of diabetes can be treated by externally supplying the necessary insulin to the body; however, if insulin is not given, the glucose levels in the blood can increase to a point where the eyes, kidneys, heart, and nerves can be damaged (Shaw and Cummings 2005). Both monitoring and careful control of the glucose level in the blood are necessary for the appropriate diagnosis and treatment of diabetes. Therefore, frequent testing of physiological glucose levels is crucial in order to avoid the emergency situations, such as hypoglycemia, and to prevent long-term complications from arising, which include heart attack, stroke, high blood pressure, kidney failure, blindness, and limb amputation (Diabetes Atlas 2006; Nichols et al. 2013). It was recommended that diabetes patients have their blood glucose levels tested several times a day to make sure they are within a safe range. Thus, for the proper care and management of diabetes, accurate blood glucose level measurement is crucial. Recently, there is an overwhelming demand for the development and improvement of the glucose sensors. The number of people who need these sensors significantly has increased over the last years and so does the demand to make sensors that are both biocompatible and have increased sensing capabilities compared to current technologies. To meet these requirements and to move toward nonenzymatic glucose, sensors had begun. These new sensors have great significant importance because of their ability to achieve continuous glucose monitoring, high stability compared with traditional glucose sensors, and ease of their fabrication. Research has been extensively aimed at the preparation of these nonenzymatic glucose sensors from novel materials, often with small micro- or nanostructures, which possess the ideal properties for the applications of electrochemical biosensor. Authors in Tian et al. (2014) highlight the most recent advances in nonenzymatic glucose sensors. There has been an increase in research in the last decade on the neural interface technology and the use of microelectrodes and signal transduction technology. The concept of interfacing with cortical architecture to both detect and introduce signaling into neural networks has developed rapidly from basic animal work occurring not more than four decades ago (Keefer et al. 2008). The work in Konrad and Shanks (2010) reviews and encompasses both directions of the brain computer interface: extraction of neural signaling and insertion of signals to neural structures in the cortex. Furthermore, the challenges to translate these concepts from the last decades of studies on animals and human beings deserve consideration when considering future applications. In Vaddiraju et al. (2010) authors survey the status of implantable biosensors with particular focus on the progress on the basis of the nanotechnology. There are other groups of implantable devices that are intensively researched, which include sensors for nerve stimulation capable of alleviating acute pain (Schneider and Stieglitz 2004), sensors for detecting electric signals in the brain as in Hu and Wilson (1997), and sensors for monitoring bio-analytes in the brain (O'Neill 1994), together with implantable drug delivery systems for controlled delivery at the site of pain and stress (McAllister et al. 2000; Ryu et al. 2007). Reliability of the system of implantable sensors is often undermined by some factors like biofouling (Wisniewski et al. 2001; Gifford et al. 2006) and foreign body response (Wisniewski et al. 2000), and sensor drifts and lack of temporal resolution (Kerner et al. 1993). To alleviate these issues, researchers have taken clues from the success of synergism between biosensors and nanotechnology that has led to highly reliable point-of-care diagnostic devices (Hahm and Lieber 2004) and biosensors for early detection of cancer (Liu et al. 2004; Zheng et al. 2005; Yu et al. 2006).

3.3 Motivation and Contribution

Currently, IBANs technologies have achieved development and solutions to the applications of healthcare. This chapter aims to contribute in research in that critical issue by providing an overview of ISs along with IBANs technologies, features, some of the most common applications, and its future that benefit in different aspects in healthcare applications. Existing works will be analyzed; challenges and new directions are presented. This chapter explores the importance and necessity of ISs technology and also provides opportunities for further research and highlights new directions of research.

3.4 Fundamentals of IBANs for Healthcare Monitoring

3.4.1 ISs in Biomedical Systems

ISs systems offer great advantages to increase the medical care and improve the quality of life style, consequently leading to substantial investment in biomedical systems. Biomedical sensors represent the main component in the medical diagnostic and monitoring systems and play an important role in a wide range of applications in healthcare. Some of the ISs can be implemented in measuring enzymes, while others are used to measure blood pressure. In other words biomedical sensors are classified according to the quantity to be measured and categorized as physical, electrical, or chemical, depending on their use in an application. ISs form an important class of biosensors according to their ability to provide metabolite(s) level(s) continuously without the need for the intervention of patient and regardless of the patient's physiological state (rest, sleep, exercise, etc.). The ISs should be extremely small so that it can be easily implanted and explanted with less damage to the tissues nearby (Reach and Wilson 1992).

ISs should have long operational lifetime than other sensors. When a sensor comes into contact with body fluids, the host may affect the function of the sensor, or the sensor may affect the site in which it is implanted. For example, protein absorption and cellular deposits can alter the permeability of the sensor packaging that is designed to protect the sensor and allow free chemical diffusion of certain analysis between the body fluids and the biosensor (Mendelson 2012).

Improper packaging of ISs may lead to drift and a gradual loss of sensor sensitivity and stability over time. Furthermore, inflammation of tissue, infection, or clotting in a vascular site may produce harmful adverse effects. Thus, the used materials in the construction of the sensor's outer body must be biocompatible. To overcome these challenges, it is possible to utilize various polymeric covering materials and barrier layers to minimize leaching of potentially toxic sensor components into the body. Figures 3.3–3.5 depict the structure of ISs.

- Figure 3.3 shows a real platform with a true/false alarm or event detector for the monitoring of different targets. The data are transferred to a central database where all the inputs can be personalized for each patient. The data collected can be measured in different scenarios: when the patient is at rest, undertaking a certain type of physical activity, etc., depending on the particular medical interest. Hence an accurate prognosis and diagnosis can be obtained.

- The medical implantable device block is presented in Figure 3.4.
- Figure 3.5 shows the final product focusing on its size, main components, and the interaction in/out of the body.

In biomedical technology, biopotential measurements are made using different kinds of specialized electrodes. The function of these recording electrodes is to couple the ionic potentials generated inside the body to an electronic instrument. Biopotential electrodes are classified either as noninvasive (skin surface) or invasive (microelectrodes or wire electrodes). Biopotential measurements must be carried out using high-quality electrodes to minimize motion artifacts and ensure that the measured signal is accurate, stable, and undistorted. Body fluids are highly corrosive to the metals, so not all metals are acceptable for biopotential sensing. In addition, some of the toxic materials on the cells. For implantable applications, we typically use relatively strong metal electrodes, for example, from stainless steel or noble materials such as gold, or different alloys such as platinumtungsten or iridiumoxide. Microelectromechanical system transducers are fabricated using solid-state micromachining techniques commonly used by the semiconductor industry in the production of integrated circuits. Microelectromechanical sensor systems are used, for example, in intrauterine pressure measurement to monitor contractions during delivery, automatic noninvasive blood pressure cuffs, respiratory monitors, infusion pumps, and kidney dialysis machines. Microelectromechanical system transducers are also used as accelerometers in the implantable pacemakers to monitor the body movement of the patient to determine the level of exertion and suitably adjust the pacing rate to match

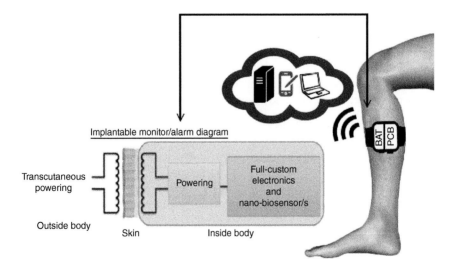

Figure 3.3 Conception of the implantable device. (Sadik et al. 2009).

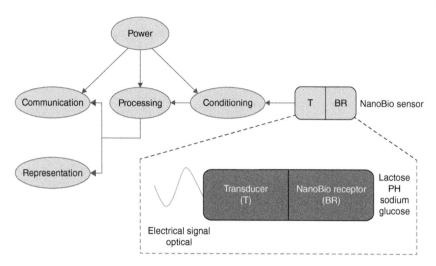

Figure 3.4 Block diagram of the implantable device. (Sadik et al. 2009).

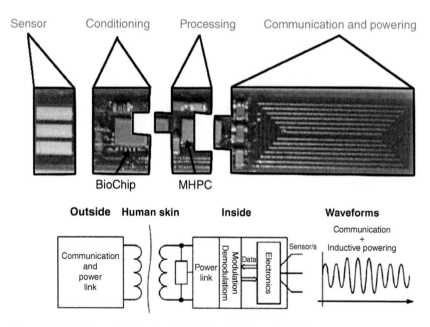

Figure 3.5 Prototype of the implantable device. (Sadik et al. 2009).

the changes in metabolic demand. The components constituting a remote monitoring system (Dubner et al. 2012) consist of the following:

1. Cardiac resynchronization therapy device.
2. *Programmer:* Manufacturer-specific devices that receive and transmit information across the telemetry from cardiac resynchronization therapy devices. Operators are able to reprogram cardiac resynchronization therapy devices via the programmer to change their behavior.
3. *Home monitor/communicator:* A remote telemetry device used for transmitting sensed data from the patient's home to a service center via telephone lines or cell phones.
4. *Remote monitor system:* Employs wireless/web technology to allow near-continuous surveillance of the device and patient-sensing parameters. Alerting events may be transmitted immediately and flagged for attention.

3.4.2 Applications of ISs in Biomedical Systems

This section presents some important applications of ISs in some real-world healthcare applications where ISs and biomedical systems are playing an important role.

3.4.2.1 Brain Stimulator

ISs and other implantable devices are attached in this application of brain stimulator. Consider an epileptic patient with a brain stimulator that can stimulate the brain by using electrical impulses in case of occurrence of seizure. Using ISs such as EEG sensor, blood flow sensor, and external sensors such as inertial accelerometers can detect the seizure occurrences. The data collected from these sensors can be processed in real time at IBAN node with controlling signals that may be sent to the implanted stimulator in the brain to stop the seizure in real time. There are some considerations in this scenario: the wireless communications between sensor nodes and other medical devices should be reliable. In addition, the battery life of the implantable brain stimulator is two to three years (Neuropace 2014). This IBAN simulation was performed to understand the effect of reliability and power consumption. However there are still other challenges and concerns in these applications that need to address some government laws.

3.4.2.2 Heart Failure Monitoring

During the last decade, there has been a surge in the number of implantations of biomedical sensors and devices for cardiac resynchronization therapy with increasing recognition of their importance in the management of medically refractory heart failure in the community. This tremendous growth the need to provide a good quality of care after the implantation procedures have gained an increase in healthcare spending. ISs in the cardiac resynchronization

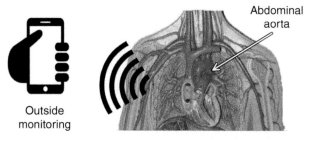

Abdominal
aorta

Outside
monitoring

Figure 3.6 Implantable wireless pressure sensor based on the RFID standard at 13.56 MHz (Khan et al. 2009).

therapy device allow a unique opportunity for continuous monitoring of a patient's clinical heart failure status by measuring cardiac rhythm, intracardiac pressures, cardiac events, and physical activity, as well as detecting any device malfunction (Liu and Tse 2013). An abdominal aortic aneurysm, which is located between the aorto-bi-iliac bifurcation and the renal arteries is shown in Figure 3.6, causes a critical problem for some people and require continuous monitoring. Several surgical operations are currently applied in the treatment procedures of this disease. But these procedures have some defects and other health problems. For example, authors in Lip et al. (2011) presented a new electronic system that aim to design an implantable pressure sensor that can be used in a network configuration. This system is remotely powered during radio transmission. Regular recordings of the pressure in the aneurysmal sac during postsurgical consultations provide a means to monitor the evolution of the abdominal aortic aneurysm, which is a critical problem.

With the aging of the world's population and the resulting increase of major cardiovascular risk factors, heart failure has become an important medical problem that imposes a great economic burden on healthcare. To effectively prevent heart failure-related hospitalizations, one needs to detect early clinical deterioration and initiate earlier intervention to avert acute decompensated heart failure problem. Telemonitoring parameters, such as body weight and natriuretic peptides, lack sensitivities in predicting the imminence of heart failure; they did not grant any living advantage or reduce the number of hospitalizations compared to usual care (Chaudhry et al. 2010). ISs provide a new means for the early detection of heart failure in a way that has not been possible before. A newly emerging technology has played an increasingly important role for such sensors in continuous heart failure monitoring. At the present time, various commercial companies are establishing novel interface-linking systems that allow remote monitoring through the transmitting of data from continuous home monitoring to a service center via a cellular network or Web application so physicians and nursing team can access and review the monitoring parameters and can initiate interventions accordingly.

3.4.2.3 Blood Glucose Level

Thanks to the availability of designing miniaturized components combined with advanced packaging techniques, dimensions of wireless electronics devices can be scaled down to implantable size. Although blood pressure is one of the most important physiological parameters, there is at present no means of continuous monitoring of this quantity without limiting a patient's mobility.

Continuous long-term monitoring of blood pressure over longer periods, such as a day or longer, would provide considerably more physiological insights than isolated clinical measurements (Fang and Dutkiewicz 2009), but the results until now are unsatisfactory. For this purpose, the structure of implantable system for continuous monitoring of blood glucose level is shown in Figures 3.7–3.9.

Figure 3.7 shows the acceleration sensor mounted perivascularly directly on an artery. As a reference, electrocardiographic and intra-arterial blood pressure signals from the descending aorta were measured. The 3.5 F blood pressure catheter (Millar Instruments) was inserted from the femoral artery and forwarded throughout the aortic bifurcation to the accelerometer position.

The accelerometers were mounted directly on the artery as shown in the photograph in Figure 3.8. The device was able to detect acceleration plethysmograms also for an awake animal.

3.4.3 Security in Implantable Biomedical Systems

Implantable systems need to be small, lightweight, and separated from the harsh places. These systems should also consume a little power to allow a

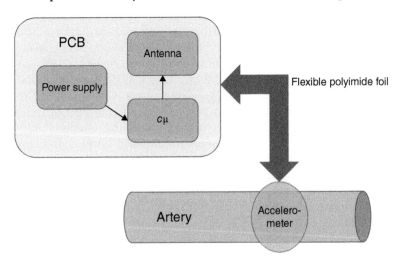

Figure 3.7 Implantable system for blood monitoring. (Theodor et al. 2014).

Figure 3.8 Sensor
mounted on an artery in a
rabbit using elastic silicone
strips (Theodor et al. 2014).

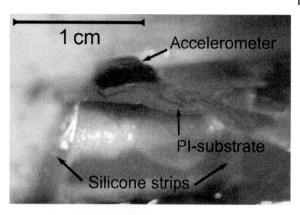

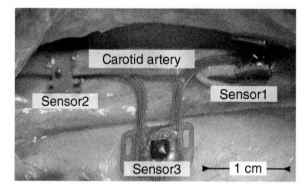

Figure 3.9 The implantable accelerometer system is mounted to the carotid artery of a domestic pig. Sensor 1 is fixated on top and Sensor 2 on the bottom of the artery using highly elastic silicone strips. Sensor 3 is placed next to the artery for compensation of movement artifacts. The system was implanted over 14 days without complications [24].

long-term processing in order to allow for data transmission to and from the implanted devices. The development of advanced implantable systems requires a great amount of expertise and knowledge in different disciplines such as materials, electronics, signal processing, chemistry, biology, physiology, etc. (Inmann and Hodgins 2013). There are some problems to protect data confidentiality and patient privacy such as user authentication. In addition to securing user access to information of medical sensing is a mutual authentication protocol between healthcare professional and accessed node to ensure medical data is not exposed to unauthorized persons. It also ensures medical data sent to healthcare professionals are not from a malicious node. Therefore, security of data collection and transmission in IS networks is a critical issue. Several research works in the wireless networks security field have identified serious security and privacy risks in implantable medical systems that could compromise the implant and even the health of the patient who carries it. In the end of this chapter, we provide security issues for the next generation of implantable medical devices and analyze the most relevant protection mechanisms proposed till now. On the one hand, the security mechanisms must have into consideration the inherent constraints of these small and implanted devices: energy, storage, and power computing. On the other hand, the proposed solutions must achieve an adequate balance between the safety of the patient and the security level offered, with the battery lifetime being another critical parameter in the design phase (Camara et al. 2015). The development of nanotechnology together with elegant multidisciplinary research involving new sensing concepts is well suited to provide a combinatorial sensing motif similar to point-of-care array detection methodologies. Such capability would certainly open the door for the development of highly sensitive, multi-analyte and multi-metabolite sensing platforms. This is expected to provide the user with the capacity not only to monitor disorders but also to identify which of user daily habits exacerbate metabolic imbalances. The integration of body area networks systems with ISs and nanomachines also creates a completely new level of security related challenges.

3.5 Challenges and Future Trends

There are some challenges to be overcome to obtain the ideal implantable systems (Sadik et al. 2009). The device must be biocompatible to avoid negative reactions inside the body. In addition, the medical device must provide long-term stability, selectivity, calibration, miniaturization and repetition, as well as power in a downscaled and portable device. In terms of the sensors, label-free electrical biosensors are ideal candidates because of their low cost, low power, and ease of miniaturization. Nanocommunication is considered to become a major building block for many novel applications in the healthcare and fitness sector. Given the recent developments in the scope of nanomachinery, coordination and control of these devices becomes the critical challenge to be solved. One of the main challenges in the widespread application of ISs is that they gradually lose their functions with time. Problems with biocompatibility have been proven to be the barriers to the development of reliable implantable systems that represent one of the most important challenges of IBANs.

Advances in nanotechnology of implantable devices area have opened up great opportunities and at the same time raised some concerns. One pressing issue to address is the biocompatibility of nanomaterials that are used to enhance IS performance. Another effort would be the realization of biodegradable implantable devices that can be triggered to biodegrade at the end of its useful lifetime similar to biodegradable sutures used for surgery. The combination of biocompatible and biodegradable materials within the same implantable device is not trivial but not impossible considering the tremendous growth in nanotechnology in the coming years. In addition, efforts to develop ISs for a particular analyte (mostly glucose) should be supplemented with research on implantable biosensors for multiple analyte detection. Researches in nanotechnology have been focused on the fabrication and integration of nanomaterials. However, there are still a lot of challenges ahead with respect to utilization in the human body, before the commercialization of these techniques is possible. Researchers are investigating new ways to improve the limited sensitivity and specificity of current heart failure sensors by using a combination of sensors to predict heart failure events. Future trends in the field of biosensor technology lean toward the miniaturization of ISs and possible biologic energy-capturing technology to minimize battery consumption have been limited due to their poor biocompatibility, high cost, and very time-intensive preparation processes. There are challenges in the use of high selectivity materials, low detection limit, a wide detection range, and fast response time, all while trying to make these sensors are ready for continuous glucose measurement. In the future, research will continue to work for detecting infinitesimally small concentrations of glucose via different bodily fluids and in forming sensors that are capable of being incorporated into portable, subcutaneous, and miniaturized implantable devices. All these requirements urge the continuous exploration to revolutionize the glucose biosensor industry. Communications in IBAN must be energy efficient and reliable in order to provide long-term operations and access. MAC protocols are an important issue in wireless communications. Different MAC protocols are presented with wireless communications for healthcare applications such as BodyMAC (Ibarra et al. 2013), HHH-MAC (Huq et al. 2012), and MEB-MAC (Kesler 2013) using different methods such as time division multiple access (TDMA), Carrier Sense Multiple Access (CSMA), and frequency division multiple access (FDMA) have been presented in different researches. However, there are still some challenges with these protocols in order to increase reliability such as idle listening, overhearing, and packet collision. New protocols in radio-frequency communication are an important feature and represent challenges for the researchers that affect reliability and energy efficiency in wireless communications as in Neuropace (2014). The proposed new protocols in this work should be analyses with the existing MAC protocols in order to understand their features and functions. Recently a number of MAC protocols have emerged to deal with these problems in a separate fashion; however there is no single protocol that addresses them in general. All modern electronic devices of smartphones to laptops still use cords and plugs for charging. When the battery dies, after a period of time, these devices have become useless and there is nowhere to charge them. The reality of wireless power is about having power everywhere we are. However, it is still too early to publicize any optimal solution or even any assumptions on the nature of such solution. Despite the numerous and different applications of consumer devices, the main goal is to eliminate the use of power cable. Although a piece of wire is the best means of transferring energy, the inherent deficiencies and advantages of wireless power transfer technologies make us think about the electrical devices and appliances from a substantive point of view. Among various wireless power transfers, the use of magnetic resonant coupling scheme will prevail in many areas of human life in the coming years due to its high efficiency and wide-range application space. At the present time, the emerging applications and growing demand for portable mobile appliances (e.g. mobiles, tablets, laptops, etc.), remote charging and powering of these portable devices, contactless radio-frequency identification for security applications and transportation, and power harvesting of battery-free CMOS devices for biomedical engineering all are playing critical role in promoting and pushing forward of highly resonant coupled wireless power transfer system. The marketing of this promising technology has started with some special applications (e.g. medical applications, automotive charging, etc.), and some of the leaders of the industry and company owners are also working in collaboration to standardize the vehicle-charging infrastructure. Some common interoperability guidelines for resonant coupled wireless charging system are being developed by standards development organizations to ensure that mobile devices from different vendors can charge anywhere in a common wireless ecosystem (Kesler 2013). If all these efforts progress, then we expect the use of wireless power technology spread out in more areas and will certainly promise the beginning of an exciting future in the energy industry with massive impact throughout our everyday lives. There are three concepts of implantable brain computer interface devices that are designed for human use: neural signal extraction primarily for motor commands, signal insertion to restore sensation, and technological challenges that remain. During the last few years, extraordinary human examples of brain computer interface implant potential have been provided. Although technological obstacles, proof-of-concept animal, and human studies provide significant encourage-ment, the provision of brain computer interface implants may find their way into the mainstream of medical practice in the foreseeable future. However, there are a number of challenges that exists to the development of brain com-puter interface devices before such implants become available to surgeons for implantation in the patients. Some of these obstacles are physiological, some are technical, and others are commercial. Physiological barriers to further development of the brain computer interface include understanding of spatial coding in sensory systems in particular. Although motor cortex physiology has been nicely demonstrated for hand movement, there are minimal reports on efforts to decode walking and postural control from implanted electrodes. Furthermore, involuntary motor control has significant clinical impact that have not been discussed enough in the literature other than in the context of spasticity management or pain related to spasticity and rigidity. Clinically, some patients complain abnormal muscle tone and resting motor state more so than the inability to initiate voluntary movement. The same issues that need further investigations also apply to sensory brain computer interface implants. Technological hurdles are numerous in the design of stable, long-term brain computer interface implants that are clinically viable. There are numerous lessons to be learned from auditory prosthesis regarding signal processing, stimulus coding, and spatial distribution through implanted electrodes of auditory implants that span over years of clinical experience. A number of technological problems have been highlighted in recent years that have driven research funding to specific goal-directed solutions. These focused research agendas should provide more usable solutions for medical products in the next decade. The increasing incidence of cancer has stimulated research on the development of novel implantable devices for the localized treatment of cancer. Cancer is currently the second largest cause of death worldwide, after cardiovascular disease. Current trends also suggest that cancer will become the leading cause of death by 2030 (Danyuo et al. 2014). Furthermore, standard treatment methods, such as bulk systematic chemotherapy (Hildebrandt and Wust 2007; Oni et al. 2011; Perry 2011) and radiotherapy (Gutierrez 2008), have exhibited severe side effects. There is, therefore, a need to develop localized cancer treatment methods that mitigate these side effects. One approach that can be used to reduce the potential side effects of cancer treatments is to use localized chemotherapy to reduce the concentrations of cancer drugs that are needed for effective treatment. This can be achieved by using implantable drug eluting devices for localized drug delivery. Such systems will need controllers and local ISs for the management of local drug release and heat diffusion.

3.6 Conclusion and Recommendation

Recent years have witnessed an increasing demand in the use of smart ISs for healthcare applications. In addition, new emitters are constantly entering the marketplace and more medical procedures are based on electromagnetic fields as well. Technical design improvements will enhance the functions of ISs for the quality of life and longevity. This chapter presented a comprehensive and state-of-the-art IS biomedical technology. In particular, IS technology, some critical applications, privacy and security of ISs, and challenges and future trends to overcome some issues in the development of this technology have been presented along with applications such as brain stimulator and monitoring of heart failure and blood glucose level. Challenges, new trends, and future work are discussed. The author recommends that embedding ISs in healthcare applications play an important role especially in monitoring patient's in their daily life, after medical operations, and in other activities. However, governments need to issue the appropriate resolutions, laws, and legislations for regulation and security of human life.

Bibliography

Aziz, O., Lo, B., Yang, G.-Z. et al. (2006). Pervasive body sensor network: an approach to monitoring the postoperative surgical patient. In: Proceedings of International Workshop on Wearable and implantable Body Sensor Networks, 13–18. Cambridge, MA.

Barman, S.D., Reza, A.W., Kumar, N. et al. (2015). Wireless powering by magnetic resonant coupling: recent trends in wireless power transfer system and its applications. *Renewable and Sustainable Energy Reviews* **51**: 1525–1552.

Camara, C., Peris-Lopez, P., and Tapiador, J.E., (2015). Security and privacy issues in implantable medical devices: a comprehensive survey. *Journal of Biomedical Informatics* **55**: 272–289.

Chaudhry, S.I., Mattera, J.A., Curtis, J.P. et al. (2010). Telemonitoring in patients with heart failure. *New England Journal of Medicine* **363**: 2301–2309.

Clark, L.C. Jr. and Lyons, C. (1962). Electrode systems for continuous monitoring in cardiovascular surgery. *Annals of the New York Academy of Sciences* **1021**: 29–45.

Diabetes Atlas (2006). *Introduction to Biomedical Engineering*, 3e. International Diabetes Federation.

Danaei, G., Finucane, M.M., Lu, Y. et al. (2011). National, regional, and global trends in fasting plasma glucose and diabetes prevalence since 1980: systematic analysis of health examination surveys and epidemiological studies with 370 country-years and 2.7 million participants. *Lancet* **378** (9785): 25–28.

Danyuo, Y., Obayemi, J.D., Dozie-Nwachukwu, S. et al. (2014). Prodigiosin release from an implantable biomedical device: kinetics of localized cancer drug release. *Materials Science and Engineering* **42**: 734–745.

Darwish, A. and Hassanien, A.E. (2011). Wearable and implantable wireless sensor network solutions for healthcare monitoring. *Sensors* **11** (6): 5561–5595.

Dressler, F. (2015). Connecting in-body nano communication with body area networks: challenges and opportunities of the internet of nano things. *Nano Communication Networks* **6**: 29–38.

Dubner, S., Auricchio, A., Steinberg, J.S. et al. (2012). ISHNE/EHRA expert consensus on remote monitoring of cardiovascular implantable electronic devices (CIEDs). *Europace* **14**: 278–293.

Espina, J., Falck, T., Muehlsteff, J. et al. (2008). Wearable body sensor network towards continuous cuff-less blood pressure monitoring. In: The 5th

International Workshop on Wearable and Implantable Body Sensor Networks, 28–32. Rome, Italy.

Fang, G. and Dutkiewicz, E. (2009). BodyMAC: energy efficient TDMA-based MAC protocol for wireless body area networks. In: 2009 9th International Symposium on Communications and Information Technology, 1455–1459. IEEE.

Gifford, R., Kehoe, J.J., Barnes, S.L. et al. (2006). Protein interactions with subcutaneously implanted biosensors. *Biomaterials* **27** (4): 2587–2598.

Gutierrez, D. (2008). *Cancer Facts and Figures*, 2e. America Cancer Society.

Hahm, J. and Lieber, C.M. (2004). Direct ultrasensitive electrical detection of DNA and DNA sequence variations using nanowire nanosensors. *Nano Letters* **4** (1): 51–54.

Hanna, S. (2009). *Regulations and Standards for Wireless Medical Applications*. ISMICT.

Hildebrandt, B. and Wust, P. (2007). *Peritoneal Carcinomatosis: A Multidisciplinary Approach*. New York: Springer.

Hu, Y. and Wilson, G.S. (1997). Rapid changes in local extracellular rat brain glucose observed with an in vivo glucose sensor. *Journal of Neurochemistry* **68** (4): 1745–1752.

Huq, M.A., Dutkiewicz, E., Fang, G. et al. (2012). MEB MAC: improved channel access scheme for medical energy traffic in WBAN. In: International Symposium on Communications and Information Technologies (ISCIT), 371–376.

Ibarra, E., Antonopoulos, A., Kartsakli, E., and Verikoukis, C. (2013). Energy harvesting aware hybrid MAC protocol for WBANs. In: 15th IEEE International Conference on e-Health Networking, Applications Services (Healthcom), 120–124.

Inmann, A. and Hodgins, D. (2013). *Implantable Sensor Systems for Medical Applications*. Woodhead Publishing Limited.

Keefer, E.W., Botterman, B.R., Romero, M.I. et al. (2008). Carbon nanotube coating improves neuronal recordings. *Nature Nanotechnology* **3** (7): 434–439.

Kerner, W., Kiwit, M., Linke, B. et al. (1993). The function of a hydrogen peroxide-detecting electroenzymatic glucose electrode is markedly impaired in human sub-cutaneous tissue and plasma. *Biosensors and Bioelectronics* **8** (9): 473–482.

Kesler, M. (2013). *Highly Resonant Wireless Power Transfer: Safe, Efficient, and Over Distance*. WiTricity Corporation.

Khan, P., Hussain, M.A., and Kwak, K.S. (2009). Medical applications of wireless body area networks. *JDCTA* **3**: 185–193.

Konrad, P. and Shanks, T. (2010). Implantable brain computer interface: challenges to neurotechnology translation. *Neurobiology of Disease* **38**: 369–375.

Kotanen, C.N., Moussy, F.G., Carrara, S., and Guiseppi-Elie, A., (2012). Implantable enzyme amperometric biosensors. *Biosensors and Bioelectronics* **35**: 14–26.

Lip, Le, Ijlra et al. (2011). ENDOCOM: implantable wireless pressure sensor for the follow-up of abdominal aortic aneurysm stented. *IRBM* **32** (3): 163–168.

Liu, G., Wang, J., Kim, J. et al. (2004). Electrochemical coding for multiplexed immunoassays of proteins. *Analytical Chemistry* **76** (23): 7126–7130.

Liu, P.S. and Tse, H.-F. (2013). Implantable sensors for heart failure monitoring. *Journal of Arrhythmia* **29**: 314–319.

McAllister, D.V., Allen, M.G., and Prausnitz, M.R. (2000). Microfabricated microneedles for gene and drug delivery. *Annual Review of Biomedical Engineering* **2** (1): 289–313.

Mendelson, Y. (2012). *Introduction to Biomedical Engineering*, 3e. Elsevier Inc.

Mohseni, P. and Najafi, K. (2005). A 1.48-mW low-phase-noise analog frequency modulator for wireless biotelemetry. *IEEE Transactions on Biomedical Engineering* **52**: 938–943.

Neuropace (2014). Neural simulator for treating epilepsy. http://neuropace.com/product/overview.html (accessed 08 March 2019).

Nichols, S.P., Koh, A., Storm, W.L. et al. (2013). Materials science and engineering. *Chemical Reviews* **113**: 25–28.

O'Neill, R.D. (1994). Microvoltammetric techniques and sensors for monitoring neurochemical dynamics in vivo. A review. *Analyst* **119** (5): 767–779.

Oni, Y., Theriault, C., Hoek, A.V., and Soboyejo, W.O. (2011). Effects of temperature on diffusion from PNIPA-based gels in a BioMEMS device for localized chemotherapy and hyperthermia. *Materials Science and Engineering* **31**: 67–76.

Perry, M.C. (2011). Approach to the patient with cancer.

Ponmozhi, J., Frias, C., Marques, T., and Frazão, O. (2012). Smart sensors/actuators for biomedical applications: review. *Measurement* **45**: 1675–1688.

Ramachandran, V.R.K., van der Zwaag, B.J., Meratnia, N., and Havinga, P.J.M. (2014). Evaluation of MAC protocols with wake-up radio for implantable body sensor networks. *Procedia Computer Science* **40**: 173–180.

Reach, G. and Wilson, G.S. (1992). Medical applications of wireless body area networks. *Analytical Chemistry* **64** (6): 381–386.

Ryu, W.H., Huang, Z., Prinz, F.B. et al. (2007). Biodegradable micro-osmotic pump for long-term and controlled release of basic fibroblast growth factor. *Journal of Controlled Release* **124** (1–2): 98–105.

Sadik, O.A., Aluoch, A.O., and Zhou, A. (2009). Status of biomolecular recognition using electrochemical techniques. *Biosensors and Bioelectronics* **24**: 2749–2765.

Schneider, A. and Stieglitz, T. (2004). Implantable flexible electrodes for functional electrical stimulation. *Medical Device Technologies* **15** (1): 16–18.

Schwiebert, L., Gupta, S.K.S., and Weinmann, J. (2001). Research challenges in wireless networks of biomedical sensors. In: Proceedings of the 7th Annual International Conference on Mobile Computing and Networking, 151–165. Rome, Italy.

Shaw, K.M. and Cummings, M.H. (2005). *Diabetes Chronic Complications*. Wiley.

Shults, M.C., Rhodes, R.K., Updike, S.J. et al. (1994). A telemetry-instrumentation system for monitoring multiple subcutaneously implanted glucose sensors. *IEEE Transactions on Biomedical Engineering* **41**: 937–942.

Theodor, M., Fiala, J., Ruh, D. et al. (2014). Implantable accelerometer system for the determination of blood pressure using reflected wave transit time. *Sensors and Actuators* **206**: 151–158.

Tian, K., Prestgard, M., and Tiwari, A., (2014). Materials science and engineering. *Neurobiology of Disease* **41**: 100–118.

Vaddiraju, S., Tomazos, I., Burgess, D.J. et al. (2010). Emerging synergy between nanotechnology and implantable biosensors: a review. *Biosensors and Bioelectronics* **25**: 1553–1565.

Valdastri, P., Susilo, E., Förster, T. et al. (2009). Wireless implantable electronic platform for blood glucose level monitoring. In: Proceedings of the Eurosensors XXIII conference, Procedia Chemistry, Volume 1, 1255–1258.

Wisniewski, N., Moussy, F., and Reichert, W.M. (2000). Characterization of implantable biosensor membrane biofouling. *Fresenius' Journal of Analytical Chemistry* **366** (6–7): 611–621.

Wisniewski, N., Klitzman, B., Miller, B., and Reichert, W.M. (2001). Decreased analyte transport through implanted membranes: differentiation of biofouling from tissue effects. *Journal of Biomedical Materials Research* **57** (4): 513–521.

Yu, B., Long, N., Moussy, Y., and Moussy, F. (2006). A long-term flexible minimally-invasive implantable glucose biosensor based on an epoxy-enhanced polyurethane membrane. *Biosensors and Bioelectronics* **21** (12): 2275–2282.

Yuce, M.R. (2010). Implementation of wireless body area networks for healthcare systems. *Journal of Sensors and Actuators* **162**: 116–129.

Yuce, M.R., Keong, H.C., and Chae, M.S. (2009). Wideband communication for implantable and wearable systems. *IEEE Transactions on Microwave Theory and Techniques* **57**: 2597–2604.

Zheng, G., Patolsky, F., Cui, Y. et al. (2005). Multiplexed electrical detection of cancer markers with nanowire sensor arrays. *Nature Biotechnology* **23**: 1294–1301.

4

Social Network's Security Related to Healthcare

Fatna Elmendili, Habiba Chaoui, and Younés El Bouzekri El Idrissi

Systems Engineering Laboratory, National School of Applied Sciences, Ibn Tofail University, Kenitra, Morocco

4.1 The Use of Social Networks in Healthcare

The health sector for example (in Morocco) suffers from several problems and on the other hand, several acquired to take into consideration. The implementation of the technologies and the tools of communication and sharing in this sector in our country. Will certainly help to resolve the majority of its problems and refit its acquits (Bigdata 2012). In 50 years the Moroccan population has almost tripled from 11.6 million in 1960 to 32 million in 2011. During the same period the annual rate of population growth is increased from 2.6% to 1.05%.

The priority of the Minister of Health in its sectorial strategy for the period 2012–2017 are essentially linked on the one hand to the consolidation of the acquits and the development of responses to new priorities were mainly related to the satisfaction of the right of access to essential care and to the protection of the health and on the other hand to the method with which the strategy will be implemented, and the development of actions which is necessarily based on the participation and transparency, and the surrenders of the accounts. Today is aware of the need for the computerization and the use of the tools of technology to make the sharing and communication between patients and doctors as well to make the sharing of any information related to the health sector (Bellare et al. 2014). Morocco has launched several initiatives of reforms of information systems and the use of technology in the health sector. The use of technologies, tools, and technical communication and sharing can help significantly to improve the quality of care offered by the hospital centers, Moroccan to reduce the expenditures of the Department of Health, as well as those of individuals in the acquisition of care, and to ensure the interoperability more flexible and effective between the various medical organizations of the country. Use the tools of the technologies to track and monitor the medical condition of the population old, will enable them to maintain good health and a good quality

Intelligent Pervasive Computing Systems for Smarter Healthcare, First Edition.
Arun Kumar Sangaiah, S.P. Shantharajah, and Padma Theagarajan.

Table 4.1 Moroccan population in healthcare.

Year	Total population	Rate of increase (%)
1960	11 626 470	2.58
1971	15 379 259	2.58
1982	20 419 555	2.61
1994	26 073 717	2.06
2004	29 891 708	1.38
2011	32 187 000	1.05

of life without having recourse to medical organizations of the country. Social networks among the tools the more popular to communicate and share information of medical A very fast between patients and physicians (Bellare et al. 2014) (Table 4.1).

Nearly 60% of the French are turning in priority to the Internet to search for information in health. A revolution that has not escaped the attention of the National Council of the order of physicians (Cnom), which organized on 14 November, a round table on "The Dr. Google and the cyberpatients" in the framework of its day of ethics. For the CNOM, the "Dr. Google," in other words this inexhaustible source of information via search engines to scope of click of patients, must meet two requirements: the protection of the confidentiality of personal health data and medical ethics. A useful reminder, because now, the sick do not simply to seek the information health on the Internet, but they are no longer reluctant to share the results of their assessments and analyzes with a community, virtual, on forums and social networks (type Twitter or Facebook). Dr. Michel Legmann, President of the CNOM, invites however to caution: "These data are information of which the exploitation inappropriate, could have negative consequences if they were disclosed without control."

4.2 The Social Media Respond to a Primary Need of Security

Internet users behave virtually as they would do in their real life. In a recent study, Forrester has established a close link between the hierarchy of needs of Maslow and willingness of populations to share content online. According to analysts, Internet users congregate and exchange on virtual communities, before all, in order to respond to a primary need of safety corresponding to the second level of the pyramid. Driven by a strong desire to socialize, many move the discussion forums to Facebook or Twitter to find information, ask

Figure 4.1 Health Pyramid.

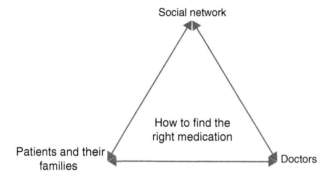

Figure 4.2 The relationship between patients, practitioners, and social networks.

for advice, acquire the experience, and mainly be reassured about their state of health (Figure 4.1).

The exponential growth of content published each day on the social media has had a significant impact on the relations formerly established between physicians, laboratories, and patients. The patients now use the Internet to find information on their symptoms, before to consult their physician. Thus, they do not hesitate to go on specialized sites such as DOCtissimo patients Like me or to establish their own health diagnosis from information published by other Internet users. The laboratories, clinics, hospitals and practitioners, find themselves more and more often confronted to patients on informed that cater to their doctor with a precise idea of their disorder, of the associated treatment and drugs are the most adapts (Figure 4.2).

In the context of hyper communication, the reputation of professionals has become a critical topic in 2010 of new social platforms such as Vitals.com are even emerged, offer the possibility to patients to assess the work of their practitioner. Forced to adapt to this new mode of consumption of the medical information, some have chosen to meet in virtual communities to exchange between health professionals and to remove new information on diseases, their developments and the expectations of patients (Sahama et al. 2013). Today thousands of patients and doctors interact heavily on social networks dedicated to their disorders such as cancer, depression, or diabetes. They meet in super focus group to share their experience of the disease and the different treatments associated. These new media provide the directorates marketing a unique opportunity to build an intimate relationship with consumers q they rub shoulders usually only through the distorting mirror of focus traditional groups. Using social media, as a source of returns of consumers, the laboratory can also be overcome the structural costs related to focus traditional groups (Sahama et al. 2013). The massive use of social networks offers patients and physicians a space for sharing and communication, but in this exchange there is always a risk of find profiles with identities falsified under the name of the doctor who give bad recommendation and medical information, which can directly influence on the life and the entourage of patients. The medical data, contain a lot of information very personal and very sensitive about patients. The protection of these data against any unregulated disclosure should be a priority of any organization (Sahama et al. 2013). However, this is not easily achievable in the social media, or the data comes from a fraud diversity of sources and are processed by the policies of security already exists in the social networks, then the protection of the life of the patients against the attacks and malicious profiles becomes very difficult (Sahama et al. 2013). The reason for which we sum focused essentially on the security profiles and the groups who are dedicated to the health sector to offer a place well secured. Among the challenge linked to the respect of the private life of the patients in the use of technologies "Social Networks" in the medical sector (Sahama et al. 2013):

Intellectual property: In studies conducted in respect of the privacy of patients by protecting effectively their personal and medical data, it is important not to neglect the question of the intellectual property of these data. Indeed, the creation of the data during the process of medical care is a mutual effort between the two parties to know: the patient and the provider of the care (Sahama et al. 2013).

Financial gains: Knowing that these data are really valuable for several companies: in this case the companies which manufacture the drugs. The provider of care may therefore want to benefit financially for these data in the selling. On the other side the patient will not tolerate that such medical data are sold or provided such that they are to third parties for fear that his reputation is not damaged, since these data can contain very sensitive information and very private (Sahama et al. 2013).

The sharing of data: The availability of large volumes of data and the possibility to treat and analyze all font that the medical organizations seek to share a greater number of data with third parties and to correlate more data from several sources, in order to have more knowledge in the health sector, and thus improve their practice while minimizing the costs. This can therefore cause a random sharing of these data without do not really consider if they are sensitive or not. Medical organizations cannot manage and analyze effectively the medical data on a massive scale even if they have, they generally appeal to professionals and experts to analyze these data. It is for these reasons and others that the policies of security and protection of the private life currently used must be readjusted in order to optimize the implementation of technologies "social networks" in the health sector while protecting the privacy of patients and the safety and security of medical data (Sahama et al. 2013).

4.3   The Type of Medical Data

Health data are considered sensitive information and, in this chapter, are subject to a high level of security, physical and technical. However, the media report regularly on the existence of data leakage of the patients, of hospital centers, or of medical analysis laboratories, found on the canvas. Health professionals and establishments are thus legally required to preserve the security and confidentiality of the data of their patients, the use of subcontracting for certain treatments of data or their accommodation, do not unloading the professionals of the obligations, as has just been recalled the CNIL. The information relating to the state of physical and mental health of a patient are considered by the law as sensitive data. The processing of these data, including their collection, use, communication, storage, and destruction, is subject to the special conditions set out in the Law on Information Technology and Freedoms (Articles 8, 34, and 35) and the Code of Public Health. Health professionals and establishments are required to comply with the obligations relating to the processing of personal data, in their quality of responsible for the treatment. Among these obligations, the security of data constitutes an imperative the Public Health Code provides, moreover, that any person supported by a professional or a health institution has the right to respect for his/her private life and the confidentiality of the information concerning it. Healthcare professionals, as well as those involved in the health system, are submitted to the medical secrecy (art. L.1110-4). The Public Health Code imposes on health professionals the respect of repositories of security. In practice, these professionals must take all necessary precautions to prevent that the data cannot be altered, erased by mistake, or that unauthorized third parties have access to treatment. They are therefore obliged to implement: - of physical security measures by a controlled access to premises hosting servers and by the implementation of a procedure of empowerment to restrict access to only the persons empowered, and technical measures by the protection of servers by firewalls, filters, anti-spam and anti-virus, the access to working positions by individual passwords and regularly renewed, the use of the health professional card to access the data, the data encryption, etc. in order to ensure the security and confidentiality of data, it is recommended to the directors of health institutions, public and private, to sensitize their staff to the good practices to adopt. This awareness will for example by internal plans for training in computer security and the adoption of a computer charter adapted to the tools and other computing means put at the disposal of the staff.

4.3.1   Security of Medical Data

Who said security, said confidentiality, availability, integrity, and authentication. It is important to protect the medical data by ensuring these five characteristics (Synthsesio 2016).

The confidentiality: The implementation of the tools of technology in the health sector involves the use complementary to different means: Internet, cloud, social networks, personal sensors … different actors come into play, and the medical data are thus increasingly exposed to unauthorized access and malicious users. The confidentiality is therefore difficult to control is very important since the individuals do not tolerate the disclosure of their personal data of the patient if they are not kept confidential (Synthsesio 2016).

The availability: The medical data still need to be accessible by several stakeholders: doctors, scientific researchers, insurance. This is indeed one of the strong points of the "social networks" that arises on the principle of "open data" in order to ease the access to and the sharing of data, and thus increase their values. It is therefore important that the medical data are available at any time to authorized users to have access. However, ensure the availability in the platforms of social media requires the risk of flies of medical data for uses illegal (Synthsesio 2016).

The integrity: The "Social Networks" are of platforms of communication and sharing of information, so it is important to ensure that the medical data are integrity and relevant and that no change there has been brought to an internship of their process and especially during a communication between a physician/patient. But this up to today cannot be completely insured in an environment of communication, or the data are so voluminous, varied and occur at a frequency without precedent, that it becomes very difficult to know what data are correct and what data is there are not (Synthsesio 2016).

Authentication: The medical data are accessible by several actors. It is essential to ensure that these actors have all the right to access the data by putting in place the mechanisms and policies for access control, which require the authentication of each actor before any use of the data (Synthsesio 2016).

4.4   Problematic

The great family of social networks public such as Facebook, Twitter, Google, Foursquare, Instagram, Viadeo, Linkedin, Xing, Pinterest and YouTube all propose options for security and/or confidentiality but who do not delight not always Internet users the most refractory. The professionals and health institutions are more and more present on the social networks. These networks have become the privileged means for health institutions to expand their external communication via the users. Healthcare professionals are becoming more and more numerous on the networks large public or professional networks for the exchange of information, news. Patients individually or in the framework of associations of users are without doubt the most regular users of social networks. Close to the majority of Internet users are turning in priority to the Internet to search for information in health. A revolution that has not escaped the attention of the National Council of the order of physicians (Cnom), which organized on 14 November, a round table on "The Dr. Google and the cyber patients" in the framework of its day of ethics. For the CNOM, the "Dr. Google," in other words this inexhaustible source of information via search engines to scope of click of patients, must meet two requirements: the protection of the confidentiality of personal health data and medical ethics. A useful reminder, because now, the sick do not simply to seek the information health on the Internet, but they are no longer reluctant to share the results of their assessments and analyzes with a community, virtual, on forums and social networks (type Twitter or Facebook). Dr. Michel Legmann, President of the CNOM, invites however to caution: "These data are information of which the exploitation inappropriate, could have negative consequences if they were disclosed without control." But the irruption of the Internet in the doctor–patient relationship is also a chance according to Dr. Jacques Lucas, Vice President of the Cnom and General Delegate to information systems in health, because "it should not have the nostalgia of a consultation idyllic which has never existed." Without going so far as to put the patient at the same level of expertise with that the doctor, it is undeniable that the tool now allows to expand the knowledge of the sick on his illness. A type of new partnership, according to the oncologist Franck Chauvin, professor of public health: "Internet fact pass the doctor–patient relationship of a model extremely paternalistic and completely asymmetric to a relationship much more balanced." The discussions between the sick are also a double-edged sword, because what was true for a patient in a given situation and at a particular time is not necessarily so for another, reached by example of a cancer of genetic profile different or having other priorities in its daily life. This time, it is the experience of the doctor, who has known to other patients with the same disease, which will allow to individualize the best options that are available to the patient. Less present that patients on the forums, physicians are on the other hand very open to medical applications: "Nearly a third of them uses his smartphone in consultation to prescribe. With a priority for the consultation of drug databases and drug–drug interactions," stresses Lucie Tesquier specialist in the social networks in health. According to it, the applications intended to improve the observance and follow-up of the patient between two consultations will develop in the years to come: "It is estimated that there will be 500 million users of health applications in 2015." Another trend of substance, pointed to by the expert, the development of "Serious Game," these games which allow to transmit a pedagogical message in a playful way. There are already, for example, to raise the awareness of young people to an excessive consumption of alcohol or help the sick to identify the factors triggering of allergic crises. Social networks on the Internet have become a fact of society which continues to grow with the years. It is therefore to define this new phenomenon and to understand the challenges that it creates for individuals. Among the effective methods to be able to detect these malicious users on social networks are the honeypots. Honeypots is a concept developed by the experts in computer security whose purpose is not to prevent hackers to enter on their systems, but on the contrary to trap them when they come. And therefore to study their behavior to better protect.

4.5 Presentation of the Honeypots

Of our days, the attacks against computer systems have become many, more specific, powerful, and intelligent and cause considerable damage. Unfortunately, most of these attacks are new and unknown by the systems of protection, which sometimes asks of complex interventions and costly for the recovery and maintenance after attack. In this context, a good approach is to observe and study the behavior of pirates and exploit this knowledge to better understand the threat and to establish a knowledge base. Analyzes based on this last should enable us to know when and how to protect themselves from hackers. This knowledge could then be exploited to guide the development of the techniques of the computer security, in order to define appropriate mechanisms to deal with malicious intent. Honeypots are one of the tools used in the computer systems to study and gain knowledge on the behavior and the techniques used by hackers to attack the computer systems (Chiny et al. 2012).

4.5.1 Principle of Honeypots

The idea behind a honeypot is simple. It is to put in place a means to control the attacks and the activities of the attackers in giving them access to some services, emulated sometimes, so that they can interact with them while limiting the damage caused by these attacks can that the attacker has no access to real servers in production (Chiny et al. 2012). However, the quantity and the quality of the information collected is directly proportional to the degree of interaction offered by the honeypot. As well, if the services offered are very limited, the honeypot will not be very attractive for hope to gather good information and the catch implementation risk to be easily detected and avoided by intruders (Chiny et al. 2012). However, the current versions offer more interaction (more services), therefore more attractive and offer an analysis of data the virtually automatic incorporating the same advanced technologies of excavations of data (data mining).

4.6 Proposal System for Detecting Malicious Profiles on the Health Sector

Computer security experts are studying these threats to put in place of the counter-measures. Among the strategies used are the honeypots (honeypots). Honeypots is a technique widely used in the security of networks and the detection of malicious profiles in social networks. The honeypots are tools adapted to the observation of the behavior of the attackers. A honeypot is a computer system voluntarily vulnerable to one or several vulnerabilities and aimed to attract the attackers in order to study their behavior. They are divided into several categories, low or high interaction, depending on the level of interaction proposed to hackers. They allow to collect data from real processes, important to establish realistic assumptions about the behavior of the attackers. Recently, the honeypots are also used to combat malicious behaviors on the most popular social networking such as Facebook and Twitter. This is called type of honeypots "honeypots social." Social networks are now part of our daily life, we have certainly several accounts said "social," that this relates to our daily lives (Facebook or Twitter, for example), our professional life (Viadeo or Linkedin), our sporting life or associative (we can cite jogg.in) and why not on sites of meeting (Adopteunmec, Meetic, Lovoo tinder or) (El Idrissi Younes et al. 2016). That this either on social networks do not promote the anonymity (Facebook, Viadeo, Linkedin) or on the contrary on social networks promoting the anonymity (of general way all the sites of meeting, but also of services of Visio-conference as Skype), we have certainly received requests for connections from persons completely unknown. These applications are, for most of the cases, issued by malicious profiles (El Idrissi Younes et al. 2016). That they emanate from the robots or that they are created to spoof the identity of a user, the malicious profiles are in constant increase on the Internet. In 2012, 8.7% of the users of the social network Facebook were malicious users. In 2014, they reached 11.2 %. Same bell sound on the side of Twitter, with 8.5% of malicious profiles, and Instagram, which accounts 10%. On social networks, the malicious profiles can be generated by machines or be the result of identity theft and their motivations are various: Spy A PERSON, increase the number of fans of a page (Facebook, Twitter...), spammer friends in impunity, fit all types of scams (very often of blackmail), harm the reputation of a person or a company, etc. (El Idrissi Younes et al. 2016).

4.6.1 Proposed Solution

We propose to monitor malicious activity on OSNs through the creation of social honeypots. We define social honeypots as information system resources that monitor malicious profiles behaviors and log their information. Social honeypots and traditional honeypots (e.g. in domains such as network systems and emails Goodman et al. 2005; Nazir et al. 2008; Ghosh et al. 2012) share a similar purpose in that they both monitor and log the behaviors of attackers. In practice, we deploy a social honeypot consisting of a legitimate profile and an associated bot to detect malicious behavior (Lee et al. 2010). If the social honeypot detects suspicious user activity (e.g. the honeypots profile receiving an unsolicited friend request), then the social honeypots bot collects evidence of the malicious candidate (e.g. by crawling the profile of the user sending the unsolicited friend request plus hyperlinks from the profile). As the social honeypots collect malicious (El Idrissi Younes et al. 2016) profiles as evidence, we extract observable features from the collected candidate malicious profiles (e.g. number of friends, text on the profile, age, etc.) (https://fr.wikipedia.org/wiki/Twitter). Coupled with a set of known legitimate profiles that are more populous and easy to extract from social networking communities, we call this type of strategy feature-based strategy (El Idrissi Younes et al. 2016). A new method used in our approach to improve our classification and increase the possibility of detecting an attacker on social networks is honeypot feature based strategy, this strategy uses the feature of the deployed honeypots that interact with users to refine our ranking. The collected data becomes part of the initial training set of a malicious profiles classifier. Through iterative refinement of the features selected and using a set of automatic classification algorithms that are implemented on Waikato Environment for Knowledge Analysis (Weka) machine learning toolkit, we can explore the wider area of malicious profiles. The overall architecture, include human inspectors in the loop for validating the quality of these extracted malicious profiles candidates. Based on their feedback, the malicious profile classifiers are updated with the new evidence and the process continues. The proposed approach is based on three phases including the deployment of social honeypots, the collection of user data through the deployed honeypots, and classification of these users based on their characteristics and the characteristics of deployed honeypots (El Idrissi Younes et al. 2016).

4.6.1.1 Deployment of Social Honeypots

For many years, researchers have been deploying honeypots to capture examples of nefarious activities (Sridharan et al. 2012; Yang et al. 2012. In this chapter, we utilize honeypots to collect deceptive malicious profiles in social networking communities. Specifically, we created and deployed 50 Twitter profiles within the Twitter community to serve as our social honeypots. To collect timely information and increase the likelihood of being targeted by malicious profiles, we created custom Twitter bots to ensure that all of our profiles are logged in to Twitter 24 hours a day, 7 days a week. We also created joint Twitter profiles to see which profiles can attract the most malicious profiles. There are seven types of Twitter accounts identified by the Bluebird Network: the Social Star, the Butterfly, the Distant Star, the Private Eye, the Cycler, the Listener, and the Egghead. Four behaviors of our social honeypots including following back, mentioning, retweeting, and posting tweets with sensitive keywords are observed to analyze how our social honeypots can be attractive to malicious profiles.

Social honeypots follow back their followers: Some existing works (Stringhini et al. 2010; Naruoka et al. 2015) find that malicious profiles tend to follow those accounts that will follow them back. In order to verify whether social honeypots are exactly this type of accounts, a study was conducted that calculated the follow back ratio (FB-ratio) of each account, which is defined (El Idrissi Younes et al. 2016):

$$\frac{||(\text{friend set} \cap \text{follower set})||}{\text{follower set}} \tag{4.1}$$

This study compared the FB-ratio between the social honeypots and random influential accounts. According to the results of this study, only 21% social honeypots have FB-ratio larger than 0.5 (El Idrissi Younes et al. 2016). While 57% social honeypots have FB-ratio smaller than 0.05. Obviously, a significant portion of active honeypots does not follow back their followers.

Social honeypots mention malicious profiles and unrelated accounts: Generally, social honeypots like to mention malicious accounts and unrelated accounts. To prove this conclusion, a study was conducted that analyzed users mentioned by social honeypots in tweets. This experience analyze the ratio of malicious profiles among mentioned users for social honeypots and random influential accounts. According to the results of this study, about 88% of random influential accounts and only 27% social honeypots have never mentioned malicious accounts (El Idrissi Younes et al. 2016). About 38% social honeypots have more than 25% mentioned users as malicious profiles. So social honeypots are more willing to mention malicious users than random influential accounts.

Social honeypots retweet for malicious profiles: Social honeypots offer retweeting service for malicious profiles. To prove this, a study was conducted that compare the retweet ratio and retweet count of original posters between social honeypots and random influential accounts. Retweet ratio is the ratio of retweeted tweets among all the posted tweets of a user. According to the

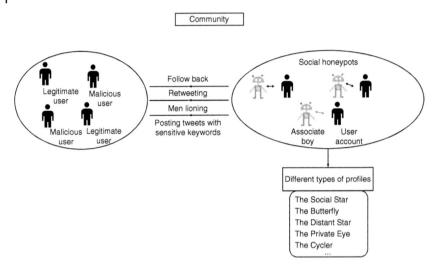

Figure 4.3 The features of a social network.

results of this study, about 70% social honeypots and only 35% random influential accounts have a retweet ratio higher than 0.5 (El Idrissi Younes et al. 2016). In addition, about 13% random influential accounts have a retweet ratio smaller than 0.05. Overall, active honeypots are more willing to retweet tweets for others.

Social honeypots post sensitive keywords in tweets: Social honeypots post in their tweets certain sensitive keywords, which are attractive to malicious accounts. According to an investigation by Sridharan et al. (El Idrissi Younes et al. 2016), malicious users will pick their targets based on the content of tweets from Twitter users. We guess social honeypots also post such kinds of keywords in their tweets. To prove it, a study was conducted that use the term frequency inverse document frequency (TF-IDF) statistic which reflects how important a word is to a document in a collection to extract the most important keywords in tweets of social honeypots as well as random influential accounts (El Idrissi Younes et al. 2016). According to the results of this study, the keywords posted by random influential accounts are mainly related to retweet and follow. Besides, there are a few keywords expressing the feeling such as hate, fucking and thank. In contrast, fewer keywords posted by social honeypots are related to retweet and follow (El Idrissi Younes et al. 2016). Based on our previous observation of social honeypots, we can identified several user behaviors that probably make social honeypots attractive to malicious accounts. The potential attractive behaviors include following back, retweeting, posting tweets with sensitive keywords, and mentioning unrelated accounts (Figure 4.3).

4.6.1.2 Data Collection

After implementing our honeypots and interact with different types of users, we selected a set of profiles, and for each profile we extracted the traditional characteristics feature-based strategy and the features based on honeypots honeypot features based strategy.

Feature-based strategy: Many features can be extracted from all user data: follower number (FLN), FF-ratio, account age (AA), tweet number (TWN), default profile image (DPI), follower fame (FAM), mention ratio (MR), hashtag ratio (HR), URL ratio (UR), tweets interval (TWI), etc. We will also measure the tweet similarity (TS), the similarity among the tweets posted by an account. It can be calculated with the following equation introduced in

$$\text{TS} = \frac{\sum_{p \in P} c(p)}{l_a l_p} \tag{4.2}$$

P is the set of possible tweet-to-tweet combinations among any two tweets posted by a certain account, p is a single pair, $c(p)$ is a function calculating the number of words two tweets share, l_a is the average length of tweets posted by that account, and l_p is the number of tweet combinations. When we sampled users' data, we considered two conditions: the profiles did not have a verified account badge and the number of tweets had to be over zero. The verified account badge is one way Twitter ensures that profiles belong to known people.

Honeypot features based startegy A new kind of features named honeypot-based features is introduced in our malicious profile detector. The intuition behind honeypot based feature is quite simple (El Idrissi Younes et al. 2016):
  If an account interacts with a social honeypot that attracts a high proportion of malicious users, this account is probably a malicious account.
  If an account interacts with many social honeypots, then this account is also probably a malicious account.
  If the new followers of a social honeypot are densely created within a short time period, these followers are probably malicious accounts.
  Based on the intuitions, four properties are used in social honeypot-based features for accounts interacting with social honeypots:
  The first one is the ratio of malicious accounts interacting with a social honeypot in the last time period (MAR).
  The second one is the average daily new follower number of a social honeypot (DFN).
  The third one is how many social honeypots an account interacts with (AIN).
  The last one is whether a social honeypot follow back an account (AFB).
  We calculate the first and second properties for each social honeypot and the third and fourth ones for each account interacting with social honeypots.

4.6.1.3 Classification of Users

Machine learning is a type of artificial intelligence (AI) that provides computers with the ability to learn without being explicitly programmed (Elmendili et al. 2017). The process of machine learning is similar to that of data mining. Both systems search through data to look for patterns. However, instead of extracting data for human comprehension as is the case in data mining applications, machine learning uses that data to detect patterns in data and adjust program actions accordingly. Machine learning algorithms are often categorized as being supervised or unsupervised. Supervised algorithms can apply what has been learned in the past to new data (logistic regression, Bayes classifier, support vector machine [SVM]). Unsupervised algorithms can draw inferences from datasets (k-means, expectation maximization (EM), hierarchical grouping) (Elmendili et al. 2017) (Figure 4.4).

Weka machine learning toolkit: In our experiment, after selecting all the characteristics of users and deployed honeypots, we use *Weka machine learning toolkit* to form the classifier and we assess the results with *10-fold cross-validation* (Elmendili et al. 2017).

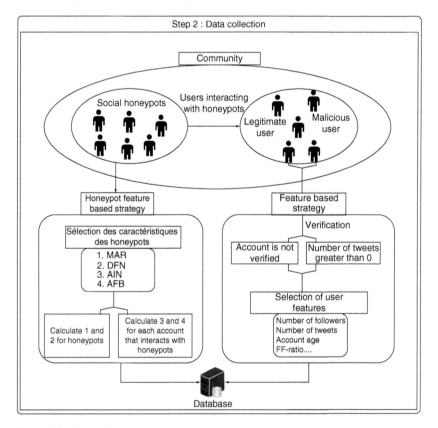

Figure 4.4 Data collection.

Weka is a popular suite of machine learning software written in Java, developed at the University of Waikato, New Zealand. Weka is free software available under the GNU General Public License. The Weka workbench contains a collection of visualization tools and algorithms for data analysis and predictive modeling, together with graphical user interfaces for easy access to this functionality.Weka supports several standard data mining tasks, more specifically (Elmendili et al. 2017) data preprocessing, clustering, classification, regression, visualization, and feature selection. All of Weka's techniques are predicated on the assumption that the data is available as a single flat file or relation, where each data point is described by a fixed number of attributes (normally, numeric or nominal attributes, but some other attribute types are also supported) (Elmendili et al. 2017). Weka provides access to SQL databases using Java Database Connectivity and can process the result returned by a database query. It is not capable of multi-relational data mining, but there is separate software for converting a collection of linked database tables into a single table that is suitable for processing using Weka (Elmendili et al. 2017). Another important area that is currently not covered by the algorithms included in the Weka distribution is sequence modeling.

Decorate algorithm: One of the major advances in inductive learning in the past decade was the development of ensemble or committee approaches that learn and retain multiple hypotheses and combine their decisions during classification (Elmendili et al. 2017).

Diverse Ensemble Creation by Oppositional Relabeling of Artificial Training Examples (*DECORATE*) is a meta-learner that uses an existing strong learner (one that provides high accuracy on the training data) to build an effective diverse committee in a simple, straightforward manner (http://blog.cozic.fr/twitter-presentation-du-concept-de-ses-differents-usages-et-de-quelques-applications-connexes-188). This is accomplished by adding different randomly constructed examples to the training set when building new committee members.

In *DECORATE*, we initialize the ensemble to contain the classifier trained on the given training data. The classifiers in each successive iteration are trained on the original training data combined with some artificial data. In each iteration, artificial training examples are generated from the distribution, where the number of examples to be generated is specified as a fraction of the training set size (http://blog.cozic.fr/twitter-presentation-du-concept-de-ses-differents-usages-et-de-quelques-applications-connexes-188). We train a new classifier on the union of the original training data and the diversity data, thereby forcing it to differ from the current ensemble. Therefore adding this classifier to the ensemble will increase its diversity. This process is repeated until we reach the desired committee size or exceed the maximum number of iterations.

To classify an unlabeled example, x, we employ the following method. Each base classifier, C_i, in the ensemble C^* provides probabilities for the class membership of x. If $P_{C_{i,y}}(x)$ is the probability of example x belonging to class y according to the classifier C_i, then we compute the class membership probabilities for the entire ensemble as (http://blog.cozic.fr/twitter-presentation-du-concept-de-ses-differents-usages-et-de-quelques-applications-connexes-188):

$$P_y(x) = \frac{\sum_{C_i \in C^*} P_{C_{i,y}}(x)}{C^*} \qquad (4.3)$$

where C is a classifier, a function from objects to classes. C^* is an ensemble of classifiers. C_i is the ith classifier in ensemble C^*. $P_y(x)$ is the probability of x belonging to class y. We then select the most probable class as the label for x, i.e.

$$C^*(x) = \underset{y \in Y}{\operatorname{argmax}} P_y(x) \qquad (4.4)$$

K-fold cross-validation (KFCV): In our classification, we use the *10-fold cross-validation* (CV) method. CV is a popular strategy for algorithm selection. The main idea behind CV is to split data, once or several times, for estimating the risk of each algorithm: part of data (the training sample) is used for training each algorithm, and the remaining part (the validation sample) is used for estimating the risk of the algorithm. Then, CV selects the algorithm with the smallest estimated risk. In K-fold partition of the dataset, for each of K experiments, use $K - 1$ folds for training and a different fold for testing. In 10-fold cross-validation, the original sample is randomly divided into 10 equally sized subsamples. Nine sub-samples are used as a training set and the remaining one is used as a testing set; the classifier is evaluated, then the process is repeated for a total of 10 times. Each sub-sample is used as a testing set once in each evaluation. Classification results are presented in the form of a confusion matrix as in Figure 4.5.

To measure the effectiveness of classifiers based on our proposed features, we used the standard metrics such as precision, recall.

Precision is the fraction of retrieved documents that are relevant to the query:

$$\text{precision} = \frac{\text{nb of documents correctly assigned to the class}}{\text{nb of documents assigned to the class}} \qquad (4.5)$$

For example, precision (P) of the malicious class is $a/(a + c)$.

		Predicted	
		Malicious	legitimate
Actual	Malicious	a	b
	legitimate	c	d

Figure 4.5 Confusion matrix example.

Recall is the fraction of the documents that are relevant to the query that are successfully retrieved[1] :

$$recall = \frac{\text{nb of documents correctly assigned to the class}}{\text{nb of documents belonging to the class}} \qquad (4.6)$$

For example, recall (R) of the malicious class is $a/(a + b)$. Accuracy is the total number of correct predictions. In our case the accuracy is: $(a + d)/(a + b + c + d)$.

A false positive is a result that indicates a given condition has been fulfilled, when it actually has not been fulfilled. The false positive of the malicious class is c (Figure 4.6).

In this chapter we have presented the design of a new approach based on the social honeypots to detect the malicious profiles in social networks. Our overall objective of this research is to study the techniques and developing effective tools to automatically detect and filter the malicious profiles that target the

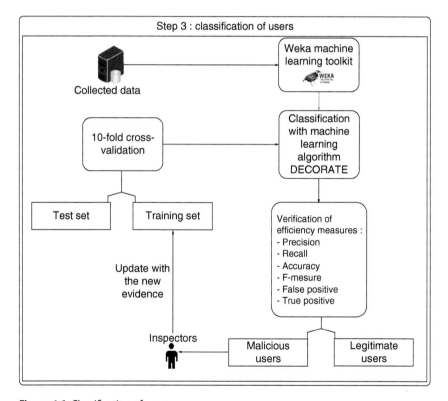

Figure 4.6 Classification of users.

1 https://en.wikipedia.org/wiki/Precision_and_recall.

social systems and especially in the area of health in order to detect those who use the identity falsified to share of bad information on the identity of the physicians. More specifically, our approach deploys the social honeypots in order to attract the malicious accounts. By focusing on the Twitter community, we used a set of characteristics of the users as well of the honeypots deployed to create a classifier of malicious profiles based using the algorithm for automatic learning decorate to identify malicious accounts with a high precision and a low rate of false positives.

4.7 Results and Discussion

After implementing our honeypots and interact with different types of users, we selected 90 profiles among 300 profile strapped by our honeypots and for each profile we selected traditional characteristics "traditional features" such as (follower number, FF-ratio, account age, tweet number, mention ratio, ratio URL) and features based on honeypots "honeypot based features" such as (the number of honeypots with whom one interacts account, the daily average of new followers fora honeypot). The size of the database is 90 profiles. Now that we have gathered our dataset, we used DECORATE machine learning algorithm to model the problem and make predictions and we chose CV, which lets WEKA build a model based on subsets of the supplied data and then average them out to create a final model. In previous work, generally the métas Classifiers (Decorate, Lo-gitBoost, etc.) Product of Best performance that the classifiers to trees (BFTree and FT) and classifiers based on functions (SimpleLogistic and libsvm) (Melville 2003). For our approach we chose decorate as classifier. For different reasons: -The speed and the execution time; -Best Performance Compared to Other; -Of Results approximately correct. Figure 4.7 shows estimates of the trees predictive performance, generated by WEKAs evaluation module. It outputs the list of statistics summarizing how accurately the classifier was able to predict the true class of the instances under the chosen test module. The set of measurements is derived from the training data. In this case 97.7778% of 90 training instances have been classified correctly. This indicates that the results obtained from the training data are optimistic compared with what might be obtained from the independent test set from the same source. In addition to classification error, the evaluation output measurements derived from the class probabilities assigned by the tree. More specifically, it outputs mean output error (0.132) of the probability estimates, the root mean squared error (0.1929) is the square root of the quadratic loss. Theme an absolute error calculated in a similar way by using the absolute instead of squared difference. The reason that the errors are not 1 or 0 is because not all training instances are classified correctly. Kappa statistic is a chance-corrected measure of agreement between the classifications and the true classes. It's calculated by taking the agreement

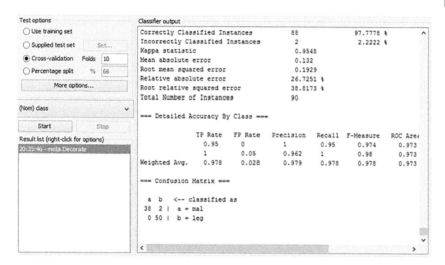

Figure 4.7 Estimates of the trees predictive performance

expected by chance away from the observed agreement and dividing by the maximum possible agreement.

The true positive (TP) rate is the proportion of examples that were classified as class x, among all examples that truly have class x, i.e. how much part of the class was captured. It is equivalent to recall. In the confusion matrix, this is the diagonal element divided by the sum over the relevant row, i.e. $38/(38 + 2) = 0.95$ for class malicious and $50/(50 + 1) = 1$ for class legitimate in our example. The Precision is the proportion of the examples that truly have class x among all those that were classified as class x. In the matrix, this is the diagonal element divided by the sum over the relevant column, i.e. $38/(38 + 0) = 1$ for class malicious and $50/(2 + 50) = 0.962$ for class legitimate. From the confusion matrix in Figure 4.8, we can see that two instances of a

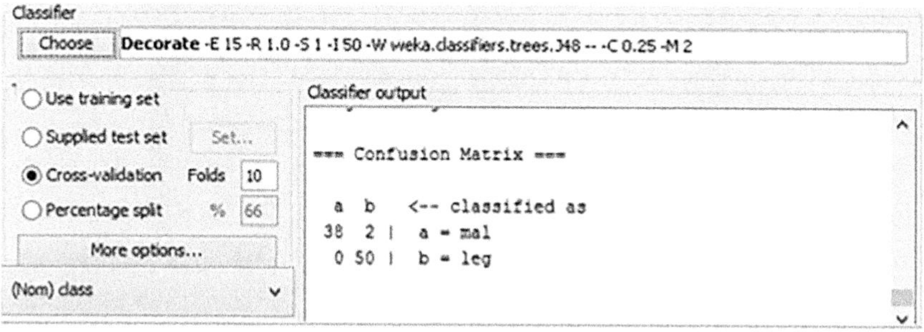

Figure 4.8 Confusion matrix.

class "legitimate" have been assigned to a class "malicious," and zero of class "malicious" are assigned to class "legitimate."

Figure 4.9 presents the threshold curve for the prediction.

This figure shows a 97.28% predictive accuracy on the malicious class.

In Figure 4.10 we present the performance of our malicious users detector trained with traditional features, honeypot based features and two sets of features together, respectively.

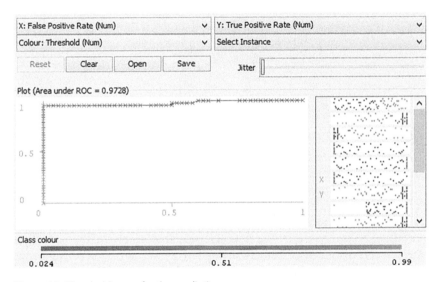

Figure 4.9 Threshold curve for the prediction.

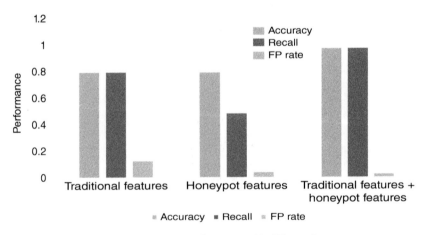

Figure 4.10 Malicious user's detector performance with different feature set.

We can find that after we combine a traditional feature set with honeypot-based feature set, we can achieve an accuracy of 0.979, a recall of 0.978, and a false positive rate of 0.028. The accuracy and recall are much better than simply using the other two feature sets independently. Though the FP rate is higher than simply using honeypot-based feature set, we can modify the threshold to make a trade-off between FP rates and recall (Elmendili et al. 2017). From the results obtained, we can point out that with the hybrid method used (traditional feature set with honeypot-based feature), we can detect the more wide space of malicious users on social networks and why not apply the same approach to other communities. This hybrid approach gives results relevant to other methods.

4.8 Conclusion

The social networks are online services that allow a user to share personal and professional information and interact more or less closely with other Internet users according to their degree of proximity. These services host more and more data, the growth is exponential. This makes the management of the confidentiality of these shared information very difficult. The adaptation of this approach to a social network will allow, not only to finalize this study but also to extend on a set of social networks in the framework of a policy of overall network security. The application of this approach on the social networks in the health sector allows not only to protect this platform but also to detect the profiles that use of falsified identities, and who can share and spread of information unnecessary for the health of the patient, as well as the profiles that use the name of physicians recognized for the purposes of illegal. This approach is new application to detect the malicious profiles and especially is a new innovation applied in this sector. The health sector is very sensitive in terms of shared data and information already mentioned that this either by the patient or the doctor. However, the sensitivity of this sector attracts the attackers and malicious users to apply their desires, and wait for their illegal goals.

Bibliography

Bellare, M., Paterson, K.G., and Rogaway, P. (2014). Security of symmetric encryption against mass surveillance. In: *Advances in Cryptology - CRYPTO 2014. CRYPTO 2014. Lecture Notes in Computer Science*, vol. **8616** (ed. J.A. Garay and R. Gennaro). Berlin, Heidelberg: Springer.

Bigdata (2012). Big data in healthcare hype and hope.

Chiny, M., Lahmaim, M., Kalam, A.A.E., and Ouahman, A.A. (2012). Evaluation de la cybercriminalité au Maroc: Cas d'un établissement universitaire. 2012

National Days of Network Security and Systems, Marrakech, 56–61. https://doi.org/10.1109/JNS2.2012.6249242.

El Idrissi Younes, E.B., Fatna, E.M., and Nisrine, M. (2016). A security approach for social networks based on honeypots. 2016 4th IEEE International Colloquium on Information Science and Technology (CiSt), Tangier, 638–643. 10.1109/CIST.2016.7804964.

Elmendili, F., Maqran, N., Idrissi, Y., and Chaoui, H. (2017). A security approach based on honeypots: protecting Online Social network from malicious profiles. *Advances in Science, Technology and Engineering Systems Journal* **2** (3): 198–204.

Ghosh, S., Viswanath, B., Kooti, F. et al. (2012). Understanding and combating link farming in the twitter social network. In: Proceedings of the 21st International Conference on World Wide Web, 6170. ACM.

Goodman, J., Heckerman, D., and Rounthwaite, R. (2005). A stopping spam. *Scientific American* **292** (4): 4288.

Intelligence Artificielle Weka: Présentation février 2004.

Lee, K., Caverlee, J., and Webb, S. (2010). The social honeypot project: protecting online communities from spammers. In: Proceedings of the 19th International Conference on World wide web (WWW'10), 1139–1140. New York, NY: ACM. http://dx.doi.org/10.1145/1772690.1772843.

Melville, P. (2003). *Creating Diverse Ensemble Classifiers*. The University of Texas at Austin.

Naruoka, H., Matsuta, M., Machii, W. et al. (2015). ICS Honeypot System (CamouflageNet) based on attacker's human factors. 6th International Conference on Applied Human Factors and Ergonomics (AHFE 2015).

Nazir, A., Raza, S., and Chuah, C.-N. (2008). Unveiling facebook: a measurement study of social network based applications. In: SIGCOMM.

Rosenblatt, B. (1997). The digital object identifier: solving the dilemma of copyright protection online. *Journal of Electronic Publishing* **3** (2). https://quod .lib.umich.edu/j/jep/3336451.0003.204?view=text;rgn=main.

Sahama, T., Simpson, L., and Lane, B. (2013). Security and privacy in eHealth: Is it possible?. In: 2013 IEEE 15th International Conference on e-Health Networking, Applications and Services (Healthcom 2013), Lisbon, 249–253. http://dx.doi.org/10.1109/HealthCom.2013.6720676.

Sridharan, V., Shankar, V., and Gupta, M. (2012). Twitter games: how successful spammers pick targets. In: Proceedings of the 28th Annual Computer Security Applications Conference, 389–398. ACM.

Stringhini, G., Kruegel, C., and Vigna, G. (2010). Detecting spammers on social networks. In: Proceedings of the 26th Annual Computer Security Applications Conference, 19. ACM.

Synthsesio (2016). les médias sociaux dans le secteur de la santé.

Yang, C., Harkreader, R., Zhang, J. et al. (2012). Analyzing spammers social networks for fun and profit: a case study of cyber criminal ecosystem on twitter. In: Proceedings of the 21st International Conference on World Wide Web, 7180. ACM.

(2012). http://formation-e~reputa-tion.fr.

5

Multi-Sensor Fusion for Context-Aware Applications

Veeramuthu Venkatesh[1], Ponnuraman Balakrishnan[2], and Pethru Raj[3]

[1] School of Computing, SASTRA Deemed University, Thanjavur, Tamilnadu, India
[2] Department of Analytics, SCOPE, VIT University, Vellore, Tamilnadu, India
[3] Site Reliability Engineering (SRE) Division, Reliance Jio Infocomm. Ltd. (RJIL), Bangalore, India

5.1 Introduction

The intelligent pervasive system is a new archetype in the field of technological innovation developed by people's experiences using digital encompassment. This model is highly profound, adaptive, and highly forthcoming to the needs of an individual's habits, signs, and sentiments. This impressive hallucination of the daily atmosphere will allow a pioneering human–machine communication categorized through intelligent, pervasive, modest, and proactive infrastructures. Such advanced communication archetypes make the intelligent pervasive systems as an appropriate applicant for evolving several real-world resolutions in healthcare domain especially for the needs of elderly people. It is necessary to look at the facilities and technology prerequisites intended for realizing the perspective of an intelligent pervasive system, for example, smart surroundings and body worn sensor devices. The state-of-the-art intelligent pervasive system approaches are intended for evolving the pervasive system in the healthcare area, together with various machine learning methods, reasoning methods, and planning methods. The following sections discuss the vision of pervasive system and also about how it can upkeep one's pretentious knowledge about chronic diseases, several physical, and mental disabilities.

5.1.1 What Is an Intelligent Pervasive System?

Intelligent pervasive healthcare is a flourishing area, concentrating on the advancements and applications of pervasive and ubiquitous computing technology, for ambient healthcare and wellness of any patients. Let us consider a real-time example of a biosensor, which is attached to a patient's body.

Intelligent Pervasive Computing Systems for Smarter Healthcare, First Edition.
Arun Kumar Sangaiah, S.P. Shantharajah, and Padma Theagarajan.
© 2019 John Wiley & Sons, Inc. Published 2019 by John Wiley & Sons, Inc.

The sensor will continuously record the patient's body temperature, glucose, and blood pressure signs inevitably and send it to a specialist of a laboratory. This type of mechanism can be called as intelligent pervasive computing. This paradigm characterizes the futuristic vision of intelligent computing wherever the surroundings can upkeep the people who are occupying them (Mitchell et al., 2000; Vasilakos and Pedrycz, 2006; Sordo et al., 2008; Aarts and Wichert, 2009; Cook et al., 2009; Augusto et al., 2010; Baig and Gholamhosseini, 2013; Benavente-Peces et al., 2014; Rahmani et al., 2015; Soh et al., 2015). Such computing archetype, the Orthodox input, and output broadcasting no longer occur, and relatively the sensors and processing element are combined into day-to-day individual objects, which will interact with each other in coordination to endorse the residents (Cook et al., 2009; Benavente-Peces et al., 2014). By depending on several intelligent pervasive healthcare methods, the pervasive system guarantees the fruitful understanding of the wealth of a contextual evidence that is acquired from the embedded devices and will acclimatize the location to the inhabitant requests in an apparent and anticipatory way. Intelligent pervasive computing is predominantly known by several characteristics:

- *Context awareness*: It uses the situational and contextual information.
- *Anticipatory*: It can figure out the necessities of any individual without aware intervention of the individual.
- *Adaptive*: To adjust to the varying needs of any personalities.
- *Personalized*: It is personalized and made to measure to the necessities of any individual.
- *Ubiquitous*: It is entrenched and is assimilated into every real-world surroundings.
- *Transparency*: It moves away into the contextual everyday lifestyle in a moderate way.

Moreover, several features such as context management and transparency, the characteristic of pervasive computing, have no bounds. Through illustration from developments in pervasive computing, this method proves to be even more profound, personalized, adaptive, and ubiquitous, in addition to application subareas such as cognitive, activity monitoring, and decision support system. The example for application domain includes "wireless sensor networks" (WSNs) to assist any environment in getting the real data. "Industrial robotics" to control actuators and "humanoid computing" to form more and more natural interfaces. Globally, every human being is besieged by a variety of computing components such as personal digital assistants, radio-frequency identification (RFID) tags, various sensors, smartphones, tablets, global positioning systems (GPS), and infrared sensors, in addition to biometric sensors. The extensive existence of this electronic gadget and sensing devices and associated facilities, which include situation aware facility, has previously flashed the consciousness from pervasive computing. Furthermore, modern computational and electronics developments have made it likely for the new researchers to work on the motivated ideas such as smart environments that bring people one step nearer from the complete consciousness of pervasive computing into our real-world surroundings.

5.1.2 The Significance of Context Awareness for Next-Generation Smarter Environments

Context awareness is a primary function of the intelligent pervasive healthcare systems, and it has been utilized since the early 1990s. Over the last decade, the ubiquitous Web and desktop applications focused on context-aware computing in the Internet of things (IoT). Nevertheless, context-aware computing became well known with enhancements of the world as per the phrase ubiquitous computing introduced by Mark Weiser. Later Schilit and Theimer used the word "context aware."

In the last two years, the symbolic quantity of prototypes and techniques, along with the alternatives, has been designed by engineers and scientists using context-aware processing methods. Although they concentrate differently based on each venture, looking after the work stays the same: that is, the amount of data origins like hardware and software sources. Very few virtual and physical sensors are used to collect the data, which are to be proposed. In these circumstances, accumulating and analyzing sensor data from all the available resources is not feasible and also is viable because of restricted models. On the other hand, IoT visualizes that point of time where the Internet was linked to an immeasurable number of sensors, making it infeasible to process the data, which was collected by all the available sensors. For this reason, context awareness is the best suitable way to determine what information needs to be handled and how many more information can be accommodated.

With increasing developments in sensor strategies, they promise to be more compact in dimension with minimum cost and also with high dominance factor, which has activated comprehensive distribution. As a result, the sensors are deployed in the early stages of manufacturing, and it is believed that the figures will improve at par with the emerging technology. Eventually, these active sensors produce a large volume of data. If we are going to interpret and evaluate the available information, then it becomes insignificant for use by the users. Context-aware computing has been proven to be an important factor especially in fields as ubiquitous and pervasive, guiding us to rely on the IoT framework. With context-aware computing, we can rule the context information associated with the sensor data for a meaningful and an easy interpretation. Furthermore, understanding data in this way makes it much easier to perform bidirectional communication between machines, which makes it the primary element in the IoT process.

From the moment after placing each sensor in their respective slot, they start to produce data, and the conventional task-centered approach becomes inefficient. Significant quantities of middleware alternatives are presented by researchers to deal with this inefficiency. In IoT, each middleware solution concentrates on different factors in system control, interoperability, system mobility, context awareness, protection, comfort, etc. Though there are some alternatives dealing with several factors, a perfect middleware alternative that details all the factors necessary for IoT is, however, to be designed. Context-aware computing requires relevant characteristics and functionalities, which are required by the pervasive healthcare system, which is recognized as the key process for this section.

5.1.2.1 Context-Aware Characteristics

An application that can support context awareness scenario comes in three typical flavors: starting with labeling, then to present, and finally to execute. Even if, the IoT perspective was not known at the initial period, these characteristics are identified to be appropriate to the IoT paradigm. Here these features are explicated from an IoT viewpoint.

Presentation: Information and services, which are presented to the consumer, are by present context. In a scenario like smart environment, a person depends on his or her smartphone to contain the list of items to be purchased for a better satisfaction. For this, the kitchen equipments are connected to mobile apps that support context awareness phenomenon such as a refrigerator getting the shopping list and then presenting it to the customer. The information that is being offered depends on the context of including time, location, etc. From the survey, IoT has the potentials to offer any 24/7 round the clock service.

Accomplishment: In the IoT paradigm services, automatic accomplishment is also a critical feature. In a scenario like smart environment, once a person starts driving from their office to home, the deployed IoT diligence in the home environment would turn on the coffee machine, and air condition has to be ready at the time of arrival at home. Such activities need to be considered with high priority, which is centered on the context.

Labeling: A number of sensors are involved every day to the physical object in the IoT framework. Large volumes of sensor data will be produced by the physical object that has to be composed, studied, fused, and inferred. The data, which are produced by any sensor, will not deliver the required information that can be used to completely recognize the state of context. In IoT paradigm data from multiple sources are fused. To perform a fusion of sensor data, in the application environment, all contexts should be gathered. Context needs to be labeled unitedly with the data, which is collected from every sensor to be processed and recognized later. In a context-aware computing, context notation performs a significant part in context-aware processing analysis. Labeling operation is called as one of the notations in the context.

5.1.2.2 Context Types and Categorization Schemes

Context types are defined by some leading mechanisms. They are location identification, personal identity, period, and action and are considered as primary context categories. Additionally, the secondary context is identified as a context that originates from the primary context. In a person's identity example, the primary context-related information is nothing but his or her address, phone numbers, email addresses, etc. Let us consider another example based on two GPS sensors, which are positioned in two different locations. Based on these two GPS values, it is easy to locate the position of each sensor. After getting the raw values, which are generated by two sensors performing some calculation over the values, it is then possible to get the distance between those two sensors. Here the important context is whether the context distance is belonging to the primary or secondary category. By fusing the values of two sensors, the distance may be computed. However, the above example lacks clarity regarding the same. Thus it is necessary to have context categorization scheme, which is used to realize the given data value (e.g. current time of the single data) of the context in relation to functional perspective (i.e. in what method the data is acquired). Nevertheless, in one scenario, similar data value is also considered as a primary context, and, in another scenario, it is considered as secondary context. In another example, if it is necessary to determine the level of the blood pressure from a patient directly with the attached sensor, it might be recognized as the primary context. But if similar information is derived from the health record of the patient through linking to the database in the hospital, then it will be recognized as secondary context. Consequently, the same context can be derived using different methods. It is significant to recognize the effort of acquisition that the accuracy, validity, and cost may differ based on the methods used in the above scenario.

In the IoT archetype, this should be more challenging because the same data value can be retrieved through an enormous volume of information sources that in turn can be used later. It is a difficult task to decide which source and technique to use, for example, in the case where the GPS derives the raw data value such as location (e.g. shopping mall) or sometimes the name of the location, name of the city, and name of the road. It is inaccurate to categorize a location as a primary context without analyzing in what way the information has been collected. Table 5.1 shows how the context can be identified based on context definitions.

Primary context: Without using the existing context, the data can be retrieved and without the accomplishment of any the fusion processes (e.g. location information from GPS sensor interpretations).

Table 5.1 Characteristics of context awareness through three levels.

	Primary	Secondary
Location	From GPS (longitude and latitude) of location, data is identified	GPS values are used to compute the distance between two sensors
Identify	RFID tag is used to identify the user	Facebook profile used to retrieve friends list
		Facial recognition system is used to identify a face of a person
Time	Clock is used to get the time	Weather information used to calculate seasonal data
Activity	Door sensor is used to identify whether door is opened or closed	With help of accelerometer, GPS, gyroscope user activity is identified

Secondary context: By means of primary context, the information can be processed. By performing the operations like sensor data fusion, secondary context can be computed or through Web service calls such as data retrieval. For example, sensor data fusion processes with twofold raw GPS sensor values find out the distance between two sensors by applying these values. Additionally, context through a list of contacts, mailing addresses, email, date of birth, and friend's details and also personal characteristics such as the primary context and the secondary context can also be recognized. It is necessary to acknowledge the significant context information based on activity time, identity, and location. The IoT framework aspires to look at more extensive categorization techniques in an ordered way with significant groups, subgroups, and so on. Functional categorization techniques permit to comprehend the problems, difficulties in data acquirement model, in addition to QoS and cost aspects connected to context.

Centered on the consumer interaction, context awareness can be identified as three levels.

Personalization: Any users are allowed to set their predilections, expectations, their wishes, and dislikes manually in the system. In a smart home environment, the preferred temperature is set by users so that heating system in all rooms are maintained at the same temperature as specified by the users.

Passive context awareness: The environment is continuously monitored by a system, and it offers the suitable options to the users for taking necessary actions. In a supermarket example, as soon as the user enters into the customer premises, they can be alerted through their mobile phones, related to items that are currently in discount and also according to their needs and preferences.

Active context awareness: The context-aware computing system consistently and originally looks for the situation and acts independently. In a smart home environment example, a fire in a room can be detected by the smoke sensors and temperature sensors, and the monitoring system will instantly determine the cause of fire and inform all the persons living there through suitable approaches, for example, mobile phone.

Context is identified as comprehensively based on eight characteristics:

- Sensed through WSNs.
- Detected by miniaturized and resource-constrained devices.
- Initiates from disseminated sources.
- Endlessly varying.
- Originates from mobile objects.
- Through temporal character.
- Through spatial character.
- Inadequate and ambiguous.

5.1.2.3 Context Awareness Management Design Principles

Only the most important design aspects are considered.

Architecture stages and components: The functions and features must be divided into a number of stages and components in a significant manner. Limited amount of task will be carried out by each component, and it should be able to accomplish independently.

Scalability and extensibility: Dynamically each component can be added or removed from an infrastructure. For example, in a smart home a new feature can be added or removed without changing the existing components in that environment (OSGi). To improve the scalability and extensibility, the hardware component must be developed to allow the standards through the different solutions (e.g. plug'n play designs).

Application programming interface (API): It is an easy and comprehensive way to learn and use the available functionalities in an application environment. Further, in context management, framework binding can be done on the application environment through API. Interoperability between different IoT deeply depends on API and their functionalities.

Context life cycle management through automata: Context-aware computing is to be comprehended by the existing context sources based on physical and virtual sensors and also through data structure. It inevitably deploys classified data models to assist them. With a minimum human intervention, it is necessary to retrieve and transform the appropriate context to suitable models.

Context model independency: Code and data structures related to the context from a context-aware framework want to be modeled and stored distinctly so that both can be transformed independently.

Extended, rich, and comprehensive modeling: It is easy to extend the context models. In IoT they deal with large amount of participating devices, and for a domain-specific context, it is required to handle a large amount of data. Constrains and complex relationships also need to be supported by context awareness. In an IoT framework based on ideal context awareness, to increase their efficiency and effectiveness, different and multiple context representation framework should be combined.

Multi-model reasoning: To adapt the difficulties of the IoT, single reasoning model is not sufficient. There are some own strengths and weaknesses on each reasoning model. To mitigate the weaknesses and strength, which are complement to each other, it is necessary to integrate multiple reasoning models together in an ideal IoT framework.

Mobility support: Most of the devices would be mobile in an IoT framework, wherever each device takes a diverse set of hardware and software potentialities. Multiple flavors (i.e. versions) have to be developed for context-aware frameworks, which are able to run on diverse hardware and software versions (e.g. more skills for software in a server and fewer skills for mobile phones).

Information sharing: Normally there is no single point of control in the IoT, which means that it employs distributed architecture. Different levels of context sharing should be utilized, framework to framework and framework to application. There is independency in the context model and is also very critical in sharing of resources.

Resource optimization: When more and more devices are connected in an IoT framework, even a small change in processing and improvement in data structures can lead to very high influence in bandwidth, power, and energy depletion. It remains fatal for some kind of resource active in the IoT.

Event detection and monitoring: Events play an important part in the IoT, whereas monitoring is complement to the event. In an IoT paradigm event triggers an action independently whenever an event is detected. To bring out their day-to-day work effortlessly and fruitfully, it helps the human in an IoT. The foremost difficulty for context-aware computing in the IoT archetype is to detect the events in real time.

5.1.2.4 Context Life Cycle

In a software system a data life cycle indicates the way in which way data transfers from stage to stage (e.g. application, middleware). Where the information is produced and information is expended is explained specifically by the life cycle. In context-aware systems movement of context is also considered. Normally context awareness is not restricted to mobile apps, Web, or desktop. It has been considered as context as a service (CXaaS). In software systems, context management has emerged to be of vital functionality. This development will also propagate in the IoT archetype. Context information management is provided all the way through the context's life cycle using

Web-based context management services (WCXMS). Data life cycles are classified into two approaches: enterprise lifecycle approaches (ELA) and context lifecycle approaches (CLA).

ELA are motivated on context. However, these life cycles remain robust and deep rooted, centered on industry standard approaches for data management. In contrast, CLA are specialized in context management.

A classical context management system has three stages besides life cycles, namely, information processing, context acquisition, and verdict and logical thinking. Upon analyzing these, an apt (least stages with all vitals) context life cycle has been developed, which is given in Figure 5.1. It has four stages as follows. Initially, context is gained from several sources, which can be physical or implicit sensors (context acquisition). Then, the context is simulated and interpreted in a substantive way (context modeling). Next, the modeled context is treated to infer sophisticated data from subsidiary unprocessed sensor data (context reasoning). Last, the context is disseminated to the end users having context interests (context dissemination).

Context acquisition: Here, we present five aspects to be taken into account while building context-alert middleware outcomes in the IoT exemplar. Context is obtained using techniques that vary upon frequency, liability, sensor type, and acquisition process and context source. Context acquisition is the basic stage in a context development. These are the crucial steps in context management systems and middleware solutions. The remaining operations are nothing but value-added services provided by systems.

Based on accountability context (e.g. sensor facts): Push and pull are the two main schemes by which acquisition is done. *Pull*: To gain sensor data from

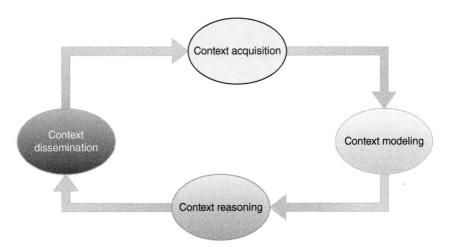

Figure 5.1 The compact view of context life cycle.

sensors, software modules hold a query from the sensor hardware once in a while or immediately. *Push*: The implicit sensor (otherwise physical) drives information into the software module liable to obtain sensor data at once or occasionally, which gets used in aiding a subscriber as well as publishing a framework.

Based on the rate of recurrence: Instant and interval events are the two types by which context is generated in the IoT paradigm.

Instant (threshold violation): These events take place immediately, which extend across a certain time period. Some examples are switching the light on, animals coming into the observational crop field, and opening a door. To sense this event, sensor data has to be obtained. Pull and push routines find their application here also.

5.1.2.5 Interval (Called Occasionally)

They cover some time period. Examples of interval events are an animal eating a plant, raining, winter, etc. Push and pull methods come into play in detecting this event as well and sensor data is gained sporadically.

Based on source: Three more categories of context acquisition methods are presented below:

Acquire directly from sensor hardware: Here, communication between the sensor hardware and the concerned APIs directly yields the context. Local installation of libraries and software drivers is emphasized. This method is recommended to recover data from local sensors. Sensors and devices, nowadays, necessitate driver support to some extent, which can be linked through COM, USB, or serial ports. Conversely, wireless technologies catch the attention in our time-permitting data transmission devoid of driver installations. This principle is used in the IoT paradigm

Acquire through a middleware infrastructure: Here, the context is incurred via middleware solutions like GSN. The applications salvage information of the software and not from the hardware. For instance, certain GSN unswervingly make use of sensor hardware, and the rest will commune with other GSN exemplars to recollect info.

Obtain from context servers: This technique gets data of different context storages (e.g. databases, Really Simple Syndication (RSS) feeds, Web services) through unlike routines like Web service calls. This is a promising means when it comes to limited computing supplies. Servers having boundless resources are exploited to obtain and process context.

Based on the kinds of sensor: Usually, sensor refers to substantial sensor hardware devices. Nevertheless, it also signifies any data resource that affords pertinent context. Thus, sensors are categorized into three types: physical, virtual, and coherent.

Physical sensors: Physical sensors are very common and are palpable. They develop sensor data on their own. Many present day devices are outfitted with diverse sensor (e.g. temperature, humidity, microphone, touch). These sensors yield subsidiary context information, which are not so evocative, trifling, and susceptible to even minute alterations. IoT solutions have to study the corporal world by infringing, deficient in addition to vague information.

Virtual sensors: They do not produce sensor information on their own but regain from various resources and issue that as one (e.g. datebook, contacts list, chat, and twitter statuses). They do not possess any substantial existence and utilize Web services expertise for transmitting plus accepting information.

Logical sensors (or software sensors): Logical sensors generate significant information by combining physical and virtual sensors. They are nothing but an out-and-out Web service to provide weather information. Metrological centers exploit numerous physical sensors to gather climate information. Facts from virtual sensors like historic data, calendars, and maps are also taken into account. Both the sensors' data are utilized to get weather information. Besides these, android OS has various software sensors like gravity, linear accelerometer, rotation vector, and orientation sensors.

Based on acquisition procedure: Context is gained by three ways: sense, derive, and manually provided.

Sense: Here, the data is perceived via sensors, together with detected data kept in databases (for instance, recollect temperature from a sensor, get back appointments specifications from a calendar).

Derive: The data gets spawned through computational operations on sensor data that are very effortless like Web service calls or intricate like mathematical operations performed on attained information (e.g. compute distance flanked by two sensors by means of GPS coordinates). The required context should be accessible for implementing arithmetic and rational reasoning schemes.

Manually provided: Here, context information is offered by the users physically through predicted settings selections like priorities (as an example, know that user does not like to have event appraisals between 10:00 p.m. and 6:00 a.m.). It is used to get any form of information.

5.1.3 Pervasive Healthcare-Enabling Technologies

In general, the pervasive computing applications are in continuous operation and should be highly available. The quality is characterized by their capability to acclimatize to the present situations in the current environment. For instance, in a mobile environment, present physical location and the orientation define the characteristics of that environment. Hence, in e-healthcare applications, identifying the patient's identity and understanding his/her present situation is equally important as capturing the patient's health data.

5.1.3.1 Bio-Signal Acquisition

The quantifiable representation of an actual phenomenon is called signal. Bio-signals are the signals that represent the stimuli of any biological process of a biological system. To understand the health status of a patient, firstly, the bio-signals need to be captured through either (i) external measurement (e.g. temperature measurement) or (ii) internal measurement (e.g. endoscopy). Secondly, the noise in the captured bio-signals is removed, and the signal enhancement is done through preprocessing. The measured bio-signals are analog and need to be converted to a digital signal for further processing. The analog signals (A) can be converted to digital signals (D) by using an analog-to-digital converter (A/D). Once the bio-signals are converted to digital signals, the computer can easily perform the required analysis. Some of the common bio-signals in pervasive applications are provided in Table 5.2. Besides the patient-related bio-signals, the contextual information such as current location, present situation, age, and physiological information like body movement are also considered by the pervasive applications in decision making. Here, the patient-related data are collected using the sensors, whereas the contextual information is obtained from cameras, microphones, vibration, and movement sensors.

5.1.3.2 Communication Technologies

The collected bio-signals have to be communicated to the system for the process. Communication can take place in two ways: (i) direct/wired data transfer and (ii) wireless data transfer. In case of wired data transfer, the bio-signals collected from a patient's body are directly transferred to the computer using wires (e.g. electrocardiogram, ECG). Wireless data transfer can be subclassified into (i) wireless local area network (WLAN) or (ii) Bluetooth. WLAN is very useful for transmitting the bio-signals collected from wearable sensors using the wireless network to the desired location/system. Bluetooth is another technique that employs a license-free frequency band

Table 5.2 Common bio-signals and their metrics.

Bio-signals	Volt-(V)	Sensor count	Data rate (b/s)
ECG	0.5–4 mV	5–9	15 000
Heart sound	Extremely small	2–4	120 000
Heart rate	0.5–4 mV	2	600
EEG	2–200 μV	20	4 200
EMG	0.1–5 mV	2+	600 000
Respiratory rate	Small	1	800
Body temperature	0–100 mV	1+	80

to transfer data between devices such as mobiles and PDAs. Bluetooth is comparatively a low-cost and low power technology with restricted data transfer speed and range (10-15 m). Hence Bluetooth is useful for short-range data transfer, and wireless networks are apt for long-range data transfer in pervasive health systems. Table 5.3 represents the different characteristics of discussed technologies. The assessment of the pervasive healthcare systems is highly dependent on energy, cost, power, connectivity, portability, and coverage trade-offs. The real communication network can be constructed via (i) infrastructure-based networks and (ii) ad hoc networks by careful design of the trade-off of the above parameters. The amount of energy used by the computer depends on its storage and communication resources. Regarding data storage, if the bio-signal data is collected using less number of sensors, the data has sparse coverage, and employing a large number of sensors not only improves the bio-signal data quality but also increases storage and energy requirements of the system. The power savings in the network can be implemented by changing the redundant nodes to the power-saving mode.

Table 5.3 Wireless communication technologies for pervasive health systems.

Technology	Data rate	Range	Frequency
IEEE 802.11a	54 Mbps	150 m	5 GHz
IEEE 802.11b	11 Mbps	150 m	2.4 GHz ISM
Bluetooth (IEEE 802.15. 1)	721 Kbps	10 m–150 m	2.4 GHz ISM
HiperLAN2	54 Mbps	150 m	5 GHz
Home RF (shared wireless access protocol, SWAP)	1.6 Mbps (10 Mbps for Ver.2)	50 m	2.4 GHz ISM
DECT	32 kbps	100 m	1880–1900 MHz
IEEE 802.15.3 (high data rate wireless personal area network)	11–55 Mbps	1 m–50 m	2.4 GHz ISM
IEEE 802.16 (local and metropolitan area networks)	120 Mbps	City limits	2–66 GHz
IEEE 802.15.4 (low data rate wireless personal area networks), ZigBee	250 kbps, 20 kbps, 40 kbps	100 m–300 m	2.4 GHz Ism, 868 MHz, 915 MHz ISM
IrDA	4 Mbps (IrDA-1.1)	2 m	IR (0.90)

5.1.3.3   Data Classification

The application of efficient data classification approaches over the acquired bio-signals enables the faster decision making on patient's health. The classification approach may either be supervised or unsupervised. During the training phase of supervised classification, the classifier learns the appropriate key features of an input pattern that represents the output pattern. During the testing phase, it utilizes this knowledge to assign the test input pattern with one of the output patterns. In unsupervised learning, the input patterns, which are having similar characteristics, are grouped as a cluster of unknown class.

5.1.3.4   Intelligent Agents

The agents that have the capability to execute the predefined tasks or adjust itself to the environment and make appropriate decisions are known as intelligent agents. The intelligent agents can:

- execute any task in the best interests of the users or other agents;
- interact with users to obtain instructions and respond;
- functions independently without any direct interference from the users while observing the environment or reacting to the environment changes;
- intelligently interpret the events to obtain suitable decisions.

An intelligent agent also communicates with other agents, analyzes the patient information, and makes their decisions that will be beneficial to the patients in a pervasive healthcare system.

5.1.3.5   Location-Based Technologies

Assisted healthcare facilities such as sensor monitoring of the patient, radio frequency ID (for patient identification), and communication techniques will be useful for patients. Location-based health services are extremely useful in emergency and natural disaster situations. The location-based health services would be very helpful for elderly and physically challenged people. Mobile-based positioning and satellite-based positioning are two of the location-based service technologies. In mobile-based sensing the signals communicated through the network antennas are used to identify the patient's location. In satellite-based positioning, the signals that are communicated through various receivers, and the signal travel path are calculated based on the GPS information. Time delay is a vital parameter in identifying the patient's location as the signal may get affected if the timing delay has not been included in the calculations. Some of the practical applications that employ satellite positioning are Ekahau Positioning Engine, MS RADAR, and Nibble.

5.1.4   Pervasive Healthcare Challenges

In recent decades, a greater number of industrial peoples are confronting noteworthy difficulties concerning the trustworthiness and functional and nonfunctional monetary value of numerous healthcare and comfort facilities. These complications aggravate more and more in the growing elderly population, which results in a variety of health issues demanding several healthcare facilities. The budget allocated for healthcare might not be viable, and so, manufacturing republics want to determine design and strategies to custom the restricted cost-effective resources further competently and effectually. Based on this, there is a demand for viable healthcare solutions that can be transformed into several gains for the people as well as our worldwide economy. Within the development of any specific information, secured message passing for realizing independent and active healthcare facilities will be particularly more helpful.

In the recent years, Internet-based market-driven healthcare devices combined with automated health records lead to an array of value-added results in healthcare. The latter reviews also have countersigned the need for a large number of apps in a smartphone that are willingly offered for physical conditioning

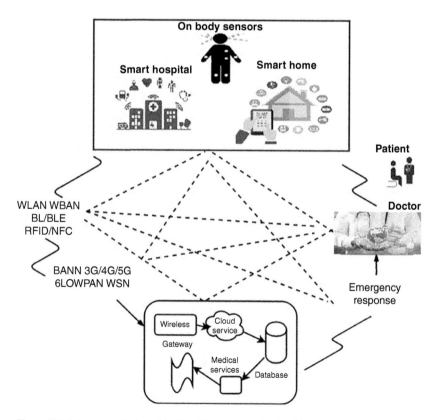

Figure 5.2 Interconnected world of intelligent pervasive healthcare.

detection (Mitchell et al., 2000; Cook et al., 2009; Baig and Gholamhosseini, 2013; Benavente-Peces et al., 2014; Rahmani et al., 2015). Nevertheless, these outcomes often undergo different challenges relating to issues on interoperability, reusability, information safety, and confidentiality. Additionally, these outcomes are capable toward delivering a footprint of physical status relatively more than a constant outlook of the fitness throughout the development for several months. By using the current advancement in WSNs, a low-cost healthcare monitoring research is embedded into smart home and living environments for the elderly people (Augusto et al., 2010; Soh et al., 2015). For example, the pervasive computing helps the elderly to provide an extreme care to monitor the health condition with physical or mental restrictions. The persuasive services are developed to motivate elderly people to lead the life independently without any help from any caretaker. Eventually, it can give an extreme level of support for the healthcare specialists regarding allowing to have advanced data communication and monitoring utensils. The pervasive system will offer elderly healthcare in a well cobwebby and unremarkable way. Figure 5.2 shows how pervasive computing may be employed as interconnected and combined into diverse situations and heterogeneous devices.

5.2 Ambient Methods Used for E-Health

The following discussion will bring together and define the supportive framework and innovative technologies that are utilized in the intelligent pervasive system in the background of ambient healthcare domain.

- Body area networks (BANs).
- Home M2M sensor networks.
- Microelectromechanical system (MEMS).
- Cloud-based intelligent healthcare.

5.2.1 Body Area Networks (BANs)

The extensive use of WSNs and the support of body-worn devices (sometimes referred as moot devices) have endowed the growth of BANs. In BANs, numerous sensing materials are seized on wearables or the human body or even embedded in the skin. This innovative type of communication furnishes plentiful new, real-world, and advanced applications for refining the health of every individual, by endlessly observing health-related features such as blood pressure, physical activity, ECG, body temperature, heartbeat, electromyography (EMG), and electroencephalography (EEG) to improve the quality of life. BANs afford a highly technological setup for remotely streaming censored information to a physician site. For an exact diagnosis, the BANs can autonomously and proactively send an exigency alert with which appropriate activities to correct the health of every individual has been carried out. In healthcare applications, there are some advantages by using wireless BANs, efficiency over communication and effectiveness in size and cost. Indeed, to obtain reliable and accurate predictions from the body-worn sensors, the sensors have to process the information effectively. And at the same time, the lifetime of the sensor batteries (used) also increases accordingly. Furthermore, with the mass increasing requirement of body-worn sensors in the consumer microelectronics market, reasonably low-cost sensors will be produced with high demand, particularly in the field of medical sciences. The important additional advantage of BAN is their integration and scalability with any one of the network infrastructure. It can interface with video surveillance, WSNs, Bluetooth, RFID, and WiBree, wireless personal area network, cellular networks, and the Internet. Every one of these has their important features and advantages of the new market, thereby expanding and opening for consumer electronics and also with new marketing opportunities in the area of pervasive computing specifically in healthcare applications.

5.2.2 Home M2M Sensor Networks

Using the connection establishment of various network models and developments in smart environment technologies, home M2M novel network frameworks are continuously developing to livelihood with added functions and improved QoS. M2M can be enhanced significantly for an enormous amount of deployment in pervasive healthcare applications, which is an innovative development in fitness monitoring or remote health monitoring. In the M2M method, body-worn sensors independently communicate with access points (APs) directly through radio transmitters based on ZigBee. Nevertheless, this method demands that manifold APs be seized to a wall. WBASN and M2M scheme does not have any integrated control for communication to form a mesh structure whenever patients' body-worn sensors publish all appropriate information. The self-organizing capability and the ad hoc-based ability of the structure, interconnecting several wireless sensor devices, turn into the straightforward method. Also, it also has an ability of flexible security model to prearrange the vital messages. M2M is mainly used for remote healthcare systems that are integrated with wireless sensor environment. Integration, reliability, scalability, performance, and security are the features offered by M2M along with WBASN. It offers features such as high reliability, performance, scalability, security, and integration with the Internet-based platform that allows caretakers to access a medical database that is connected through an M2M network.

5.2.3 Microelectromechanical System (MEMS)

MEMS is a state-of-the-art technology for sensor-based design, which includes miniaturized mechanical and electromechanical elements (i.e. physical devices and design structures). The techniques that are used here are called as micro-fabrication. The actual dimensions of MEMS products differ from well below 1 μm of the comprehensive wide range on the lower end to several millimeters all the way. As an impact, they start up new circumstances for popular medical care applications. In recent times, MEMS technological innovation has been used for the design of diverse kinds of sensors such as gyroscope, accelerometer, carbon dioxide (CO_2) gas sensor, ECG, EEG, EMG, blood glucose, blood pressure, pulse oximetry, etc., used in WSNs. Considering one real-time example, bedside monitoring using ECG, nonreusable electrodes are usually made of silver chloride (AgCl). Nevertheless, long-term practice of these kinds of electrodes might induce electrical contact failure and skin irritation problems. MEMS technological innovation can resolve this issue by embedding textile-structured electrodes into clothes fabrics. These embedded textile-structure electrodes may be woven into clothes, which will not irritate the skin, and it is more suitable and comfortable for continuous monitoring. In comparison with the normal electrodes, they are also much more versatile, since their form can be adjusted to human motion.

5.2.4 Cloud-Based Intelligent Healthcare

A health monitoring system is integrated with cloud computing, which uses ambient sensors. They are usually used for accumulating data such as glucose, ECG, and BP from patients. The data is then sent to the server through gateways. Using cloud intelligently envisages a patient's health-related information by using a method called storing/mining. The feedback is also provided to the patient through any one of the computing devices. The patient directly gets necessary precautions through a communicating device or is directly taken care by a physician. Besides, there is no automated medical computing device so far in the field of healthcare. Indirectly it increases the need for a large number of medical consultants to take care health-related issues in the field of medical sciences. It encourages us to create a framework for an intelligent medical server connected with the cloud for fitness applications that will aid more medical consultants in the healthcare domain. The information, which are gathered from the physician and patient, are collected, and finally, it is stored in the cloud. Normally the cloud is outfitted with the computational element that receives the new arrival of data from an individual who is suffering and does some processing over the information. Finally, it then relates the acquired result with the information already stored in the cloud. The patient will get the feedback through any one of the communicating devices if any appropriate values are found. Otherwise, the physician will be called through a smartphone or be sent an SMS. The physician will then download the patient information from the cloud. Then he/she may perform several processes to identify the disease and deliver the review to the individual patient.

5.3   Algorithms and Methods

The main objective of activity recognition model remains to recognize actions as they are centered on information collected by each one of the sensors. In the literature, there are some methods available for activity recognition that differ depending on the sensor-innovative methods that are employed to look after the daily activities. The alternate machine learning procedures, which are applied to realize the actions and their complexity, present the activity recognitions needed for their further development. Improvements in intelligent pervasive computing and sensor networks have led to the growth of a huge number of sensor methods that are beneficial for collecting data related to human actions. Environmental sensors such as motion detectors, door sensors, and pressure mats have been utilized to collect information related to complicated activities such as food preparation, rest, and food consumption. These sensors are programmed to execute activity recognition based on the location, which is already available in internal home environments. Particularly they are mainly applied to exercise and identify events that are as diverse as the sensor methods, which are then used to detect events. Current approaches can be classified into template matching, discriminative and reproductive. Template matching methods implement a nearby neighbor classifier centered on Euclidean distance. Gaussian mixtures modeled are used by naïve Bayes classifiers for generative approaches that yield predicted results for any batch learning models. For any activity sequences, Bayesian techniques are used as an ensemble classifier for smooth recognition.

5.3.1   Behavioral Pattern Discovery

Intelligent pervasive systems concentrate on basic requirements of a human, and, therefore, they need information related to the actions being accomplished. While acknowledging predetermined actions that often depend on unsupervised learning, supervised learning procedures are preferred, especially for their means to determine periodic series of unlabeled sensor actions. This includes events of attentiveness and means for activity finding construct based on an ample history of research findings, approaches comprising regular expressions for frequent patterns, sequences frequent mining based on constraint, and pattern mining for periodic frequents. Other methods have been suggested for complicated discontinuous patterns to mine with ease from data streaming done in intervals and also in diverse series of information sets and to agree for variants in events of the patterns. To infer using sensor data, valuable interactive patterns can be discovered, and prototypes can be made since these patterns can be used to classify and predict their occurrences.

5.3.2 Decision Support System

In healthcare decision support systems, the most commonly used include assisting physicians and experts in the healthcare domain for accurate decision-making processes. Knowledge based and non-knowledge centered are the two mainstream methods of DSSs. The knowledge-based method involves two key components: The first method consists of knowledge database that includes the rules for the compiled data and also an association for them regarding if–then rules. The second method includes an inference engine from the patient's real-time data and forms a rule from the knowledge database to make new knowledge that is then recommended to a set of appropriate actions. For designing healthcare, different methodologies have been proposed based on knowledge databases and inference engines, for example, information-based ontological representation. In healthcare domain, sometimes no clinical data is directly available due to no knowledge-based information, and also time, based on the past experiences, are used to formulate clinical rules, by determining patterns from the clinical data. Sensitive and adaptive nature of the intelligent pervasive system is more suitable for framing decision support system. In particular, DSS will be more suitable for helping the physician in a critical situation to take an accurate decision.

5.4 Intelligent Pervasive Healthcare Applications

In a bounded environment like hospitals, the pervasive healthcare systems (Sordo et al., 2008) are employed to manage the patient health records efficiently as well as to provide location/context-aware services.

5.4.1 Health Information Management

The computerization of traditional hospital environments produces a huge amount of healthcare data. Besides, the transaction details give the knowledge about routine activities. This huge volume of data poses challenges while storing, managing, and extracting the knowledge from them. Hence, the patient health record information system should provide secure access to sensitive data, support search related to hospitals or doctors in a particular location, and manage the appointments with doctors. Apart from this, the pervasive healthcare system should be patient-friendly (guiding them to take medication at correct instances), doctor-friendly (collecting all the medical information of the patient), and highly secure (to avoid unnecessary data retrieval from unauthorized individuals). The patient's healthcare history, the medical procedures that he has underwent, and those logs are separately available as islands of information within an organization. Further, interconnection and interaction among organizations enable information sharing and decision making. Agent-based communication supports this kind of interaction wherein the application components are designed as agents. For instance, query optimization agents (refer to Figure 5.3) are responsible for handling the queries related to patient data. The information retrieved can be presented by the presentation agent. Finally, the mobile and ubiquitous agent interface mediate the access to the abovementioned health information.

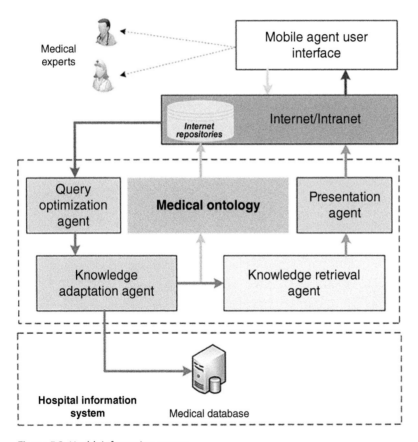

Figure 5.3 Health information system.

5.4.2 Location and Context-Aware Services

Location and context-aware services are used to enhance the treatment process by allocating an appropriate number of physicians by considering the patient's status and location. Figure 5.4 describes intelligent pervasive systems hosted inside the hospital that helps to reduce the time spent on attending to false alarms, unnecessary supervision, and control task and therefore to increase the direct patient interaction time. Here, RFID tags are used to obtain the patient location, whereas the Bluetooth technology is used to schedule a suitable number of physicians among the patients. Also, this architecture aims at multimedia data exchange that helps in knowing the patients' current context, for example, QoS DREAM framework (Mitchell et al., 2000) emergency notifications along with the location information and multimedia content. Apart from these services, special entertainment can be provided to the patients like context-aware hospital bed and context-aware pill container.

5.4.3 Remote Patient Monitoring

Telemedicine supports remote monitoring as well as treatment of the patients who reside in their home, remote locations where full-fledged medical services are not available, or in an ambulance. The telemedicine architecture for remote patient monitoring is given in Figure 5.5. It contains the following components:

On-body monitoring devices: The wearable sensor devices are fastened to the patient's body to capture the bio-signals such as ECG, temperature,

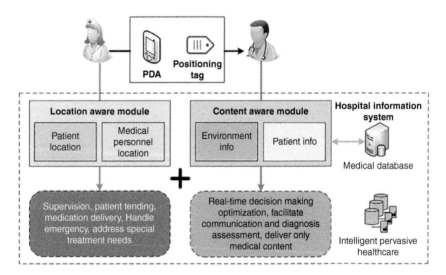

Figure 5.4 Intra-hospital intelligent pervasive systems.

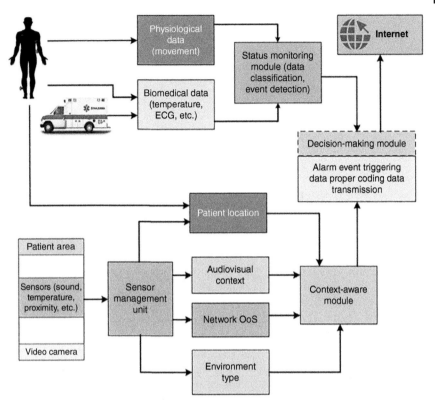

Figure 5.5 Remote patient monitoring.

respiration, and blood oxygen levels and the physical data like movement, location, and weight. **Patient area devices**: The patient's present condition and his/her current environment can be traced using the devices like video cameras, microphones, proximity sensors, and thermal mapping. Smart interactivity devices are also utilized to enable advanced communication with the patients.

Status monitoring module: Intelligent tools have the capability to mine the sensor data to identify the emergency events that need immediate medical assistance. For example, adaptive neuro-fuzzy inference system fuses the both bio-signals with the physical data to identify the cardiovascular diseases. Periodically the home spirometers are used to detect lung dysfunctions. Intelligent programs detect the person fall from the accelerometer data and alarm a trigger with the aid of the software agents.

Context-aware module: It is the intelligent software that collects and interprets the patient environment data. Special middleware components and agents are utilized in development and deployment of this module. For example, visual information telling the body orientation that has been calculated from the posture extraction tells the inactivity time duration, which may be a crucial sign of an emergency. Further, the activity classification is obtained from the floor vibration signals.

Decision-making module: It decides the triggering of alarm events using the information obtained from status monitoring and context-aware services.

5.4.4 Waze: Community-Based Navigation App

Mobile devices may obtain their context information in either direct or indirect fashion. Direct context awareness of mobile devices demands one or more embedded sensors as well as algorithms for extracting the context from the raw sensor data that must be present in the device itself. In contrast, the indirect context awareness, the sensing, and the processing happened in the external infrastructure, whereas the mobile devices get the context by means of communication. Waze is one such indirect context awareness-enabled mobile application. It gathers the routes, traffic, and travel-related information of other drivers and sends it to the centralized Waze server. Also, it allows the Wazers to update the accidents and traffic jams together with the landmarks. After that, the Waze server conducts the analytics over the gathered data and suggests the alternative traffic routes as well as real-time traffic updates. In addition, it sends the red alert messages while the user is approaching accident zones, high crime rate areas, road hazards, and dead ends. Apart from this, Waze coordinates you with your friends who are heading toward the same destination. With the help of community-shared gas price data, it also suggests the location of cheapest gas station on the user's path. In concise, Waze is an outstanding real-time application that utilizes the crowd-sensed data to extract the context and suggests the users to act accordingly

5.5 Conclusion

Recent advancements in mobile communication and the advent of location, as well as context awareness, lead to the evolution of pervasive computing. The natural sync between the characteristics of the pervasive computing and the requirements of healthcare applications facilitates the development of pervasive healthcare applications in conjunction with multi-sensor data fusion and mining algorithms. Though the integration of healthcare applications with pervasive computing yields numerous benefits such as secure distributed access to health data, good quality medical service at reduced cost, and personalized healthcare services, still some of the following issues and challenges are open: interoperability among organizations that share health data and data and location privacy.

Bibliography

Aarts, E. and Wichert, R. (2009). Ambient intelligence. In: *Technology Guide* (ed. H.J. Bullinger), 244–249. Berlin, Heidelberg: Springer-Verlag.

Augusto, J.C., Nakashima, H., and Aghajan, H. (2010). Ambient intelligence and smart environments: a state of the art. In: *Handbook of Ambient Intelligence and Smart Environments* (ed. H. Nakashima, H. Aghajan, and J.C. Augusto), 3–31. Boston, MA: Springer.

Baig, M.M. and Gholamhosseini, H. (2013). Smart health monitoring systems: an overview of design and modeling. *Journal of Medical Systems* **37** (2): 9898.

Benavente-Peces, C., Ahrens, A., and Filipe, J. (2014). Advances in technologies and techniques for ambient intelligence. *Journal of Ambient Intelligence and Humanized Computing* **5** (5): 621–622.

Cook, D.J., Augusto, J.C., and Jakkula, V.R. (2009). Ambient intelligence: technologies, applications, and opportunities. *Pervasive and Mobile Computing* **5** (4): 277–298.

Mitchell, S., Spiteri, M.D., Bates, J., and Coulouris, G. (2000). Context-aware multimedia computing in the intelligent hospital. In: Proceeding EW 9 Proceedings of the 9th workshop on ACM SIGOPS European workshop: beyond the PC: new challenges for the operating system, 13–18.

Rahmani, A.-M., Thanigaivelan, N.K., Gia, T.N. et al. (2015). Smart e-health gateway: bringing intelligence to internet-of-things based ubiquitous healthcare systems. In: 2015 12th Annual IEEE on Consumer Communications and Networking Conference (CCNC), 826–834. IEEE.

Soh, P.J., Vandenbosch, G.A.E., Mercuri, M., and Schreurs, D.M.M.-P. (2015). Wearable wireless health monitoring: current developments, challenges, and future trends. *IEEE Microwave Magazine* **16** (4): 55–70.

Sordo, M., Vaidya, S., and Jain, L.C. (2008). An introduction to computational intelligence in healthcare: new directions. In: *Advanced Computational Intelligence Paradigms in Healthcare – 3*, Studies in Computational Intelligence, vol. **107** (ed. M. Sordo, S. Vaidya, and L.C. Jain), 1–26. Berlin, Heidelberg: Springer-Verlag.

Vasilakos, A. and Pedrycz, W. (2006). *Ambient Intelligence, Wireless Networking, and Ubiquitous Computing*. Artech House Inc.

6

IoT-Based Noninvasive Wearable and Remote Intelligent Pervasive Healthcare Monitoring Systems for the Elderly People
Stela Vitorino Sampaio

Department of Computer Science and Engineering, Heart Hospital Dr. Carlos Alberto Studart, Fortaleza, Ceará, Brazil

6.1 Introduction

With the advent of electronic remote health monitoring systems, elderly healthcare has been revolutionized promisingly. Life expectancy has been increasing continually over a several few decades across the globe. In general, it has been recorded that increased longevity has resulted in the promoted lifespan of older people above 60 years. The oldest old age segment (80 years and above) is the fastest growing segment, and by 2050, about 20% of older persons will be 80 years and above. This is because of the growing awareness on healthcare and medical expansions as well as personal asepticism toward health. Though increased life expectancy is the most wanted boon and welcoming change for the healthcare practitioners and the individuals too, the cost associated with healthcare services continues to soar because of the increasing price of prescription drugs, medical instruments, and hospital care. Hence, it is an utmost necessity to develop and implement technology-based solution in order to provide better healthcare services at an affordable price to the elderly.

6.2 Internet of Things (IoT) and Remote Health Monitoring

Recent advances in Internet technologies have led to the emergence of Internet of things (IoT). In the modern healthcare environment, the usage of IoT brings convenience to physicians and patients, since they are applied to various medical areas like remote and real-time monitoring and patient management. IoT is defined as connecting the sensors and actuators over living and nonliving

Intelligent Pervasive Computing Systems for Smarter Healthcare, First Edition.
Arun Kumar Sangaiah, S.P. Shantharajah, and Padma Theagarajan.
© 2019 John Wiley & Sons, Inc. Published 2019 by John Wiley & Sons, Inc.

objects as presented by Bajpayee and Rana (2015). IoT is not only to gather data but also to view that data locally and connect to the healthcare practitioners and generate value therein through access to information. IoT enables the healthcare industry to reduce its dependency on humans, and they are steadily improving healthcare and providing early diagnosis and treatment of serious issues. It is very important to monitor various physiological parameters of the elderly when they are living independently. To access elderly or patients' medical parameters in local and remote areas, healthcare communication using IoT is used. The main objective is to transmit the patients/elderly health monitoring parameters through wireless communication. These input data are uploaded in the cloud server and transmitted to the computer and mobile for family and doctor's reference. The body area network (BAN) is one of the most imperative technologies used in IoT-based modern healthcare system. It is basically a collection of low-power and lightweight wireless sensor nodes that are used to monitor the human body functions and surrounding environment. BAN nodes are used to collect sensitive (life-critical) information and may operate in hostile environments; accordingly, they require strict security mechanisms to prevent malicious interaction with the system.

IoT-based remote health monitoring systems have become a boon to the improvement of the elderly people's quality of life as suggested by Guidi et al. (2012). The number of elderly people is increasing over the time where today, in developed countries, it is quite normal that elderly people usually live independently in their own homes. Further, IoT makes healthcare remote monitoring systems technically feasible, and even the decreasing cost of sensors makes it economically feasible. With the advent of smartphone technology, it is also expected that population is already prepared to accept this kind of solutions, collecting in real-time people's private and sensitive data like temperature, blood pressure (BP), heartbeat, and pulse rate (PR). This kind of systems informs about elderly or monitored patients' physiological parameters, making real smart home medication dispensers to, for instance, automatically alert when medication is not taken. Several healthcare remote monitoring systems use different technologies for monitoring and tracking patients within hospitals and at their homes. This chapter presents an IoT-aware architecture for healthcare remote monitoring systems to the elderly/patients.

IoT-based patient health tracking system effectively uses the Internet to monitor patient health status and save lives on time. There is an imminent need to promote and support through technology-initiated attention for the elderly to lead a peaceful and healthier life. This model is also suitable where there is limited access to healthcare facilities while ensuring maximum comfort, independence, and participation among the people. Confluence of IoT into these healthcare systems can further increase intelligence, flexibility, and interoperability. IoT-based devices in remote health monitoring systems perform sensing tasks and exchange information with other devices. Also, they automatically connect to and exchange information with hospitals through the Internet, significantly simplifying the painstaking tasks. These remote monitoring systems are able to provide services such as automatic alarm to the nearest hospitals in the event of critical and emergency situations of patients/elderly exclusively. Remote healthcare monitoring allows people to continue to stay at home rather than in hospitals. However, if there is a medical emergency and need to be given treatment in the hospitals, then these persons are admitted to suitable critical/emergency care units. Such systems equipped with noninvasive and unobtrusive wearable sensors can be viable diagnostic tools to the healthcare personnel for monitoring important physiological signs and activities of the patients in real time from a distant facility.

6.3 Wearable Health Monitoring

6.3.1 Wearable Sensors

Wearable sensors play a critical role in health monitoring systems that have attracted the attention of many healthcare professionals, researchers, entrepreneurs, and tech giants in recent years. A variety of application-specific wearable sensors and physiological and activity monitoring systems are available. These systems provide an efficient and remote health monitoring, based on noninvasive and wearable sensors, actuators, and modern communication, and information technologies offer an efficient and cost-effective solution that allows the elderly to continue to live in their comfortable home environment instead of expensive healthcare facilities as advocated by AlSharqi et al. (2014). These systems will also allow healthcare personnel to monitor important physiological signs of their patients in real time, assess health conditions, and provide feedback from distant facilities.

Bajpayee and Rana (2015) stated that monitoring elderly health, supporting them, and being with them become a difficult task in the modern-day life for the family members or caretakers. Keeping track of the health status of elderly at home is a difficult task. Especially old age people/patients should be periodically monitored, and their loved ones need to be informed about their health status from time to time while at work. Mobile devices and wearable sensors can be integrated in monitoring the elderly people's health more flawlessly as suggested by Haghi et al. (2017). Recent technological developments have been empowered and made it easier in terms of design and implementation of lightweight, intelligent wearable biocompatible sensor nodes to measure the abnormalities in the body temperature (BT), pressure, heart rate (HR), and pulse, and this kind of early warning systems saves the lives of many people due to the immediate attention and appropriate treatment at the right time as presented by AlSharqi et al. (2014). These nodes, capable of sensing, processing, and communicating one or more vital signs, can be seamlessly integrated into wireless personal or BAN for mobile health monitoring.

An innovative IoT-based system, which automated this task with ease, is proposed and presented, and this system puts forward a smart patient health tracking system that uses sensors to track patients' health and uses the Internet to inform their loved ones in case of any issues. This system uses temperature as well as heartbeat sensing to keep track of patient health. The sensors are connected to a microcontroller to track the status, which is in turn interfaced to an LCD display as well as Wi-Fi connection in order to transmit alerts through voice also. If system detects any abrupt changes in patients/elderly people's heartbeat or BT, the system automatically alerts the family members or caretakers about the patients' status. Also, this system is designed in such a way that it shows details of heartbeat and temperature of patient live over the Internet. Remote health monitoring systems are the application of IoT and mobile computing technologies for improving communication among patients, family members/caretakers, physicians, and other healthcare workers.

It enables the delivery of accurate medical information anytime anywhere by means of smartphones, and the system automatically alerts the family members or caretakers about the elderly health status. Also, this system is designed in such a way that it shows details of various physiological parameters like heartbeat and temperature of patient live on the Internet.

Presently, there exist technologies that hold great promise to expand the capabilities of the healthcare system, extending its range into the community, improving diagnostics and monitoring, and maximizing the independence and participation of elderly. This chapter will discuss these remote monitoring systems based on wearable sensors. With the unprecedented growth in information technology and IoT technologies, recent developments in wearable sensors have led to abundant and exciting healthcare applications.

Wearable sensors have diagnostic as well as monitoring applications. Their current capabilities include physiological, biochemical sensing, and motion sensing. Physiological monitoring could help in both diagnosis and ongoing treatment of a vast number of elderly persons and disabled community with neurological, cardiovascular, and pulmonary diseases. Remote monitoring systems have the potential to mitigate problematic patient access issues. Access may get worse over time as many organizations are predicting a shortfall in primary care providers as healthcare reform provides insurance to millions of new patients. Compared with people in urban areas, those in rural areas travel farther to meet healthcare specialists and have worse outcomes for such common conditions like heart attack or other emergency situations. Wearable sensors and remote monitoring systems have the potential to extend the reach of specialists in urban areas to rural areas and decrease these disparities.

6.4   Related Work

Recently, researchers are greatly involved in developing IoT-based healthcare systems to address various practical challenges in remote monitoring of the elderly. Research trends in IoT-based healthcare include various technologies such as wireless sensor networks, cloud computing, and wearable devices. The challenge lies in developing suitable network architectures and platforms, new services and applications, interoperability, and security, among others, for remote health monitoring. The objective of this section is to review wearable healthcare devices in measuring the effective parameters of elderly in a remote fashion.

Mohammed et al. (2014) and AlSharqi et al. (2014) have presented the wire-based wearable smart clothing in medical IoT to measure the vital signs. The system enables measurement and investigation of health through body monitoring by using 10 sensors in order to study electroencephalogram (EEG), electrocardiogram (ECG), and body temperature. The major drawbacks of smart clothing are it is necessary to customize the smart clothing for the patient and communication to the outside world. Mukherjee et al. (2014) proposed an e-health monitoring system in which medical and environmental sensors are used. Bed sensor is an environmental sensor equipped with a set of piezoelectric elements for detecting the presence of the patients on the bed. These sensors can also be programmed with a microcontroller to detect a fall or collapse of the patients and mobility of the patient is highly restricted.

Guidi et al. (2012) developed an ECG Android application to visualize end-user ECG waves and data logging functionality. The system utilizes various technologies such as IOIO microcontroller, signal processing, communication protocols, secure and efficient mechanisms for large file transfer, database management system, and a specific medical cloud. The monitored data can be uploaded to a cloud to keep track of it, which can be further analyzed by the medical personnel.

Bajpayee and Rana (2015) has collected patients' vital health parameters and stored it in the cloud setup to enable data access from anywhere and anytime. Their system is also capable of sending alerts to caretakers and doctors for immediate action in case of emergencies. The system has provided systematic analysis and evaluation of a secure communication network as well as more reliable health-related information. Though enough measures have been taken by the authors for security issues, still certain aspects of security and privacy are unaddressed.

Sharma et al. (2011) have proposed the use of wireless body area network (WBAN) for pervasive remote monitoring of the patients' physiological abnormal signs at hospitals and remote environment. The system has employed sensor nodes, and a network coordinator is connected in a star network using proprietary components. In spite of using the wireless technologies, this system

Table 6.1 Research gaps in remote health monitoring for elderly.

Methodology/ technology		Limitations	Recommendations
Wire-based wearable	Smart clothing	Patient-specific customization	Wireless wearable
		Comfortless	
	Bed sensor	Less mobility	
		Intrusive	
		Expensive	
Wireless sensor network	Bluetooth	Low energy	ZigBee
		Low bandwidth	
Cloud	Centralized	High latency	Edge/fog computing (cloudlets)
		Privacy and security	

is prone to having issues related to capturing the parameters that are expected at critical situations.

Heart failure analysis dashboard is designed by Guidi et al. (2012), which is used to measure the clinical parameters. It is combined with a handy device for the automatic acquisition of a set of patients' clinical parameters to support telemonitoring functions. The authors have incorporated artificial intelligence (AI)-based techniques to diagnosis, prognosis, and follow-up management. This intelligent dashboard is designed to assist the clinical decision of nonspecialist caring personnel.

Nicolas Schmidt from Nokia designed a dashboard for keeping track of the health data. It is also integrating the patient-generated data within their electronic health records. This patient care dashboard supports the patients when they are in emergency situations. Healthcare practitioners and caretakers can access patient-generated data. This dashboard is designed with high security concerns and ease with a comprehensive set of health metrics such as weight, BP, HR, and even pulse wave velocity. The successful implementation of this system circumvents unnecessary hospitalizations as suggested by Guidi et al. (2012). Table 6.1 shows the research gaps observed from the literature review, and the authors would like to recommend the choice of alternative approaches that will be implemented in the proposed system.

6.4.1 Existing Status

In spite of the advancement in computer-enabled healthcare technology, the elderly still fall prey to the most common and anticipated diseases that could have been treated if they were attended to at the earliest. This scenario is prevailing even in the most developed cities, and this leads to an emergent need of a combination of IoT and analytics technology implications in remote health monitoring. Many projects have been developed to incorporate various technologies at different scales. For example, small-scale platforms target exclusively in providing one or two core services such as sleep or diet monitoring, while medium- and large-scale platforms provide services at a mediocre and wider range, respectively. Since the aim is to effectively monitor the health of elderly in remote fashion, various approaches have been adopted and are taken into consideration with respect to their properties and benefits in daily life.

In general, a multilayer IoT-based system for remotely monitoring the elderly would comprise a suitable BAN consisting of sensors through smart wearable to capture vital physiological parameters, mobile devices, and network access as stated by Sharma et al. (2011). The fixed devices such as smart appliances, bed sensors, and audiovisual devices are widely in use. Internet access is considered as a vital setup that enables cloud technology to be used for a wider coverage of patient data and to enhance the storage capacity to a greater extent. Localized servers are also utilized for maintaining the data needed to be reviewed frequently. Hospital information system has also been employed to closely track the health status of the patient. This system empowers the inclination toward attending the patient at emergencies. Such systems not only lack quick response time in-house as the number of patients to be treated increases but also suffer affordability in terms of cost per patient. Interface devices are most commonly Web based, mobile application based, and short message services (SMS). SMS facility is pertinent for serving a minimal group, Web-based service handles when the group size is moderate, and mobile application-based services is used to a greater extent due to its simplicity and high precision.

6.5   Architectural Prototype

Even though researchers have made attempts to solve those challenges aforesaid in the previous sections, a comprehensive streamlined approach is yet to be devised. Hence, this section presents an appropriate approach for pervasive mobile health monitoring to the elderly. Figure 6.1 shows the architecture of an intelligent Internet of things-enabled mobile-based pervasive health monitoring system (IITMPHMS) that contains three phases: collection phase, transmission phase, and utilization phase. BAN is constructed to collect the required data from the patient. The parameters used to diagnose the disease may vary from one disease to another. Therefore, each parameter is sensed by separate IoT devices, which are connected to the patient. All the devices connected in the body of the patient are networked to form BAN. BP module, HR

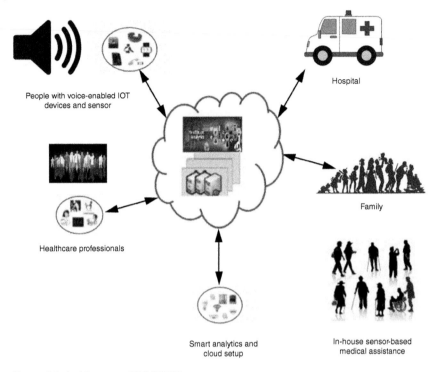

People with voice-enabled IOT devices and sensor

Hospital

Family

Healthcare professionals

Smart analytics and cloud setup

In-house sensor-based medical assistance

Figure 6.1 Architecture of IITMPHMS.

monitor, and thermometer are the basic devices used to collect the BP, HR, and the temperature of the patients.

Wrist IITMPHMS band (a wearable device) can monitor and record real-time information about the elderly's physiological conditions. The sensors attached to this wearable device are capable of measuring physiological signs such as HR, BT, BP, and PR. Continuous monitoring of physiological signals could help to detect and diagnose several cardiovascular and pulmonary diseases at the earliest. The data collected in the collection phase is communicated to the doctor to evaluate the parameter for diagnosis. The collected data is communicated to the medical professionals through different communication channels depending on the patient's position as mentioned by Haghi et al. (2017). The transmission device used in the transmission phase are Wi-Fi or Bluetooth devices. All the information collected from the IoT devices are communicated to the local system that contains the software to check the threshold levels of parameter. HR, BT, BP, and PR are measured by the sensors and transmitted to the monitoring system through the wireless device. Integrated circuit (IC)-based temperature sensor is a two-terminal integrated circuit temperature transducer that produces an output current proportionate to absolute temperature. This sensor is small and has the fastest response time.

The hydraulic bed sensor measures the HR and PR. HR sensor is based on the change in volume of blood through the organ of the body, and the flow of blood volume is decided by the rate of heart pulses. The light is absorbed by the blood, and the signal pulses are equivalent to the heart beat pulses. This kind of noninvasive sensor is designed to be part of an integrated sensor or wearable hybrid sensors for the early detection of emergency situations in the elderly. The advantages of these sensors are that it acquires enhanced and quantitative data related to pulse and respiration. It can be connected to a microcontroller, which is used to monitor the heartbeat of the patients. The collected data is updated in the IITMPHMS.

Recently, the incidence of cardiovascular morbidity and mortality is going up. BP is a vital signal, which is a key concern for those who have hypertension and other cardiovascular diseases. Therefore, the noninvasive method using oscillometric method is the best choice, especially for the elderly. BP sensors can send signals across wireless BP monitoring information system. User-friendly software design and high automation can record the results through the ZigBee wireless transmission in real time as mentioned by Kim et al. (2007). Microcontroller-based processing circuitry and the sensors assembled on PCBs are placed in the wrist band. This requires a 9 V battery. The RF transmission using ZigBee's has been tested to operate successfully at 10–20 m range.

IITMPHMS is connected to the Internet for global communication and is also able to inform the healthcare professionals and caretakers about any unusual health conditions of a patient/elderly. The doctors can also use the publishing system incorporated with the system. When the measured data exceeds the allowable normal range, the system can send an alarm message to the concerned healthcare professionals. The system can facilitate healthcare professionals to perform immediate medical diagnosis and to administer the medical treatment if needed. The wearable health monitoring systems discussed here are equipped with a variety of sensors to measure the different physiological parameters of a patient. The measurements obtained by the sensors connected in a WBAN are transmitted to a nearby processing node using a low power and short-range wireless medium, ZigBee (Kim et al. (2007)). The microcontroller receives the signals from the sensors and processes them before sending them to a ZigBee transmitter module. The transmitter module transmits the signal that is received by the receiving antenna of the ZigBee receiver.

A wireless transmitter is used to send the data to a wireless receiver connected to a local monitoring unit. To monitor heartbeat rate, temperature, BP, and PR of a patient, four biomedical sensors are deployed. These sensors convert the physiological changes of the patient's bodily parameters into biomedical signals. The conditioning circuit (i.e. Arduino microcontroller) reads the data from the sensors and controls the transmission of data to a monitoring unit. The monitoring unit displays the data that is used by the physicians for necessary medical advices. The wireless receiver receives the data and sends it to the local monitoring unit. The monitoring unit can record, display, and analyze the data. It can send reports as well as alarming messages to the healthcare professionals and caretakers.

The processing node, which could be a personal digital assistant (PDA), smartphone, computer, or a custom-made processing module based on a microcontroller or a field-programmable gate array (FPGA), runs advanced processing, analysis, and decision algorithms and may also store and display the results to the stakeholders. It transmits the measured data over the Internet to the healthcare personnel, thus functioning as the gateway to remote healthcare facilities. If the system is reliable and used over long-term monitoring purposes, then this system should be comfortable, convenient, small in size, and especially nontoxic and nonallergenic to the users (elderly). Toward this attempt, IITMPHMS is designed in such a way that the best choices of technological components were added. The objectives of the proposed system are as follows:

1. Design and develop a smart customized IoT-based lifeline aid for the elderly to save their lives during emergencies.
2. Envisage the meaningful and useful patterns from existing cases of issues prevailing in elderly's health data so as to create a knowledge base of possible incidence to strengthen preventive treatment and healthcare supporting services via appropriate technologies (in Tamil Nadu).
3. Utilize edge analytics and machine learning (ML) techniques to discover the inherent knowledge and actionable insights available in the patient's/elderly's health record.
4. Create a voice-enabled prioritized gesture-based real-time remote health monitoring system that provides the appropriate healthcare services in a very timely fashion.
5. Development of a customized, unique, and responsive dashboard to facilitate medical professionals, caretakers, and dear ones for ease of communication.

6.5.1 Data Acquisition and Processing

Data collection has been done by conducting a pilot study at old age home. A questionnaire has been designed especially for this purpose with the guidance of healthcare professionals and caretakers who give personal attention to the elderly. The questionnaire is designed in such a way that the required choice of attributes is collected appropriately from the elderly to obtain sufficient information. The significant attributes include current health issues, medications, normal/abnormal behaviors, previous medical history, and treatments. Then, suitable data acquisition parameters such as sampling rates and amplification levels will be individually determined for all sensors.

The data from each sensor will then be collected on a continual basis to allow both real-time notifications and pattern recognition over time. The data will be collected from the elderly persons who are deemed capable of living independently. Before giving input into the decision-making system, the sensor outputs will undergo various preprocessing steps. They will first be converted into data formats that are readable by the processing software. The formatted data will then go through a procedure of normalization, segmentation, signal enhancements, and data fusion. The parameters of interest for each sensor will then be extracted and stored for use in the system. The signals acquired from the intelligent sensors will be processed in the processing unit which is located in the home. It will therefore be necessary to investigate data storage needs, transmission bandwidth, and reliability of this distribution.

6.5.2 Pervasive and Intelligence Monitoring

Healthcare monitoring through the latest technological intervention will become more personalized to the elderly. Though the challenges of providing high-quality healthcare in developing countries are more than those in developed countries, they share a common goal: to provide access to health monitoring and assessment technologies to people with limited access to hospitals and caregivers. However, successful collection of abnormal parameters and further taking appropriate decisions relevant to the abnormality can be achieved using pervasive computing.

Pervasive computing promises efficiency, accuracy, and availability of medical treatment. IITMPHMS can provide medical feedback to the patients through mobile devices based on the biomedical and environmental data collected by deployed sensors, and this system is to provide convenient healthcare services to patients, caregivers, and caretakers. To diagnose patient's health condition lucidly with ease, pervasive computing has made the interaction between humans and computational devices completely natural, and user can get the desired data in a transparent manner. Smartphones, laptops, and PDAs have made ubiquitous computing possible. They are available anywhere at any time. Pervasive or ubiquitous computing is used widely in hospitals, emergency, and critical situations.

These systems are designed to continuously monitor and implement initial medical diagnosis. These systems often adopt PDA as the data receiver and Web-based interface for home healthcare in daily lives for remote monitoring. It is very easy and seamless, observing immediate pulse signals and HR to support remote treatment. The framework integrates the sensors and a robust mesh network that routes patient data to a remote base station within a hospital via router node, which is required for monitoring and detecting potential parameters.

Instead of simply collecting and storing a patient's vital signs and providing raw data, the role of an intelligent remote healthcare monitoring system for elderly is to perform data interpretation and validation to offer the health professionals the information actually needed. These systems are responsible to assess a patient's physiological status, notify of alarming conditions, give expert advice, react to critical event, make diagnostic decisions, and take, if possible, therapeutic actions. In addition, they contribute to the automation of the clinical workflow, carry routine clinical tasks, and control the function of life-supporting devices. This would be possible with the support of AI and ML technologies.

AI intervention aims to simulate in the remote patient monitoring system as a medical professional how he/she analyzes, interprets, and diagnoses decisions in elderly care. AI systems can represent, organize, and/or learn the practical and theoretical medical knowledge of experienced specialists. They are autonomous and automated systems endowed with large quantities of knowledge on relations among elderly/patient's symptoms, signs which are given by the integrated sensors initially. Once a healthcare professional interferes and recommends them to undergo the relevant tests and prepare reports, those laboratory results, other clinical findings, and their underlying pathologies help them acquire diagnostic and therapeutic decisions. In addition, these systems can be a part of clinical environments for the collection and processing of data from various medical devices that may also be connected to the hospital information systems with the approval of the hospital management. These systems save time and make the patient management more effective even after they are discharged and optimum or minimum length of stay in hospitals are envisaged. This will benefit both hospitals and patients to admit emergency cases and who can be monitored at the home environment to make them feel comfortable without any unnecessary anxiety and fear.

One of the major components of this system is to develop intelligence-based expert system. This system will correlate information from all of the sensors and make decisions regarding the elderly people status and physiological conditions. The AI-based expert system extends the monitoring capabilities to consider various options as to the person's behavior after dismounting the bed and provides corresponding alerts or alarms.

The expert system will implement adaptive architectures to allow the modeling of daily behavior as well as the response to changes observed over time. The information provided by the various sensors are fused together to make an analysis of the situation. The system can generate alerts to inform the persons about their regular schedule if they violate it. The example alerts are breakfast/mid-day snacks/lunch/tea/dinner timing, bedtime exercise, and walking time. Finally, any expressions of pain or cries for help by the patient could be monitored by the voice alert system located at home.

Different pattern recognition and hybridized artificial neural networks classification algorithms are used to construct the model. The expert system will detect pattern abnormalities in real time, reported through a different level alerts and voice messages. In level 1, unusual patterns like food overdue timing, bed, and exercise overdue time will be reported to the elderly directly. In the next level, alerts are sent to caregivers if their pressure readings are slightly abnormal (+ or −20 values). And in the last level, two or more abnormal values in BP, heartbeat, PR, and temperature readings are taken, and then the alerts will be given to both caretakers and registered hospitals. This alert will also enable healthcare practitioners in hospitals to get associated with this system to analyze the situation to send emergency vehicle to the needy if required; otherwise the caretakers can bring them to the hospitals. The alert systems can also be further integrated with the first aid information through the voice system. The first aid has to be classified according to the abnormality of the various parameters.

6.5.3 Communication

There will be two levels of communication at the output of the AI expert system: online database and automated alarms/alerts. An Internet-based database containing real-time patient statistics will be created in such a way that it can be accessed by medical practitioners, specialists, and caregivers. The displays will be visual and audio displays controlled by the privacy level assigned to the user. The medical practitioners will have full access to all medical data and sensor outputs, while the caretakers will be given only information regarding the status of the monitored persons. These will be transmitted through emails, cell phones, pagers, or SMS, depending on the severity of the detected abnormalities. For the non-dangerous level alerts, the communication will only reach the immediate caregivers. In the low-danger level, alerts will be given to the registered medical practitioners that these persons monitored. In the next level, based on the emergency signs, occupant's caregivers or medical practitioners will urge the emergency vehicle to collect the occupants.

The notification system will require the communication between several partners: the smart home processing unit, the central monitoring facility, the caregivers, the medical specialists, emergency services, and the next of kin. In view of this, the use of wireless technology will be investigated, along with the power requirements, data compression, and storage capabilities at each location. Issues of privacy and encryption will remain of prime importance throughout the consideration of all options.

6.5.4 Predictive Analytics

Analytics for interconnected medical devices and sensors are designed to capture data and enable organizations to base decisions on real-time or near-real-time information and to process the insights in order to make effective operational analytics decisions. In order to pay high and immediate attention, the proposed solution will facilitate the needy community appropriately. Clinical decision support system (CDSS) is used for analyzing patient data, and it consists of two principal components: the knowledge base and the inference engine. The knowledge base contains the rules and associations of compiled data that often take the form of IF-THEN rules, whereas the inference engine combines the rules from the knowledge base with the real patients' data in order to generate new knowledge and to propose a set of suitable actions. Different methodologies have been proposed for designing healthcare databases and inference engines. Indeed, sensitive, adaptive, and unobtrusive nature of intelligent health systems is particularly suitable for designing the decision support system capable of supporting medical staff in critical decisions. In particular, intelligent health systems move away from the simple reactive approach and adopt a proactive strategy capable of anticipating emergency situations. As a result, CDSS could be used with multimodal sensing and wearable computing technologies to constantly monitor all vital signs of a patient. Predictive analytics is performed on those data to support the medical professionals to make real-time decisions. CDSSs are jointly used with the intelligent health systems paradigm for enhancing communications among health personnel such as doctors and nurses. These systems are aimed at facilitating the communication and improving the capability to take decisions remotely among different healthcare professionals.

6.5.5 Edge Analytics

Generating value from the connected devices of elderly, data will not be contingent upon just with sensors. The value of the IoT lies on how the applications incorporate their data into processes they use to derive useful prescription or any other appropriate diagnostics. Rather than sending data to various places for analysis, it must instead focus on performing the analytics in the deployed wearable IoT device. This trend will be driven by healthcare organizations and patients who are in need of emergency medical services, which are analyzed instantaneously, despite operating in a geographically distributed manner. To continue to derive value from their data, this remote IoT-based elderly healthcare monitoring must use edge analytics infrastructures. IoT-based healthcare remote monitoring operates with far fewer sensors that are just processed in its edge network. If it has to be processed in the cloud every time it has to be brought here for extracting the insights, the analysis will be slow and may overlook many local insights. Moving data to the cloud, especially as the volume grows, introduces latency and higher costs. Hence, the data gets processed quickly bringing insights to the data at the edge of the network where sensors reside. The very important reason behind choosing edge analytics is that the healthcare applications must analyze and act on the data immediately, and they must send other pieces of information to a central repository for storage and eventual analysis.

Sending data from distributed locations to a centralized location for analytics and then back to the disparate locations for action takes time. The analytics infrastructure adopted here is that in tandem with its added server locations at the edge of its network. Performing analytics at each of its distributed servers allows the organizations to ingest, analyze, and take action on its data in real time without much time to save the lives of elderly.

6.5.6 Ambient Intelligence

It is an emerging multidisciplinary area based on ubiquitous computing, which influences the design of protocols, communications, systems, and devices. Ambient intelligence provides interaction between people and technology, making it suitable to the needs of individuals and the environment that surrounds those. It tries to adapt the technology to the people's needs by means of omnipresent computing elements, which communicate among them in an ubiquitous way. It puts together all the resources to provide flexible and intelligent services to users acting in their environments. It provides services for those who suffer from various illnesses and the need for constant healthcare monitoring of elderly, and it ensures to provide them better assistance. Therefore, improve their lifestyle. It is believed that support for people with chronic diseases and elderly through this infrastructure is the most wanted bliss of the present-day situations. Ambient intelligence is to develop intelligent and intuitive systems and interfaces, capable of recognizing and responding to the elderly necessities and providing capabilities for ubiquitous communication, considering the elderly in the center of the development, and creating technologically feasible environments in domestic and other living environment like gated community and old age homes.

6.5.7 Privacy and Security

Remote monitoring of elderly people yields more information about the individuals and their lives. While this information is intended to promote the well-being of individuals, it could be used for malicious purposes either intentionally or unintentionally. In the ambient intelligent systems, privacy issues are highlighted by the fact that one can infer the insights even from the aggregated data without even intentionally intruding and collecting the information. For this reason, a number of approaches are being developed to ensure that important information cannot be gleaned from mined patterns.

Securing health information may not be the immediate concern of elderly who are under observation. Patients would not restrict themselves from using any service as long as they perceive health benefits resulting from it. Phishing attacks would be one of the malicious attacks that are anticipated when the information is sent in networks. Health conditions may create added safety risks for patients when using a particular health application or device, for instance, hackers would like to attract them via the respective online forums by embedding flashing animations to guide them inappropriately and collect data from them. Mostly, elderly may not have awareness to understand the potential risks and security consequences of using health-related services. These people have to be advised by the implementers about the potential problems in sharing their data and using the adversary services or tools.

6.6 Summary

This chapter summarized the use of wearable technology, which is witnessed by a great deal of work toward the integration of pervasive, mobile technologies, and communication as well as data analytics technologies. Thus, the goal of remote monitoring the elderly in the home environment could be achieved. In addition, when monitoring has been performed in the home, researchers and clinicians have integrated ambient sensors in the remote monitoring systems. It has also been observed that there is a growing need for establishing such a home setting to implement clinical interventions. Research toward achieving remote monitoring of elderly undergoing clinical interventions will surely face the need for establishing business models to serve the community at large. It is ensured that the wearable sensors and systems deliver on their promise of improving the quality of care provided to elderly and may be extended to disabled community whom are affected by chronic conditions. Monitoring could be done remotely for the wellness and health of the individuals at the home environment and in critical care units. Some of the future applications that would be possibly envisaged are personalized and context-sensitive medicine prescription by considering tools that scale easily to multiple disparate locations.

Bibliography

AlSharqi, K., Abdelbari, A., Elnour, A.A., and Tarique, M. (2014). ZigBee based wearable remote healthcare monitoring system for elderly patients. *International Journal of Wireless and Mobile Networks* **6**: 53.

Bajpayee, A. and Rana, J. (2015). Healthcare monitoring and alerting system using cloud computing. *International Journal on Recent and Innovation Trends in Computing and Communication* **3**: 102–105.

Guidi, G., Pettenati, M.C., Miniati, R., and Iadanza, E. (2012). Heart failure analysis dashboard for patient's remote monitoring combining multiple artificial intelligence technologies. In: International Conference of the IEEE Engineering in Medicine and Biology Society, 2210–2213. https://10.1109/EMBC.2012.6346401.

Haghi, M., Thurow, K., and Stoll, R. (2017). Wearable devices in medical Internet of things: scientific research and commercially available devices. *Healthcare Informatics Research—* **23**: 4–15.

Kim, B., Kim, Y., Lee, I.S., and You, I. (2007). Design and implementation of a ubiquitous ECG monitoring system using sip and the zigbee networks. In: Proceedings of the Future Generation Communication and Networking, 599–604.

Mohammed, J., Lung, C.-H., Ocneanu, A. et al. (2014). Internet of things: remote patient monitoring using web services and cloud computing. In: IEEE International Conference on Internet of Things (iThings) and Green Computing and Communications, 256–263.

Mukherjee, S., Dolui, K., and Datta, S.K. (2014). Patient health management system using e-health monitoring architecture. In: IEEE International Conference on Advance Computing, 400–405.

Sharma, S., Vyas, A.L., Thakker, B. et al. (2011). Wireless body area network for health monitoring. *International Conference on Biomedical Engineering and Informatics* **4**: 15–17.

7

Pervasive Healthcare System Based on Environmental Monitoring

Sangeetha Archunan and Amudha Thangavel

Department of Computer Applications, Bharathiar University, Coimbatore, India

7.1 Introduction

Environmental pollution is a global ecological problem, caused by the rapid economic growth, industrialization, and urbanization that harm the human health and other living beings either directly or indirectly (Sangeetha and Amudha (2016b)). Environmental pollution assessment is an important task that can be performed using statistical techniques and computational techniques like ant colony optimization, bee colony optimization, particle swarm optimization, and many more (Alaa et al. (2013); Behrang et al. (2011); Reza (2013); Sangeetha and Amudha (2016a)). Rather than assessment, monitoring the environmental pollution has become the need of the hour. The goal of monitoring is to acquire facts regarding the environment process and thus to understand and manage the environment in order to prevent its degradation. Continuous monitoring of pollution can lead to preparedness, which could optimize the hazardous impact on human health and environment. Figure 7.1 represents the evolution of computers from large devices to the present-age miniaturized devices and sensors.

Pollution from different sources severely affects human health, which leads to mortality in association with cardiovascular and respiratory diseases. An assessment of health damages due to heavy pollution exposure in 126 cities globally reveals that pollution leads to about 1 30 000 premature deaths, 5 00 000 new cases of chronic bronchitis and many more issues every year (Gunasekaran et al. (2012)). Several technological trends have paved the way for continuous monitoring of environmental pollution and the corresponding health hazards. Powerful sensing systems and smart devices can be connected to create a pervasive infrastructure that provides accessibility to environmental information and healthcare services, thereby improving the quality of life. This chapter is organized as follows: Section 7.2 focuses on intelligent

Intelligent Pervasive Computing Systems for Smarter Healthcare, First Edition.
Arun Kumar Sangaiah, S.P. Shantharajah, and Padma Theagarajan.
© 2019 John Wiley & Sons, Inc. Published 2019 by John Wiley & Sons, Inc.

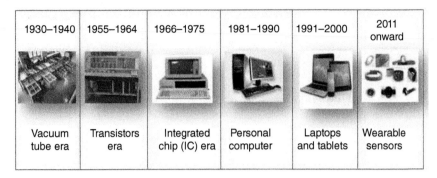

1930–1940	1955–1964	1966–1975	1981–1990	1991–2000	2011 onward
Vacuum tube era	Transistors era	Integrated chip (IC) era	Personal computer	Laptops and tablets	Wearable sensors

Figure 7.1 Computer evolution over time period.

pervasive computing system (IPCS) and its applications. Section 7.3 discusses the biosensors for environmental monitoring. Section 7.4 deals with IPCS for healthcare and presents a system architecture for healthcare based on environmental monitoring.

7.2 Intelligent Pervasive Computing System

Pervasive computing referred as "Ubiquitous Computing" or "Internet of things (IoT)" or "Ambient Systems," devised by Xerox PARC Chief Scientist Mark Weiser describes the seamless integration of computing to the everyday physical world (Weiser (1999)). IPCS integrates the unique capabilities of existing and emerging wireless networks, mobile devices, and middleware. IPCS is coined by 4As "Anywhere, Anytime, by Anyone and Anything." Pervasive computing environment consists of heterogeneous devices, network interface, operating system, and communication protocols (da Rocha and Endler (2006)), as shown in Figure 7.2. Hardware heterogeneity denotes to the existence of the different computing devices such as computers, laptops,

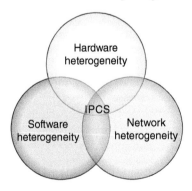

Figure 7.2 IPCS heterogeneity environment.

Table 7.1 Pervasive hardware.

Pervasive hardware	Description
Sensors	Detect the behavior of user, environmental changes through remote commands
Processors	Microsized electronic chips used to analyze and interpret the input data
Actuators	Receive the data, alter, or update environmental variables by using electrical or mechanical resources

palmtops, and smartphones. It demands for the middleware infrastructure, which is deployable on workstations, servers, and portable devices. Pervasive hardware (Guelzim and Obaidat (2011)) includes sensors, processors, and actuators defined in Table 7.1 to make the system intelligent.

Software heterogeneity refers to the environment that executes different operating systems and applications that requires software interoperability and adoption of context model for specific applications. Network heterogeneity refers to the interconnection of networks among the devices in the system that does not rely upon single architecture or technology. This heterogeneity demands scalable and adaptable middleware to support seamless communication. IPCS is used in diverse applications, which include intelligent transport system, healthcare, military, environmental monitoring, agriculture, disaster management, and many more. Pervasive computing makes use of different technologies for the creation of the system that is transparent and accessible to the users. Recent advancements in sensors and embedded computing technologies have led to upsurge in sensor networks that can be integrated within the home environment without affecting the people's routine activities. Digital information and their services are provided through handheld devices and it can be retrieved from any location. Every object in IPCS is "smarter" (connected across networks) reacts based on their environment, and interacts with the end users (Jaydip (2010)). Pervasive computing is not an independent technology; it is composed of heterogeneous technologies as shown in Figure 7.3 and explained as follows (Wäger et al. (2006)).

Context-aware system: Context awareness is a characteristic of pervasive computing environment, which acts as a middleware to accomplish human–computer interaction. This component integrates information regarding the user continuously with the computing devices. The context uses different hardware and software to collect information with the aid of sensors.

Miniaturization: Components of ICT are becoming smaller and more portable due to this miniaturization technology. It has its own advantages, namely, low cost, high speed, and greater density.

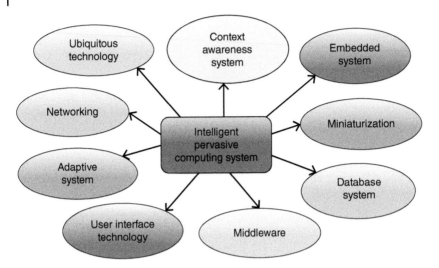

Figure 7.3 IPCS characteristics paradigm.

Embedded systems: These systems are dedicative for specific applications that embed the hardware peripherals, operating system, and other components to work independently and are also used to achieve control, management, and monitoring. Its primary goal is to react or to respond to the environmental signals. Everyday objects are integrated with ICT components, thus transforming objects into smart objects.

Networking: Networking is used to connect systems either through satellite, optical cable, or wireless communication to transmit various data, communication, and resources globally. Pervasive systems are connected through distributed network for the purpose of global accessibility. ICT components are linked to each other and the communication occurs among them through technology empowerment.

Ubiquity system: ICT components are gradually appearing anywhere and anytime naturally, and at the same time they are less noticeable. Ubiquity provides easy access to data through which anyone can access data from anywhere and reduces the complexity in data storage and data retrieval. It automatically senses the environmental changes based on the user need or behavior.

Middleware: Middleware, also referred to as "kernel," acts as a bridge between the operating system and the application software. It enables the communication and data management for distributed applications. It covers the primary complexity of the operating system, thereby creating a simple and unified environment for the developers to work with. It also reduces the complexity of the program design and supports different technologies. It enables mobility, adaptability, and transparency to the users.

User interface technology: Pervasive computing environment makes use of sensors, laptops, and other equipment that varies widely in nature. User interface technology includes adaptive interfaces and allows application user interface based on abstract definition, which leads to human–computer interaction and the physical world information to be incorporated with the computers.

Adaptive system: Adaptive system is a system that changes its behavior as per the individual based on the information acquired from users and its environment. In pervasive computing, different devices that vary in power consumption, storage, bandwidth, and many more factors are used.

Database system: Database plays an eminent role in pervasive computing; it provides a persistent storage mechanism for data storage. A large amount of data can be stored and operations will be performed with no loss in data. Data synchronization ensures availability of consistent data anytime for the users, and processing of data will be high.

7.2.1 Applications of Pervasive Computing

Pervasive computing aims to interconnect all areas of life, thus enabling the flow of data and information in a ubiquitous way. It is used in various real-time applications, namely, logistics management, e-commerce, military, environmental monitoring, and medical technology. Several challenges faced globally by environmental monitoring and healthcare were given effective solutions through pervasive computing, which are represented in Table 7.2.

7.3 Biosensors for Environmental Monitoring

According to International Union of Pure and Applied Chemistry (IUPAC), a biosensor is defined as a self-contained integrated device consisting of a biological recognition element interfaced to an analytical device, which together reversibly respond in a concentration-dependent manner (Rodriguez-Mozaz et al. (2005)). A biosensor is clearly distinguished from a bioanalytical system, because it requires an additional processing step known as reagent addition. A device that is disposable after single use and incapable to monitor the analyte concentration after rapid and reproducible regeneration should be designated as a single-use biosensor (Thévenot et al. (2001)). It is referred to as a self-sufficient integral tool that provides precise, quantitative, and analytical information with a biochemical receptor that is in direct contact with a transduction element. Biosensors are made up of three constituents, namely, a biological recognition element, a transducer, and a signal processing system (Sethi (1994)). Biosensors are used in several applications such as food analysis, development of drugs, crime detection, medical diagnosis, agriculture, defense

Table 7.2 Challenges overwhelmed by pervasive computing.

Application	Challenges	Current system	Pervasive computing
Environmental monitoring	Long-term monitoring for detecting changes	Satellite/radar systems to provide automatic image investigation	Miniaturized environmental sensors for intelligent event detection
Chronic diseases, Postoperative recovery	Physiological parameter includes activity measurement and sleep assessment	Snapshot measurement, surveys/observations, personal feedback/surveys	Continuous monitoring of activity, pervasive sensors for monitoring sleep quality
Elderly care	Fall detection or risk assessment	Pendants with push buttons, regular clinic visits or surveys, and clinical observations	Automatic fall detection based on wearable sensors for balance or stability
Rehabilitation	Encouraging activity	Attending rehab clinics and clinical observation	Remote rehabilitation monitoring sensors for quantifying performance
Maternal and neonatal care	24-hour monitoring of neonates	Clunky uncomfortable sensor	Miniaturized sensors embedded in clothes or surroundings for minimal disruption to neonates

Source: Reproduced from (Atallah. et al., 2012). © Elsevier.

and security, biomolecules and their interactions, environmental monitoring, marine applications, and manufacturing pharmaceuticals (Mehrotra (2016)). Biosensor appears to be well suited for environmental monitoring applications rather than standard analytical methods. Biosensor technology is an emerging technique and it has been recently reviewed from the perspectives of agricultural monitoring, groundwater management and screening, ocean monitoring, and global environmental monitoring. Biosensors are also developed for the assessment of a variety of organic and inorganic pollutants in the environment, with limited scope for biosensors in air pollution measurement. The key advantage of using biosensors instead of conventional analytical techniques are the possibility of miniaturization, portability, and working on-site, and its ability to measure pollutant level in complex matrices with least sample preparation. However, most of the biosensors are restricted for a specific toxicant or can be applied for a limited number of pollutants as given in Table 7.3 (Roda et al. (2001); Rodriguez-Mozaz et al. (2006); Rogers (2006)).

Table 7.3 Biosensors used in environmental pollution monitoring.

Name of biosensor	Description
Gas biosensors	Thiobacillus-based biosensors can detect the pollutant sulfur-dioxide (SO_2) gas, immobilized methalomonas detect the methane (CH_4) gas, pseudomonas is used to monitor carbon dioxide levels
Immunoassay biosensors	Immunoelectrodes as biosensors are used to detect low concentrations of pollutants
BOD biosensor	Biological oxygen demand (BOD) is widely used as a test to detect the levels of organic pollution
Miscellaneous biosensors	To measure the degree of electron transport inhibition during the photosynthesis due to certain pollutants

7.3.1 Environmental Monitoring

Air is the primary source to survive in this ecosystem. Air gets contaminated through different anthropogenic activities. Globally, air pollution is considered as a serious environmental problem. Over last few years, air pollution has drawn a lot of interest among researchers and policy makers to evaluate and make decisions on environmental degradation. The significant increase in air pollution has a major effect on human health, worldwide economy, and the global environment. Air pollutants such as carbon dioxide (CO_2), carbon monoxide (CO), nitrogen dioxide (NO_2), particulate matter (PM), and volatile organic compounds (VOCs) cause multiple effects on the human health, which are represented in Table 7.4. It is well known that haze, acid rain, and climate change in the ecosystem are due to air pollution. In order to mitigate the ill effects of pollution, government has put numerous efforts on air quality monitoring. Air quality monitoring is used to determine the level of air pollution in rural and urban environments. Traditionally, the level of air pollution is monitored through conventional air pollution monitoring system with stationary monitors. These monitoring stations make use of conventional monitoring instruments, which are highly accurate, reliable, and capable of measuring wide range of pollutants in the environment (Amorim et al. (2008)). These conventional monitoring instruments are large in size, highly expensive, and heavy weight, which leads to thin deployment of the monitoring stations. For the purpose of effective monitoring, the localities of the monitoring stations were carefully investigated because the air pollution is vastly related to anthropogenic activities (e.g. construction activities, consumption of fuels) (Hasenfratz et al. (2012); Richards et al. (2006);

Table 7.4 Air pollutants: sources and impacts.

Pollutants	Sources	Impacts on human health
Carbon dioxide (CO_2)	Tobacco smoke, wood and gas stoves, combustion of fuels, oxidation of automobile products	Respiratory problems
Carbon monoxide (CO)	Leaking chimneys and furnaces, wood and gas stoves, burning process	Impaired vision, headaches, dizziness, nausea
Nitrogen dioxide (NO_2)	Kerosene heaters, gas stoves, tobacco smoke	Irritation in eyes, nose and throat, Impaired lung function Increase in respiratory infections
Particulate matter (PM)	Oxidation of automobile products Tobacco smoke	Irritation in the eye, nose, and throat bronchitis, lung cancer
Volatile organic compounds (VOCs)	Paints, aerosol sprays, air fresheners, stored fuels, automotive products	Damages the liver, kidneys, and central nervous system

Source: Based on data from Choi et al. (2009).

Völgyesi et al. (2008)). The conventional monitoring instruments comprises long-term time-consuming average models that updates the air pollution situation hourly or daily. Therefore, the air pollution maps made by the conventional air pollution monitoring systems are with extremely low temporal and spatial resolutions. These low spatiotemporal determinations are only sufficient for ambient background monitoring but not adequate for the public to be conscious regarding their personal exposure to air pollution. To overcome the low spatiotemporal determinations, the researchers are insisting to use biosensors, wireless sensor networks (WSNs) and low-cost portable ambient sensors for the purpose of air pollution monitoring. The combination of WSNs and low-cost portable ambient sensors with intelligent mobile devices will provide current information regarding pollutant level, which can be updated every second or minute (Ma et al. (2008)). Recent studies have emphasized the effectiveness and feasibility of environmental monitoring based on the WSN technologies. Moreover, the low-cost portable sensors enable the feasibility and the mobility in large-scale deployment in sensor nodes. Many studies were developed for the purpose of environmental monitoring through information and communications technology (ICT), WSN, and portable devices. Jiang et al. (2009) developed a water environment monitoring system that includes monitoring nodes, base stations, and remote monitoring based on WSN technology. Lin et al. (2017) applied ICT-based monitoring system to evaluate the risks in the agricultural environment based on the pollutants and discussed about the importance and functions of the ICT in the field of agricultural engineering. Lorincz et al. (2006) used WSN technology to collect the volcanic data through triggered event detection and data retrieval based on bandwidth and data quality standards. Martinez et al. (2006) designed WSN to collect the data from the nodes that were deployed inside the glaciers and discussed about the impact of wind in coastal areas. Ma et al. (2008) developed an air pollution monitoring system based on a sensor network to gather instantaneous, large-scale, and comprehensive data from road traffic emissions, which induce air pollutants in the urban environment. With the help of ICT, WSN, and portable and wearable devices, the public can measure their personal exposure to pollutants.

7.3.1.1 Influence of Environmental Factors on Health

Environment and climate change are being regularly monitored by environmentalist, meteorologists, geologists, biologists, and biochemists. Monitoring is done through remote sensing technologies and by installing air pollutant sensors in urban/rural areas. Traditional sensing technologies are expensive and they were used to capture the macro measurements around large regions, and actions will be taken after environmental incidents occurred. Therefore, the direct effect of environmental factors on human health is often very challenging to identify. Rapid development in ultralow power and low-cost wireless sensing technologies can significantly enable real-time monitoring and improve the environmental monitoring of microenvironments, which can be done with the help of biosensors. With the detailed environmental and health information acquired using the new wireless environmental sensors and health sensors, environmental impact on human health can be identified accurately.

7.4 IPCS for Healthcare

Health monitoring involves testing an individual to find any changes in their health status because of exposure to certain health hazards arising from their environment, such as contaminants in the air like hazardous dusts, vapors, or fumes. In recent years, sensor technology and wearable computing with healthcare provide an innovative and leading solution to improve the quality of patient's life. IPCS plays a vital role in healthcare monitoring system, which integrates the wearable and ubiquitous sensor with the personal mobile devices for the purpose of continuous monitoring of patients during their daily activities in order to prevent them from critical situations. Use of mobile devices and wireless technologies in healthcare are typically related to bio-monitoring and home monitoring. Mobile networks are used in bio-monitoring, which includes physiological parameters, namely, heartbeat rate, body temperature, electrocardiogram (ECG), oxygen saturation, blood pressure, and other physiological signals (Vouyioukas and Maglogiannis (2012)). Considering the patient context such as indoor and outdoor temperature, location, and activity status, data can

Figure 7.4 IPCS services in healthcare.

be acquired using various sensor and mobile technologies (Maglogiannis and Doukas (2014)). Healthcare professionals can have a ubiquitous access to the patient's data, laboratory results, and pharmaceutical data from any location through the interconnected network. IPCS provides a wide range of services to the public and healthcare professionals, namely, patient monitoring, pervasive access to data, telemedicine, incident detection, emergency response and management, and location-based services (Varshney (2003)) as shown in Figure 7.4.

Patient monitoring focuses on observing the health conditions of the patients remotely through sensor technology, and the data will be accessed by healthcare professionals to view the health status of the patient.

Pervasive access to data permits patient and healthcare professionals to view and update the clinical records with the help of portable devices.

Telemedicine enables the healthcare professionals such as doctors and specialists to diagnose and recommend the treatment in normal or critical situations from any location using handheld devices.

Incident detection delivers the notification immediately to healthcare professionals if there is any change in patients' health condition.

Emergency response and management provides facilities to the public efficiently by dispatching the nearby ambulatory vehicles to the location where the emergency takes place and directing the patients to nearby hospitals.

Location-based services help the healthcare professionals to supervise elderly patients or mentally degraded patients who are in need of ambulatory but restricted to certain areas. This service also helps people to locate the nearby healthcare facilities in critical situations.

Over the last decades, numerous healthcare systems were developed to monitor health status. A remote monitoring system for ECG signals was developed by (Khanja et al. (2008)). The system utilizes a device equipped with ZigBee module connective based on WSNs. The system records data to an online database, and the ECG signals are analyzed on a server. If there exists any serious heart anomalies, an alarm will be sent to the authorized medical staffs or to the physician through the telecommunication network. An embedded system designed by (Cheriyan et al. (2009)) capable of tracking relevant bio-signals from the individuals in real time and facilitating a dependable decision-making process that delivers alerts for potential brain activity changes. The design focuses around the use of sensors and a processing element. It integrates the use of electroencephalography (EEG) and oxygen saturation (SpO2) signals. An ECG measurement system provided by (De Capua et al. (2010)) based on a Web service-oriented architecture to monitor the heart condition of cardiac patients. The projected device is a smart patient-adaptive system, able to provide personalized diagnoses by using personal data and clinical history of the monitored patients. Code Blue system (Malan et al. (2004)) was based on wireless infrastructure to enhance the capability of rescue workers and allow patients to examine during their normal activities. mobi-Health monitoring system (Konstantas et al. (2004)) was based on body area network (BAN) and mobile health (m-health) platform service for the utilization of next-generation wireless network that includes general packet radio service (GPRS) and universal mobile telecommunications system (UMTS) for point-to-point care for mobile patients. @Home system (Sachpazidis (2002)) uses portable sensors to monitor the patient's health status, which includes blood pressure, body temperature, and oxygen saturation, and the information will be transmitted to healthcare professionals by Bluetooth remotely from their home. TeleCARE (Camarinha-Matos and Afsarmanesh (2004)) was designed especially for helping elderly people and their caretakers. It uses multi-agent systems, federated information management, safe communications, hypermedia interfaces, rich sensorial environments, and increased intelligence technologies to integrate the Internet with mobile agent technology. My-heart system (Habetha (2006)) uses an intelligent system for monitoring and prevention of cardiovascular diseases. ALARM-NET (Wood et al. (2006)) is a WSN that incorporates environmental and physiological sensors in a heterogeneous architecture for pervasive, adaptive healthcare and monitor the individuals in their residence. A query protocol permits real-time collection and processing of sensor data for authorized care providers and program analysis. SNAP (Malasri and Wang (2007)) is a medical sensor network architecture that focuses on security. In this architecture, one or more wireless sensors are attached to an individual patient. The patient's data are forwarded by a number of wireless relay nodes throughout the hospital zone. These nodes are categorized into unlimited-powered and limited-powered nodes. WBAN

Table 7.5 Healthcare system: An empirical view.

Healthcare system	Description	Year, reference
IOTC – bringing IoT and cloud computing toward pervasive computing	IoT architecture for acquisition and management of sensor data on the cloud infrastructure	2012, (Doukas and Maglogiannis (2012))
Commodity – A personal health system (PHS)	A healthcare system specially designed for diabetic patients	2013, (Ozgur et al. (2013))
Managing wearable sensor data through cloud computing (MWCS)	System uses sensor to monitor heartbeat information and motion data, stored in cloud infrastructure	2011, (Doukas and Maglogiannis (2011))
An IoT-based personal device for diabetes therapy management in ambient assisted living (AAL)	Personal diabetes management device based on IoT provides mobile assistance services	2011, (Jara et al. (2011))
Cloud-enabled wireless body area network for pervasive healthcare	Mobile cloud computing capabilities and cloud-enabled wireless body area network (WBAN) for pervasive healthcare applications	2013, (Wan et al. (2013))
Personal health service framework (PHSF)	PHSF uses new advancements of service-oriented architecture to develop healthcare systems and enable remote and self-monitoring	2013, (Ghorbani and Du (2013))
Pervasive healthcare system	Software architecture based on pervasive computing for healthcare system and modeled about the system	2016, (Tahmasbi et al. (2016))

group (Warren et al. (2005)) developed wearable health monitoring systems using ZigBee wireless sensor platforms, custom signal conditioning boards, and the TinyOS software environment. Sensor nodes are strategically placed on the user's body. They process and store information about user's physiological signals for further reference. All these healthcare systems are utilized for patient's welfare but were not designed based on cloud infrastructure, hence leading to issues such as inadequate data access, inadequate data storage, and less computing power. To provide an effective healthcare system, cloud computing can be incorporated with pervasive computing, which will improve the scalability, adaptability, efficiency, storage capacity, computing power, and overall performance of the system (Mandal et al. (2015)). Recently, various studies were done on healthcare system based on wireless technology and portable devices with cloud infrastructure, which are represented in Table 7.5. Healthcare systems use various sensors to monitor the physiological parameters of the patients based on the diseases, which are represented in Table 7.6.

Table 7.6 Sensors used in healthcare systems.

Measuring sensor	Physiological parameter	Syndrome
Accelerometers, gyroscopes, glucose monitors, vision sensor	Gait patterns, visual and sensory impairment	Diabetic disorder
Wearable heart rate or respiration sensors, and accelerometers	Heartbeat rate, oxygen saturation, respiration and activity level	Chronic obstructive pulmonary disease (COPD)
Accelerometers, gyroscopes, and optical or vision sensors	Muscle tone, gait, activity level	Parkinson's disorder
Wearable blood pressure sensor, accelerometers	Blood pressure	Hypertension
Accelerometers, gyroscopes, and optical or vision sensors	Gait patterns, stiffness, body temperature	Arthritis disorder
ECG sensors, wearable heart rate and blood pressure sensors	Heartbeat rate, blood pressure	Cardiac disease

7.4.1 Healthcare System Architecture Based on Environmental Monitoring

This section describes an architecture for healthcare system based on environmental monitoring. It comprises of wireless sensors or biosensors, monitoring devices, cloud infrastructure, electronic platforms (e-platform), computing devices, and gateways. The system utilizes the concept of cloud computing for efficient management of data from heterogeneous devices. Cloud infrastructure provides the facilities to access the data, resources, direct communication between the sensors, and common infrastructure in a ubiquitous manner. The layered architecture consists of six layers, namely, physical layer, mobile computing layer, interoperability layer, affective computing layer, context-aware computing layer, and application layer as described below and shown in Figure 7.5.

Physical layer: Physical layer is the first layer in this architecture; it holds heterogeneous hardware to perform intelligent pervasive computing. The heterogeneous hardware includes microprocessor, wired or wireless network interface card, sensors, and input and output devices to perform monitoring and computation. All the heterogeneous devices are interconnected through wired or wireless technologies; this monitoring information will be useful for making decisions regarding the health and preventive actions in the environment. For effective pervasive computing, either the physical user or an application will send and receive the signals. The entities in the physical layer are compatible with each other.

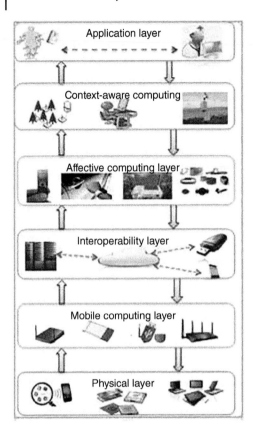

Figure 7.5 Healthcare system architecture based on environmental monitoring.

Mobile computing layer: Mobile computing layer lies between physical layer and interoperability layer. This layer sits at higher level of abstraction than the physical layer and defines about the resources available for the devices. It includes communication, computing, and handheld devices for the purpose of acquiring data from different remote locations that can be accessed by any user from anywhere. Sensors in the centralized mode transmit data to a server, which consolidates and analyzes the data it receives. There are several artificial intelligence and data mining techniques, namely, neural networks, fuzzy rules, decision making, spatiotemporal reasoning, and machine learning, which are used in analyzing sensor data from different environment.

Interoperability Layer Interoperability layer is in between mobile computing layer and affective computing layer. This layer utilizes the cloud server to provide robust and scalable data for user or service providers from different sources. By using cloud infrastructure, acquisition of data, management, and communication with external applications become easier. Several services of cloud computing are utilized for managing the data, namely, database services, queue storage, table storage, cloud service Web role, and traffic manager. System security can be improved due to centralization of data and increased availability of the resources.

Affective computing layer: Affective computing layer is an intermediate layer between interoperability layer and context-aware computing layer. Its main goal is to solve multimodal input issues and identifying their effects. It holds different types of environmental monitoring sensors (e.g. greenhouse gases (GHGs), temperature, humidity, wind speed, and wind direction). This layer holds the measured environmental pollutants value from multiple devices and transmits the values to the context-aware computing layer for analysis and decision making. Human–computer interaction is made available through intelligent systems that include wearable sensors, biosensors, and portable devices for communication and computing needs. Data integration and analysis from various sensors are done for further processing.

Context-aware computing layer: Context-aware computing layer is the second topmost layer in this architecture, which is mainly used for the purpose of decision making. This layer makes use of pollutant information transmitted by the affective computing layer. It provides the high-level context data about the user's activity, location, and other contextual data. The context information on the environmental pollutants will be generated automatically and provided to the healthcare service providers or users based on the current situation. This layer delivers the services to the authenticating user and resources on the network. It is also responsible for making connection and disconnection of resources and provides information to update the network. This layer is helpful for formation of pollution related guidelines by government organizations and to provide appropriate services.

Application layer: Application layer is the topmost layer in this architecture. This layer holds a variety of applications through which various users can be benefited. In the pervasive computing architecture, the application layer consists of healthcare system. This layer contains an interface component that specifies pervasive application on user handheld devices. The component allows the user or developer to define the required user interface and to identify the mode of communication. It includes continuous patient monitoring that updates health status of patients to healthcare professionals through communication devices. Based on the context-aware computing layer information, changes in the environmental pollutant levels will send necessary alerts to the application layer. Through this information, healthcare professionals can take safety measures and essential steps to overcome the risks by alerting the patients with the help of portable devices or wireless sensors.

Several types of wireless networking and sensing technologies, namely, on-body sensors with long-range radios, BANs of short range, on-body sensors with a long-range gateway, sensors implanted in body with wireless communication and power delivery, wireless sensors embedded in assistive devices carried by individuals, wireless sensors embedded in the environment, and sensors embedded in the ubiquitous mobile smartphones, can be used in the architecture to provide scalable, flexible, and heterogeneous environment. Naturally, more than one type of sensing technology will be used for a single application. The above architecture uses various sensors, mobile devices, and cloud computing technologies for environmental modeling in view of cost reduction and effective resource utilization, even though data security is one of the challenging issues pertaining to cloud computing.

7.5 Conclusion

Tremendous increase in the level of environmental pollutants causes ill effects to human health and damages the ecosystem. Recent advances in the field of biosensors, WSNs, cloud system, and communication devices have led to improvements in real-time environmental monitoring and assessment of health vulnerabilities. Development of intelligent pervasive healthcare systems can provide an efficient methodology for pollution information processing and decision making on healthcare to adopt preventive measures against the environmental threats. The healthcare system architecture deals with environmental monitoring through biosensors and other sensors to manage and maintain the health status of the people with the help of handheld devices. The adaptability and scalability of the system is ensured by using the cloud infrastructure for efficient data management and sharing the resources in pervasive manner.

Bibliography

Alaa, A., Mokhtar, S.A., Alaa, S., and Basma, S. (2013). Forecast global carbon dioxide emission using swarm intelligence. *International Journal of Computer Applications* **77**: 5.

Amorim, L.C.A., Carneiro, J.P., and Cardeal, Z.L. (2008). An optimized method for determination of benzene in exhaled air by gas chromatography-mass spectrometry using solid phase microextraction as a sampling technique. *Journal of Chromatography B* **865**: 141–146. https://doi.org/10.1016/j.jchromb.2008.02.023.

Atallah, L., Lo, B., and Yang, G.-Z. (2012). Can pervasive sensing address current challenges in global healthcare? *Journal of Epidemiology and Global Health* **2**: 1–13. https://doi.org/10.1016/j.jegh.2011.11.005.

Behrang, M.A., Assareh, E., Assari, A., and Ghanbarzadeh, M.R. (2011). Using bees algorithm and artificial neural network to forecast world carbon dioxide emission. *Energy Sources, Part A: Recovery, Utilization, and Environmental Effects* **33**: 1747–1759. https://doi.org/10.1080/15567036.2010.493920.

Camarinha-Matos, L.M. and Afsarmanesh, H. (2004). TeleCARE: collaborative virtual elderly support communities. Proceedings of the 1st Workshop on Tele-Care and Collaborative Virtual Communities in Elderly Care, TELECARE 2004.

Cheriyan, A.M., Kalbarczyk, Z., Iyer, R. et al. (2009). Pervasive embedded real time monitoring of EEG & SpO2. In: 2009 3rd International Conference on Pervasive Computing Technologies for Healthcare, 1–4.

Choi, S., Kim, N., Cha, H., and Ha, R. (2009). Micro sensor node for air pollutant monitoring: Hardware and software issues. *Sensors* **9**: 7970–7987. https://doi.org/10.3390/s91007970.

De Capua, C., Meduri, A., and Morello, R. (2010). A smart ECG measurement system based on web-service-oriented architecture for telemedicine applications. *IEEE Transactions on Instrumentation and Measurement* **59** (10): 2530–2538.

Doukas, C. and Maglogiannis, I. (2011). Managing wearable sensor data through cloud computing. In: 3rd IEEE International Conference on Cloud Computing Technology and Science. https://doi.org/10.1109/CloudCom.2011.65.

Doukas, C. and Maglogiannis, I. (2012). Bringing IOT and cloud computing towards pervasive healthcare. In: 2012 6th International Conference on Innovative Mobile and Internet Services in Ubiquitous Computing (IMIS). https://doi.org/10.1109/IMIS.2012.26.

Ghorbani, S. and Du, W. (2013). Personal health service framework. *Procedia Computer Science* **21**: 343–350. https://doi.org/10.1016/j.procs.2013.09.045. The 4th International Conference on Emerging Ubiquitous Systems and Pervasive Networks (EUSPN-2013) and the 3rd International Conference on Current and Future Trends of Information and Communication Technologies in Healthcare (ICTH).

Guelzim, T. and Obaidat, M.S. (2011). *Security and Privacy in Pervasive Networks*. Chichester: Wiley. https://doi.org/10.1002/9781119970422.ch10.

Gunasekaran, R., Kumaraswamy, P.P., Chandrasekaran, K., and Punithavathi, J. (2012). Analysis of ambient gaseous pollutants in and around coal based thermal power plant - a case study. *International Journal of Current Research* **4**: 268–274.

Habetha, J. (2006). The myheart project–fighting cardiovascular diseases by prevention and early diagnosis. In: IEEE Engineering in Medicine and Biology Society. Conference Proceedings, Volume 36. https://doi.org/10.1109/IEMBS.2006.260937.

Hasenfratz, D., Saukh, O., Sturzenegger, S., and Thiele, L. (2012). Participatory air pollution monitoring using smartphones. 2nd International Workshop on Mobile Sensing.

Jara, A.J., Zamora, M.A., and Skarmeta, A.F.G. (2011). An Internet of things-based personal device for diabetes therapy management in ambient assisted living (AAL). *Personal and Ubiquitous Computing* **15**: 431–440.

Jaydip, S. (2010). Ubiquitous computing: potentials and challenges. In: International Conference on Trends & Advances in Computation & Engineering, 1323–1346.

Jiang, P., Xia, H., He, Z., and Wang, Z. (2009). Design of a water environment monitoring system based on wireless sensor networks. *Sensors* **9**: 6411–6434. https://doi.org/10.3390/s90806411.

Khanja, P., Wattanasirichaigoon, S., Natwichai, J. et al. (2008). A web base system for ECG data transferred using ZigBee/IEEE technology.

Konstantas, D., Halteren, A.V., Bults, R. et al. (2004). MobiHealth: ambulant patient monitoring over public wireless networks. *Studies in Health Technology and Informatics* **106**: 107–122. https://doi.org/10.3233/978-1-60750-948-6-107.

Lin, Y.-P., Chang, T.-K., Fan, C. et al. (2017). Applications of information and communication technology for improvements of water and soil monitoring and assessments in agricultural areas-a case study in the Taoyuan irrigation district. *Environments* **4** (1): 6.

Lorincz, K., Welsh, M., Marcillo, O. et al. (2006). Deploying a wireless sensor network on an active volcano. *IEEE Internet Computing* **10**: 18–25. https://doi.org/10.1109/MIC.2006.26.

Ma, Y., Richards, M., Ghanem, M. et al. (2008). Air pollution monitoring and mining based on sensor grid in London. *Sensors* **8**: 3601–3623. https://doi.org/10.3390/s80603601.

Maglogiannis, I. and Doukas, C. (2014). Intelligent health monitoring based on pervasive technologies and cloud computing. *International Journal on Artificial Intelligence Tools* **23**: 1460001. https://doi.org/10.1142/S021821301460001X.

Malan, D., Thaddeus, F.J., Welsh, M., and Moulton, S.B. (2004). CodeBlue: an Ad Hoc sensor network infrastructure for emergency medical care. In: Proceeding Workshop on Wearable and Implantable Body Sensor Networks, 3–6.

Malasri, K. and Wang, L. (2007). Addressing security in medical sensor networks. In: HealthNet '07: Proceedings of the 1st ACM SIGMOBILE International Workshop on Systems and Networking Support for Healthcare and Assisted Living Environments, 7–12.

Mandal, A.K., Sarkar, A., and Chaki, N. (2015). Flexible cloud architecture for healthcare applications. In: *Applied Computation and Security Systems. Advances in Intelligent Systems and Computing*, (eds. R. Chaki, K. Saeed, S. Choudhury et al.) **304**: 103–121. New Delhi: Springer.

Martinez, K., Padhy, P., Elsaify, A. et al. (2006). Deploying a sensor network in an extreme environment. In: IEEE International Conference on Sensor Networks, Ubiquitous, and Trustworthy Computing. https://doi.org/10.1109/SUTC.2006.1636175.

Mehrotra, P. (2016). Biosensors and their applications - a review. *Journal of Oral Biology and Craniofacial Research* **6**: 153–159. https://doi.org/10.1016/j.jobcr .2015.12.002.

Ozgur, K., Stefano, B., Michal, S. et al. (2013). COMMODITY12: a smart e-health environment for diabetes management. *Journal of Ambient Intelligence and Smart Environments* **5**: 479–502. https://doi.org/10.3233/AIS-130220.

Reza, S. (2013). Application of ant colony optimization (ACO) to forecast CO_2 emission in Iran. *Bulletin of Environment, Pharmacology and Life Sciences* **2**: 95–99.

Richards, M., Ghanem, M., Osmond, M. et al. (2006). Grid-based analysis of air pollution data. *Ecological Modelling* **194**: 274–286. https://doi.org/10.1016/j .ecolmodel.2005.10.042.

da Rocha, R.C.A. and Endler, M. (2006). Middleware: context management in heterogeneous, evolving ubiquitous environments. *IEEE Distributed Systems Online* **7**: 1. https://doi.org/10.1109/MDSO.2006.28.

Roda, A., Pasini, P., Mirasoli, M. et al. (2001). A sensitive determination of urinary mercury (II) by a bioluminescent transgenic bacteria-based biosensor. *Analytical Letters* **34** (1): 29–41. https://doi.org/10.1081/AL-100002702.

Rodriguez-Mozaz, S., de Alda, M.J.L., Marco, M.-P., and Barceló, D. (2005). Biosensors for environmental monitoring. *Talanta* **65** (2): 291–297. https://doi .org/10.1016/j.talanta.2004.07.006. ISSN: 0039-9140. Evaluation/Validation of Novel Biosensors in Real Environmental and Food Samples.

Rodriguez-Mozaz, S. de Alda, M.J.L., and Barceló, D. (2006). Biosensors as useful tools for environmental analysis and monitoring. *Analytical and Bioanalytical Chemistry* **386** (4): 1025–1041. https://doi.org/10.1007/s00216-006-0574-3. ISSN: 1618-2650.

Rogers, K.R. (2006). Recent advances in biosensor techniques for environmental monitoring. *Analytica Chimica Acta* **568** (1): 222–231. https://doi.org/10.1016/ j.aca.2005.12.067. ISSN: 0003-2670. Molecular Electronics and Analytical Chemistry.

Sachpazidis, I. (2002). @HOME: A modular telemedicine system. In: 2nd Conference on Mobile Computing in Medicine, 87–95.

Sangeetha, A. and Amudha, T. (2016a). An effective bio-inspired methodology for optimal estimation and forecasting of CO_2 emission in India. In: *Innovations in Bio-Inspired Computing and Applications*. Advances in Intelligent Systems and Computing, vol. **424** (ed. V. Snášel, A. Abraham, P. Krömer et al.), 481–489. Springer International Publishing. https://doi.org/10.1007/978-3-319-28031-8_ 42. ISBN: 978-3-319-28031-8.

Sangeetha, A. and Amudha, T. (2016b). A study on estimation of CO_2 emission using computational techniques. In: International Conference on Advances in Computer Applications, 244–249. https://doi.org/10.1109/ICACA.2016 .7887959.

Sethi, R.S. (1994). Transducer aspects of biosensors. *Biosensors and Bioelectronics* **9**: 243–264. https://doi.org/10.1016/0956-5663(94)80127-4.

Tahmasbi, A., Adabi, S., and Rezaee, A. (2016). Behavioral reference model for pervasive healthcare systems. *Journal of Medical Systems* **40**: 270. https://doi .org/10.1007/s10916-016-0632-0.

Thvenot, D.R., Toth, K., Durst, R.A., and Wilson, G.S. (2001). Electrochemical biosensors: recommended definitions and classification1international union of pure and applied chemistry: physical chemistry division, commission I.7 (biophysical chemistry); analytical chemistry division, commission v.5 (electroanalytical chemistry).1. *Biosensors and Bioelectronics* **16** (1): 121–131. https://doi.org/10.1016/S0956-5663(01)00115-4. ISSN: 0956-5663.

Varshney, U. (2003). Pervasive healthcare. *IEEE Computer Magazine* **36** (12): 138–140.

Völgyesi, P., Nádas, A., Koutsoukos, X., and Lédeczi, A. (2008). Air quality monitoring with sensorMap. In: *Proceedings of the 7th International Conference on Information Processing in Sensor Networks, IPSN '08*, 529–530. IEEE Computer Society. https://doi.org/10.1109/IPSN.2008.50. ISBN: 978-0-7695-3157-1.

Vouyioukas, D. and Maglogiannis, I. (2012). Communication issues in pervasive healthcare systems and applications. In: *Pervasive and Smart Technologies for Healthcare: Ubiquitous Methodologies and Tools* (eds. A. Coronato and G. De Pietro), 197–227. Hershey, PA: IGI Global.

Wäger, P.A., Hilty, L.M., Arnfalk, P., and Erdmann, L. (2006). Experience with a system dynamics model in a prospective study on the future impact of ICT on environmental sustainability. International Congress on Environmental Modelling and Software.

Wan, J., Zou, C., Ullah, S. et al. (2013). Cloud-enabled wireless body area networks for pervasive healthcare. *IEEE Network* **27** (5): 56–61. https://doi.org/10.1109/ MNET.2013.6616116.

Warren, S., Lebak, J., Yao, J. et al. (2005). Interoperability and security in wireless body area network infrastructures. In: Proceedings of the 27th Annual International Conference of the IEEE Engineering in Medicine and Biology Society, 3837–3840.

Weiser, M. (1999). The computer for the 21st century. *SIGMOBILE Mobile Computing and Communications Review* **3** (3): 3–11. https://doi.org/10.1145/ 329124.329126. ISSN: 1559-1662.

Wood, A., Virone, G., Doan, T. et al. (2006). Alarm-Net: Wireless Sensor Networks for Assisted-Living and Residential Monitoring. Technical Report CS-2006-01. Charlottesville, VA: Department of Computer Science, University of Virginia.

8

Secure Pervasive Healthcare System and Diabetes Prediction Using Heuristic Algorithm

Patitha Parameswaran[1] and Rajalakshmi Shenbaga Moorthy[2]

[1] Department of Computer Technology, MIT Campus, Anna University, Chennai, India
[2] Department of Computer Science and Engineering, St. Joseph's Institute of Technology, Anna University, Chennai, India

8.1 Introduction

Pervasive computing, also coined as ubiquitous computing, is the field where microcontrollers are embedded in day-to-day objects, which enable them to share information. Pervasive/ubiquitous computing is anytime/anywhere through any network in the form of any data. Pervasive devices are completely connected to the network and are constantly available to provide unobtrusive connection. With telehealth a person can monitor his/her health from anywhere. The importance of pervasive healthcare system is to provide optimal treatment, required care, and healthcare services to patients in any location. Since a large number of users have pervasive devices, the amount of data that is generated is huge. Thus storing is a primary concern, which can be solved by cloud computing. Cloud computing utilizes the advantages of parallel, distributed, cluster, and grid computing and makes the services available all the time. It provides three kinds of service delivery models, namely, software as a service (SaaS), platform as a service (PaaS), and infrastructure as a service (IaaS). The IaaS service delivery model provides the infrastructure or platform for hosting the PaaS and SaaS applications.

The medical data produced by pervasive devices are stored in the cloud. The proposed SMDAP system should be able to predict the likelihood that person will suffer from diabetes based on the observations from pervasive devices. It plays a major role in increasing the accuracy of clustering similar data, predicting the likelihood of disease, and enhancing security. Figure 8.1 shows the major components of proposed SMDAP system.

The system contains pervasive devices, security manager, clusterer, and diabetes predictor. Several professionals can access the medical data stored in the cloud at any time from anywhere. Hence there is a possibility of hacking the

Intelligent Pervasive Computing Systems for Smarter Healthcare, First Edition.
Arun Kumar Sangaiah, S.P. Shantharajah, and Padma Theagarajan.

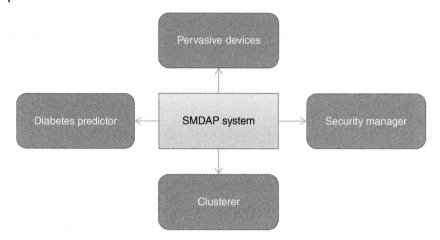

Figure 8.1 Major components of SMDAP system.

data or change or mutation of data. Hence, the proxy re-encryption algorithm (PRA) based on Elgamal cryptosystem (Stallings, 2006) is used to ensure security. The data is encrypted at the client side (patient) before storing in the cloud. In the cloud, the data is again encrypted. The data gathered through pervasive devices are clustered using the clusterer. Clustering is unsupervised learning, where the centroid plays a prominent role. K-means clustering approach selects the initial centroid value randomly, which leads to poor clusters. The sensitive medical data should be clustered properly since it may lead to wrong prediction and improper treatments, which is very crucial. Hence, HPSO-K algorithm is proposed to cluster the data of patients. This HPSO-K aims to find the optimal cluster centroid, which is given as input to K-means. HPSO-K provides optimal clusters with the maximum similarity of the patients within a cluster.

Having identified the group of healthy patients, diabetes predictor is used to forecast diabetes. The hidden Markov model (HMM)-based predictor is preferred because the conventional prediction mechanism needs historical values to predict future values and it requires usage of a training set, which builds a model that will be used to predict data. In comparison, the proposed HMM-based predictor does not use a training set as it uses its own historical values to predict the future values. Thus the contributions of the research work are given as follows:

- To design a security manager using PRA to secure sensitive medical data.
- To design a clusterer using HPSO-K to efficiently cluster the patient's data based on the severity of the symptoms.
- To design a predictor using HMM-VA to efficiently predict the likelihood of suffering from diabetes.

The rest of the chapter is organized as follows: Section 8.1 starts with an introduction and motivation behind the proposed work. Sections 8.2–8.5 describe related work, the proposed system architecture, the implementation of proposed mechanism, and simulation results. Section 8.6 concludes the proposed work and explores the feasibility of future work.

8.2 Related Work

Doukas and Maglogiannis (2012) proposed that pervasive healthcare applications generate the vast amount of heterogeneous data that need to be optimally managed for future analysis and processing. Further, the authors stated that cloud computing serves as the best platform to store and analyze pervasive healthcare data. The privacy of medical data is not addressed. Hanen et al. (2016) proposed an enhanced healthcare system in mobile cloud computing environment, where a security mechanism was imposed for securing private data. However, the man-in-the-middle attack was not addressed, as the encryption happens only on the data owner side. The authors focused only on securing health data and not on continuous monitoring and prediction of health conditions of patients. Poorejbari and Vahdat-Nejad (2014) proposed a pervasive healthcare system as they addressed that pervasive data can be stored and processed in the cloud. However, securing private data and monitoring and providing optimal treatment to patients are not addressed. Doukas et al. (2010) designed a mobile application using Google's Android operating system that can provide management of patient's record. The authors addressed efficient storage and retrieval but did not focus on security. Chen and Ye (2012) proposed the particle swarm optimization (PSO) for finding cluster centers in any dataset. PSO is a metaheuristic algorithm that tends to find the global best value rather than local value. Harb and Desuky (2014) proposed a feature selection using PSO. The features play a prominent role in increasing the accuracy of any machine learning algorithms. The features are selected by PSO and are given as input to the decision tree, radial basis function, k-nearest neighbor, and naïve Bayes. Suresh et al. (2015) proposed to predict the waiting time of the patient in the hospital. A stochastic PSO is used to build a training model. The PSO is compared with neural networks in terms of error convergence, sensitivity, specificity, positive precision value, and accuracy. Kawamoto et al. (2013) proposed HMM for analyzing time series health checkup data. HMM is a probabilistic approach and it can find the most likely sequence. The author represents the HMM with six states. An HMM model had been constructed to find any transition, which indicates likelihood, whether a person will suffer from disease. Stolfo et al. (2012) proposed Fog Computing: Mitigating Insider Data Theft Attacks in the Cloud for securing the cloud data using an offensive decoy technology. The data security has become a major challenge in the cloud computing paradigm. Existing data protection mechanisms such as encryption have failed in preventing data theft attacks, especially those perpetrated by an insider to the cloud provider. Hence in this paper they have proposed a different approach for securing data in the cloud using offensive decoy technology. Lang et al. (2017) proposed a self-contained data protection mechanism called RBAC-CPABE by integrating role-based access control (RBAC), with the ciphertext-policy attribute-based encryption (CP-ABE).

8.3 System Design

The proposed SMDAP system shown in Figure 8.2 includes:

1. Data collector
2. Security manager
3. Analytic engine

The first component is achieved using the various Internet of things (IoT) devices. Nowadays, various sensors are embedded in smartphones and other handheld devices to gather health data of the patient. Since the patient health

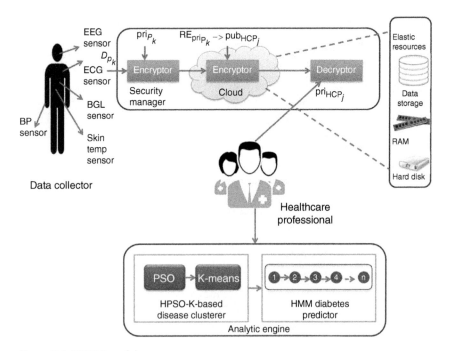

Figure 8.2 SMDAP model.

data is sensitive, security is a prime concern, which is done using the second component, security manager. The security manager encrypts the patient data with his/her private key. While the data is stored in the cloud, the data is again re-encrypted using the re-encryption key, which is the private key of the patient and public key of an assigned healthcare professional. Having seen the patient data, in order to produce optimal insight, an analytic engine is designed. Analytic engine includes two components: (i) HPSO-K clusterer clusters the patient in an optimal manner. The outcomes are cluster of healthy patients, cluster of patients having diabetes, cluster of patients having heart disorder, cluster of patients having lung disorder, and so on. (ii) HMM-based diabetes predictor for the healthy patient, which takes healthy cluster as input and forecast whether the patient will be subjected to diabetes or not, based on the observations.

8.3.1 Data Collector

The data collector aims to collect medical data from IoT devices. The patients are represented as $P \leftarrow \{P_1, P_2, \ldots, P_n\}$. The list of symptoms associated with medical data is represented as $S \leftarrow \{s_1, s_2, s_3, \ldots, s_n\}$.

8.3.2 Security Manager

In SMDAP model, the patient need not be in hospital. The patient from anywhere can use IoT sensors and send the information to healthcare professionals through the cloud. There is a need for security to the medical data in the cloud. The objective of security manager represented in Eq. (8.1) is to provide security to the sensitive medical data.

$$D_{P_k} \leftarrow \text{Decrypt}\left(\text{Encrypt}\left(\text{Encrypt}\left(D_{P_k}\right)_{\text{Pub}_{P_k}}\right)_{\text{RE}_{\text{Pri}_{P_k} \to \text{Pub}_{\text{HCP}_j}}}\right)_{\text{Pri}_{\text{HCP}_j}} \tag{8.1}$$

subject to

$$\text{Pub}_{P_k} \in G \tag{8.2}$$
$$\text{Pub}_{\text{HCP}_j} \in G \tag{8.3}$$
$$\text{RE}_{\text{Pri}_{P_k} \to \text{Pub}_{\text{HCP}_j}}; k \neq j \tag{8.4}$$

8.3.2.1 Proxy Re-encryption Algorithm
The medical data are very sensitive; when the data is stored in the cloud, it is possible for a third party to reveal the data. Thus, proxy re-encryption is proposed to protect the data. To protect the patient data, Elgamal-based encryption is used. Elgamal encryption is public key cryptography method proposed by Taher Elgamal in 1985. Elgamal encryption consists of three components:

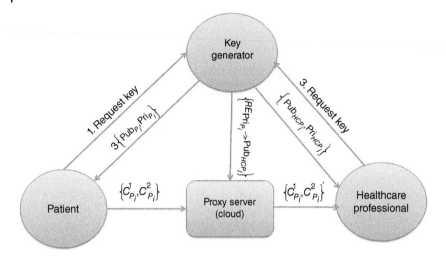

Figure 8.3 Proxy re-encryption algorithm (PRA).

key generator, Elgamal encryptor, and Elgamal decryptor. The aim of the key generator is to generate and distribute keys. Elgamal encryptor will encrypt the patient data. Elgamal decryptor will decrypt the encrypted patient data. Elgamal encryption algorithm is used because the computation of discrete log on large prime is very difficult. Figure 8.3 represents the working procedure of PRA. The steps in PRA are given as follows:

1. Patients encrypt their data using Elgamal encryption.
2. The encrypted data is sent to proxy server (cloud) for storage and transmission.
3. The key generator sends the key for re-encryption to the proxy server.
4. The proxy server encrypts the encrypted patient data.
5. Finally, the healthcare professional decrypts the received data using a private key.

8.3.2.2 Key Generator
The key generator is responsible for generating keys for the parties involved in SMDAP model.

- For each healthcare professional
    1. Chooses a large prime, $\text{Prime}_{\text{HCP}_j}$
    2. Chooses a primitive element, $\alpha_{\text{HCP}_j} \bmod \text{Prime}_{\text{HCP}_j}$
    3. Chooses an integer, $\text{Pri}_{\text{HCP}_j}$
    4. Computes

$$\beta_{\text{HCP}_j} \equiv (\alpha_{\text{HCP}_j})^{\text{Pri}_{\text{HCP}_j}} \bmod \text{Prime}_{\text{HCP}_j} \tag{8.5}$$

The public and the private keys of the healthcare professional are represented as $\{\text{Prime}_{\text{HCP}_j}, \alpha_{\text{HCP}_j}, \beta_{\text{HCP}_j}\}$ and $\text{Pri}_{\text{HCP}_j}$, respectively.

- For each patient
  1. Chooses a random integer, Pub_{P_i}
  2. Chooses a random integer, Pri_{P_i}

  The public key and the private key of the patient are represented as $\{\text{Pub}_{P_i}, \text{Pri}_{P_i}\}$.

- For proxy server (cloud)
  1. Computes re-encryption key as

$$\text{RE}_{\text{Pri}_{P_i} \to \text{Pub}_{\text{HCP}_j}} \equiv \frac{\text{Pub}_{\text{HCP}_j}}{\text{Pri}_{P_i}} \tag{8.6}$$

8.3.2.3 Patient

The patient encrypts the data before sending across the network. For each character in plain text, two ciphertexts are generated. Equations (8.7) and (8.8) represent the ciphertext pair for a plain text:

$$C_{P_i}^1 \leftarrow (\alpha_{\text{HCP}_j})^{\text{Pri}_{P_i}} \bmod \text{Prime}_{\text{HCP}_j} \tag{8.7}$$

$$C_{P_i}^2 \leftarrow (\beta_{\text{HCP}_j})^{\text{Pri}_{P_i}} D_{P_i} \bmod \text{Prime}_{\text{HCP}_j} \tag{8.8}$$

The ciphertext is sent to the proxy server (cloud).

8.3.2.4 Proxy Server

The proxy server re-encrypts the ciphertext pair with the re-encryption key represented in Eqs. (8.9) and (8.10). After creating re-encrypted ciphertext pair $\{\{C_{P_i}^2\}'\{C_{P_i}^1\}'\}$, the proxy server sends it to the healthcare professional for analysis.

$$\{C_{P_i}^1\}' \leftarrow \{C_{P_i}^1\}^{\text{RE}_{\text{Pri}_{P_i} \to \text{Pub}_{\text{HCP}_j}}} \bmod \text{Prime}_{\text{HCP}_j} \tag{8.9}$$

$$\{C_{P_i}^2\}' \leftarrow \{C_{P_i}^2\}^{\text{RE}_{\text{Pri}_{P_i} \to \text{Pub}_{\text{HCP}_j}}} \bmod \text{Prime}_{\text{HCP}_j} \tag{8.10}$$

8.3.2.5 Healthcare Professional

The healthcare professional decrypts the re-encrypted ciphertext pair using the private key of the healthcare professional. Equation (8.11) represents the decryption of re-encrypted ciphertext pair to get the original medical data:

$$\{C_{P_i}^2\}'\{\{C_{P_i}^1\}'\} \equiv \left[(\beta_{\text{HCP}_j})^{\text{Pri}_{P_i}} D_{P_i} \bmod \text{Prime}_{\text{HCP}_j}\right]^{\text{RE}_{\text{Pri}_{P_i} \to \text{Pub}_{\text{HCP}_j}}}$$

$$* \left[\left[(\alpha_{\text{HCP}_j})^{\text{Pri}_{P_i}} \bmod \text{Prime}_{\text{HCP}_j}\right]^{\text{RE}_{\text{Pri}_{P_i} \to \text{Pub}_{\text{HCP}_j}}}\right]^{-\text{Pri}_{\text{HCP}_j}} \tag{8.11}$$

Substitute Eq. (8.5) in Eq. (8.11):

$$\{C_{P_i}^2\}'\{\{C_{P_i}^1\}'\}^{-\mathrm{Pri}_{\mathrm{HCP}_j}}$$

$$\equiv \left(\left(\left(\alpha_{\mathrm{HCP}_j}\right)^{\mathrm{Pri}_{\mathrm{HCP}_j}}\right)^{\mathrm{Pri}_{P_i}}\right)^{\mathrm{RE}_{\mathrm{Pri}_{P_i}} \to \mathrm{Pub}_{\mathrm{HCP}_j}} D_{P_i} \bmod \mathrm{Prime}_{\mathrm{HCP}_j}$$

$$* \left(\left(\left(\alpha_{\mathrm{HCP}_j}\right)^{\mathrm{Pri}_{P_i}}\right)^{\mathrm{RE}_{\mathrm{Pri}_{P_i}} \to \mathrm{Pub}_{\mathrm{HCP}_j}}\right)^{-\mathrm{Pri}_{\mathrm{HCP}_j}} \bmod \mathrm{Prime}_{\mathrm{HCP}_j} \qquad (8.12)$$

$$\{C_{P_i}^2\}'\{\{C_{P_i}^1\}'\}^{-\mathrm{Pri}_{\mathrm{HCP}_j}} \equiv D_{P_i} \bmod \mathrm{Prime}_{\mathrm{HCP}_j} \qquad (8.13)$$

8.3.3 Clusterer

The objective is to cluster the medical data in such a way that patients with similar symptoms will be clustered so that necessary treatment can be taken. This is essential in order to avoid the risk of improper treatment and to correctly diagnose diseases. Clustering algorithm should maximize the similarity within the instances of a cluster. Thus the objective function is to maximize the intra-cluster distance of medical data within a cluster, which is represented in Eq. (8.14). A good clustering algorithm should have high intra-cluster distance and low inter-cluster distance. In SMDAP model, HPSO-K algorithm is used to cluster the medical data. Once the data are clustered, optimal treatment will be given accordingly.

$$\mathrm{Max}(f(Pa_i)) \leftarrow \frac{\sum_{i=1}^{N_c} \sum_{j=1}^{n_i} S(c_i, (D_{P_i})_i)}{n_i}}{N_c} \qquad (8.14)$$

subject to

$$\forall D_{P_i} \in P \qquad (8.15)$$

$$\forall d_i S(c_i, (D_{P_i})_i) > S(c_i, (D_{P_i})_j) \qquad (8.16)$$

8.3.3.1 Hybrid Particle Swarm Optimization K-Means (HPSO-K) Algorithm

HPSO-K is the integration of PSO with K-means (Kennedy 2011). Used to cluster the medical data, the PSO is a swarm intelligence technique designed by Kennedy and Ebherat in 1995. It is initialized with a swarm of particles. Each particle in the swarm represents a feasible solution. Initially, all the particles will be located in their current position. For each iteration, the particles move toward the global best position, where each particle is driven by its own velocity. Thus, the particles try to reach the global best position of the swarm. When there is no more improvement in the fitness value, the PSO stops and returns. Cluster centroid obtained from HPSO is used as input in K-means algorithm.

K-means clustering algorithm works as follows: At each iteration, the similarity is found between medical data and optimal cluster centroid. The medical data will fall into a cluster when the similarity measure for the cluster is high.

At the end of each iteration, centroid value is computed as ratio of sum of attributes of health data in a cluster to the number of health data in that cluster. Equation (8.17) represents the calculation of centroid.

$$c_i \leftarrow \sum_{i=1}^{|n_i|} \sum_{j=1}^{|dim|} D_{P_j} \tag{8.17}$$

The K-means algorithm is a partitioning-based algorithm, which takes an initial centroid randomly. The probability of forming outliers is high and also as the iteration exceeds, the model is subjected to overfit. But the proposed HPSO-K algorithm, which is the integration of nature-inspired PSO algorithm and partitioning K-means algorithm, tends to overcome the problem of outlier formation and overfitting. Table 8.1 represents the comparison of proposed HPSO-K with K-means.

Representation of Particles in HPSO
1. *Size of swarm*: Swarm represents the number of particles. The number of dimensions of each particle is the number of clusters. In the proposed HPSO,

Table 8.1 Comparison of HPSO-K and K-means.

S.No	Characteristics	HPSO-K	K-means
1	Input	"N" number of particles, each representing cluster centroid	K centroid, where centroids are randomly chosen
2	Output	Optimal centroid and data assigned to each cluster	Data assigned to each cluster
3	Measure of similarity	High	Low
4	Similarity metric	Cosine similarity	Euclidean distance
5	Fitness function	Average of distances of datasets fall into each centroid to the total number of clusters	—
6	Quantization error	Lower	Higher
7	Intra-cluster distance	Minimum between datasets within a cluster	Maximum than HPSO-K
8	Inter-cluster distance	Maximum between one centroid and other centroids	Minimum than HPSO-K
9	Convergence	Fast	Slow
10	Formation of outlier	No	Yes
11	Proximity	Maximum	Minimum
12	Scalability	Yes	No

swarm represents the cluster centroid shown in Eq. (8.18). Let the number of particles and dimensions be represented as $|N_p|$ and $|N_d|$, respectively.

$$\text{swarm}_{|N_p|*|N_d|} \leftarrow \begin{bmatrix} D_{Pa_{11}} & D_{Pa_{12}} & \cdots & D_{Pa_{1|N_d|}} \\ D_{Pa_{21}} & D_{Pa_{21}} & \cdots & D_{Pa_{2|N_d|}} \\ \cdots & \cdots & \cdots & \cdots \\ D_{Pa_{|N_p|1}} & D_{Pa_{|N_p|2}} & \cdots & D_{Pa_{|N_p||N_d|}} \end{bmatrix} \quad (8.18)$$

where each $D_{Pa_{ij}} \leftarrow \{s_1, s_2, \ldots, s_n\}$.

2. *Velocity*: Initially, for all the particles, velocity is initialized randomly. Equation (8.19) represents the velocity of the swarm:

$$V_{|N_p||N_d|} \leftarrow \begin{bmatrix} v_{11} & v_{12} & \cdots & v_{1|N_d|} \\ v_{21} & v_{22} & \cdots & v_{2|N_d|} \\ \cdots & \cdots & \cdots & \cdots \\ v_{|N_p|1} & v_{|N_p|2} & \cdots & v_{|N_p||N_d|} \end{bmatrix} \quad (8.19)$$

where the size of v_{ij} is equivalent to $D_{P_{ij}}$.

3. *Personal best position (PBestPos)*: As iteration proceeds, each particle will have its new best position it had ever reached. Equation 8.20 represents the PBestPos of the swarm:

$$\text{PBestPos}_{|N_p|*|N_d|} \leftarrow \begin{bmatrix} D_{Pa_{11}} & D_{Pa_{12}} & \cdots & D_{Pa_{1|N_d|}} \\ D_{Pa_{21}} & D_{Pa_{21}} & \cdots & D_{Pa_{2|N_d|}} \\ \cdots & \cdots & \cdots & \cdots \\ D_{Pa_{|N_p|1}} & D_{Pa_{|N_p|2}} & \cdots & D_{Pa_{|N_p||N_d|}} \end{bmatrix} \quad (8.20)$$

4. *Personal best (PBest)*: For each particle, PBest is represented as the fitness of corresponding Personal Best Position. Equation (8.21) represents the PBest for all particles in the swarm.

$$\text{PBest}_{|N_p|*} \leftarrow \begin{bmatrix} f(Pa_1) \\ f(Pa_2) \\ \cdots \\ f(Pa_{|N_p|}) \end{bmatrix} \quad (8.21)$$

5. *Global best position (GBestPos)*: For the entire swarm, there will be only one GBestPos. Equation (8.22) represents the GBestPos for the swarm:

$$\text{GBestPos}_{\text{swarm}} \leftarrow \begin{bmatrix} D_{Pa_{k1}} & D_{Pa_{k2}} & \cdots & D_{Pa_{k|N_d|}} \end{bmatrix} \quad (8.22)$$

6. *Global best (GBest)*: GBest is represented as fitness of corresponding GBestPos. Equation (8.23) represents the GBest for the swarm:

$$\text{GBest}_{\text{swarm}} \leftarrow f(\text{GBestPos}_{\text{swarm}}) \quad (8.23)$$

As mentioned earlier, each particle is driven by its own velocity. The particles in the swarm will move toward the GBestPos. The calculation of velocity and displacement for all particles in the swarm is represented in Eqs. (8.24) and (8.25), respectively.

$$\overrightarrow{v_{Pa_i}(t+1)} \leftarrow \overrightarrow{v_{Pa_i}(t)} + w * \left(\text{rand1} + C1 * \left(\overrightarrow{\text{PBestPos}_{Pa_i}(t)} - \overrightarrow{Pa_i(t)} \right) \right)$$

$$+ w * \left(\text{rand2} + C2 * \left(\overrightarrow{\text{GBestPos}_{\text{swarm}}(t)} - \overrightarrow{Pa_i(t)} \right) \right) \qquad (8.24)$$

$$\overrightarrow{Pa_i(t+1)} \leftarrow \overrightarrow{Pa_i(t)} + \overrightarrow{v_{Pa_i}(t)} \qquad (8.25)$$

Flow of HPSO-K   The flow of HPSO given in Figure 8.4 is as follows:

1. Initiate particles.
2. Compute fitness.
3. Compute PBestPos.
4. Compute GBestPos and global best value.
5. After termination criteria, return GBestPos.
6. Invoke K-means to compute optimal clusters.

Algorithms 1 and 2 implement proposed HPSO-K algorithm for medical data.

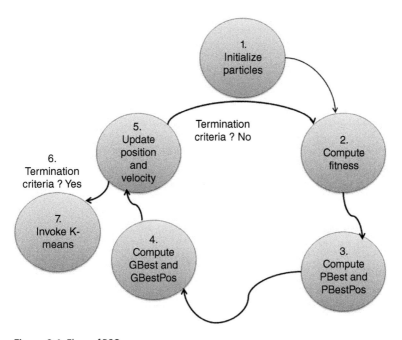

Figure 8.4 Flow of PSO.

Algorithm 1: Hybrid particle swarm optimization for clustering

---

input : Number of particles $\left|N_{\mathrm{p}}\right|$

output: A particle Pa_i which represents the centroid $\left[c_1, c_2, \ldots, c_{|N_d|}\right]$

1 $Pa_i \leftarrow \left\{Pa_1, Pa_2, \ldots, Pa_{|N_p|}\right\}$

2 $c_i \leftarrow (s_1, s_2, \ldots, s_n)$

3 $|N_i| = 0$

4 **foreach** *Particle* $Pa_i \in Pa$ **do**

5     $PBest_{Pa_i} \leftarrow \infty$;

6     $GBest_{swarm} \leftarrow -\infty$;

7     $PBestPos_{Pa_i} \leftarrow \left[\begin{array}{cccc} 0_1 & 0_1 & \ldots & 0_{N|d|} \end{array}\right]$;

8     $GBestPos_{swarm} \leftarrow \left[\begin{array}{cccc} 0_1 & 0_1 & \ldots & 0_{N|d|} \end{array}\right]; v_{Pa_i} \leftarrow rand \in_U [-1, 0]$;

9 **end**

10 **while** *until max iteration* **do**

11   **foreach** *Particle* $Pa_i \in Pa$ **do**

12   **foreach** *Medical data* D_{P_k} **do**

13   **foreach** *cluster centroid* c_k **do**

14                 $SimMat_{jk} \leftarrow S\left(D_{P_j}, c_k\right)$;

15   **end**

16             $index \leftarrow FindMinIndex\left(SimMat_{jk}\right); // N_{index} + +;$

17   **end**

18         $f\left(Pa_i\right) \leftarrow \dfrac{\sum_{index=1}^{|N_d|} \sum_{q=1}^{N_c} s\left(c_{index} \cdot \left(D_{P_q}\right)_{index}\right)}{\dfrac{N_{index}}{|N_d|}}$;

19   **end**

20   **foreach** *particle* $Pa_i \in Pa$ **do**

21   **if** $PBest_{Pa_i} > f\left(Pa_i\right)$ **then**

22             $PBest_{Pa_i} = f\left(Pa_i\right)$;

23             $PBestPos_{Pa_i} \leftarrow \left[\begin{array}{cccc} c_1 & c_2 & \ldots & c_{|N_d|} \end{array}\right]_{Pa_i}$;

24

25   **end**

26     $GBest_{swarm} \leftarrow FindMax\left(PBest_{Pa_i}\right)$;

27     $GBestPos_{swarm} \leftarrow \left[\begin{array}{cccc} c_1 & c_2 & \ldots & c_{|N_d|} \end{array}\right]_{l \leftarrow FindMinIndex\left(PBest_{Pa_i}\right)}$

28   **foreach** *particle* $Pa_i \in Pa$ **do**

29   Calculate Velocity using Equation 8.24

30   Calculate Position using Equation 8.25

31   **end**

32 **end**

33 **return** $GBestPos_{swarm}$;

Algorithm 2: K-means

---

    input : $GBestPos_{swarm} \leftarrow \begin{bmatrix} c_1 & c_2 & \cdots & c_{|N_d|} \end{bmatrix}$
    output: Optimal Assignment of Medical Data to each cluster

1 **while** *until max iteration* **do**
2   **foreach** $c_i \in GBestPos_{swarm}$ **do**
3   **foreach** D_{P_j} **do**
4             $SimMat_{ij} \leftarrow S\left(D_{P_j}, c_i\right)$
5   **end**
6   **foreach** D_{P_j} **do**
7             $index \leftarrow FindMinIndex\left(SimMat_{ij}\right)$
8             $N_{index} + +$
9   **end**
10   **end**
11    $c_i \leftarrow \sum_{i=1}^{|N_{c_i}|} \sum_{j=1}^{|dim|D_{P_i}} D_{P_j}$
12 **end**

8.3.4 Predictor

The HPSO-K algorithm outputs the cluster of healthy, cluster of diabetes, and cluster of other diseases. Predictor is used for predicting whether the healthier patient will subject to diabetes or not based on the observations of that patient. The objective of predictor is to maximize accuracy of prediction represented in Eq. (8.26):

$$\text{Max}(A_M) \leftarrow \frac{TP + TN}{|P|} \tag{8.26}$$

subject to

$$\frac{(FP + FN)}{|P|} < \frac{(TP + TN)}{|P|} \tag{8.27}$$

8.3.4.1 Hidden Markov Model-Based Viterbi Algorithm (HMM-VA)

HMM (Bishop (2006), Wikipedia (2017)), a statistical modeling, is used to forecast whether a healthier person will suffer from diabetes. Figure 8.5 represents the HMM for prediction of diabetes in a healthy patient with two hidden states and five known states. The blood glucose level before and after meals is monitored and the known state is found. For example, if blood glucose level before meals is greater than a threshold and blood glucose level after meals is greater than a threshold, then the known state is S1. Similarly rules had been written for other known states also. Algorithm 3 represents the implementation of HMM-VA for forecasting diabetes.

Algorithm 3: HMM-VA

---

input : Patient P_i

output: $Result_{P_i}$

1 **foreach** $PatientP_i$ **do**

2     $t \leftarrow 0$;

3     $Status_{P_i} \leftarrow PatientMonitor\,()$ **while** $t \le TimePeriod$ **do**

4   **if** $t == 0$ **then**

5           $P\left(ND_{P_i}|Status_{P_i}\right) \leftarrow P\left(Start \to D_{P_i}\right) * P\left(Status_{P_i}|ND_{P_i}\right)$

6           $P\left(ND_{P_i}\right) \leftarrow P\left(ND_{P_i}|Status_{P_i}\right)$

7           $P\left(D_{P_i}|Status_{P_i}\right) \leftarrow P\left(Start \to D_{P_i}\right) * P\left(Status_{P_i}|D_{P_i}\right)$

8           $P\left(D_{P_i}\right) \leftarrow P\left(D_{P_i}|Status_{P_i}\right)$

9   **else**

10          $P\left(ND_{P_i}|ND_{P_i}, Status_{P_i}\right)_t \leftarrow$

11          $P\left(ND_{P_i}\right)_{t-1} * P\left(ND_{P_i}|ND_{P_i}\right) * P\left(Status_{P_i}|ND_{P_i}\right)_{t-1}$

12          $P\left(D_{P_i}|ND_{P_i}, Status_{P_i}\right)_t \leftarrow P\left(D_{P_i}\right)_{t-1} * P\left(D_{P_i}|ND_{P_i}\right) *$ $P\left(Status_{P_i}|D_{P_i}\right)_{t-1}$

13   **if** $P\left(ND_{P_i}|ND_{P_i}, Status_{P_i}\right)_t > P\left(D_{P_i}|ND_{P_i}, Status_{P_i}\right)_t$ **then**

14            $P\left(ND_{P_i}\right)_t \leftarrow P\left(ND_{P_i}|ND_{P_i}, Status_{P_i}\right)_t$

15   **else**

16            $P\left(ND_{P_i}\right)_t \leftarrow P\left(D_{P_i}|ND_{P_i}, Status_{P_i}\right)_t$

17   **end**

18          $P\left(D_{P_i}|D_{P_i}, Status_{P_i}\right)_t \leftarrow P\left(D_{P_i}\right)_{t-1} * P\left(D_{P_i}|D_{P_i}\right) *$ $P\left(Status_{P_i}|D_{P_i}\right)_{t-1}$

19          $P\left(ND_{P_i}|D_{P_i}, Status_{P_i}\right)_t \leftarrow P\left(ND_{P_i}\right)_{t-1} * P\left(ND_{P_i}|D_{P_i}\right) *$ $P\left(Status_{P_i}|ND_{P_i}\right)_{t-1}$

20   **if** $P\left(D_{P_i}|D_{P_i}, Status_{P_i}\right)_t > P\left(ND_{P_i}|D_{P_i}, Status_{P_i}\right)_t$ **then**

21            $P\left(D_{P_i}\right)_t \leftarrow P\left(D_{P_i}|D_{P_i}, Status_{P_i}\right)_t$

22   **else**

23            $P\left(D_{P_i}\right)_t \leftarrow P\left(ND_{P_i}|D_{P_i}, Status_{P_i}\right)_t$

24   **end**

25   **if** $P\left(ND_{P_i}\right)_t > P\left(D_{P_i}\right)_t$ **then**

26            $Result_{P_i} \leftarrow D$

27   **else**

28            $Result_{P_i} \leftarrow ND$

29   **end**

30   **end**

31   **end**

32 **end**

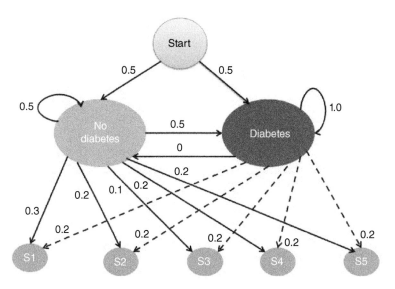

Figure 8.5 HMM model for diabetes prediction.

8.4   Implementation

Lichman (2013) dataset, which has 70 patients and 4 attributes, is used. Date, time, code, and its corresponding value are the attributes present in the dataset. The code is the numerical value that corresponds to observation of the patient.

The security manager aims to provide security to the medical data. It encrypts the data while traveling across network and storing in the cloud. Figure 8.6

```
def test():
        count=0
        start_time = datetime.now().replace(microsecond=0)
        print(start_time)
        print("preparing algorithm for encryption")
        assert (sys.version_info >= (3,4))
        keys = generate_keys()
        priv = keys['privatekey']
        pub = keys['publickey']
        list_patient_details = read_PatientDetails()
        enc_end_time = datetime.now().replace(microsecond=0)
        print("Time taken to prepare for encryption")
        print(enc_end_time - start_time)
        print("preparing for encryption")
        for patient_info in list_patient_details:
                count = count + 1
                patient_info = patient_info. strip ()
                cipher = encrypt(pub, patient_info)
                print(cipher)
```

Figure 8.6 Elgamal encryption.

```
            }
            r1++;
    }       while (r5<res.length);
//calculating fitness function
for(int i=0;i<r;i++)
{
fitness[r1] = ((fitness[r1]+dist[i]/index[i])/k; //particle's fitness
}
} //end of computing fitness for all particles
// choosing pbest
for(int pa=0;pa<num_particles;pa++)
{
        if(fitness[pa] < Pbest[pa]);
        {
                Pbest[pa] = fitness[pa];
                for(int rt=0;rt<K;rt++)
                {
                        for(int hg=0;hg<res_T.getColumnCount();hg++)
                        {
                            PbestPos[pa][rt][hg] =Par[pa][rt][hg];
                        }
                }
        }
}
// choosing Pbest
float invalue = Pbest[0];
for(int pa=1;pa<num_particles;pa++)
{
        if (Pbest[pa]<minvalue)
```

Figure 8.7 HPSO-K cluster.

represents the encryption of medical data by security manager. The medical data is encrypted using the public key of the patient. While storing the data in cloud, proxy server encrypts it using a re-encryption key. The intended healthcare professional decrypts the medical data using a private key.

The design of clusterer involves handling all medical data and groups them as Healthy Patients, Patients with Diabetes, and so on. Figure 8.7 shows the implementation of HPSO-K for finding optimal cluster centroid and assigning medical to optimal centroid. The particles are cluster centroids assigned randomly. At each iteration, fitness value is computed and the particle is drifted by its own velocity to displace from its current position toward GBestPos. The HPSO stops while returning to optimal cluster centroid.

```
                    fp = i;
                    }
          }
//st_NUM[er][1] = start_trans[1][0] * hid_tp_ka[1[choice]; //
probability that a patient(nr+1) is unhealthy
}
else
          {
                    for(int i=0;i<num_hidden_state;i++)
                    {
                              for(int j=0;i<2;j++)
                              {
                                        mid_NUM[i][j] = p[i] *
hid_trans[i][j]*hid_to_ks[i][choice];
                              }
                    }
          float mindf = mid_NUM[a][a];
          p[a] = minuM;
          for(int i=1;i<num_hidden_state;i++)
          {
                    if(mid_NUM[0][i]<minuM)
                    {
                              minuM = mid_NUM[0][1];
                              p[0] = minuM;
                    }
          }
          float minH = mid_NUM[1][0];
          p[1] = minH;
          for(int i=1;i<num_hidden_state;i++)
          {
                    if(mid_NUM[1][j]<minuM)
                    {
                              winH=wid_NUM[1][i];
                              p[1]=winH;
                    }
          }
}
```

Figure 8.8 HMM-VA predictor.

Then K-means is used to find optimal assignment of medical data to cluster centroid.

The design of a predictor based on HMM-VA involves designing probability distribution table. Each patient has two hidden nodes for whether he/she will suffer from diabetes or not. The sum of probability of transition at any level is 1. The probability of healthy and unhealthy at t is found by HMM-VA diabetes predictor. Figure 8.8 represents the design of HMM-VA diabetes predictor.

8.5 Results and Discussions

The simulation is carried out and the results are observed. The SMDAP model is simulated using Python, Java in Eclipse IDE, and MATLAB. The simulation model generates 200–1000 medical data with different values for blood glucose level before meals, blood glucose level after meals, and blood pressure.

8.5.1 Analyzing the Performance of PRA

The performance of any algorithm relies on secure transmission of the message between the parties involved in communication. The proposed SMDAP model encrypts the message twice, which puts additional security over the data. Figures 8.9 and 8.10 represent the original medical data of the patient and re-encrypted medical data, respectively.

8.5.1.1 Time Taken for Encryption

The time taken for encryption of original medical data is represented in Figure 8.11a. When the size of the medical data is increased, the time taken for encryption also increases. Table 8.2 represents the time taken for encryption obtained for various simulation of medical data.

8.5.1.2 Storage Space for Re-encrypted Data

The PRA produces a ciphertext pair for each plaintext message. The storage space required to store the re-encrypted data of medical data is more than that of original data represented in Figure 8.12. This plays a vital role: that intruder cannot recover the original data. Table 8.2 represents the simulation details of storage space for original data and re-encrypted data.

8.5.1.3 Time Take for Decryption

The re-encrypted ciphertext is decrypted with the private key of the healthcare professional. Figure 8.11b represents the time taken for decryption of re-encrypted data over the re-encrypted file size. Table 8.2 represents the simulation details of time taken for decryption.

Name: ABCDF
Age: 32
Sex: male
Blood Glucose level before meals: 5.2 mmol/L
Blood Glucose level after meals: 7.3 mmol/L
Blood Pressure:120/80
Vision: Normal
Location: Madurai;
Any other Symptoms: Headache, Nausea;
Cause: Stress

Figure 8.9 Original medical data.

531050140471270295737243190893311823479499237673963098489791442971461791048 68
278046940585057978929951658056061467553337480120690164228039604171866347465 25
352908927956486261016221378561850694234006825096487783503807939799051578327 61
284634407196146400621437010396921970091880284007495658564538154942572460239 17
398915221504090273426946643409853217346635690384987088576335362132974372112 23
702641187997183339834434074515115482845587458571005293091793835806494194478 45
228557466325811183198686749228570929023525796560852121774072200153048075056 20
355899021252446733960746877042587743835516034486024177754006006990977994595 2
443472722956464626207121175541694698979220508915184815389155585689422056876 54
780832577292937648245721768881206320049535799695141650203561615237316403205 43
683393044407536884634599810379027433273741937797438174678161056928767797773 61
213123981642931920423660817172502582104313928339471615135263061801277779793 12
191504847788767615077907726573362745050202682002058614037478458588341723951 76
153545321095984565933777446276693578428837356627831954260325127610369136347 52
467083232847025099053053305147408269204135682631909316546426078339382061676 61
642746230589052415989352415024656159642367921493639102462353816754174593613 46
239776223479739682597187457285898480688207175327634064735072176124438237339 5
472856331852560837027754259733186131371861444503650404597904341938734379065 63
722454325778112590066888032273461811571214955255187903652698512991553594830 04
431404127452849097522097675261311890597612130575350318950402978874873935360 52
756770698143392431967760324372485633589058814788871262240069521896116143892 21
823986941427744079363536650161854125413174065670083213596623807649929182472 16
522905020791102950108186150729968659884606023397094920584867775952374348281 14
897113434629885997846729388264658797597672006854156383261827456136990567503 19
974018748161587375710658462604352991736634788250355652967326186900894746413 42
555348803005670388668552253271439940915487583328447968479951708698319074827
296562274922696847998749102865231726790577697808489005508520474499991408752 68
467186250001784877314640379427638071218125218675786186047796936942813028522 15
156592871561407365884462996290691040503567601059570860490989250082856888075 20
768870824680219610595886595864065891563118262448187019376047944263076864553 11
275543566093272974446317738145612750822503826833288687892055227342811747738 39
829624499094082922320402677549679233456568418985478428159907792740299159606 39
525115477112826929524275612686596051942133985286764334238744703100436687004 36
368230258319502611123172076505776323457248905841801901565855209229966013010 33
240062412049099068650255698719431573670772906823842293435168630044166424357 39
916161209958249947506342725995773615778326367658551554149492640081291975689

Figure 8.10 Re-encrypted medical data.

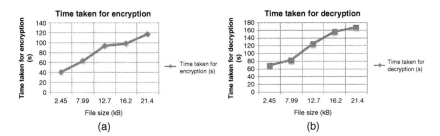

Figure 8.11 Time taken in PRA. (a) Encryption. (b) Decryption.

8.5.2 Analyzing the Performance of HPSO-K Algorithm

The HPSO algorithm is used to obtain optimal cluster centroid, which is taken as input for K-means to produce optimal clusters. The performance of clustering algorithm is measured by intra-cluster distance, inter-cluster distance, and computational complexity.

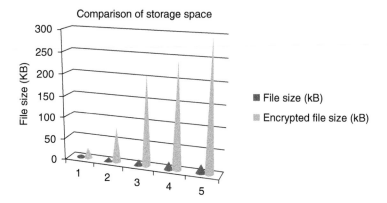

Figure 8.12 Storage space in PRA.

Table 8.2 Performance of PRA.

S. No	File size (kB)	Time taken for encryption (s)	Re-encrypted file size (kB)	Time taken for decryption (s)
1	2.45	41	24.2	69
2	7.99	63	80.3	82
3	12.7	93	208	124
4	16.2	98	244	156
5	21.4	117	296	167

8.5.2.1 Number of Iterations (Generations) to Cluster Patients

The simulation is carried to cluster the patients based on the attributes blood glucose level before and after meals. HPSO-K algorithm finds the global optimal solution rather than local optimum. At each iteration, the position of the particle will be changed and all the particles move toward the global best position. All the particles are driven by a small amount of negative velocity uniformly distributed between $[-1, 0]$. The convergence occurs when the values remain the same for minimum number of iterations. Figure 8.13a,b represents the rates of convergence, when the number of patients is 500 and 1000, respectively.

8.5.2.2 Comparison of Intra-cluster Distance

The intra-cluster distance represents the sum of distances between all the instances of the cluster. It should be minimum for good clustering algorithm. Equation (8.28) represents the calculation of intra-cluster distance:

$$\text{IntraClusterDistance} = \sum_{i=1}^{N_c} \left[\sum_{j=1}^{N_p} d(P_j, C_i) \right]_{\forall P_j \in C_i} \tag{8.28}$$

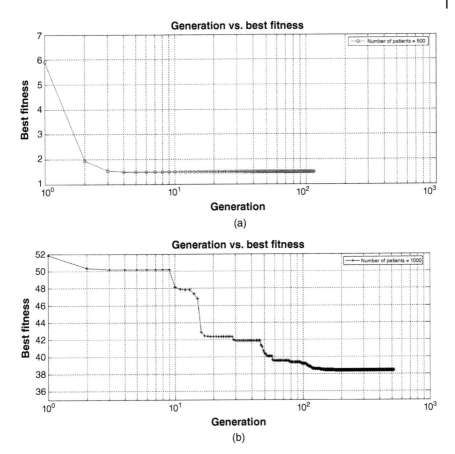

Figure 8.13 Rate of convergence. (a) Number of patients = 500. (b) Number of patients = 1000.

Table 8.3 contains the intra-cluster distance of HPSO-K algorithm for clustering medical data. HPSO-K chooses the optimal cluster centroid and those centroids are used for further clustering. Figure 8.14a represents that the similarity of the patients within the cluster is more than K-means.

8.5.2.3 Comparison of Inter-cluster Distance
The inter-cluster distance represents the sum of the distance between each of the cluster centroid as shown in Eq. (8.29). Inter-cluster distance should be maximum for good clustering algorithm. Figure 8.14b represents that HPSO-K achieves maximum inter-cluster distance than K-means. The reason behind is optimal centroid chosen by HPSO-K, whereas K-means chooses centroids randomly, which leads to poor cluster formation.

$$\text{IntraClusterDistance} = \sum_{i=1}^{N_c} \left[\sum_{j=1}^{N_p} d(P_j, C_i) \right]_{\forall P_j \in C_i} \tag{8.29}$$

Table 8.3 Performance of HPSO-K.

Number of patients	Intra-cluster distance		Inter-cluster distance	
	HPSO-K	K-Means	HPSO-K	K-Means
200	542.345	855.292	7.81	2.8
400	931.21	1683.24	10.04	14.21
600	1334.34	2344.271	16.117	11.09
800	1133.09	4732.24	18.61	13.89
1000	6003.28	8871.32	18.103	13.07

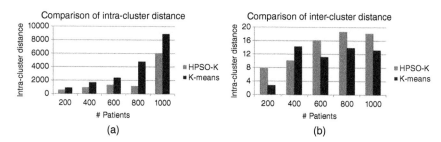

Figure 8.14 Performance of HPSO-K. (a) Intra-cluster distance. (b) Inter-cluster distance.

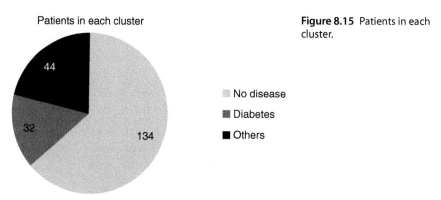

Figure 8.15 Patients in each cluster.

8.5.2.4 Number of Patients in Cluster

The simulation groups the patients into three clusters. Cluster 1 contains persons having no disease. Cluster 2 represents the patients who suffered from diabetes, and Cluster 3 represents patients with other symptoms. Figure 8.15 represents the number of patients in each cluster given by HPSO-K.

8.5.2.5 Comparison of Time Complexity

The time required by the algorithm to complete a task is known as time complexity. The time complexity of K-means and HPSO-K algorithm is represented in Eqs. (8.30) and (8.32), respectively. The time complexity of HPSO-K is less than K-means, since K-means randomly initializes centroid and computes the similarity of the medical data with cluster centroid, which takes more time for convergence. On the other hand, HPSO-K chooses optimal centroid and computes the similarity of the medical data with cluster centroid, which results in faster convergence. Table 8.4 represents the simulation results of time complexity of HPSO-K and K-means:

$$T_{K\text{-Means}} = O(|P| * K * N_t) \tag{8.30}$$

Equation (8.32) represents that the time complexity of HPSO-K algorithm is the maximum time required for HPSO and K-means (Figure 8.16).

$$T_{HPSO-K} = Max\{(O(N_p * N_c * m * N_t)), O(|P| * K * \text{NumIter})\} \tag{8.31}$$

$$T_{HPSO-K} = O(N_p * N_c * m * N_t) \tag{8.32}$$

8.5.3 Analyzing the Performance of HMM-VA

The HMM-VA is used to predict whether a normal person will suffer from diabetes or not. The HMM-VA prediction is based on probabilistic value. The performance of HMM-VA is measured using the error rate.

8.5.3.1 Forecasting Diabetes

The simulation is carried for 200 persons, and, among them, 134 persons are found to be healthy. Figure 8.17 shows the simulation result of HMM-VA for forecasting diabetes. The 134 persons are monitored, and based on the observation of blood glucose level before and after meals, HMM-VA predicted

Table 8.4 Computation of time complexity.

Number of particles	HPSO-K	K-means
10	9 000	60 000
20	18 000	120 000
30	27 000	180 000
40	36 000	240 000
50	45 000	300 000

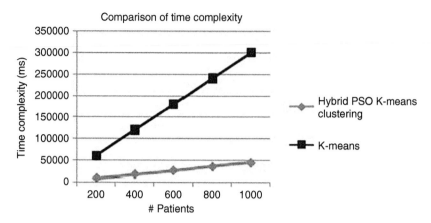

Figure 8.16 Time complexity of HPSO-K and K-means.

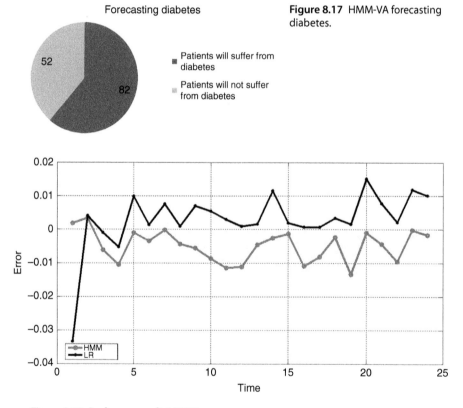

Figure 8.17 HMM-VA forecasting diabetes.

Figure 8.18 Performance of HMM-VA.

that 82 patients are at risk of diabetes. Figure 8.17 shows the simulation result of HMM-VA for forecasting diabetes.

8.5.3.2 Comparison of Error Rate

The error rate is difference between observed value and the predicted value. The proposed HMM-VA is having minimum error rate, since it is a probabilistic approach that does not depend on historical data. On the other hand, linear regression required historical data to build a model. Figure 8.18 represents the error rate of HMM-VA and linear regression.

8.6 Conclusion

The SMDAP model is proposed for securing and analyzing the medical data. The model consists of a security manager, clusterer, and predictor. Security manager, designed using PRA, re-encrypts the medical data while storing in the cloud. The clusterer designed using HPSO-K clusters the medical data as cluster of healthy persons, cluster of persons having diabetes, and cluster of persons having other symptoms. The predictor designed using HMM-VA predicts whether a healthy person will have diabetes or not. The simulation results shown that the SMDAP model has to be applied for pervasive medical data.

Currently this model is developed only to address diabetic-related information. In the future, this model has to be enhanced to predict blood pressure and other chronic disorders. With a better view of medical data, the scalability of SMDAP model could potentially be improved.

Nomenclatures Used

P_i	patient i
s_j	symptom j
Pub_{P_k}	public key of patient k
$\text{Pub}_{\text{HCP}_j}$	public key of healthcare professional
Pri_{P_k}	private key of patient k
$\text{Pri}_{\text{HCP}_j}$	private key of healthcare professional
$\text{RE}_{\text{Pri}_{P_k} \to \text{Pub}_{\text{HCP}_j}}$	re-encryption of patient k and healthcare professional j
$\text{Prime}_{\text{HCP}_j}$	prime number of healthcare professional
α_{HCP_j}	primitive element of healthcare professional
$C^1_{P_i}$	first ciphertext of patient i
$C^2_{P_i}$	second ciphertext of patient i

$\{C_{P_i}^2\}'$	re-encrypted second ciphertext of patient i
$\{C_{P_i}^1\}'$	re-encrypted first ciphertext
Pa_i	particle i
N_c	total number of cluster
n_i	number of instances in cluster i
D_{P_i}	medical data of patient i
c_i	cluster centroid i
$|dim|$	number of dimensions
$D_{\mathrm{Pa}_{ij}}$	dimension j in particle i
v_{ij}	velocity of dimension j in particle i
A_M	accuracy of the model
TP	true positive
TN	true negative
FP	false positive
FN	false negative
$P(D_{P_i})_{t-1}$	probability of patient i will suffer from diabetes at time $t-1$
$P(ND_{P_i})_{t-1}$	probability of patient i will not suffer from diabetes at time $t-1$

Bibliography

Bishop, C.M. (2006). *Pattern Recognition and Machine Learning*. Springer.

Chen, C.-Y. and Ye, F. (2012). Particle swarm optimization algorithm and its application to clustering analysis. In: 2012 Proceedings of 17th Conference on Electrical Power Distribution Networks (EPDC), 789–794. IEEE.

Doukas, C. and Maglogiannis, I. (2012). Bringing IOT and cloud computing towards pervasive healthcare. In: 2012 6th International Conference on Innovative Mobile and Internet Services in Ubiquitous Computing (IMIS), 922–926. IEEE.

Doukas, C., Pliakas, T., and Maglogiannis, I. (2010). Mobile healthcare information management utilizing cloud computing and android OS. In: 2010 Annual International Conference of the IEEE Engineering in Medicine and Biology Society (EMBC), 1037–1040. IEEE.

Hanen, J., Kechaou, Z., and Ayed, M.B. (2016). An enhanced healthcare system in mobile cloud computing environment. *Vietnam Journal of Computer Science* **3** (4): 267–277.

Harb, H.M. and Desuky, A.S. (2014). Feature selection on classification of medical datasets based on particle swarm optimization. *International Journal of Computer Applications* **104** (5): 14–17.

Kawamoto, R., Nazir, A., Kameyama, A. et al. (2013). Hidden Markov model for analyzing time-series health checkup data. *MedInfo* **192**: 491–495.

Kennedy, J. (2011). Particle swarm optimization. In: *Encyclopedia of Machine Learning* (ed. C. Sammut and G.I. Webb), 760–766. Springer.

Lang, B., Wang, J., and Liu, Y. (2017). Achieving flexible and self-contained data protection in cloud computing. *IEEE Access* **5**: 1510–1523.

Lichman, M. (2013). UCI machine learning repository. http://archive.ics.uci.edu/ml (accessed 05 November 2017).

Poorejbari, S. and Vahdat-Nejad, H. (2014). An introduction to cloud-based pervasive healthcare systems. In: Proceedings of the 3rd International Conference on Context-Aware Systems and Applications, 173–178. ICST (Institute for Computer Sciences, Social-Informatics and Telecommunications Engineering).

Stallings, W. (2006). *Cryptography and Network Security: Principles and Practices*. Pearson Education India.

Stolfo, S.J., Salem, M.B., and Keromytis, A.D. (2012). Fog computing: mitigating insider data theft attacks in the cloud. In: 2012 IEEE Symposium on Security and Privacy Workshops (SPW), 125–128. IEEE.

Suresh, A., Harish, K., and Radhika, N. (2015). Particle swarm optimization over back propagation neural network for length of stay prediction. *Procedia Computer Science* **46**: 268–275.

Wikipedia (2017). Hidden Markov model — Wikipedia, the free encyclopedia. https://en.wikipedia.org/w/index.php?title=Hidden_Markov_model&oldid=813449939 (accessed 5 December 2017).

9

Threshold-Based Energy-Efficient Routing Protocol for Critical Data Transmission to Increase Lifetime in Heterogeneous Wireless Body Area Sensor Network

Deepalakshmi Perumalsamy[1] and Navya Venkatamari[2]

[1] Department of CSE, Kalasalingam Academy of Research and Education, Anand Nagar, Krishnankoil 626126, Tamil Nadu, India
[2] Department of ECE, Kalasalingam Academy of Research and Education, Anand Nagar, Krishnankoil 626126, Tamil Nadu, India

9.1   Introduction

Pervasive computing envisions a world of communicating tiny medical devices, namely, body area network (BAN), integrating information and communication technology into people's life and environments, with built-in communication facilities. Pervasive computing technology is used in various healthcare applications, ranging from wearable and embedded sensors that assist in self-care to hospital environments. Patients under the coverage area could utilize the facilities of tracking, configuring, and monitoring of vital signs during daily routine activities.

Pervasive computing tends to play a very important role in wireless body area networks (WBANs). A wide range of biosensors (BS) are commercially available; based on patient's condition specific sensors can be fixed in, on, and around the human body to monitor, store, and transmit the patient's vital signs for further investigation, decisions, and treatment. BS are heterogeneous in nature and the available ones are used for measuring various vital signs such as blood pressure (BP), respiration rate (RR), heart rate (HR), blood glucose level (BSL), body temperature (BT), body mass index (BMI), oxygen saturation (OS), giant speed (GS), etc. Key elements for the WBAN to be embedded in pervasive computing technology are patient's vital signs being monitored and the actual data generation time. Data generated must be handled with proper care to ensure less power consumption during processing and communication with high accuracy of received data, low latency, high reliability, enhanced throughput with efficient bandwidth utilization, synchronization with other WBANs technologies, etc., since all these parameters will have vulnerable effects on person's life and computing techniques used.

Intelligent Pervasive Computing Systems for Smarter Healthcare, First Edition.
Arun Kumar Sangaiah, S.P. Shantharajah, and Padma Theagarajan.
© 2019 John Wiley & Sons, Inc. Published 2019 by John Wiley & Sons, Inc.

Lifestyle of a person can be enhanced in e-healthcare, if disease and syndromes are found prior, before they become life threatening. WBANs use different routing strategies for data forwarding from body sensors to the BS. Sensed data should be reliably transferred to the BS for further investigation. The routing schemes play a very important role in the data transmission. The growing popularity of using pervasive computing technologies in WBANs for health monitoring continues to increase; thus there is a need to minimize unnecessary usage of energy consumption. Connection of sensors to a device to measure one's vital signs condition and their related behaviors is being limited by the battery life due to wireless aspect of WBAN technology.

Short-range wireless communication techniques are used to interconnect wearable health sensors in order to form a BAN. Transferring sensor data to the central server, however, needs long-range wired or wireless communication techniques. Patients use e-health technology that is connected to Internet always, frequently, or quite frequently when there is a need for information gathering about health, diseases, and treatment methods. Thus for a WBAN to operate accurately, it is essential to understand the amount of energy being spent by the device and then use energy-effective schemes to operate a WBAN. A WBAN designer always has a scope for selection of range of alternatives to deal with limited battery by considering many other important metrics.

In this chapter, we modified previous work of SIMPLE (Nadeem et al., 2013) and M-ATTEMPT (Javaid et al., 2013) in WBANs by adding threshold values not only to sensor data being monitored but also to their required energy levels to carry out data transmission to reach the sink. If both the conditions are satisfied, data is forwarded directly to sink or else forwarder-based communication is carried out by finding the nearest neighbor having high residual energy and less distance to sink using the cost function parameter. Therefore, depending upon the threshold values assigned, direct or forwarder-based routing is utilized to make the network more efficient in terms of remaining energy and immediate transmission of sensed information. In this protocol, continuous transmissions are avoided, which will result in minimum energy consumption and thus increasing stability period, overall network lifetime, throughput, and remaining energy in the network.

The rest of the chapter is organized in the following order. Related works on some of the existing routing protocols for WBANs are discussed in Section 9.2. Section 9.3 contains the background and motivation behind our research work and explanation to basic radio model. In Section 9.4, details of our proposed protocol including the system model consisting of four phases are presented. In Section 9.5 analysis on energy consumption of sensor nodes is discussed. Simulation results are discussed in Section 9.6. In Section 9.7 conclusion and future work are stated.

9.2   Related Works

A BS is an analytical device that is affixed in or on the human body to monitor physiological and environmental changes. They are easy to use and they provide real-time information by allowing information computing in a wide range of wearable forms. The amount of energy spent for transmitting data packets in the sensor nodes can be minimized by applying threshold-based techniques. Many energy-efficient protocols in the network layer are proposed to minimize the energy consumption in sensor nodes, during network activities in WBANs. Some of the major issues and challenges in WBANs are aforementioned in Ovesh et al. (2014), Movassaghi et al. (2014), Javed et al. (2014) are energy constraints, body postural movements, heterogeneous nature of sensor nodes, short transmission range, poor computational capabilities, limited storage capacity, less bandwidth, antenna radiation absorption, power consumption of circuitry, and frequent battery replacement. Here, the challenging task is to come up with routing protocols that try to overcome all these issues. Existing routing protocols (Javed et al., 2014; Movassaghi et al., 2014; Ovesh et al., 2014) are classified as quality of service (QoS)-based routing protocols (Razzaque et al., 2011; Khan et al., 2012, 2014; Anand and Vidya Raj, 2017), thermal-aware-based routing protocols (Henry et al., 2013; Javaid et al., 2013), cluster-based routing protocols (Culpepper et al., 2004; Watteyne et al., 2007), cross-layered-based routing protocol (Braem et al., 2006; Bag and Bassiouni, 2009), and postural movement-based routing protocols (Javaid et al., 2013; Kim et al., 2017). Some of the existing routing protocols are explained below.

In this section, we provide a comprehensive coverage of several common communication protocols addressed by pervasive healthcare systems in recent years.

In Ovesh et al. (2014), Ovesh et al. presented a survey on WBAN challenges, its architecture, difference between wireless sensor network and WBANs, MAC protocols and technologies used in WBANs, and various healthcare applications.

In Movassaghi et al. (2014), Movassaghi et al. presented a survey on WBAN challenges, applications, characteristics, different layers, routing algorithms, address allocation, and radio technologies used in WBANs. Comparison with other wireless networks, challenges, and open issues for future and on-going research of WBANs are discussed.

In Javed et al. (2014), Javed et al. presented a comprehensive survey on existing data routing approaches and their classification based on nature and structure along with a critical analysis of each protocol. Architecture of the WBANs, different routing issues, and challenges of WBANs are also discussed.

In Cong Vo (2013), Cong Vo presented a broad overview on the different aspects, such as focused on objectives, characteristics, requirements, challenges, research areas, visions, reasons for failure, recent developments in technologies and societies, classification, programming models used, and context techniques used in pervasive healthcare systems.

In Ni et al. (2015), Ni et al. presented a detailed explanation to smart home technology for elder people to live their life independently. Context characterization and formalized representation are the techniques used to identify different activities performed by the user. Based on the classification of sensors and data processing methods, suitable sensor is selected for the detection of activities. As a scope to future challenge, coexistence problem between the multiple users to be carried out.

In Sarkar and Sinha (2017), Sarkar and Sinha presented an overview on existing works and also comparative analyses on machine learning algorithms used in different aspects of pervasive healthcare applications are explained in detail.

In Uniyal and Raychoudhury (2014), Uniyal and Raychoudhury presented a comprehensive survey on different tools and techniques used in pervasive healthcare related to diseases or disorders mostly attributed to different age groups, like children, elderly, and adults. Several open issues associated with pervasive healthcare research are also discussed.

In Lathies (2013), Lathies discussed a detailed explanation about the pervasive computing technologies, architecture, applications, issues, and challenges related to pervasive healthcare.

In Rastegari et al. (2011), Rastegari et al. developed a context-aware hospital system that analyzes data streams in different spaces such as public spaces, private spaces, and isolated spaces. RFID technology is used to acquire contextual information about the usable objects resources and the staff locations in different parts of the hospital. As a future work, data transmission using different communication technologies are studied.

In Shahriyar et al. (2009), Shahriyar et al. developed an intelligent system for the mobile condition of patient. The system is used for monitoring and gathering the patient's data. Automatic feedback is provided to the patient based on the health condition. Compatibility of the device, for specific disease under serious condition of a patient, should be tested.

In Bastiani and Librelotto (2013), Bastiani and Librelotto presented an architecture for development of pervasive home-care monitoring system to treat dementia patients, in order to reduce the burden of a caregiver, while the patients continues to receive the necessary care. Machine learning modules are used on individual patient profile to differentiate among them with respect to disease and to use in real environments.

In Nadeem et al. (2013), Nadeem et al. proposed a routing algorithm to minimize energy consumption and increase network lifetime. Cost function was used to select an advanced node and send data to the sink. Nodes placed nearer to the sink forwarded data directly to the sink. There was a quick energy depletion of nodes placed near to the sink, as they were over loaded by data that as to be transmitted.

In Javaid et al. (2014), Javaid et al. proposed an extension of their previous work in SIMPLE (Nadeem et al., 2013) by considering mobility of nodes and used linear integer equations to minimize energy consumption of overall network and results showed increased stability period, network lifetime, and throughput of the network.

In Javaid et al. (2013), Javaid et al. proposed a routing algorithm that was thermal- aware senses the hot sensors and transmits the data away from these established paths. Sensors producing high data rates are fixed on less mobile places on the human body. Energy management schemes were used to overcome the disconnection of established paths. An optimization technique such as linear programming model was used to reduce energy consumption of nodes.

In Ahmed et al. (2014), Ahmed et al. proposed a routing protocol that used priority-based route selection mechanism for the transmission of normal and critical data. Multihop delay was overcome by using minimum hop count and energy consumption was overcome by lowering the number of relays and thereby maintains the balance with respect to the energy levels. Time domain and linear programming-based mathematical modeling were used and explained.

In Yousaf et al. (2014a), Yousaf et al. proposed a cooperative-based routing protocol to increase the average packet rate. First, shortest path route was selected and then the cooperation between the nodes was improved. Results showed higher throughput and minimum energy consumption.

In Yousaf et al. (2014b), Yousaf et al. proposed a routing algorithm considering body mobility. Efficient choice of the next node is made by using a minimum hop count metric. Critical data was forwarded, thus reducing the repeated transmissions of similar data, thereby reducing the energy consumption of nodes.

In Chen and Pompili (2011), Chen and Pompili proposed a cross-layer communication protocol by considering together the services of MAC, communication, and scheduling modules. Interference-aware prioritization mechanism is used based on the data content and health condition of patients. Wireless channels were provided for quick services and scheduling of packets based on health condition and data requirement, which leads to less delay and high reliability. As an extension of their proposed work, advanced signal processing techniques for data recovery and real-time vital signs at the receiver can be used to evaluate the performance.

In Khan et al. (2012), proposed a routing mechanism for both in home and hospital environment. Nearby devices were discovered with the help of a routing table that minimizes traffic load of the network and energy consumption and enhances reliability of the network.

In Aminian and Naji (2013), Aminian and Naji proposed a system consisting of wireless relay nodes used for performing multihop routing. Coordinator node forwards the information to the nearest relay node and from there to base station. An emergency alert service was also added to the proposed system. With large users or high contention rate, the improvement on energy consumption can be done by considering the patient's mobility.

In Chung et al. (2012), Chung et al. proposed a bidirectional minimum cost routing protocol, for the hybrid healthcare data transmission in multihop environment. Results showed low wireless data packet and high reliability. Furthermore, QoS was also considered.

In Rafatkhah and Lighvan (2014), Rafatkhah and Lighvan proposed a routing protocol that used a direct path for critical and real-time data and a multihop path for normal data delivery. It was thermal aware and sensed the hotspot path and replaced the established path with the new path. Thus, multimodal and mobility support minimized the energy consumption and overcame the problem of disconnection of the path. As an extension to this work, data association algorithms and dedicated sensors could be developed to increase the quality of data.

In Jovanov et al. (2005), Jovanov et al. proposed a multitier telemedicine system that performed analysis on real-time sensors data for home-based patient rehabilitation, remotely provided suggestions to the user, and generated alerts based on the patient's condition, activity being performed, and surrounding conditions. All recorded information were transferred to a medical server. Further improvement can be made in the system design, configuration and customization of device, integration of various components, security, and privacy.

In Otto et al. (2006), Otto et al. proposed a system consisting of sensors that measured a patient's heart rate and movement activity and periodically uploaded time-stamped information to the home server. Simulation results showed the increased packet delivery ratio and throughput. Further improvement could be performed on accurate step recognition and user activity conditions.

In Crilly and Muthukkumarasamy (2010), Crilly and Muthukkumarasamy proposed a routing protocol during patient's mobility. A smartphone was used to store and perform initial data processing of vital signs measurements and sending of emergency alerts to a central data server. Due to this there was a large memory storage leading to increase in device cost.

In Khan et al. (2014), Khan et al. proposed a framework that used a hybrid communication mode that helped to increase privacy and save energy consumption. The routing protocol consists of two components, namely, MAC and network layer, and three algorithms consisting of neighbor table, routing table, and path selector tables. The two modules' performance was tested on a real hospital scenario and showed good performance in terms of packets received at the sink, less packets dropped, and lower network traffic.

In Iftikhar et al. (2014), Iftikhar et al. developed a Markov chain, a closed form expression, and extracted the various parameters related to QoS such as queue length, queue delay, bandwidth, packet loss rate, and throughput for different kinds of traffic. Queuing models with polling schemes could be developed as a future work.

In Razzaque et al. (2011), Razzaque et al. used lexicographic optimization technique in which the location information and the residual energy levels were considered as important metrics. Individual modules for delay and reliability-critical packets were built separately and they worked in coordination to provide the required service. System design lacked the knowledge of modification of tuning parameters to select the perfect values to adjust to different circumstances.

9.3 Proposed Protocol: Threshold-Based Energy-Efficient Routing Protocol for Critical Data Transmission (EERPCDT)

9.3.1 Background and Motivation

In recent years, in many developed countries there is a lot of innovation in pervasive healthcare as it is an upcoming technology that helps to provide real-time monitoring of patients data by using different BS, specialized WBAN routing protocols, and intelligent context-aware applications. Pervasive healthcare applications consists of tiny and smart devices called BS that are capable of sensing the information, processing the data, and communicate the data to the nearby service provider if any change occurs in the health status of a monitored patient. Pervasive healthcare has been a great benefit in continuously monitoring the disabled, older, and weak patients, whose vital signs keep varying based on activity and the stress that they undergo during their routine activities.

BS can be connected wired or wirelessly to monitor health condition but has to deal with technical challenges like mobility support, less energy consumption, increased stability, and reliability. To enhance the lifetime of the network, more importance should be given to energy-efficient parameters. The life of a BS is dependent on the type of activity it performs, and it may operate for days or weeks without user's interference. It is very much important to impose the limitations not only on communication but also on the data being transferred. Thus, making the communication to happen for a cause rather than forwarding the actual data during continuous operation.

In case of emergency situations, immediate response is required by the patient. Thus, the significance of any WBAN could be accurate and immediate transmission of data with minimum energy consumption in mind. Therefore, depending upon the situation, single hop or multihop communication is carried out to make WBAN more efficient. The main objective behind this research is to carefully utilize single hop path and multihop path for continuous transmission of data with less energy consumption by sensor nodes as it is one of the issue in pervasive healthcare application. In SIMPLE (Nadeem et al., 2013) and M-ATTEMPT (Javaid et al., 2013) routing algorithms, single hop and multihop paths are used for regular data transmission to the sink, respectively. Thus, regular and repeated data transmission increases the workload and energy consumption of forwarding sensor nodes. This motivated us to come up with an energy-efficient routing algorithm for a pervasive healthcare system that has the tendency to avoid unnecessary data transmissions so that stability period, throughput, and network lifetime can be extended.

Here we make use of threshold-based data transmission technique. Each time the sensor node senses the information, comparison of the sensed value with the assigned threshold value is done. Data transmission happens only if variations are observed and thereby avoiding unnecessary transmissions. A sink, which is placed at the center of the human body, collects critical information from all sensor nodes and transmits to the BS. In case, if sensor node does not satisfy the energy condition to transmit critical data to the sink, data is then transmitted by multihop transmission to the sink. If energy condition is satisfied and particular sensor nodes energy is decreasing below the threshold value, then single hop/direct transmission takes place. Efficient selection of transmission distance plays a significant role in the selection of the next hop in case of WBANs. This kind of dynamic routing technique minimizes energy consumption as a sensor node selects less distant next hop for further data forwarding by using the cost function metric in case of finding nearest neighbors to perform multihop communication.

In our proposed work, we try to reduce energy consumption and improve throughput at the sink. Our contribution in this new scheme includes achieving longer stability period to pervasive healthcare applications, which contributes to high throughput and making sensor nodes to be alive for longer duration of time as the algorithm that we developed here try to minimize energy consumption at sensor technology level and also at communication network level.

9.3.2 Basic Communication Radio Model

Different radio models were proposed in the number of literature survey papers (Javaid et al., 2013, 2014; Nadeem et al., 2013; Ahmed et al., 2014; Yousaf et al., 2014a,b). The first-order linear equations for computational radio model are

Table 9.1 Energy parameters of transceivers used in WBAN.

Parameter	nRF2401A	CC2420	Unit
DC (tx)	10.5	17.4	mA
DC (rx)	18	19.7	mA
Supply voltage (min)	1.9	2.1	V
E_{txelect}	16.7	96.9	nJ/bit
E_{rxelect}	36.1	172.8	nJ/bit
e_{amp}	1.97	0.0271	nJ/bit/mn

given below (Javaid et al., 2014):

$$E_{\text{tx}}(L, D) = E_{\text{txelect}} * L + e_{\text{amp}} * L * D^2 \tag{9.1}$$

$$E_{\text{rxelect}}(L) = E_{\text{txelect}} * L \tag{9.2}$$

where E_{tx} and E_{rx} are the energies absorbed by the transmitting node and receiving node during the data communication process. E_{txelect} and E_{rxelect} are the energies needed to run the electronic circuit of transmitter and receiver, respectively. The amount of energy needed by the amplifier circuitry is e_{amp}, size of the packet is L, and the distance between transmitting node and receiving node is D.

In WBANs, during the data communication process between the transmitting and receiving nodes, the radio signals undergo attenuation due to interferences. In radio model, n is the path loss coefficient and its value depends on the propagating medium. In free space, its value is considered as two and varies in line of sight (LOS) communication from 3 to 4 and 5 to 7.4 for non-line of sight (N-LOS) communication. The energy consumption expression becomes as follows:

$$E_{\text{tx}}(L, D, n) = E_{\text{txelect}} * L + e_{\text{amp}} * L * n * D^n \tag{9.3}$$

In pervasive healthcare system, vital parameters are monitored using various sensors and thus form a WBAN. Transceivers, commonly used in WBAN technology for communication, are Nordic nRF 2401A and Chipcon CC2420 and their related parameters are given in Table 9.1.

9.4 System Model

In our proposed work, eight sensor nodes are placed at fixed locations, a sink is placed at the center position of the human body, and connection to BS is treated

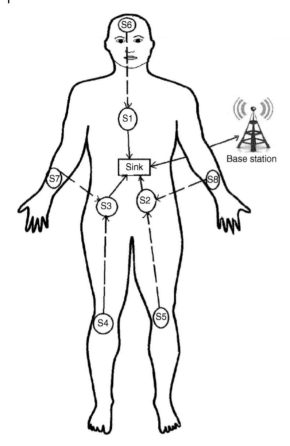

Figure 9.1 Sensor nodes placement on the human body.

as an external network. Figure 9.1 shows placement of eight sensor nodes and a sink on the human body. Proposed work follows three phases, namely, initialization, routing, and data transmission.

9.4.1 Initialization Phase

Sensor nodes that act as BS are having different computational demands in different situations and are equipped with different resources regarding the data rate, reliability, and energy consumption. They are heterogeneous and deployed to record patient's physiological parameters and their activities in a regular and continuous manner. Sink forwards the hello information packet to all the sensor nodes about its position and placement on the human body. On receiving this packet, sensor node forwards information packet consisting of node identification, location of node, threshold information, and energy level information. On receiving these packets, all the nodes become aware of their neighboring sensor nodes' location and sink.

Normal ranges of various biomedical sensors – BP, 120/80 mmhg; BT, 36.5–37 °C; HR, 60–100 bpm; RR at rest, 12–16 breaths/min; EEG (gamma wave frequency), 30–80 Hz; EMG, <50 to 30 mv; PO, 90–100%; BSL (before meal and after meal), 4–7 mmol/l and 5–9 mmol/l – are adopted from different literature (Chen and Pompili, 2011) as well as after medical consultation. Normal range may be different for some (age/gender) but it is acceptable by majority of population.

9.4.2 Routing Phase Selection of Forwarder Node

Deployed sensor nodes on human body have limited energy constraints. Battery power of sensor nodes should be properly utilized during the communication for enhancing network lifetime. To conserve energy, we applied forwarder-based routing scheme using cost function metric, which is dependent on both distance between the nodes and residual energy of a node. Sink is aware of all the sensor nodes information for any further communication. It computes and sends cost function values for each and every node. Based on this value, each sensor node takes decision whether to become a forwarder node or not in each and every round. If i is a sensor node's ID and i ranging from $i = 1, 2, 3, 4, 5, 6, 7, 8$, $D(i)$ refers to the distance between the sensor nodes i and sink and RE(i) refers to the residual energy of the sensor node. Then CF_{S_i}, cost function, is computed by the expression given as follows:

$$CF_{S_i} = \frac{D(i)}{RE(i)} \forall i \in S_i \tag{9.4}$$

A sensor node with least cost function is selected as a forwarder node. The forwarder node ID is sent to the remaining nodes. All the neighboring nodes try to transmit data to this forwarder node. Forwarder node is selected, as maximum residual energy and minimum distance to the sink and from their aggregated data is transmuted to the sink. Sensor nodes which are very closer to the sink send their data directly.

9.4.3 Scheduling Phase

In order to avoid collisions between the nodes during transmission, time schedules are set. Based on this time slots, data transmission takes place. Once the forwarder node is selected, time division multiple access (TDMA) slots are assigned by the sink to the forwarder node as well as to other nodes. Forwarder node then assigns slots to its neighbor nodes for data transmission. Thus, the neighboring nodes transfer sensed data in their scheduled time slots and from there the aggregated data is forwarded to the sink. Node remains in idle mode when it has no data to send and in wake mode during the transmission time.

9.4.4 Data Transmission Phase

In case of emergency situation, immediate response is required by the patient when using pervasive healthcare system. Thus the significance of our protocol lies on quick transmission of data and having more reliability for data being transmitted, keeping minimum energy consumption in mind. For each and every sensor node, we assign certain threshold value and energy level required for data transmission. These values are fixed and are being monitored for a continuous period. Data transmission takes place only when there is a variation in the sensed value compared with the stored threshold value and also if the energy of a sensor node is decreasing below the threshold value. These values act as a warning signal or an alert data to a doctor who is monitoring a particular patient. This strategy saves the energy consumption of the overall network and reduces the communication overload.

If a node transmits data to the sink directly, then its transmission energy should be greater than threshold energy, or else, it performs multihop communication to transmit data to the sink. Therefore, depending upon the threshold values, single hop or multihop paths are used to make the network more efficient in terms of energy efficiency and immediate transmission of sensed data. This results in minimum energy consumption, increase in stability period, and also increase in the total network lifetime.

9.5 Analysis of Energy Consumption

In this section, we introduce set of linear equations for single hop communication and multihop data communication. Amount of energy consumed by different sensor nodes in WBAN varies during communication process. Energy absorbed in single hop data communication process is given by the equation as Javaid et al. (2014):

$$E_{sh} = E_{tx} \tag{9.5}$$

where E_{tx} is the transmitting node energy, given by the equation as

$$E_{tx} = (e_{amp} + E_{txelect}) * L * D^2 \tag{9.6}$$

The amount of energy absorbed by the amplifier is e_{amp} and $E_{txelect}$ is the energy absorbed during transmission by the electronic circuit. L is the packet size, and D corresponds to the distance between the transmitting and receiving nodes.

Energy absorbed by nodes in multihop data communication process is given by the equation as

$$E_{mh} = L * h \left[E_{tx} + (E_{da} + E_{rx}) * \left(\frac{(h-1)}{h} \right) \right] \tag{9.7}$$

In (9.7), h denotes number of hops and energy absorbed in data aggregation process is denoted by E_{da}. Furthermore, we assume that transmission energy to be equal to reception energy (E_{rx}) and is given by the expression as

$$E_{tx} = E_{rx} \tag{9.8}$$

9.6 Simulation Results and Discussions

Simulations are conducted in MATLAB under static condition, to evaluate and compare the performance of proposed work with existing SIMPLE (Nadeem et al., 2013) and M-ATTEMPT (Javaid et al., 2013) routing algorithm in terms of network lifetime defined as the network operation being performed till the death of the last node, throughput, stability period, residual energy with reference to the number of iterations(r). Initial energy for each sensor node is 0.2 J. Eight sensor nodes are placed on the front side of the body at different locations. Sensor nodes locations followed in this experiment are S1 (0.3, 0.1), S2 (0.5, 0.3), S3 (0.3, 0.55), S4 (0.5, 0.55), S5 (0.7, 0.8), S6 (0.1, 0.8), S7 (0.3, 0.75), and S8 (0.4, 0.9), and the sink is placed at (0.4, 0.9) m in the x and y directions, respectively. The sink is placed at the center of the human body to receive maximum data efficiently from all its neighboring nodes. Different performance parameters are compared and discussed in the following subsections. Simulation parameters as stated in Table 9.1 for transceiver nRF2401A is utilized here, and other parameters used are presented in Table 9.2.

9.6.1 Network Lifetime and Stability Period

Figure 9.2 shows the comparison of network lifetime and stability period of the proposed TEERPCDT compared with SIMPLE and ATTEMPT routing protocols, respectively. Here, the first node dies at 5900th round, whereas for ATTEMPT is at 2100th and for SIMPLE routing protocol is at 2400th round,

Table 9.2 Simulation parameters for proposed work.

Parameter used	Value	Units
d_0	0.1	m
E_{th}	0.2	J
Packet size (L)	4000	bits
f	2.4	GHz
Sink	(0.4, 0.9)	m
Area	(1, 1.4)	m

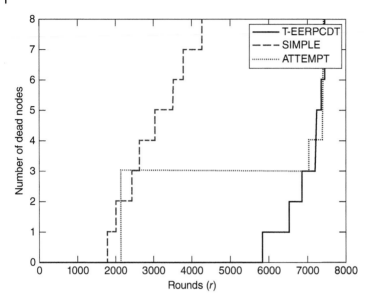

Figure 9.2 Analysis of network lifetime and stability period.

respectively. Sensor nodes are alive for longer duration of time as the number of iterations increases, in our proposed work. This is because redundant data packet transmissions are avoided due to threshold-based approach applied on each sensor nodes, which results in minimum energy consumption. From the figure above, we could observe that there is an increased stability period and network lifetime compared to SIMPLE and ATTEMPT, respectively.

9.6.2 Residual Energy

The average energy consumption of network in each round is shown in Figure 9.3. Our proposed protocol, TEERPCDT, uses cost function metric for the selection of the next forwarder node for multihop communication; nodes which are away from the sink and not able to transfer data to the sink will forward the data with the support of a forwarder node. Appropriate selection of forwarder node in each round helps to save energy and helps in load balancing over sensor nodes. Simulation results show that our algorithm dissipates less energy and have more residual energy. As more number of

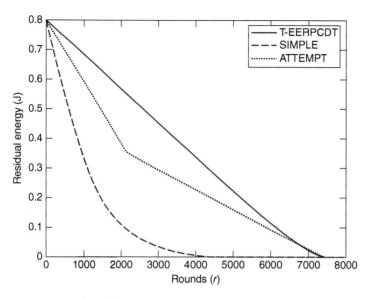

Figure 9.3 Analysis of averaged residual energy.

nodes has enough energy with them, they can transfer more data packets to the sink. Figure 9.3 depicts that the proposed work performs better than existing SIMPLE and ATTEMPT protocols in terms of minimum energy consumption of nodes. As mentioned earlier, data transmission in our proposed work occurs only when there is a variation in the sensed values compared to threshold values. Due to this, there is a slow decrease in average residual energy of the network as the number of rounds increases.

9.6.3 Throughput

The proposed work achieves increased throughput as compared to SIMPLE and ATTEMPT protocols, as shown in Figure 9.4. The number of packets sent to the sink depends on the number of alive nodes in the network. More alive nodes (as shown in Figure 9.2) send more data packets to the sink, which enhances the overall throughput of the network. Longer stability period signifies increase in throughput of the overall network. The network lifetime of proposed work is more compared to SIMPLE and ATTEMPT routing algorithms, respectively. Thus the sink receives more number of packets successfully as shown in Figure 9.4.

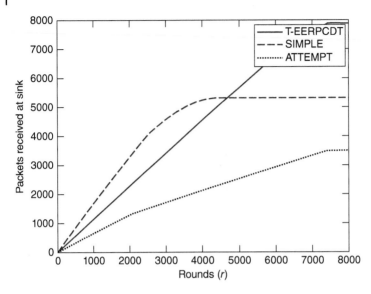

Figure 9.4 Analysis of averaged throughput.

9.7 Conclusion and Future Work

In this chapter, we proposed routing protocol for a WBAN that supports threshold-based approach for data transmission of sensor nodes and during data communication cost metric is used for the selection of forwarder node. The proposed cost metric depends on node's residual energy and the distance between two communicating nodes in LOS. Node with minimum cost metric value is chosen to be a forwarder node. Other sensor nodes try to transmit their critical data to this forwarding node only if the energy condition is satisfied. In this work, we first apply threshold-based approach to all the sensor nodes and analyze the required energy for the transmission of the particular data by each node during the communication. Continuous transmissions are avoided, which results in low energy absorption, and nodes are monitored for continuous time interval that supports pervasive healthcare system. Simulation results show that our proposed routing protocol increases the lifetime and stability period of the overall network, residual energy, and throughput compared to the existing protocols SIMPLE and M-ATTEMPT. Future directions can focus on adding a learning module that can be used to adapt the inference rules of the system according to which the real-time sensor data can be studied and used for classification based on the data being monitored more frequently during emergency conditions.

Bibliography

Ahmed, A., Javaid, N., Qasim, U. et al. (2014). RE-ATTEMPT: a new energy efficient routing protocol for wireless body area sensor networks. *International Journal of Distributed Sensor Networks* **2014**: Article ID 464010.

Aminian, M. and Naji, H.R. (2013). A hospital healthcare monitoring system using WSNs. *Journal of Health & Medical Informatics (JHMI)* **4** (2). https://doi.org/10 .4172/2157-7420.1000121.

Anand, K.M. and Vidya Raj, C. (2017). A comprehensive survey of QoS-aware routing protocols in wireless body area networks. *International Journal of Advanced Research in Computer and Communication Engineering* **6** (1). https://doi.org/10.17148/IJARCCE.2017.6132.

Bag, A. and Bassiouni, M.A. (2009). Biocomm—a cross-layer medium access control (MAC) and routing protocol co-design for biomedical sensor networks. *International Journal of Parallel, Emergent and Distributed Systems* **24** (1): 85–103.

Bastiani, E. and Librelotto, G.R. (2013). Pervasive computing applied to the care of patients with dementia in homecare environments. *International Journal of UbiComp (IJU)* **4** (3). https://doi.org/10.5121/iju.2013.4301.

Braem, B., Latre, B., Moerman, I. et al. (2006). The wireless autonomous spanning tree protocol for multihop wireless body area networks. In: Proceedings of 3rd Annual International IEEE Conference on Mobile and Ubiquitous Systems: Networking and Services, San Jose, CA, USA (17–21 July 2006), 1–8.

Chen, B. and Pompili, D. (2011). Transmission of patient vital signs using WBANs. *Mobile Networking Application* **16**: 663–682.

Chung, W.-Y., An, S.-M., and Lee, S.-C. (2012). Real time multi-hop routing protocol for healthcare system based on WSN. In: 14th International Meeting on Chemical Sensors (IMCS). https://doi.org/10.5162/IMCS2012/P1.9.30.

Cong Vo, C. (2013) A Survey and Taxonomy of Pervasive Computing Research.

Crilly, P. and Muthukkumarasamy, V. (2010). Using smart phones and body sensors to deliver pervasive mobile personal healthcare. 6th International Conference on Intelligent Sensors, Sensor Networks and Information Processing (ISSNIP), ISSNIP 2010.

Culpepper, B.J., Dung, L., and Moh, M. (2004). Design and analysis of Hybrid Indirect Transmissions (HIT) for data gathering in wireless micro sensor networks. *ACM SIGMOBILE Mobile Computing and Communications Review* **8** (1): 61–83.

Henry, C., Oey, W., and Moh, S. (2013). A survey on temperature-aware routing protocols in wireless body sensor networks. *Sensors* **13** (8): 9860–9877. https://doi.org/10.3390/s130809860.

Iftikhar, M., Al Elaiwi, N., and Aksoy, M.S. (2014). Performance analysis of priority queue model for low power WBANs. *Procedia Computer Science* **34**:

518–525. The 2nd International Workshop on Communication s and Sensor Networks (ComSense-2014). 1877-0509@2014 published by Elsevier Ltd.

Javaid, N., Abbas, Z., Fareed, M.S. et al. (2013). M-ATTEMPT: a new energy efficient routing protocol for wireless body area sensor networks. *Procedia Computer Science* **19**: 224–231. The 4th International Conference of Ambient Systems, Networks and Technologies (ANT 2013).

Javaid, N., Ahmad, A., Nadeem, Q. et al. (2014). iM-SIMPLE: iMproved stable increased-throughput multi-hop link efficient routing protocol for Wireless Body Area Networks. *Computers in Human Behavior*. https://doi.org/10.1016/j .chb.2014.10.005.

Javed, I.B., Abdul, H.A., Mohammad, H.A., and Abdul, W.K. (2014). A survey of routing protocols in wireless body area network. *Journal Sensors*. https://doi .org/10.3390/s140101322.

Jovanov, E., Milenkovic, A., Otto, C., and de Groen, P.C. (2005). A wireless body area network of intelligent motion sensors for computer assisted physical rehabilitation. *Journal of Neuro Engineering and Rehabilitation* **2** (1): 6.

Khan, Z., Aslam, N., Sivakumar, S., and Phillips, W. (2012). Energy-aware peering routing protocol for indoor hospital body area network communication. *Procedia Computer Science* **10**: 188–196.

Khan, Z.A., Sivakumar, S., Philips, W., and Robertson, B. (2014). ZEQOS: a new energy and QoS-aware routing protocol for communication of sensor devices in healthcare system. *International Journal of Distributed Sensor Networks* **2014**: Article ID 627689, 18 p.

Kim, B.-S., Kim, K.H., and Kim, K.-I. (2017). A survey on mobility support in wireless body area networks. *Sensors* **17** (4): 797. https://doi.org/10.3390/ s17040797. Multidisciplinary Digital Publishing Institute. www.mdpi.com/ journal/sensors.

Lathies, B.T. (2013). Pervasive computing issues, challenges and applications. *International Journal of Engineering and Computer Science* **2** (12): 3337–3339.

Movassaghi, S., Abolhasan, M., Lipman, J. et al. (2014). Wireless Body Area Networks: A Survey, IEEE Communications Surveys & Tutorials, 1553-877X/13/2013.

Nadeem, Q., Javaid, N., Mohammad, S.N., and Khan, M.Y. (2013). SIMPLE: stable increased-throughput multi-hop protocol for link efficiency in wireless body area networks. In: 8th International Conference on Broadband and Wireless Computing, Communication and Applications (BWCCA) (28–30 October 2013), 14000642. https://doi.org/10.1109/BWCCA.2013.42.

Ni, Q., Belén, A., Hernando, G., and de la Cruz, I.P. (2015). The Elderly's independent living in smart homes: a characterization of activities and sensing infrastructure survey to facilitate services development. *Sensors* **15**: 11312–11362. https://doi.org/10.3390/s150511312.

Otto, C.A., Jovanov, E., and Milenkovic, A. (2006). A WBAN-based system for health monitoring at home. In: 3rd IEEE/EMBS International Summer School on Medical Devices and Biosensors, 20–23.

Ovesh, S.M., Sharma, A.K., Khandelwal, S., and Salim, S.F.M. (2014). A survey on wireless body area network. *IJSRD - International Journal for Scientific Research and Development* **2** (09). ISSN (online): 2321-0613.

Rafatkhah, O. and Lighvan, M.Z. (2014). M^2E^2: a novel multi-hop routing protocol for wireless body sensor networks. *International Journal of Computer Networks and Communication Security* **2** (8): 260–267.

Rastegari, E., Rahmani, A., and Setayeshi, S. (2011). Pervasive computing in healthcare systems. *International Journal of Computer, Electrical, Automation, Control and Information Engineering* **5** (11): 1166–1172.

Razzaque, A., Hong, C.S., and Lee, S. (2011). Data-centric multi-objective QOS-aware routing protocol for body sensor networks. *Sensors* **11**: 917–937. https://doi.org/10.3390/s110100917.

Sarkar, P. and Sinha, D. (2017). Application on pervasive computing in healthcare–a review. *Indian Journal of Science and Technology* **10** (3). https://doi.org/10.17485/ijst/2017/v10i3/110619.

Shahriyar, R., Bari, F., Kundu, G. et al. (2009). Intelligent mobile health monitoring system. *IMHMS - International Journal of Control and Automation* **2** (3): 5–12.

Uniyal, D. and Raychoudhury, V. (2014). Pervasive healthcare-a comprehensive survey of tools and techniques. arXiv:2014, preprint arXiv:1411.1821.

Watteyne, T., Augé-Blum, I., Dohler, M., and Barthel, D. (2007). Anybody: a self-organization protocol for body area networks. In: Proceedings of the ICST 2nd International Conference on Body Area Networks (11-13 June 2007), 06.

Yousaf, S., Ahmed, S., Akbar, M. et al. (2014a). Co-CEStat: cooperative critical data transmission in emergency in static Wireless Body Area Network. In: 9th International Conference on Broadband and Wireless Computing, Communication and Applications (BWCCA) (November 2014), 127–132. https://doi.org/10.1109/BWCCA.2014.54.

Yousaf, S., Akbar, M., Javaid, N. et al. (2014b). CEMob: critical data transmission in emergency with mobility support in WBANs. In: 2014 IEEE 28th International Conference on Advanced Information Networking and Applications. https://doi.org/10.1109/AINA.2014.111.

10

Privacy and Security Issues on Wireless Body Area and IoT for Remote Healthcare Monitoring

Prabha Selvaraj[1] and Sumathi Doraikannan[2]

[1] CSE, Malla Reddy Institute of Engineering and Technology, JNTUH, Secunderabad, Telangana, India
[2] CSE, Malla Reddy Engineering College, JNTUH, Hyderabad, Telangana, India

10.1   Introduction

The recent developments in electronics have brought the growth of biomedical sensors, which can be attached or embedded in the body of the human. Healthcare monitoring systems (Yuce, 2010) provide a way to monitor the changes closely in human vital signs, give information to maintain optimal health status, and alert the physician when something goes serious, thus the increased usage of healthcare monitoring system. This chapter discusses the components required for the healthcare monitoring system and pursues with different methods to preserve the privacy and security of the health information. It also discusses about wireless body area network (WBAN) using Internet of things (IoT) to provide solutions for healthcare monitoring and investigates privacy and security issues in IoT healthcare monitoring.

10.2   Healthcare Monitoring System

10.2.1   Evolution of Healthcare Monitoring System

The temperature and pulse rate monitoring is introduced in 1625 in Italy by Santorio. John Floyer published the first report on "Pulse-Watch" in 1707. The course of fever for a patient was first done by Ludwig Taube in 1852. With successive improvements in the clock and the thermometer, the temperature, pulse rate, and respiratory rate became the standard vital signs. In 1896, Scipione Riva-Rocci introduced the sphygmomanometer, which allowed the fourth vital sign, arterial blood pressure, to be measured. Nikolai Korotkoff, a Russian physician, applied Riva-Rocci's cuff. The development of stethoscope by the French physician Rene Laennec allowed measuring both systolic and diastolic

Intelligent Pervasive Computing Systems for Smarter Healthcare, First Edition.
Arun Kumar Sangaiah, S.P. Shantharajah, and Padma Theagarajan.
© 2019 John Wiley & Sons, Inc. Published 2019 by John Wiley & Sons, Inc.

arterial pressure. Harvey Cushing, a preeminent US neurosurgeon of the early 1900s, insisted the need for routine arterial blood pressure monitoring in the operating room. Einthoven invented electrocardiogram (ECG) measurement in 1903, and since 1920 they have started recording blood pressure, pulse rate, temperature, and respiratory rate in all medical charts. The number of physiological parameters needed to be recorded increases with the introduction of transducers and electronic instruments. In the 1950s, the concept of ICU was introduced, and in the 1960s coronary care units monitoring cardiac rhythm came into the picture. Shubin and Weil in Los Angeles took computers to the ICU in 1966. The main objectives are to increase the accuracy and data availability, calculate the parameters that cannot be measured directly, improve the healthcare monitoring system efficiency, monitor and show data about the patients at regular interval, and assist computer-based decision making. There is a need to integrate data from various sources into unified medical record that also frees the end user to do more work practically and improves decision making with new information processed by new techniques. More analysis of huge data requires a well-organized system that records the data and also guarantees the data.

10.3 Healthcare Monitoring System

Health monitoring starts with collecting data and assessing the current condition of the patient at a regular interval of time. Decision making as regards treatment has to be done based on the information, and the patient's health condition is again reassessed. Continuous monitoring of the patient's physiological function like heart rate and rhythm, ECG, blood pressure, and several other parameters that are basic features of the seriously ill patients using a health monitoring system should be maintained. There is a need for accurate and instant decision making for the system to be effective. Electronic devices are used to gather the information frequently and show the physiological data. The patient monitoring system in WBAN is shown in Figure 10.1. The different WBAN sensors and their uses are given below:

- *Accelerometer*: Measures the acceleration relative to freefall in three axes.
- *Gyroscope*: Measures the orientation, based on the principles of angular momentum.
- *ECG/EEG/EMG*: Measures potential difference across electrodes put on corresponding parts of the body.
- *Pulse oximetry*: Measures ratio of changing absorbance of the red and infrared light passing from one side to the other of a thin part of the body's anatomy.
- *Respiration*: Uses two electrodes, cathode and anode, covered by a thin membrane to measure the oxygen dissolved in a liquid.

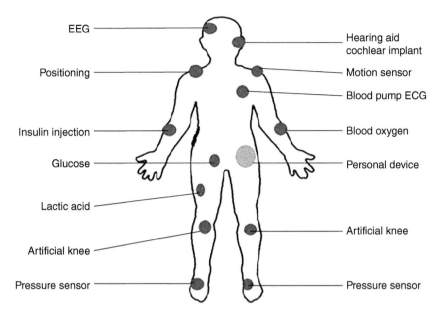

Figure 10.1 Patient monitoring in a WBAN.

- *Carbon dioxide*: Uses the infrared light and measures the absorption of the gas presented.
- *Blood pressure*: Measures the systolic pressure (peak pressure) and diastolic pressure (minimum pressure).
- *Blood sugar*: Traditionally analyzes drops of blood from a fingertip and uses noninvasive method including a near-infrared spectroscopy, ultrasound, optical measurement at the eye, and breath analysis.
- *Humidity*: Measures the conductivity changes of the level of humidity.
- *Temperature*: Uses a silicon integrated circuit to detect the temperature changes by measuring the resistance.

The challenge faced by healthcare monitoring system is to provide a solution with advanced medication in effective cost, intensive care to aged and severely diseased population, better quality, patient health-centric system, availability and moderate cost of physicians, residential care, and above all privacy and security. The growth of wearable technology has influenced healthcare monitoring system. The introduction of devices like fitness bands, blood pressure monitoring, sugar level, etc. eased the monitoring. The wearable technology communicates the information with the help of software's, which are easy to use and do not affect the normal life. The development in the technology has improved the accessibility to healthcare monitoring system especially for patients who cannot travel or are living in rural area and benefited by using this system but against cost.

10.3.1 Sensor Network

A sensor system is defined as a network of nodes that senses and controls the environment, enabling interaction between environment, person, or computers.

10.3.2 Wireless Sensor Network

A wireless sensor network (WSN) as shown in Figure 10.2. consists of spatially distributed autonomous devices that use sensors to monitor the health of the body. The nodes or devices are combined with routers and a gateway to form WSN. In case of WSN, huge number of sensor nodes, hubs, and clients are organized for health monitoring. The data sensed and collected from all the sensors are transmitted using multiple hopping through different nodes to get to the central gateway and finally reach the central node, which is interconnected to the Internet or satellite. The user can manage the configuration with WSN management to publish, collect, and monitor data. The development in WSN has facilitated new opportunities in healthcare monitoring systems. The technology in medical devices found in hospitals using sensors has replaced thousands of wires connected to these devices. In addition to enhanced mobility, it also provides reliability.

10.3.3 Wireless Body Area Network

WBAN is a wireless architecture that comprises a number of body sensor units (BSUs), which jointly form a single body central unit (BCU). The sensors

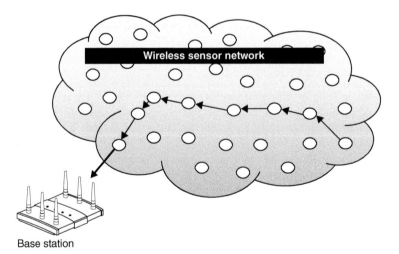

Figure 10.2 Wireless sensor network.

compose a body area network (BAN) where data are collected and sent to a base station wirelessly. The received data is stored in a database for further use. WBAN is a sensor that is implanted on-body to ease private monitoring. WBAN is implemented based on various embedded systems, sensors, and communication protocols that need the following:

- Ease of use.
- Optimal cost for maintenance.
- Fault tolerance.
- Alternate route identification in case of node failure.
- Low error rate.
- Flexible.
- Reliable.
- Latency is less.
- Immune to malicious attack.

The value of the global market for wireless sensor devices by end-vertical application from BCC Research (www.bccresearch.com/report/wireless-sensors-technologies) is shown in Figure 10.3. The sensors have the ability to collect significant data about the health condition of the body and thus enabling the introduction of WBANs. The nodes in WBAN have the capability to monitor blood pressure, pulse rate, body sugar, body temperature, etc. WBAN can be created by integrating tiny, lightweight, and low power monitoring devices and using lower power-consuming sensors for monitoring the patients in hospital or at home; data on vital parameters are sent to physicians via the Internet. It uses ZigBee or UWB standard. The data rate of different WBAN technologies is shown in Figure 10.4. WBAN comprises many inexpensive, lightweight, and small sensor platforms. Each one of them features one or more physiological sensor, e.g. motion sensor, ECGs, EMGs, and EEGs. The

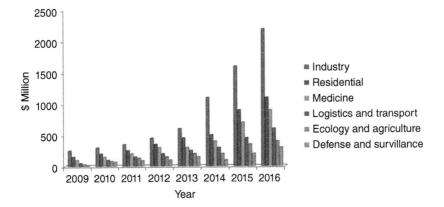

Figure 10.3 Value of the global market for wireless sensor devices.

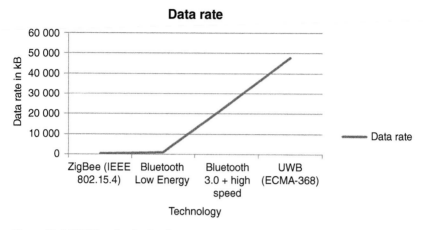

Figure 10.4 WBAN technologies data rate.

sensor could be embedded in the body as tiny intelligent patches and can also be integrated into clothing or fixed underneath the skin or muscles to monitor the physiological function. Network controller collects the information from sensors and processes it on a personal server. A personal server application runs on a personal digital assistant (PDA), cell phone, or PC. Network controller can be an add-on device, or it can be integrated into the personal server. WBAN can be implemented by a single-hop star topology in beacon mode where the data is being continuously sent without any interruption. Sensors are used to collect data and send it to the base station. Base station manages the entire activity of individual nodes in the network by requesting data periodically. The body sensor nodes can serve as a transmitter to collect the vital signs in real time. The system will operate within a specified range from the base. The main task of the base station is to coordinate the transmitting nodes, receive patient's physiological data from all transmitting nodes in real time, and communicate the data received for remote visualization. The user interface is designed in such a way that it eases the use by the user and gives sufficient details about patient's vital signs in a continuous manner. The sensor is embedded in the patient's body and transmits raw data to the receiver, which is stored in the database. As the data is updated, the changes will be reflected to the user and also stored in the server for future use. In the recovery process of patients, the information collected will be transferred to the doctor at regular interval of time as a feedback to their own doctors through Internet connectivity, which removes the distance between patients and their doctors. WBAN is classified into two parts such as in-body and on-body area network. When you consider the in-body area networks, it relies on the possibility of implanting biosensors, which allows the communication between inside and outside the body, whereas in on-body area networks it allows communication between wearable sensors and a base station. The basic need for in-body antennas is to avoid causing side effect to the human body. The materials used for implanting must have certain properties like biocompatible and having noncorrosive chemistry. Federal Communications Commission is the first licensed band for in-body communication with the frequency range of 402–405 MHz, and it is called as Medical Implant Communication Service (MICS). Conventional antennas working in this frequency will not be suitable for the human body since it is relatively too big. The designers have to face these kinds of serious challenges. To design an on-body antenna, two things have to be considered, one is antenna radiation pattern and the second is antenna sensitivity to body tissues. Due to the signal propagation features across the body surface containing surface waves, creeping waves, diffracted waves, and scattered waves, on-body communication systems are more complex, and in turn placing antennas are also crucial. The application of WBAN involved monitoring a person to assist the daily routine and activities for identifying the worsening in the health status. Buist et al. says that if a patient requires intensive care for monitoring, their vital signs can be monitored easily (Buist et al., 1999). The challenges of the WBAN explained by Fouad are the following:

- *Scale*: Embedded in human body and it is in centimeters/meters.
- *Node number*: Few nodes and limited by space.
- *Node size*: It should be small.
- *Node tasks*: It performs multiple tasks.
- *Network topology*: Based on body movement so it is variable.
- *Date rates*: It is mostly heterogeneous.
- *Node replacement*: It is difficult to replace the implanted nodes.
- *Life time of node*: Several years/months and battery capacity is smaller.
- *Power supply*: Difficult to access or replace in the implanted environment.
- *Power demand*: Lower power and supply of energy is difficult.
- *Energy source*: Vibration and thermal heat of body
- *Biocompatibility*: It is a must and for some external sensors also.
- *Wireless technology*: Low power technology is required.
- *Privacy and security*: It must be high to protect to patient information.
- *Loss of data*: Highly significant and it must facilitate measures to provide high quality of service when delivering real-time data is transferred.
- *Accuracy*: Based on robustness of node and its accuracy.

The main concern regarding wireless communication channel for healthcare monitoring is the privacy and security of the patient information and control flow.

10.4 Privacy and Security

The implementation of wireless technology has a great impact on the healthcare industry because of its capability to improve the systems, access of information in time, and storage of data (Coiera, 2004; Ilyas and Qazi, 2005; Showell and Whetton, 2005). The main use of BAN is to provide the patients' vital signs and give a snapshot of their health. It is necessary to explore the possibility of usage of BAN in monitoring patient's health. Security of the sensitive data exchange (Johnson and Turner, 2003; Zeeshan, 2003; Coiera, 2004; Security and Systems, 2005) is the major problem in adopting wireless technology in healthcare. Healthcare monitoring requires strict necessities for privacy, security, and reliability. Privacy and security of health information has essentially focused on the attacks on the wireless communication channel of the devices and also the health information online. But it is necessary to provide a scalable security, and privacy mechanism to malicious attacks is difficult. The open nature of patient's data is susceptible to eavesdrop, alteration, and loss. Even though WBAN has many open issues like communication, computation memory capacity, material, regulatory, low power, interference, quality of service, and energy efficiency, its main concern is privacy and security. The introduction of wireless technologies in medical field has a great advantage in healthcare monitoring system. There are many research works that analyze the suitable network communication, data integrity, power, delay network node failure, etc. Above all privacy and security is the most important parameter. The various types of information that leak from the human body naturally need to compromise privacy. The information transferred and stored in WBANs plays a major role in the healthcare monitoring and treatment. So it is crucial to guarantee the security for the patient information. Lack of security in WBANs is a major issue that hampers the acceptance of the technology. Sometimes it may result in life-critical events or even death. Privacy and security needs are categorized based on the data access, network communication, and data storage. This chapter also discusses about the various types of attacks and how they are classified. It also gives an insight about the issues that need to be considered while planning for privacy and security mechanism for WBANs. The effective and efficient sharing of the health information with the physicians is the requirement of wireless technology, which in turn provides more timely and effective treatment of patients. The WBAN still suffers and has issues in its capacity to secure the exchange of the sensitive health information. There is a view that WSN is not secure, so there is a necessity to address this privacy and security problem of healthcare monitoring system. The privacy of healthcare monitoring system is called as confidentiality of patient details, which contains the patient observations about vital signs, medication, and treatment history.

10.4.1 Privacy and Security Issues in Wireless Body Area Network

Various privacy and security goals that should be followed all through the BAN devices are similar to the conventional goals. WBAN systems need to adopt certain security measures so as to maintain the security properties throughout the entire life cycle of BAN devices. The most important security properties are listed below (Saleem et al., 2011):

- *Confidentiality*: Entities who access the data should be authenticated. Authorized entities must be able to access only the data, device information, and device system structures that are entitled to them.
- *Integrity*: The content, information of the device, and device system structures should not be modified.
- *Availability*: The information about the device, data, and device system structures must be provided when it has been requested by authorized entities.

WBAN systems need all these security measures to ensure confidentiality and data integrity of a patient's health records at all times, hence the necessity for the WBAN infrastructure to deploy specific security operations. The two fundamental characteristics needed in all WBAN systems are security and privacy of patient information. Security refers to the protection of data from unauthorized entities during the data transfer, data collection, data process, and data storage. Privacy refers to the issuing authority to manage one's personal information. Patient information need to be secured from unauthorized access and misuse since hackers might access the information by physically confining the node and modify the information, and, as a result, fake information might be passed on to the physician, which might lead to many critical consequences. This kind of sensitive and crucial information must be protected from unauthorized access. Figure 10.5 illustrates the security mechanisms of

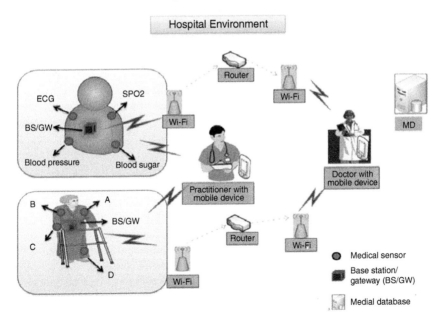

Figure 10.5 Hospital environment.

how the data has to be collected from various networking points. Data that is stored could be retrieved only by the authorized person through encryption and decryption. For example, in a hospital environment as shown in Figure 10.5, a patient's health could be monitored by implanting various sensors at the corresponding places. Patient's information has to be stored in a secured manner. The data could be transferred through the Internet to another doctor in order to get suggestions based on the critical situation of the patient and the patient's need. In order to ensure the safety of a WBAN system, the foremost security and privacy requirements are required:

- *Data confidentiality*: It is the most important issue since the data has to be protected from unauthorized entities. This could be done effectively with the help of encryption by issuing a shared key through a secured communication channel between WBAN nodes that ensure security and their coordinator.
- *Data authentication*: During the data transfer, the information that has been passed from nodes in a WBAN must be authenticated, i.e. it must ensure that the data must be from a known and trusted authority. Hence, the message authentication code (MAC) is computed, and thus it guarantees that the information is being transferred through the trustworthy node.
- *Data freshness*: This property is to ensure that the recycling of old data is not done and the data that has been sent in frames are correct. It ensures that the effective usage of integrity and confidentiality of data have been implemented in such a way that there are no chances for an adversary to record and replay the old data so as to puzzle the WBAN coordinator. Two types of data freshness that are used nowadays are as follows:

  Strong freshness: Strong freshness guarantees hindrance besides frame ordering, whereas weak freshness is restricted to frame ordering; however, there is no delay. During the time of passing signal to the WBAN coordinator, synchronization is needed to facilitate synchronization.

  Weak freshness: Weak freshness is used for WBAN nodes for low duty cycle.
- *Integrity*: The content of the message has to be protected from hackers since modifications done to the data in the case of hospital environment could result in crucial and critical health concerns and even death in severe cases. Certain measures have to be implemented so as to maintain the accuracy and consistency of the data.
- *Availability of the network*: Patient's information is highly sensitive, and it is important that the network must be accessible at all times for further suggestions and approvals of doctors who specialize in a particular field, in case of any emergency situations. If the data is not available, then there is a need to toggle to another WBAN so as to make the data available.
- *Dependability*: Retrieval of correct data is considered to be a critical concern because if any failure occurs, it causes acute severe issues in the patient. This issue could be resolved by error-correcting codes.

- *Secure localization*: The patient's location must be identified correctly in order to avoid the hacker to impose the improper details like modifying the patient's location.
- *Accountability*: The person who holds the information must have the responsibility of safeguarding the patient's information.
- *Secure management*: During the encryption and decryption process, the keys that need to be shared must be done in a secured manner. It is the role of the coordinator to add and remove WBAN nodes in a protected way.
- *Privacy rules and compliance requirement*: Presently, there exist different sets of regulations/policies for privacy all over the world. Setting out rules/policies like providing access to patient's sensitive data and ensuring security to patient's information is the predominant fact that must be adopted during providing privacy measures. As per the American Health Insurance Portability and Accountability Act (HIPAA), a set of directions/guidelines are provided for doctors, healthcare providers, and hospitals. In addition, attention is also focused on ensuring security to individual patient's health information.
- *Flexibility*: During an emergency case like consulting a doctor for second opinion and change of hospital, data must be available for the doctors. Hence the access rights have to be issued at the patient's request.

10.5 Attacks and Measures

Attacks [18] could be classified into three groups:

Service integrity: Service integrity deals with the network that is made mandatory to accept false information. For example, there is a possibility of changing the values like high blood pressure, creatinine level, urea level, thyroid levels (T3, T4, TSH), etc. These changes might create a great impact in the patient (Li et al., 2010) . Data integrity could be performed by applying MAC from these attacks.

Secrecy and authentication: The chances for a hacker to do eavesdropping, packet spoofing, and replay attacks might prevail (Javadi and Razzaque, 2013). For example, in health monitoring systems, the hacker would be interested in continuous monitoring of the patient's data through tracking the location of the patient's data. The communication channel is eavesdropped by the hacker, and the transmitted signals are captured so as to identify the location of the patient, and, in addition, the destination of the patient could also be predicted in advance. The hacker impedes the privacy of the patient since none of the patients would wish to reveal their destination. Falsifying alarms on medical data is an example of authentication attack. The hackers create bogus messages that lead to avoidable rescue missions. Secrecy and

Table 10.1 Security threats, requirement, and solutions.

Serial number	Security threats	Security requirements	Relative mean power
1	Message disclosure The message might be discovered by an hacker	Apply confidentiality and privacy	Encryption to be done in data link layer/network layer Provide access control
2	Message alteration	Apply data integrity and authenticity	Digital signatures and secure hash functions could be performed
3	Illegal access	Pertain trusting authority and do key establishment	Perform public key cryptography systems and random key distribution
4	Denial of service	Data must be available when required	Intrusion detection and prevention system
5	Compromised node	Flexibility to node compromise	Node revocation, inconsistency detection, and tamper-proofing

authentication could be protected by typical cryptographic techniques and MAC.

Network availability (DOS attacks): Hacker's focus will be on decreasing the capacity of a network. As WBANs are a variety of WSN, most of DOS attacks inherit from WSN. Even though, WBAN possess unique characteristics, few DOS attacks that occur in WBAN vary from WSN. Several threats and solutions for those threats have been given in Table 10.1.

DOS attacks that occur in different layers of OSI interconnection model (Saleem et al., 2009), i.e. from physical layer to transport layer, are depicted in Figure 10.6.

Emerging security approaches in WBAN are:

TinySec: TinySec is proposed in biomedical sensor network to achieve link layer encryption and data authentication. Communication is done through the single key, and this key has been actually implanted in the nodes before the exploitation of nodes. During the communication process, when the data has to be passed, it has to be encrypted. In this approach, encryption is done with a group key. This key is made known to all sensor nodes. MAC is computed for the entire packet, and the header is been included for the packet. Security provided through this is considered to be a minimum because the key information could be revealed if a node cooperates for a hacker and it is possible to hack the entire network.

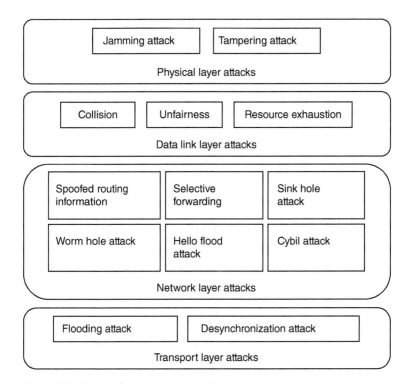

Figure 10.6 Denial of service attacks in OSI layers.

Bluetooth security protocols: It consists of protocols such as Baseband Link Manager Protocol (LMP) and Logical Link Control and Adaptation (L2CAP). LMP is applied for Bluetooth devices security, and it monitors the data that is transferred in the form of packets. Hence, LMP deals with few security issues like authentication, encryption, and exchange of the encryption keys. The L2CAP is responsible for reassembling of packets and higher level of multiplexing. Due to this, QoS could be achieved in communication.

Hardware encryption: This encryption is employed with the help of ChipCon 2420 ZigBee-compliant RF transceiver. IEEE 802.15.4 security operations have been performed through CC2420 by using AES encryption. In this 128-bit keys are used. Security operations include the countermode encryption and decryption. Power consumption in the sensor platform is not considerably increased. The disadvantage of this method is that it is dependent on the specific sensor platform.

IEEE 802.15.4 and IEEE 802.15.6 security protocols: Security system is classified into two important modes: (i) secured mode and (ii) unsecured mode. Unsecured mode is that no security set has been selected. Eight unique

Table 10.2 Security collections.

S.No	Name	Description
1	Null	No security
2	AES-CTR (counter mode of cryptographic operation with AES)	Here encryption is done Access control, data encryption, and sequence freshness are provided
3	AES-CBC-MAC-128 AES-CBC-MAC-64 AES-CBC-MAC-32 (authentication only)	Selection of different MAC lengths (32 64 128 bits) is done and is used for authentication
4	AES-CCM-128 AES-CCM-64 AES-CCM-32 (encryption and authentication)	Selection of different MAC lengths (32 64 128 bits) is done and is used for authentication

security collections have been identified as per the standard, as depicted in Table 10.2.

Biometrics: To perform the key establishment and authentication of body sensor nodes, biometrics is used. The physiological characteristics of the body are considered as a vital parameter in a symmetric key management system. Various signals such as the ECG and the timing information of heartbeats are the most proper physiological signals because they demonstrate proper time variance and randomness. Certain characteristics that have to be specified for biometric physiological values must be collectable, invulnerable, universal, random, and time variant. Biometric physiological signals could be recorded with the help of low-cost sensor devices. This results in ignoring the supplementary system, which is a prerequisite for biometric medical system in the near future.

ZigBee security services: ZigBee network layer on top of IEEE 802.15.4-defined PHY and MAC layers is implemented. Key distribution and nodes entering into the network is done through the trust center that is being identified by ZigBee standard. Certain responsibilities carried out by the trust center are as follows:

- *Trust manager*: Authenticates the nodes that put forth the request to enter into the network.
- *Network manager*: Distribution of key and maintenance is done.
- *Configuration manager*: End-to-end security is performed.

Elliptic curve cryptography: In WSN, ECC is considered as a possible option since it is famous for its fast computation and small key size and the signatures that are used for signing the document are compact. It is understood that ECC has been deployed for the purpose of establishing the key. It can also be suggested that ECC could be used for the exchange of key between the sensor nodes and base stations.

E-healthcare security models: There is a need to provide security to patient's data in order to enhance the quality of healthcare delivery. Hence, all e-health systems must be secluded and secured with security models so as to provide access controls. The conventional solution that is followed is the encryption of data. But it is not appropriate for complex electronic healthcare systems since it needs several access requirements. The main challenging task is to maintain the e-health data in a much secured manner for two reasons:

- When modification methods are deployed, the sensitivity of personal medical information must be protected.
- Computational overhead arises due to the application of encryption techniques.

10.5.1 Security Models for Various Levels

10.5.1.1 Security Models for Data Collection Level

- *Access control model*: An access control system with the enhancement of conventional role-based access control system could be suggested. In this approach, the access control policies is assigned and distributed for all sensor nodes. The current medical perspective, i.e. location, time, and health information, has to be updated since this upgradation might manipulate the access control decisions based on the current medical situation of the patient. This system works to the best until any crucial or emergency situation arises. There might be chances of overcoming the restrictions that have been employed on the patient's database.
  Drawback: No detection mechanism is available to detect the illegal access.
- *Adaptive access control model*: It provides fine-grained access control. Users start their sessions in behavior trust model. Since there exists the consideration of privilege superseding and behavior, there is no necessity of human intervention to modify authorizations and policies.
  Drawback: No prevention or detection mechanism exists to verify the user's data access during the crucial situation.
- *Key distribution scheme and key management scheme*: Maintenance of two separate key pools has to be done. One is to pass the key to mobile sink in order to access the network. The second key pool is to share the pair-wise key between the sensors.
  Drawback: The exponential operation is expensive.
- *A biometric-based security framework for data authentication*: Signal from ECG could be used as a key to facilitate the security of the patient's data. In this approach, computational complexity is reduced and the efficiency is improved due to the cryptographic key distribution. Security in this approach is increased since the patient's own biometrics is used and hence the data will not be diversified.

Drawback: Authentication is performed based on the sensors that are involved in this approach. Due to this, the process is restricted with the limited use of resources.

10.5.1.2 Security Models for Data Transmission Level
- Application of encryption techniques such as Mask-Certificate Attribute-Based Encryption (MC-ABE) by combining seven encryption algorithms, scheme based on zero knowledge protocol, etc., is used during the data transfer to make the communication in a protected manner.

10.5.1.3 Security Models for Data Storage and Access Level
There are various techniques like ABE, identity-based encryption, AES, hierarchical identity-based encryption (HIBE) schema, and the role-based access control (RBAC), or a combination of three existing role models such as DAC,MAC,RBAC into one model.

- *Privacy issues*: Various privacy issues (Ramli et al., 2010; Al Ameen et al., 2012) that might arise are:
- *Device-existence privacy*: When the patient has a device within, it must not be identified by any unauthorized user.
- *Device-type privacy*: Any hacker must not be able to find out the type of the device that has been implanted in the patient.
- *Specific-device ID privacy*: Each device possesses a unique ID. Care must be taken to protect this unique ID from illegal access.
- *Log history privacy*: Data will be stored in the server. Illicit users might try to identify private telemetry, or the patient's data could be subjected to risk factors due to the access. Hence certain access policies have to be framed during the design phase.
- *Owner privacy*: Each patient has their own attributes. These properties are vulnerable to risks.
- *Tracking*: Analog sensors could be monitored or a radio fingerprint could be used to identify the location of a patient. More attention has to be given in the form of devising a security model in such a way that the location could not be tracked.
- *Adversarial model*: An adversary could be categorized based on their goals, competence, and association to the system. The hackers could be classified as:
  Active or passive hacker: A passive hacker intervene all the communication channels in the network. An active hacker reads, alters, and inserts data over the communication channel.

External or internal hacker: A hacker might be an external or internal entity. The entity possesses a legitimate role. Entities might be employees, doctor, patient, or administrator.

Single entity or a group member:

Hacker might access the equipment that is custom or commercial. Hackers attack the components of BANs with the intension of attacking.

The patient: Hacker might desire to acquire the sensitive information about the patient. This might lead to the emotional or substantial harm to the patient

System resources: Due to various reasons, the hacker might unknowingly aim at any component of BAN. This unknown attack is due to the utilization of the system resources.

Tool: The hacker might perform hoax or corporate surveillance.

10.5.2 Privacy and Security Issues Pertained to Healthcare Applications

Patient's information might be accessible across the healthcare system as the patients may be in need of payers (Javadi and Razzaque, 2013). This transit is possible based on the patient's desire. Due to this transit, issues related to the electronic healthcare systems arise, and it could be classified into two classes:

- When the information about the patient is to be released from an individual organization: Information release could be done in two ways. This kind of inapt release of information occurs when the authorized user tries to access the information and broadcast it by violating the organizational policies purposely or accidentally under certain situations. The other way of information theft could be done by outsiders who peep into an organization's computer system.
- During the information transit from one industry to other related industries. Few industries try to hack the patient's information during the transit. These two classes possess different attributes, and they require different countermeasures.

10.5.3 Issues Related to Health Information Held by an Individual Organization

Health records that are maintained at organizations might be exposed to agents who try to violate the policies that are framed based on the security and confidentiality. The agents are known as organizational threats. Organization threats could be categorized as internal and external agents. An internal agent might wish to access the information of the person who might be a friend, neighbor, or coworker. An external agent who does not have any connection with the organization tries to access the information for his/her own personal use.

10.5.4 Categorization of Organizational Threats

Threats might arise because of the employees who access the data even when there is no necessity and hackers who work outside the organization access the data and devastate the system. The threats are differentiated based on the resources, technical capability, motives, and possibility of accessing the information system. Different levels of risk could rise in the organization due to these threats, and it could be resolved with different types of controls. Certain factors that account for threats are as follows:

Initial access: This is the association of the hacker with the target data, and it is the prior activity of the hacker before attacking the stakeholder's system. It has three essentials:

- *Data authorization*: The hacker may or may not have the consent to access the data. Data could be accessed only when the hacker has the system authorization.
- *System authorization*: If the hacker is able to access the site, then the system authorization is possible.
- *Site access*: Hacker may or may not have the permission to access the data from where the data is accessed regularly. These three elements could be combined to describe a budding hacker. In a hospital environment, a person who might have access to the system and site access could not the data due to lack of authorization. When countermeasures are considered, site access is the most important element to be involved.

Resources: Hackers might either be an individual provided with self-effacing and computing resources or intelligence agencies who are well funded. Resources that are used in the attacks could be shared by an individual or a small group.

Motive: Attacks on health information could be stimulated by economic and noneconomic factors. Information about the patient could be beneficial to insurance people and journalists. The health status of friends and relatives could create curiosity since they might help in critical situations. This is treated as noneconomic factor. Noneconomic motives might affect one's interpersonal situations. In a hospital environment, the access rights vary from person to person. As a doctor working in the hospital, he/she will be able to access the data through the site and system access rights. When a person works in the hospital as a system administrator, he/she will be able to access the data, site, and system. Information that is stored in the server could be accessed by the consultant. A worker who is working in the billing/pharmacy department could access to certain level, but they could not access the clinical information. Technical competence and the features of a hacker could not be related with each other since the hacker might or might not be a computer illiterate and an authorized user might be highly capable. The competence level of the hacker could be classified by three types, namely:

Aspiring hackers: These persons desire or wish to learn out of interest in spite of little or nil computer skill. They acquire knowledge from the published works of an organization that has been provided to the persons who survive and follow antiestablishment trade. They follow very simple techniques:

- Performing shoulder surfing, keen on finding the password that could be saved in mobile phone, and dictionary attacks.
- Inspecting the location and investigate the target site.
- Seeking the trash bin for information.
- Information gaining could be done by masquerading.
- Entering into the target location by acting as an employee of that organization.

Script runners: They are capable of acquiring typical attacks, and they execute the scripts to which they wish to enter. They do not have interest in acquiring more knowledge, and once the script fails, they cannot proceed further. The products developed must be Internet compatible. A recommendation could be provided for applying this technical competence for all developed products that use the Internet.

Accomplished hackers: They adapt to any situations such as during the failure of the scripted attacks. They are capable of realizing the system vulnerabilities. The worst scenario in the healthcare organization is that a hacker accesses the patient's information when he/she gains entry via the Internet. Technical competence of hackers in each level is enhanced with the help of available methods. Countermeasures for these threats should improve, which involves the enduring rational and monetary investment in security technology. Threat levels and its countermeasures in healthcare organizations could be categorized based on the various amalgamations of organizational threats such as resources, access, motive, and technical capability. The categorized threats have been depicted in Table 10.3.

Table 10.3 Threat categories.

Level	Type and nature of threat	Examples	Measures of threat
Level 1 low	Accidental disclosures and inexperienced mistakes	Overhearing the conversation between two persons or information left on one's personal computer	Simple techniques could be proper. Reminders about behavioral codes Authenticating the access by mistake Establish screen savers Automatic logouts to thwart access to unattended displays Reminders about behavioral codes, confirmation of actions that might route or access information erroneously, or screen savers and automatic log-outs to prevent access to unattended displays Patient's privacy has to be maintained. This could be done by encrypting the information and coded identifiers have to be deployed
Level 2 high	Exploitation of record access privilege	Violation of trust during the authorized access to the patient's information Psychiatric care episode, physical abuse, information about sports people, politicians, etc., finds an opportunity to get into media	Appeals to ethics Imposition of permits after an incident occurs
Level 3 high	Information access either for malevolence or for profit	An unauthorized access to the data A patient's information could be purchased from the organization illegally. In order to make use of the vulnerability, an employee mightacquire the data and misuse it when he/she is fired from the organization	Appeals to ethics Imposition of permits after an incident occurs
Level 4 high	Physical hacker	An individual enters into the organization with a bogus identity and try to collect as much as information needed	Strong identification authentication mechanisms and physical security measures such as badges, surveillance cameras, and physical identification

Level	Threat	Description	Countermeasures
Level 5 high	Pure technical threat	Thrashed employees or outside hackers who access the information illegally so as to damage the system and disturb operations. Outside hackers extract the patient's information by breaking into the system

It includes denial-of-service attacks. The hacker might break into the system to access the data. In addition, the hacker also injects a computer virus that makes the system to crash or all files could be deleted. On the other hand, the hacker instigates an e-mail attack in which the system gets spoiled totally by receiving virus in the form of tens of thousands of emails in a very short span of time | Technological barriers such as firewalls to segregate internal and external networks
Strong encryption-based authentication and authorization techniques |
| Level 6 high | Traffic analysis | These attacks occur due to traffic patterns. These patterns expose the information about the sensors implanted in the patient | Three traffic jumbling mechanisms such as traffic shaping, dummy noise, and dummy source have been introduced
Dummy noise: The gateway tries to infuse dummy messages in a random manner. Consequently the noise that is created due to this inculcation covers the real traffic from hackers

Dummy source simulation process is done in such a way that the gateway conjures up the transmission to make the hacker to think that the information is obtained from the sensor mounted on the patient. Due to this action, the hacker gets puzzled and not sure about the information received whether it is from the original source or dummy source.

Traffic shaping: A delay is introduced during the release of sensor readings.

The delay will be of maximum. Limited memory on the sensor nodes in order to store the data since this has to be transmitted to the gateway.

The sensor nodes plan transmission at the entry of a new sensor reading as it should be ensured that the data must not experience the delay.

This could be done by monitoring the transmission and the memory must be updated frequently |

10.6   Internet of Things

IoT is providing an excellent and unseen network that can be sensed, controlled, and coded. The IoT-based products have the embedded technology that permits the exchange of data with other devices or the Internet. It provides a different and better reformed healthcare monitoring system. IoT again stands on sensors, gateway, and wireless communication network, which allows communicating and accessing the information. Technological growth resulted in modernized healthcare system, but it is concerned with better healthcare services to the patients anywhere and at any time. The use of sensors, monitoring devices, etc., has brought many advantages in IoT by allowing the device to track the patients online and transfer the reports in time to physicians. The security of healthcare monitoring system (Abdullah et al., 2016) security as discussed by Lobna Yehia is the important criteria in healthcare applications (Yehia et al., 2015). Without privacy and security, introducing new technologies in healthcare monitoring system makes the system weak because the patient information is highly sensitive and needs to be protected from security attacks. The victory of healthcare monitoring is based on the privacy and security of patient information. E-healthcare monitoring system described by Anass Rghioui et al. explains that the patient has a set of WBAN devices (Rghioui et al., 2015) and they should still reach the medical central unit to maintain the bind with the sensors when they are moving. Temitope et al. explains that WBAN devices transfers the patient information to the medical central unit in the hospitals remotely via the Internet for tracking the patient's health status (Gia et al., 2015). Caregivers can connect through the internet via computers or mobile devices to the medical central unit to supervise patient data processed and analyzed by dedicated applications. The objective is to address the data privacy of the mobile WBAN sensors exchanged with the remote medical central unit. The age-friendly healthcare system described by Evdokimos et al. consists of Controller Application Communication (CAC) framework (www.mckinsey .com/industries/healthcare.../healthcares-digital-future) that has multiple controllers to provide communication between different entities and an XMPP network enables communication between medical devices and software components, support for aged patients, etc. The wearable and sensor devices embedded gather and share the information with each other in IoT in order to store the information for analysis by the physician.

10.6.1   WBAN Using IoT

WBAN provides the persistent information, observation, and feedback to the physician or patient. The key technology that helps in transferring the patient information is wearable device. They facilitate to monitor the patient status and provide the feedback to maintain the health in optimal condition. The wearable sensors connect to the network through an intermediate concentrator, which is located in the locality of the patient. Integrating IoT with healthcare monitoring system will further make the system interoperable, flexible, and intelligent as explained in Dimitriou and Ioannis (2008), Bazzani et al. (2012), Ray (2014). The wearable sensors form an IoT-based architecture to access data via concentrator through the Internet. If the device is using IoT, then it can be addressed uniquely and identified through the Internet. The gateway server transfers the information and stores it on a remote server via the Internet for reference. The information is transferred automatically with the healthcare monitoring system through the Internet. The three categories of traffic in WBAN are normal, on demand, and emergency traffic. The normal traffic is the data which is used to monitor if the patient is in normal status without any critical or on demand events. On demand traffic is requested by the physician to get the information for diagnosis. Emergency traffic is unpredictable traffic that is started by the nodes when they go beyond the threshold and they need to accommodate immediately.

10.7 Projects and Related Works in Healthcare Monitoring System

There are various applications (Mourad et al., 2011) and projects developed to enrich the pervasiveness of WBAN in healthcare. Many public and private organizations have taken care of some projects like monitoring glucose level in patients, cancer detection, ECG monitoring, and elderly people monitoring that covers many areas in healthcare systems. Healthcare monitoring applications or projects (Kumar and Lee, 2012a; Chen et al., 2013) implemented using WBAN are listed below.

- *CodeBlue*: It is an ad hoc-based self-organized architecture. To communicate with the access points, the sensor devices within WBAN are connected using ZigBee-enabled radio transactions (Chen et al., 2010).
- *CareNet*: It is a Web-enabled methodology with two-tier architecture for remote health monitoring and controlling. It is scalable, reliable, and secure.
- *AlarmNet*: It is for monitoring patient in the home environment (Chen et al., 2010). The three-tier architecture with the top tier as WBAN devices, the middle as the environmental sensors, and the bottom as the network based on Internet protocol AlarmGate.
- *UbiMon*: It is for capturing patient's physiological and critical symptoms (Chen et al., 2010, 2013). WBAN is with an ad hoc network of wearable and implantable sensors (Kumar and Lee, 2012a.
- *Satire*: Satire project (Milenkovic et al., 2006; Al Ameen and Kwak, 2011) is used for recording patient's daily actions calculated by sensors such as

location and motion sensors. Satire jacket worn by a patient record the daily activities of the patient. The data are updated into the repository as soon as the patient enters into the neighborhood of an access mote. These data are utilized for identifying the location and then to find the activity of a patient.

- *SMART*: The physiological signals of patients in the waiting areas of an emergency unit are monitored by SMART (Al Ameen and Kwak, 2011). Patient's health are depreciated very fast due to some critical situations when the patients are in the waiting area. This could be resolved by gathering the information that will be passed on to the central server where the data is stored and it is computed so as to produce an alarm when the patient's health deteriorates. As a result of the deployment of SMART, the treatment is given to the patient.
- *HealthGear*: A sensor that gets connected to a phone with the help of Bluetooth is deployed to investigate physiological signals (Al Ameen and Kwak, 2011).
- *MobiCare/MobiHealth*: With the help of MobiCare/MobiHealth (Chen et al., 2010; Al Ameen and Kwak, 2011; Chen et al., 2013), patient's movement could be monitored when patients are under the continual health monitoring system through GPRS and UMTS cellular networks. The patient's body data is sensed frequently, and it is broadcasted to the client. The client then accumulates all the data, which is transferred to the server to facilitate the patient's health improvement. Continual assessment and frequent examination of the physiological status of a patient is done. This MobiCare client utilizes the HTTP POST protocol of the application layer in order to send the data to the server.
- *Vital Jacket*: Heart rate and ECG waves could be monitored constantly through Vital Jacket, a wearable garment. The data could be chucked to PDA with the help of Bluetooth and accumulated in the memory. Pervasive and adaptive healthcare for nonstop scrutiny using wireless sensors for smart healthcare could be done by creating a history log while securing the patient's privacy. Compared to humans, these sensor devices are capable of observing even a minute change in critical signals like blood oxygen levels, boosting diagnostic accuracy, circadian rhythm changes, and heart rate that might specify changes in healthcare requirements.
- *AID-N*: It is same as CodeBlue but uses wireless repeaters to communicate with access points, and for localization a GPS is attached (Chen et al., 2010). Here wireless repeaters are placed in spite of access policy to facilitate the emergency course. Green lights flashed from the access policy create awareness to indicate the accurate emergency course.
- *BikeNet*: The environment is sensed mobile bicycle. The activities are assigned to a bike area networks. Wireless sensors implanted in the patient broadcast the corresponding information to the central server.

- *eWatch*: A clear audio and visual forewarning could be issued when the sensors eWatch attached on a wristwatch sense the environment and record the temperature and motion.
- *Tmote Sky*: A constant blood pressure, ECG, epicardial accelerometer, etc., could be monitored with the integration of hardware platform with sensors. As the Tmote Sky is spread on wireless communication and information, it could not be able to resolve the security issues.

10.8 Summary

Health monitoring system starts with collecting data and assessing the current condition of the patient at regular interval of time. It is done by attaching or embedding the device in the human body, which provides a way to closely monitor the changes in vital signs, gives information to maintain optimal health status, and alerts the physician when something becomes serious. The most important security properties are confidentiality, integrity, and availability. Different methods are available to preserve the privacy and security of the health information. Service integrity deals with the network that is made mandatory to accept false information. Security models deployed at various levels are data collection level, data transmission level, and data storage and access level. The IoT-based products have the embedded technology, which permits the exchange of data with other devices or the Internet. It provides a different and better reformed healthcare monitoring system, gives solutions for healthcare monitoring, and investigates privacy and security issues in IoT healthcare monitoring. Healthcare monitoring applications or projects implemented using WBAN are CodeBlue, CareNet, AlarmNet, UbiMon, SATIRE, SMART, HealthGear, MobiCare/MobiHealth, BikeNet, Vital Jacket, eWatch , AID-N, and Tmote Sky. Hence there is an increased usage of healthcare monitoring system because of its ease and accessibility.

Bibliography

Abdullah, W.A.N.W., Yaakob, N., Elobaid, M.E. et al. (2016). Energy-efficient remote healthcare monitoring using IoT: a review of trends and challenges. In: ICC '16: Proceedings of the International Conference on Internet of Things and Cloud Computing, ACM.

Al Ameen, M. and Kwak, K.S. (2011). Social issues in wireless sensor networks with healthcare perspective. *The International Arab Journal of Information Technology* **8** (1): 52–58.

Al Ameen, M., Liu, J., and Kwak, K. (2012). Security and privacy issues in wireless sensor networks for healthcare applications. *Journal of Media systems* **36** (1): 93–101.

Bazzani, M., Conzon, D., Scalera, A. et al. (2012). Enabling the IoT paradigm in e-health solutions through the VIRTUS middleware. In: 2012 IEEE 11th International Conference on Trust, Security and Privacy in Computing and Communications (TrustCom), 1954–1959.

Buist, M.D., Jarmolowski, E., Burton, P.R. et al. (1999). Recognising clinical instability in hospital patients before cardiac arrest or unplanned admission to intensive care. A pilot study in a tertiary-care hospital. *The Medical Journal of Australia* **171**: 22–25.

Chen, M., Gonzalez, S., Vasilakos, A. et al. (2010). Body area networks: a survey. *Mobile Networks and Applications* **16** (2): 171–193.

Chen, M., Wan, J., Gonzalez, S. et al. (2013). A survey of recent developments in home M2M networks. *IEEE Communications Surveys and Tutorials* **16** (1): 98–114.

Coiera, E. (2004). Four rules for the reinvention of health care. *British Medical Journal* **328**: 1197–1199.

Dimitriou T. and Ioannis K. (2008). Security issues in biomedical wireless sensor networks. 2008 1st International Symposium on Applied Sciences on Biomedical and Communication Technologies, ISABEL'08.

Fouad, H. (2014). Continuous health-monitoring for early detection of patient by web telemedicine system. In: *Recent Advances in Electrical Engineering and Computer Science*, 76–83.

Gia, T.N., Jiang, M., Rahmani, A.-M. et al. (2015). Fog computing in healthcare internet of things: a case study on ECG feature extraction. 2015 IEEE International Conference on Computer and Information Technology; Ubiquitous Computing and Communications; Dependable, Autonomic and Secure Computing; Pervasive Intelligence and Computing.

Ilyas, M. and Qazi, S. (2005). Applications of WLANs in telemedicine. In: *Handbook of Wireless Local Area Network: Applications, Technology, Security, and Standards* (ed. S. Ahson and M. Ilyas), 298–308. Boca Raton, FL: Taylor & Francis Group.

Javadi, S.S. and Razzaque, M.A. (2013). Security and privacy in wireless body area networks for health care applications. In: *Wireless Networks and Security*, Signals and Communication Technology (ed. S. Khan and A.S. Khan Pathan), 165–187. Berlin, Heidelberg: Springer-Verlag.

Johnson, B. and Turner, L. (2003). Data collection strategies in mixed methods research. In: *Handbook of Mixed Methods in Social & Behavioral Research* (ed. A.M. Tashakkori and C.B. Teddlie), 297–319. Thousand Oaks, CA: SAGE Publications.

Kumar, P. and Lee, H.-J. (2012). Security issues in healthcare applications using wireless medical sensor networks: a survey. *Sensors.* **12** (1): 55–91.

Li, M., Lou, W., and Ren, K. (2010). Data security and privacy in wireless body area networks. *IEEE Wireless Communications.* **17** (1): 51–58.

Milenkovic, A., Otto, C., and Jovanov, E. (2006). Wireless sensor networks for personal health monitoring: issues and an implementation. *Computer Communications* **29** (13–14): 2521–2533.

Mourad, F., Kallas, M., Snoussi, H. et al. (2011). Wireless sensor networks in biomedical: body area networks. In: 7th International Workshop on Systems, Signal Processing and their Applications (WOSSPA). IEEE.

Ramli, R., Zakaria, N., and Sumari, P. (2010). Privacy issues in pervasive healthcare monitoring system: a review. *World Academy of Science, Engineering and Technology, International Journal of Computer, Electrical, Automation, Control and Information Engineering* **4**: 1913–1919.

Ray, P. (2014). Home health hub internet of things (H^3IoT): an architectural framework for monitoring health of elderly people. In: 2014 International Conference on Science Engineering and Management Research (ICSEMR), 1–3.

Rghioui, A., Laarje, A., Elouaai, F., and Bouhorma, M. (2015). Protecting e-healthcare data privacy for internet of things based wireless body area network. *Research Journal of Applied Sciences, Engineering and Technology* **9** (10): 876–885.

Saleem, S., Ullah, A., and Yoo, H.S. (2009). On the security issues in wireless body area networks. *International Journal of Digital Content Technology and its Applications* **3** (3): 178–184.

Saleem, S., Ullah, S., and Kwak, K.S. (2011). A study of IEEE 802.15.4 security framework for wireless body area networks. *Sensors* **11**: 1383–1395.

Showell, C. and Whetton, S. (2005). Health informatics tools, techniques, and applications. In: *Health Informatics: A Social-Technical Perspective* (ed. S. Whetton), 214–220. Oxford: Oxford University Press.

Wireless Security and Health Care Information Systems (2005). Agder University College. http://www.mif.vu.lt/cs2/wimv/Wireless%20Security%20for %20Health%20Care.pdf.

Yehia, L., Khedr, A., and Darwish, A. (2015). Hybrid security techniques for internet of things healthcare applications. *Advances in Internet of Things* **5** (3): 21–25.

Yuce, M.R. (2010). Implementation of wireless body area networks for healthcare systems. *Sensors and Actuators A: Physical* **162**: 116–129.

Zeeshan, A. (2003). *Wireless Security in Health Care.* University of South Australia. http://www.cs.mu.oz.au/bir/auscc03/papers/ahmad-auscc03.pdf.

11

Remote Patient Monitoring: A Key Management and Authentication Framework for Wireless Body Area Networks

Padma Theagarajan[1] and Jayashree Nair[2]

[1] *Sona College of Technology, Salem, Tamilnadu, India*
[2] *AIMS Institutes, Bangalore, Karnataka, India*

11.1 Introduction

Given the present-day hectic and sedentary lifestyle, health issues like cardiac diseases, diabetes, and hypertension are widely prevalent, and these issues lead to further complications and risks over a period of time. Certain health conditions also require constant monitoring of a patient's vital parameters when not in the care of a healthcare personnel. Efficient monitoring mechanisms that collect vital parameters are the need of the hour to detect or predict worsening of any existing condition even when the patient is on the move. Advances in wireless sensor technologies and telemedicine have greatly benefitted remote human health monitoring enabled by the use of sensors to capture the relevant and vital parameters. Patients around the world can now tele-consult with any specialist doctor anywhere in the world.

Wireless body area networks (WBANs) are a promising solution to the problem of continuous monitoring of health parameters effected by a collection of wireless sensor nodes placed either on the patient's body or in close proximity to the patient. The health parameters are communicated over a wireless network involving sensor nodes, parameters aggregating nodes, and the health monitoring station (HMS). The rules regarding patient data confidentiality are governed by ethics and legislative rules. Security and integrity of data during transmission and storage are important concerns that cannot be overlooked and are one of the biggest challenges that impede the acceptance of remote healthcare monitoring. A patient's health could be seriously threatened by a malicious adversary. This wireless transmission of health parameters is prone to attacks, and the remote monitoring framework requires appropriate security mechanisms to ensure that the medical decisions are made based on actual data and not false ones. It is also important to ensure that the sensor nodes, parameter

Intelligent Pervasive Computing Systems for Smarter Healthcare, First Edition.
Arun Kumar Sangaiah, S.P. Shantharajah, and Padma Theagarajan.
© 2019 John Wiley & Sons, Inc. Published 2019 by John Wiley & Sons, Inc.

aggregating nodes, or the HMS is not compromised, and hence authentication mechanisms also need to be in place.

Wireless sensors deployed as a WBAN on a person are generally small to very small devices that have severe power and resource constraints. Traditional security mechanisms for encryption, authentication, and key exchange are heavy in terms of consumption of resources and are generally not preferred in a sensor-based environment, especially a body area network (BAN). It is crucial that the algorithms are simple in terms of resource utilization and computational requirements but at the same time robust to attacks.

The rest of the chapter is organized as follows: Section 11.2 presents related work, Section 11.3 introduces the proposed security framework, Section 11.4 details the proposed encryption and authentication scheme, and Section 11.5 is a discussion on the performance of the proposed scheme. In Section 11.6, the work is concluded.

11.2   Related Work

The findings in literature show that there is little empirical evidence on proper implementation of security in healthcare. Privacy of patient data needs to be ensured by enabling its access by only authorized medical personnel. Hence, it is essential that some kind of mechanism is available with the recipients to ensure the authenticity and integrity of the received information, i.e. ensuring credibility of the information – data or images.

Tan et al. (2008) present an identity-based cryptography approach for security in WBAN called IBE-Lite. In IBE-Lite, a sensor generates a public key on the fly using an arbitrary string. The sensors cannot create the secret keys that are derived separately by a trusted third party – the certifying authority (CA). Every time a new public/secret key pair is generated, the secret key must be stored in the CA, which then challenges the person who accesses the data. Thus, they use a trusted third party to ensure security of data in WBAN. Moving away from the conventional key generation schemes and capitalizing on the inherent random and time-variant nature of biometric data, Venkatasubramanian et al. (2008) present a scheme where the electrocardiogram (ECG) signals of a person are used to generate cryptographic keys for encrypting the communication between any pair of sensor nodes in a WBAN. In their work, sample values of EKG data are taken from a particular interval of the EKG signal, and using fast Fourier transform, coefficients are extracted. Using these coefficients, a feature vector is generated, which is used for generating the key. The derived key is then agreed upon by the sensors involved in the communication and is used to encrypt the data in their communication. The main area of focus of this work is securing the inter-sensor communication within the WBAN. The sensors in the network agree upon a common key, generated based on the EKG reading of the patient. The keys generated using the scheme will be distinct for different people, since EKG data is different for different people; it will be random given the inherent randomness associated with biometric data and time variant.

Mana et al. (2009, 2011) also use EKG signals to generate secure keys between sensor nodes and the base station, therefore focusing on securing the end-to-end communication, as well as the communication among the nodes. Use of EKG signals in these works exploits the time-variant nature and the random behavior that it exhibits with varying physiological activities.

Raazi and Lee (2009) propose a scheme that uses biometric measurements as symmetric keys (or private keys), since they are inherently random. In their scheme, the personal server issues a key refreshment schedule periodically to all the sensor nodes in the WBAN. This refreshment schedule is used to change the key allotted to it for communication. Three keys are used in the scheme a communication key for encryption of general communication in the network, an administrative key to refresh the communication key, and a basic key known only to the sensor node and the medical server, which is to be used in the rare event of the administrative key being compromised. The initial key is preloaded to the nodes and periodically the personal server chooses a value of a biometric to be used as a key for encryption by the nodes.

A notable point from the works discussed in this section is that all the encryption and key management schemes use keys that are exchanged between the transmitter and the receiver at one time or the other or use broadcasted keys in refreshment schedules. In such a scenario, if this key exchange communication was somehow intercepted, the attacker could easily get access to all the subsequent frames exchanged between the communicating entities. Thus, we can say that even though the system seems to be secure, it is still vulnerable.

Raghav et al. (2012) present a security suite for WBANs, comprised of IAMKeys, an independent and adaptive key management scheme for improving the security of WBANs and KEMESIS, a key management scheme for security in inter-sensor communication. The novelty of the schemes lies in the use of a randomly generated key for encrypting each data frame that is generated independently at both the sender and the receiver, eliminating the need for any key exchange.

Yenuganti (2016) proposed a scheme using low-cost accelerometers to authenticate sensors in BANs. In order to achieve sensor authentication, accelerometer data gathered from sensors were used to distinguish whether or not the devices are carried on the waist of same individual's body. The approach is focused on analyzing walking patterns recorded from smartphone accelerometers placed in the same location of the user's body.

Gomati (2015) proposed a scheme for implementing a secure authentication mechanism using elliptic curve digital signature algorithm (ECDSA) technique for securing the physiological signal from the human body during inter-sensor communications.

Masdari and Ahmadzadeh (2016) in their paper provide a complete survey and analysis of the various authentication schemes proposed in the literature to improve the WBANs security. It classifies the authentication schemes based on the applied techniques for authentication and highlights the advantages and limitations of the classification. The paper presents a comprehensive comparison of the capabilities and features of each of the schemes. One of the primary objectives of the work is the optimization of resource utilization, but there is a need for manual deployment of the keys in the participating entities.

A framework for authenticating and securing sensor data transmission between sensor nodes, parameter aggregating nodes, and monitoring stations is proposed in the forthcoming sections. A number of theoretic approaches using partial quotient sequences generated from continued fractions are considered in the design of the framework for effective remote patient monitoring. The proposed scheme uses sequences generated from continued fractions of certain irrational numbers as the pseudorandom sequence to encrypt and authenticate the sensor data. To ensure authenticity of health data, a simple key exchange mechanism without physically exchanging the keys is also proposed.

11.3 Proposed Framework for Secure Remote Patient Monitoring

The WBAN in consideration in this study essentially consists of two subnetworks. One is the network comprising all the sensors on the human body, which includes the individual sensors or wireless sensors on humans (WSH) and the health parameters aggregator (HPA) sensor – called the network of sensors on human and aggregators (NetSHA). The other is the network comprising the HPA sensor and the HMS – called network of aggregators and monitoring station – NetAMS. Securing the data traveling in each of the networks – NetSHA and NetAMS – is essential for effective remote health monitoring as crucial decisions may have to be taken based on the received inputs. Key management for security and authentication of sensor data is the prime concern in this proposed work given the constraints in space and cost that exists in wireless sensor nodes.

The general model for WBAN-based remote patient monitoring systems that is considered in this study is depicted in Figure 11.1. The model includes one or more than one of the various sensors or WSHs like EKG sensor, electroencephalogram (EEG), blood pressure sensor, and blood sugar level sensor. The sensors send their recorded data to the WPA sensor, which performs the role of an aggregator. The HPA aggregates the readings received from the sensors, consolidates it, and, after endorsing it with an authentication digest D, encrypts it and forwards it to personal servers (PS) like a mobile phone or wearable device

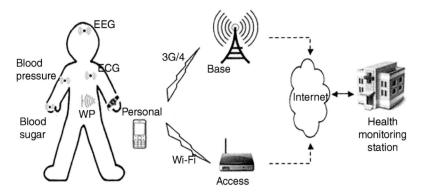

Figure 11.1 WBAN-based remote patient monitoring system.

like a watch or any other health monitoring device. The PS will transform the received data to an IP packet suitable for transmission as a wireless data packet to the HMS (health practitioner, clinic, or hospital) that is monitoring the vital parameters of the patient.

The HMS will then analyze the received data and proceed for further actions depending on the nature of the data received. It may not respond to any normal data, respond back directly to the PS for communication to the HPA and further to the WSH for routine monitoring, or refer the received input to the authorized medical practitioner for further review.

11.3.1 Proposed Security Framework

Encryption and authentication are essential elements to ensure credibility of transmitted data in any network, and the key plays an important role. In order to address secure communication in the WBAN, it is considered as two subnetworks – NetSHA and NetAMS. This is to address the power constraints of the WSHs and the HPA. Here HPA is the interface between the two subnetworks and facilitates internetwork secure communication. It has more power compared with WSHs, giving it additional computation power. Two algorithms – key establishment in NetAMS (KEAMS) and key establishment in NetSHA (KESHA) – address the security issue in NetAMS and NetSHA, respectively. Key generation algorithm – partial quotient sequence generator (PQSG) – addresses the key generation algorithm based on continued fractions. Both KEAMS and KESHA will be deployed in HPA, and choice of the algorithm will depend on the subnetwork for which authentication is being considered. It is crucial that the algorithms are efficient in terms of power and resource requirements due to the constraints because of the size of the sensor nodes. The HMS will have KEAMS deployed in it, and WSHs will have only KESHA deployed in it.

Security of sensor data transmitted between each of the networks is achieved through symmetric encryption, and authentication of the participants is done by generating authentication digests through hash operations. Symmetric encryption is a default choice for power-constrained networks like WBANs, but key management is an issue. In this scheme both algorithms generate the keys independently in each of the entities, the HPA, WSH and the HMS, without the need to physically transmit them over the wireless channel.

The patient activates the HPA, which will make the initial communication with the HMS to activate the NetAMS. The WSHs will contact the HPA to activate NetSHA.

Initially, the HPA will send initiation messages to the HMS and establish the key to secure the communication in NetAMS. Once the keys are established, the WSHs will collect the health parameters and send it to the HPA. HPA will aggregate the data received from various nodes over regular intervals of time, consolidate it, and transmit it to the HMS, which will analyze the information and send back responses either to the HPA for conveying to the WSHs or to the medical practitioner for further action and review. Once the HPA is activated, each WSH will establish its keys with the HPA, which will be further used to generate the PQ sequence. This sequence will be used to encrypt the communication in NetSHA.

The keys used in this scheme are irrational numbers that are neither transcendental nor periodic and will be used to generate the pseudorandom sequence to scramble sensor data and ensure confidentiality. The chosen keys are established in NetSHA and NetAMS without physically transmitting them.

The key generation algorithm and the authentication framework for each of the networks is discussed in the subsequent sections.

11.3.2 Key Generation Algorithm: PQSG

Good random numbers are essential to ensure safe computing systems. A random number sequence can be defined as a sequence of numbers generated using the outcomes of a process like the tossing of a fair unbiased coin, where the probability of obtaining a head or a tail is equal to half. Cryptographic applications require that the generated random sequences are cryptographically secure, which means that in addition to possessing random properties, the sequences should also be highly unpredictable, have high sensitivity to initial conditions, have zero correlation, are nonperiodic, and are robust against statistical attacks. The past output sequences of the generator should neither be predictable nor repeated to ensure resilience to attacks in spite of having some prior information about the generator like the initial input or inner state – current or previous.

A number theory-based pseudorandom number generator – PQSG – to generate pseudorandom sequences from partial quotients of continued fraction representation of certain irrational numbers that are transcendental has previously been evaluated by the authors in Pillai and Padma (2015) and Padma and Pillai (2014). The random nature and cryptographic properties of the generator based on hard mathematical problem of difficulty of retrieving an irrational number from the knowledge about some of its partial quotients was evaluated by the authors. This hardness of the problem makes it suitable to implement cryptographic services in applications for authentication, confidentiality, integrity, and related purposes. PQSG can be used to generate pseudorandom sequences that are cryptographically secure using shorter seeds, which benefits the constraints of the sensors in a WBAN.

Given a real irrational number α, which is transcendental and at the same time does not exhibit any patterns in its formation, the successive real numbers $\alpha_0, \alpha_1, \alpha_2, \ldots$ and integer numbers $b_0, b_1, b_2, \ldots$ can be defined using Euclid's iterative procedure (Hardy and Wright 1975). The iteration repeats as long as $\alpha_x \neq 0$ or as long as the required number of quotients are generated. The partial quotients, b_i so generated, are unique for the given irrational number α, and the simple continued fraction representation is given by

$$\alpha = [b_0, b_1, b_2, \ldots] \tag{11.1}$$

Given the infinite partial quotients of $\alpha = [b_0, b_1, b_2, \ldots]$, the number of partial quotients n, which will be used to form a substring, will be predetermined by the HMS prior to algorithm deployment in the nodes. loc_i will be used to identify the starting position, for partial quotient extraction is predetermined by the PRNG. The secrecy of both is to be ensured.

From loc_i, n partial quotients are selected and concatenated:

$$PQ_1(p_i \cdots p_{i+p}) = \alpha[loc_i].\alpha[loc_{i+1}] \cdots \alpha[loc_{i+n}] \tag{11.2}$$

where $\cdot$ is the concatenation operator and $PQ_1(_i \cdots p_{i+p})$ represents the p binary bits of PQ_1 and $\alpha[loc_i] = b_{(loc_i+1)}$. To PQ_1, the current value of loc_i is appended, and a digest generated using shift registers or hash functions like message digest (MD5) or secure hash algorithm (SHA) is applied to the resultant string to generate r bit digest. The binary equivalent of the digest will be the pseudorandom bits of the subsequence:

$$PQA_i(p_i \cdot p_{i+1} \cdots p_{i+s}) = (Hash(PQ_1(p_i \cdots p_{i+p}) \cdot loc_i))_2 \tag{11.3}$$

where s is the number of bits in the binary equivalent.

The current value of loc_i is added to the substring and is the salt that will eliminate any periodicity that may exist in the partial quotients. It introduces randomness into the sequences and serves as a mixing function to extract random numbers from the generated sequence. The value of loc_i is updated and the processing is continued for the next n partial quotients of α until the required number of bits for the PQ sequence is generated by concatenating the subsequences as

$$PQA = PQA_1 \cdot PQA_2 \cdot PQA_3 \tag{11.4}$$

The generated PQ sequences have a probability distribution that is very close to the uniform probability distribution and are tested using the NIST test suite (Runkin et al. 2001) to analyze them from the randomness and security perspective. Barring the initial bits of the sequences, the PQ sequences pass the tests of randomness. The initial bits (usually first 100 bits) need to be discarded due to the nature of the partial quotients so as to ensure the security of the scheme. This PQ sequence is used by the entities in NetAMS and NetSHA to encrypt the communication.

11.3.3 Key Establishment in NetAMS: KEAMS

At the heart of any secure authentication algorithm is the successful management of the key. A key compromised is considered as equivalent to the absence of a security solution. When two nodes communicate, much of the communication is for the secure key exchange. In WBANs, it is essential that the key management process is computationally inexpensive but at the same time secure to address the power issues in the wireless devices. Traditional schemes like Diffie-Hellman and elliptic curve cryptography are considered to be computationally intensive.

KEAMS is an independent key management scheme to enable the participants in the network to establish keys independently at their end without the need to physically exchange them and authenticate the HPA with the HMS and vice versa. This is coupled with the generation of a new PQ sequence to encrypt packets of sensor data for each iteration of transmission to ensure secure data communication in the network.

The successful operation of the scheme is based on some assumption:

1. A database of irrational numbers that are transcendental and nonperiodic is available with the health personnel.
2. The health personnel will deploy the WBAN on the patient.
3. Health personnel will select n irrational numbers from an available database and deploy them in both the HPA and HMS along with a random integer P.
4. All frames received are acknowledged by the receiver. Retransmission is not attempted for lost frames.

11.3.3.1 Initiation of Communication by HPA

HPA initiates the communication by randomly selecting one irrational number IR from its list and generates the continued fraction expansion using Euclid's algorithm (Hardy and Wright 1975). A random integer P, $P \geq 100$, is used to identify the position to which to extract the partial quotients that will be used to generate the initial pseudorandom sequence PQ sequence as explained in Section 11.3.2 to encrypt the initial packet to the HMS.

After generation of the PQ sequence, HPA frames a packet with the fields as shown in Figure 11.2. The packet includes a onetime nonce N_a formed by

| NONCE *N_a* | RAND_HASH *C* | DIGEST *D* |

Figure 11.2 Structure of initiation frame in NetAMS.

concatenating a time stamp and a sequence number; a random integer C given by RAND_HASH that can vary from 1 to k, $k \leq 10$, depending on the capacity of the HPA; and a digest D obtained by hashing the selected irrational number IR C number of times. Digest D is the authentication code generated by the HPA. It can also be noted that hashing is a one-way function where the Digest D can be generated from the irrational number but not vice versa.

The nonce N_a is encrypted using the PQ sequence by a simple XOR operation.

The initiation data frame is transmitted to HMS over a wireless channel that will verify the authenticity of the packet and then identify the key selected by the HPA.

11.3.3.2 Establishment of Key by HMS

HMS receives the packet transmitted by HPA and initiates the process to identify the key selected by the HPA. This is done by selecting each irrational number in its repository and hashing it RAND_HASH number of times. Each generated hash code Y is compared with the received DIGEST D. When a match is found, the corresponding irrational number IR_j in the HMS is selected as the key.

The continued fraction expansion of selected irrational number IR_j is used to generate the partial quotients and from the Pth location, the pseudorandom PQ sequence is extracted. The PQ sequence is used to decrypt the nonce N_b received in the initiation packet sent from the HPA.

11.3.3.3 Authentication of HMS

The HMS generates the acknowledgment packet using the Decrypted nonce N_b and a new random integer R given by RAND_POINT as shown in Figure 11.3. The nonce is generated using the time stamp and frame sequence number. The integer R will be used by the HPA and the HMS to extract the PQ sequence to encrypt further communications. The acknowledgment is then encrypted using the generated PQ sequence and transmitted to the HPA.

The received packet is decrypted by the HPA to get the nonce N_b and RAND_POINT R. The received nonce N_b is verified with the one previously generated nonce N_a to establish the authenticity of the HMS. The random integer RAND_POINT is then used to extract the new PQ sequence to encrypt all further communication in the NetAMS.

| NONCE *N_b* | RAND_POINT *R* |

Figure 11.3 Structure of acknowledgment frame from HMS.

| Data_Sensor1 | Data_Sensor2 | ⋯ | Data_Sensor *N* |

Figure 11.4 Structure of data frame from WSH.

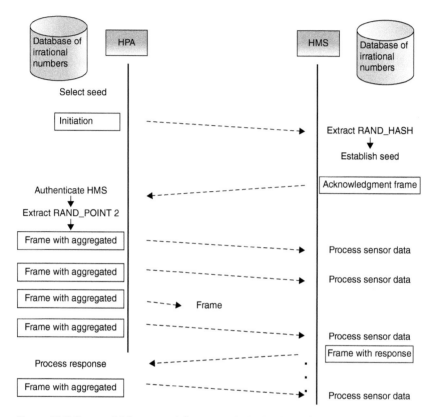

Figure 11.5 Key establishment and data transmission in NetAMS.

The HPA aggregates the sensor data from each WSH and frames them for transmission to the HMS. Every packet between HPA and HMS in the NetAMS is encrypted using the *PQ* sequences extracted from subsequent locations from *R* thus ensuring that every packet is encrypted using a different pseudorandom sequence. The structure of the data packet is depicted in Figure 11.4 and the key establishment sequence is represented in Figure 11.5.

Every time a reset happens, the key exchange procedure is repeated to establish the secret key at each of the ends without the need to transmit them over the wireless channel.

Any frame not received by the HPA and for which an acknowledge is not generated or received by it, there is no retransmission as the time lapse for the retransmission can render the information as stale in a system meant for real-time health monitoring. The packet is thus dropped and the next packet is transmitted.

11.3.4 Key Establishment in NetSHA: KESHA

To ensure key establishment and authentication in NetSHA, a lighter version of KEAMS is deployed. The algorithm is lighter as the power of each WSH deployed on the human body has more constraints than the HPA. Though it is possible that the sensor can give faulty readings, it is quite unlikely that the WSH on the patient's body can be compromised other than by the patient or personnel who deployed the sensor nodes. The algorithm eliminates the need for PQ sequences generation in each of the nodes. Rather only loc_i, for extracting the PQ sequences is exchanged by the WSH with the HPA.

Each WSH will detect the body parameters and transmit the sensed data to the HPA. The data received by HPA from multiple sensors is aggregated by the HPA and a consolidated packet containing data from each of the WSH is communicated to the HPA.

11.3.4.1 Initiation of Communication by WSH
It is assumed that

1. The personnel from HMS deploy the WSH on the patient's body.
2. From the collection of n irrationals number deployed in the HPA, and one irrational each is loaded into each of the WSH. A mutually agreed integer RSN is also deployed in the WSH with a corresponding entry in the HPA.
3. Each of the sensors will individually and independently communicate with the HPA to establish the keys.
4. WPA will not acknowledge each of the frames received by it, rather keeps track of the sequence number of the packet received.

Each of the WSH and HPA needs to be mutually authenticated to ensure that data is not compromised on transit or that the WPA or any of the WSH is compromised.

When the HPA is activated after deployment of the WBAN on the human body, it is detected by each WSH in the network. To authenticate itself, the WSH initiates communication with the HPA to establish the key. A packet is framed as depicted in Figure 11.6.

| Nonce N_c | RAND_HASH C_{SN} | DIGEST $D2$ |

Figure 11.6 Structure of initiation frame from WSN.

Nonce N_c is a onetime code generated as a time stamp, and D_2 is a digest formed by hashing the nonce C_{SN} number of times. The nonce N_C encrypted by the PQ sequence generated from the irrational number using R_{SN} and packet is transmitted to HPA.

11.3.4.2 Establishment of Key by the HPA

HPA receives the packet from each WSH and initiates the process to identify the key selected by the WSH. HPA will hash each irrational number C_{SN} number of times. When the generated hash A matches with the received hash Y, the corresponding irrational number IR_{SN} is selected as the secret key. HPA then generates the PQ sequence for the corresponding irrational number using the preestablished integer R_{SN} to extract the sequence from the partial quotients. The nonce is decrypted to get N_b.

11.3.4.3 Acknowledgment by HPA

An acknowledgment frame is created as in Figure 11.7 using the decrypted nonce N_d and RAND_POINT R_A, a random integer selected by the HPA to generate the pseudorandom sequence to encrypt further packets and is transmitted to the WSH.

On receiving the packet, WSH decrypts it to retrieve the nonce N_d and authenticates the HPA by comparing it with the selected nonce N_d. RAND_POINT R_A is then used as the input PQSG to generate the pseudorandom sequence for the further encryption of the packets.

Every subsequent packet – the sensor information from WSH to HPA and return acknowledgment or action information from WSH to HPA – is encrypted using the PQ sequences extracted from location R_A, thus ensuring that every packet is encrypted using a different key. In case of failure by HPA to identify the irrational number, the HPA will ignore the communication. The WSH will wait for acknowledgment and, on nonreceipt, will retransmit the initial authentication packet.

Every time a reset happens, the entire procedure is repeated once more to generate the secret key at each of the ends. Thus this mechanism is used to generate the key at each end without the need to transmit them over the wireless channel.

Any frame not received by the HPA and for which an acknowledgment is not generated or received by HPA, there will not be retransmission as the time lapse for the retransmission can render the information as stale. The packet is

| NONCE N_d | RAND_POINT R_A |

Figure 11.7 Structure of acknowledgment frame from HPA.

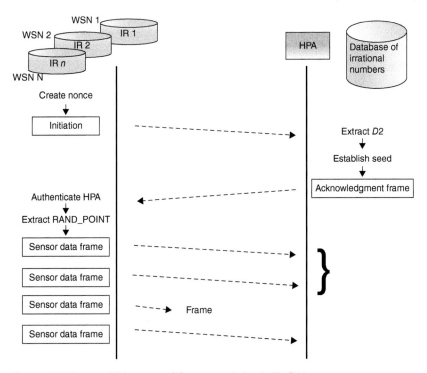

Figure 11.8 Key establishment and data transmission in NetSHA.

thus dropped and the next packet is transmitted. Figure 11.8 depicts the Key Establishment and data transmission process in NetSHA.

11.4 Performance Analysis

The proposed framework is implemented in MATLAB to analyze the performance of the scheme and the desired characteristics. The sensor readings were randomly generated using built-in functions in MATLAB. The performance of the algorithms is evaluated in terms of the number of operations performed in encrypting and authenticating the packets and users.

11.4.1 Randomness

Security of the framework is ensured using cryptographically secure pseudorandom numbers generated from continued fraction of certain irrational numbers. The strength of the system lies in its resistance to cryptanalysis.

The quality of the PQ sequences has been previously analyzed in Pillai and Padma (2015) by the authors. PQSG does not involve any type of feedback or modulus operations that will reset the PQSG and result in periodicity. The randomness properties of sequences are entirely dependent on the choice of the seed and the number of partial quotients used to generate one entity of the sequence that will also be the input to the hash function. Thus it can be assured that choice of the right irrational number as a seed that is transcendental and generates partial quotients that are infinite and nonperiodic and do not have inherent patterns and that using the hash function with a suitable salt will generate sequences without any limit or periodicity. The outcome of analysis of the PQ sequence in Pillai and Padma (2015) suggests that the sequences are suitable for implementation as a onetime pad. The same key can be used, and by varying the precision of the key and the locations of extraction of the partial quotients, a number of pseudorandom sequences that exhibit properties of onetime pad can be generated.

11.4.2 Distinctiveness

It is a measure of uniqueness of the communication between a pair of entities, in the NetSHA or the NetAMS. The pseudorandom sequence changes for every iteration of communication between the entities. This makes it quite difficult to reproduce the pseudorandom sequence at a later time to simulate a replay of the transmission. The same irrational numbers can be embedded in the sensor nodes and their precision can be varied to generate a different sequence for every iteration. Figure 11.9 shows that the correlation of multiple sequences generated from a single seed but with varying precision is negligible.

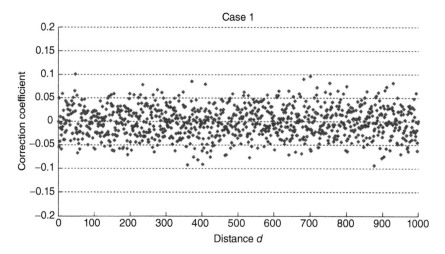

Figure 11.9 Correlation coefficient of 1000 sequences of length 1024 with the original sequence chosen as the onetime random vector selected from position 1 and the others from distance $m = 1$. Average correlation is $-0.000\,75$.

11.4.3 Complexity

Complexity of the algorithms is measured in terms of the operations performed in the encryption of a frame, transmission, and decryption of one data frame having fields of information. This is based on assumption as follows:

- Each frame has 8 bit data as each of its fields.
- Random integer selection is based on a simple RAND() function.
- The sender encrypts the nonce and the receiver encrypts the nonce and random number.

Tables 11.1 and 11.2 highlight the logical operations involved in the key identification by the sender and key establishment by the receiver.

Tables 11.3 and 11.4 illustrate the operating scenario in terms of the logical operations involved in the selection, transmission, and establishment of the keys used to introduce randomness in the authentication system. The performance of NetSHA and NetAMS are comparable. It can be observed that the

Table 11.1 Number of logical operations in key generation, encryption and decryption of one frame in NetAMS.

Operation	Encryption	Decryption
Select irrational number One of the n irrational number is selected as the key:S searches,$S \leq m$	S	–
PQ Sequence Generation		
Division, subtraction, floor function to generate x partial quotients.		
Concatenation of y partial quotients given by $\frac{x}{y}$ hashing for $\frac{x}{y}$ units to generate PQ Sequences	$x \times 3 + \frac{x}{y} + \frac{x}{y}$	$x \times 3 + \frac{x}{y} + \frac{x}{y}$
Hash operation for Digest		
Encryption: Data hashed C times to generate digest	C	$m \times C$
Decryption: m irrational numbers out of n hashed until desired key is found		
Exclusive OR		
For encryption of n bit data	8	$8 + 8$
Concatenation of fields of frame		
Sender : 4 fields	4	2
Receiver: 2 fields		
Transmission of frame	1	1
Total	$13 + 3x + 2\frac{x}{y} + C + n + s$	$19 + 3x + 2\frac{x}{y} + mC + n$

Table 11.2 Number of logical operations in NetAMS based on assumed values.

		Total Logical Operations	
	Scenario	Encryption	Decryption
Best Case	$x = 20, y = 3, C = 1, = 1, m = 1$	433	439
Worst Case	$x = 20, y = 3, C = 5, = 1, m = n = 5$	440	463
Average Case	$x = 20, y = 3, C = 3, = 1, m = 3$	442	447

Table 11.3 Number of logical operations in key generation, encryption and decryption of one frame in NetSHA.

Operation	Encryption	Decryption
PQ sequence generation		
Division, subtraction, floor function to generate x partial quotients.		
Concatenation of y partial quotients given by $\frac{x}{y}$ hashing for $\frac{x}{y}$ units to generate PQ Sequences	$x \times 3 + \frac{x}{y} + \frac{x}{y}$	$x \times 3 + \frac{x}{y} + \frac{x}{y}$
Hash operation for Digest		
Encryption: Data hashed C times to generate digest	C	$m \times C$
Decryption: m irrational numbers out of n hashed until desired key is found		
Exclusive OR		
For encryption of n bit data	8	$8 + 8$
Concatenation of fields of frame		
Sender : 3 fields	3	2
Receiver: 2 fields		
Transmission of frame	1	1
Total	$12 + 3x + 2\frac{x}{y} + C + n$	$19 + 3x + 2\frac{x}{y} + mC + n$

number of operation at the HMS is higher than that at the HPA given that logically it will also have the most computational power among the participating entities. The number of operation is the least in the WSHs, given that it has severe power constraints.

Table 11.4 Number of logical operations in NetSHA based on assumed values.

		Total logical operations	
Scenario		Encryption	Decryption
Best case	$x = 20, y = 3, C = 1, \delta = 1, m = 1$	432	439
Worst case	$x = 20, y = 3, C = 5, \delta = 1, m = n = 5$	436	464
Average case	$x = 20, y = 3, C = 3, \delta = 1, m = 3$	433	447

11.5 Discussion

Security and freshness of data is of prime concern in a WBAN-based remote health monitoring system. Freshness of data and authenticity of parties involved in the health parameters collection and transmission process is vital for the trust in the system. Security is hence of high priority and given that wireless sensor nodes have constraints in power and space; it is essential that any proposed scheme is implementable in such a system and at the same time is secure.

The complexity of the algorithms estimated in the previous section is based on assumed parameters and that one operation is equivalent to one unit of time. The actual implementation of hash functions, PQSG, and transmission process will vary in the number of operations actually implemented. The focus here is on the key management scheme that can be conveniently implemented on a constrained entity like a wireless sensor node.

KEAMS is a key management scheme where the focus is on secure exchange of the keys between the HPA and the HMS. Each packet generated from a frame of data will be unique as it was encrypted using a different PQ sequence generated from the same key but using a different set of partial quotients. HPA selects its key randomly, and the HMS goes through a sequential process of identifying the key chosen by the HPA.

KESHA focuses on key management between the WSH and the HPA. Each sensor node is preloaded with an appropriate irrational number but a random integer is used to extract different PQ sequences. It has been experimentally proved that given the partial quotients of an irrational number, barring the first few partial quotients, the PQ sequence generated by varying the starting position of selecting the partial quotients results in a totally different pseudorandom sequence as depicted in Figure 11.9. Hence randomness of the keys and ability to generate new pseudorandom sequences from a given irrational number ensures secrecy of the data encrypted by the sequence. No two data packets will have similar encrypted values making it difficult for an adversary to launch a statistical attack.

Another common attack is the man-in-the-middle attack where an adversary listens to every conversation occurring in the system and modify the data as required. The proposed algorithms have the property of dynamically changing encryption keys and are not exchanged. This makes it impossible for an adversary to launch man-in-the-middle attack.

Authentication of the communicating parties is ensured using the nonce that is generated at the initiating end, encrypted using the PQ sequences and then sent to the receiver. As the same PQ sequence is almost never used repeatedly, adversary will not be able to capture it and replay it at another point of time. Thus the data transmission in NetAMS and NetSHA are both resistant to replay attack.

One of the limitations that are evident from the scheme is the need for manual intervention to load the irrational numbers in the HPA, HMS, and the WSHs. Identifying suitable irrational number is not a task that can be done by health personnel and hence their needs to be a mechanism to identify suitable irrational numbers. To ensure a light framework, acknowledgment of sensor data packets is not incorporated, and the time spent in retransmission can render the data as stale and hence not useful. Some vital parameters could be missed out in such a design. It would be appropriate to allow authentication of each of the packets, but it would be a constraint on the resources and time.

The scheme is a very lightweight implementation for remote patient monitoring as desired in a WBAN. Though it has its own limitations, simple and efficient mechanism of key exchange and encryption without the need of complex algorithms will ensure that the scheme is implementable.

11.6 Conclusion

A remote patient monitoring system requires that accurate data be received and quick appropriate decision be made to ensure timely intervention. In this chapter, algorithms for pseudorandom number generation and secure key management and exchange are presented where the focus is on independent key generation. This enhances the security of the system as the secrecy of the key ensures security of the system. A key compromised is as good as their being no security implementation at all, and the whole system is vulnerable. The framework enables the communicating parties to establish the shared key without the need to physically transmit them over a wireless network that is vulnerable. The security of the key is thus ensured.

The algorithms proposed are also light, considering the fact that simple XOR is used in the encryption process, thus relieving the nodes of heavy computations. Each iteration of packet transmission is encrypted using a different pseudorandom sequence, thus ensuring it impossible for an adversary to sniff packets and prevent replay attacks.

To study the performance of the system, simple XOR operation is considered for the encryption process so as to focus on the key management process. Block-based symmetric schemes or asymmetric schemes can also be used, and the framework further analyzed.

Bibliography

Gomati, V. (2015). *Bio-Sensor Authentication for Medical Applications Using WBAN*, Advances in Intelligent Systems and Computing, vol. **398**. Springer AISC.

Hardy, G.H. and Wright, E.M. (1975) *An Introduction to the Theory of Numbers.* Oxford University Press.

Mana, M., Feham, M., and Bensaber, B.A. (2009). SEKEBAN (Secure and Efficient Key Exchange for Wireless Body Area Network). *International Journal of Advanced Science and Technology* **12**: 45–60.

Mana, M., Feham, M., and Bensaber, B.A. (2011). Trust key management scheme for wireless body area networks. *International Journal of Network Security* **12** (2): 71–79.

Masdari, M. and Ahmadzadeh, S. (2016). Comprehensive analysis of the authentication methods in wireless body area networks. *Security and Communication Networks* **9** (17): 4777–4803.

Padma, T. and Pillai, J.S. (2014). Image watermarking using PQ sequences. In: Proceedings of Emerging Research in Computing, Information, Communication and Applications, 740–745. Elsevier.

Pillai J.S. and Padma, T. (2015). The analysis of PQ sequences generated from continued fractions for use as pseudorandom sequences in cryptographic applications. In: *Artificial Intelligence and Evolutionary Computations in Engineering Systems*, Advances in Intelligent Systems and Computing, vol. **394** (ed. S. Dash, M. Bhaskar, B. Panigrahi, and S. Das), 633–644. Springer.

Raazi, S.M.K. and Lee, H. (2009). BARI: a distributed key management approach for wireless body area networks. In: Proceedings of 2009 International Conference on Computational Intelligence and Security, 324–329.

Raghav, V.S., Saurabh, D., Sahlini, U., and Srinivas, S. (2012). A security suite for wireless body area networks. *International Journal of Network Security & its Applications* **4** (1): 97116.

Runkin, A., Soto, J., Nechvatal, J. et al. (2001). *Statistical Test Suite for Random and Pseudorandom Number Generators for Cryptographic Applications.* Federal Information Processing Standards Special Publication 800-822, National Institute of Standards and Technology.

Tan, C.C., Wang, H., Zhong, S., and Li, Q. (2008). Body sensor network security: an identity-based cryptography approach. Proceedings of WiSec '08 (March 31-April 02 2008).

Venkatasubramanian, K.K., Banerjee, A., and Gupta, S.K.S. (2008). EKG-based key agreement in body sensor networks. In: Proceedings of IEEE INFOCOM Workshops, 1–6.

Yenuganti, N. (2016). Authentication in wireless body area networks. Graduate Theses and Dissertations. http://scholarcommons.usf.edu/etd/6442 (accessed 1 June 2018).

12

Image Analysis Using Smartphones for Medical Applications: A Survey

Rajeswari Rajendran[1] and Jothilakshmi Rajendiran[2]

[1] *Department of Computer Applications, Bharathiar University, Coimbatore, Tamilnadu, India*
[2] *Department of Physics, Veltech University, Chennai, Tamilnadu, India*

12.1   Introduction

The number of smartphone users is steeply increasing every year, and this number is expected to further increase in the forthcoming years. According to the Groupe Speciale Mobile Association (GSMA) intelligence reports (Zhang, 2017), the number of global smartphone connections is approximately 51% of the total mobile phone users in 2016. The report also predicts that the number of smartphone users will be two-thirds of the total number of mobile phone users by the end of 2020. It also predicts that the percentage of smartphone users will increase from 47% in 2016 to 62% in 2020 in developing countries where the major contributors will be countries such as India, China, and Indonesia. Moreover, smartphones are increasingly being used by all age groups of people ranging from adolescents to senior citizens and in all areas including remote areas where adequate healthcare facilities are not available. Thus smartphones can be used to provide pervasive medical solutions (Jutel, 2011).

Smartphones are currently used in a number of medical applications including evidence-based medicine, mobile clinical communication, patient assessment and disease management, remote patient monitoring, and administrative tasks in the clinic. Smartphones come with built-in sensors such as camera that can be used for detecting biological signals. The powerful processing power of smartphones enables in analyzing these images to provide diagnostic results. Smartphones are currently being used to obtain various health-related information including heart rate, breathing rate, blood oxygen saturation, diabetes, melanoma, wound status, and fatigue status from the images of fingertips, eyes, skin, and tongue. External sensors attached to smartphones have enabled medical imaging to be combined with smartphones

Intelligent Pervasive Computing Systems for Smarter Healthcare, First Edition.
Arun Kumar Sangaiah, S.P. Shantharajah, and Padma Theagarajan.

and hence provide great potential to provide diagnosis of blood cells, sweat, saliva, and serum. Apart from these characteristics, smartphones have powerful transmission capability such as cellular data connection, wireless fidelity (Wi-Fi), and Bluetooth that enables in collecting on-site disease data using image acquisition device, transmits these data to remote health center, and obtains the analyzed results.

There are many characteristics of smartphones that make them suitable for various medical applications to be used by common people and by medical practitioners (Kratzke and Cox, 2012). Section 12.2 describes the characteristics of smartphones and how they support in pervasive healthcare. Section 12.3 provides a review of recent work carried out in medical image analysis using smartphones. The applications are mainly categorized as the ones that are based on the built-in sensors of smartphones and the ones that are based on additional sensor/hardware attached to the smartphones. This survey is not exhaustive but tries to cover all important smartphone applications for medical image diagnosis. Section 12.4 gives a brief description of various libraries and tools available for developing medical image analysis-based smartphone applications. Section 12.5 describes the challenges and perspectives in developing medical image-based smartphone applications. Section 12.6 concludes the chapter.

12.2 Pervasive Healthcare Using Image-Based Smartphone Applications

Smartphones are increasingly being preferred by a large number of people over ordinary phones due to their various characteristics. Smartphones have the ability to connect to other devices through mobile data connections, local Wi-Fi, or Bluetooth. This makes them suitable for communication with other devices, which are either nearby or situated at distant places. Smartphones help in remaining connected through social networking sites such as Twitter, Facebook, and LinkedIn all the time. They also provide access to email, video calling, and conferencing. The decline in the price of smartphones without compromising their quality is also one of the reasons why smartphones are used by a large number of people. Another important characteristic of smartphones is their portability, which makes them suitable to be used anywhere and anytime.

Apart from these characteristics, the power of smartphones is increasing every day, which makes them suitable for imaging-based medical applications. Smartphones of today have processing power that is equivalent to that of a personal computer. All the topmost vendors of smartphones including Apple and Samsung give importance to the improvement of the processing power of the smartphones. With the increase in the processing power of the smartphones, their imaging capability also improves. The modern smartphones have faster image processing capability that will further improve the quality of image and speedy processing of the images and provide additional imaging capabilities. Almost all the smartphones come with cameras that can generate images with resolution approximately 10 megapixels, which makes them suitable for preliminary examination, diagnosis, and continuous monitoring of certain diseases.

Apart from the built-in camera, the smartphones can also be connected with other devices that help in capturing medical images. The smartphone manufacturers have also made efforts to improve the display quality and technology, which have greatly improved the resolution of smartphone displays. The increase in resolution helps in viewing the images with more clarity and detail. The ability to be connected with a large number of devices enables the smartphones to capture and transmit medical images at high speed with other devices. Generating images of high quality, intelligent interpretation of the captured images, lesser cost, and immediate transmission of information make them extremely suitable for pervasive healthcare.

12.3 Smartphone-Based Image Diagnosis

Smartphones have a rich set of sensors such as camera, microphone, accelerometer, proximity sensor, barometer, and magnetometer, which help in receiving various signals from the individuals/patients and their surroundings (Khan et al., 2013). Although a number of built-in sensors are available, almost all the smartphone-based medical applications make use of the capabilities of camera and microphone. The powerful processors and memories of smartphones help in processing and storage of the signals obtained. The obtained results can be used for further processing or decision making with regard to the medical conditions.

Apart from the built-in sensors additional sensors or hardware can be attached with the smartphones, which further improve the capability of the smartphones in monitoring and diagnosis of health. The signals obtained from the smartphones with the additional devices can provide vital information, which can be used for preliminary examination and self-monitoring by common people. Smartphones also have excellent data transmission capability, which allows them to transmit the received signals/processed data to be transmitted to a remote site so that guidance from medical experts can be obtained. Images of various human body parts such as eye, fingertip, and skin may be used to obtain health-related information.

The smartphone-based image diagnosis for medical applications consists of various stages including development of smartphone application, installation of the application in the smartphone, retrieval of images from patients/people

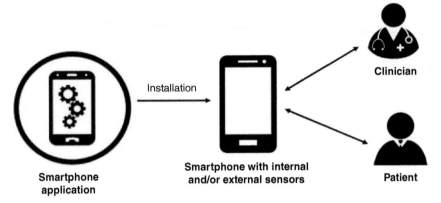

Figure 12.1 Stages in smartphone-based medical image diagnosis.

through camera/external sensors, and processing and diagnosis of the captured images. Figure 12.1 shows these generic steps involved in smartphone-based diagnosis of images for healthcare. The smartphone application incorporates various steps such as capturing images, processing them, and performing diagnosis from the obtained results. Processing of images may include image segmentation, feature extraction, and classification. These steps may be based on statistical, machine learning, or soft computing techniques. In this section a review of image-based smartphone applications that help in monitoring and diagnosis of certain diseases is given.

12.3.1 Diagnosis Using Built-In Camera

Smartphone camera itself helps in effectively capturing images that can be further processed using algorithms implemented in the smartphones. The implemented algorithms can help in measuring various physiological parameters such as heart rate, respiration rate, and blood oxygen saturation level. Thus, smartphones can be used for low-cost, noninvasive monitoring of various physiological parameters. Heart rate computed from the fingertip images captured through smartphone camera are almost accurate with the readings obtained using other clinical devices.

Zaman et al. use smartphones to record the video of fingertip images (Zaman et al., 2017). Later, the video is processed to track the changes in the curves of fingertip to obtain the heart rate. They also propose another method that keeps track of changes in fingertip image intensity to measure the heart rate. Photoplethysmogram (PPG) is a technique that detects the changes in the blood volume in tissues. Android-based smartphone cameras are used to obtain the images of fingertips by Sukaphat et al. (2016). They propose a method to compute PPG from the histograms of red channel that is

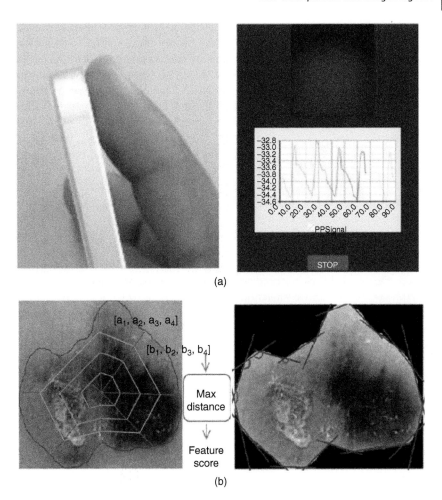

Figure 12.2 Examples of diagnosis using smartphone's camera: (a) detection of heart rate from fingertip image (Zaman et al., 2017) and (b) border fitting for skin lesion (Do et al., 2014).

then used to calculate the heart rate (Figure 12.2a). Just like images of fingertip are used to calculate the heart rate, Poh et al. have used video images of human face to calculate heart rate (Poh et al., 2010). Their method also utilizes the logic that blood volume changes in human faces can be used to compute the PPG signal. They have used region of interest extracted from human face videos and have applied independent component analysis (ICA) to divide them into three source signals. Out of the three resulting components, they have considered the second component to calculate the heart rate as it contained the strong PPG signal.

Kurylyak et al. (2011) have used PPG to calculate blood pressure using artificial neural network (ANN). They have used twenty-one parameters including times of systolic, diastolic parts, and ratio between them to train the ANN. The changes in the color signal obtained from fingertip images can also be used to calculate other physiological parameters such as oxygen saturation and respiration rate. Scully et al. have used the green band of video images obtained from the fingertip to calculate heart rate and respiration rate (Scully et al., 2012). Initially the beat rates are obtained from the green band that are then resampled to continuous heart rate signal. The power spectrum density of the obtained heart rate signal is calculated using Welch periodogram method to obtain the respiration rate. They also propose a method to compute the relative oxygen saturation using red and blue bands. The standard deviations and mean intensities of red and blue bands are computed, which are then processed using moving average filter to calculate the relative oxygen saturation.

Melanoma is one of the severe forms of skin cancer. Prescreening results using smartphone-based applications would provide an awareness about the disease. Do et al. have captured and processed dermoscopic images using smartphones to diagnose melanoma. They have used a modified feature criterion selection that takes advantage of mutual information and average neighborhood maximization (Do et al., 2014) (Figure 12.2b). Zhang et al. have proposed a method that diagnoses tongue images captured by smartphone camera (Zhang et al., 2013). The captured tongue images are segmented to obtain the region of interest, then features such as tongue thickness, coating color, and blade color are extracted from the segmented image. All the methods described in this subsection are based on only the images captured by smartphone camera, and they are summarized in Table 12.1.

12.3.2 Diagnosis Using External Sensors/Devices

Smartphones can also be attached with external imaging devices or sensors to obtain additional health information. The functionalities and capabilities of smartphones are improved by these external devices. They help in obtaining more diagnostic information such as images of various organs. Personalized nutritional information help the individuals to keep track of their health and diet. One of the most required tests is blood test, which provides the density measure of white blood cells and red blood cells. It can also be useful in diagnosing the overall health information or warning us against diseases such as anemia and blood infections.

Zhu et al. have used additional hardware components, one for counting white and red blood cells and another for calculating the hemoglobin content (Zhu et al., 2013). The hardware component has a lens and a light-emitting diode (LED). This component together with the lens of the smartphone camera forms a complete imaging system (Figure 12.3a). Oncescu et al. have used

Table 12.1 Smartphone camera-based diagnosis.

Health information	Description of diagnosis method
Heart rate	Fingertip images are used to calculate heart rate from the changes in the curves of fingertip (Zaman et al., 2017)
Heart rate	Changes in the histograms of red channel of fingertip images are used to calculate the heart rate (Sukaphat et al., 2016)
Heart rate	Changes in blood volumes obtained from applying ICA on human face images are used to calculate heart rate (Poh et al., 2010)
Blood pressure	Several parameters including times of systolic, diastolic parts, and ratio between them are used to train ANN to compute blood pressure (Kurylyak et al., 2011)
Respiration rate and oxygen saturation	Method based on Welch periodogram and a method based on moving average filter are used to compute respiration rate and oxygen saturation, respectively, from the fingertip images (Scully et al., 2012)
Melanoma	Dermoscopic images are processed to diagnose melanoma (Do et al., 2014)
Tongue-based features	Tongue-based features such as thickness, coating, and blade color are obtained from the tongue images (Zhang et al., 2013)

smartphones to detect biomarkers such as hydration level, sodium concentration, and pH level of saliva (Oncescu et al., 2013). The external hardware includes a case where the test strips containing samples of saliva or sweat are inserted. The images are captured using smartphone camera. Colorimetric quantification of the samples are carried out to detect the biomarkers. The hydration level and sodium concentration are obtained from the sweat. The pH level of saliva is also obtained. It can be used to prevent enamel decalcification.

Vitamin D deficiency is associated with other diseases such as diabetes, cardiovascular diseases, cancer, and infections. Lee et al. use an accessory consisting of LED in a polydimethylsiloxane diffuser to illuminate the prepared sample (Lee et al., 2014). They have used gold nanoparticle-based immunoassay and colorimetric tests to measure the levels of 25-hydroxy vitamin D. Seoho et al. have designed a mobile platform called Nutriphone, which helps every individual to understand the levels of B_{12} and other health markers (Seoho et al., 2014). Blood sample can be applied on a test strip to find the resulting colorimetric signals. These signals or images are captured by camera and analyzed to obtain the levels of B_{12} (Figure 12.3b).

Proper diagnosis of diabetes would help in its efficient treatment planning. A complete automated system is developed by Prasanna et al. to diagnose diabetes (Prasanna et al., 2013). They have used an ophthalmoscope along with a

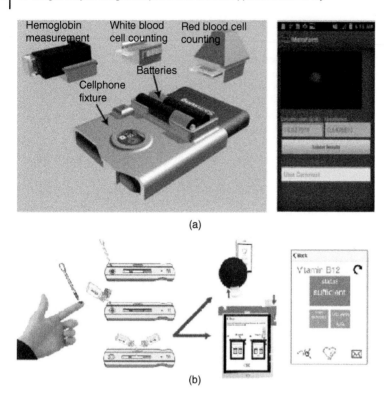

Figure 12.3 Examples of diagnosis using sensors/devices attached to smartphone: (a) platform for blood analysis (Zhu et al., 2013) and (b) system for detection vitamin B_{12} levels (Seoho et al., 2014).

smartphone to capture images of the retina. These images are processed using pattern recognition and statistical inference algorithms for decision making in diabetic retinopathy. Andrew et al. have developed a smartphone app that displays a spatially resolved pattern to the individual with the help of a pinhole attached to the smartphone. The individual aligns the patterns by a touch screen interface based on which the refractive error is estimated. This is one of the cost-effective refractive error screening tools. Retinopathy of prematurity is one of the major causes of blindness in children, and early treatment of this disease can prevent many complications. Smartphone camera along with 30D lens are used to record the fundus images as video while the examination is performed under anesthesia (Lin et al., 2014). The fundus images captured from the patients can be used for their treatment planning.

It may be difficult for some patients to repeatedly visit their doctors in person post-surgery. In order to provide some help to such patients, a smartphone-based application that can be used to remotely monitor the post-surgery wounds by doctors has been designed by Wiseman et al. (2016).

They have captured the images of post-surgery wound by smartphone camera at patient's place and transmitted them to doctors for assessment. They have shown that the inter-rater agreement of smartphone image-based assessment was almost same as the assessment done in person. Diagnosis of brain images may help us in understanding various neurological diseases. Stopczynski et al. have proposed *Smartphone Brain Scanner* (SBS2), which utilizes the characteristics of electroencephalography (EEG) sensors and open-source software for real-time neuroimaging to capture the neuroimaging responses. The stimuli they have used in their experiments include time-locked audiovisual stimuli such as text, images, and video. This SBS2 can be utilized as a software platform for developing research and end-user-oriented EEG applications. The details of health information diagnosed using smartphone with the help of additional sensors or devices attached to it are summarized in Table 12.2.

Table 12.2 External sensors or device-based diagnosis using smartphones.

Health information	Description of diagnosis method
Count of red and white blood cells and hemoglobin content	LED and smartphone camera are used as part of imaging system to count red and white blood cells (Zhu et al., 2013)
Hydration level, sodium concentration, and pH level of saliva	Colorimetric quantification of sweat and saliva samples is used to obtain values of their biomarkers (Oncescu et al., 2013)
Vitamin D	Colorimetric tests based on gold nanoparticle immunoassays are used to obtain the levels of vitamin D (Lee et al., 2014)
Vitamin B$_{12}$	Colorimetric tests from the blood samples are used to obtain the levels of vitamin B12 and other health markers (Seoho et al., 2014)
Diabetes	Retinal images are acquired using ophthalmoscope and processed by smartphone to diagnose diabetes (Prasanna et al., 2013)
Refractive measurement of the eye	Measurement of refractive error using alignment of patterns with the help of pinhole and touch screen of smartphone (Vasudevan et al., 2015)
X-ray dose rate, linearity	CMOS image sensor-based processing of images to obtain X-ray dose linearity, dose rate, X-ray dependence, and angular dependence (Kim and Youn, 2013)
Perfusion abnormalities	The thermogram images of palm or feet are used to diagnose perfusion abnormalities (Peleki and Silva, 2016)
Fundus images	Smartphone's camera and 30D lens are used to capture the fundus images of retinopathy of prematurity patients during examination procedure (Lin et al., 2014)
Wound assessment	Post-surgery wound images are captured by smartphone camera and assessed by doctors for further decision making (Wiseman et al., 2016)
Neuroimaging responses	Smartphone along with EEG sensors and neuroimaging software are used to record the neuroimaging responses (Stopczynski et al., 2014)

12.4 Libraries and Tools for Smartphone-Based Image Analysis

The two most preferred mobile devices today are iPhone and Android. The Apple iPhones are easy to use from the point of view of developers and users. Moreover, as there is only one common mobile platform with Apple, all the processes are homogenized, and this reduces the compatibility problems. Android operating system supports a range of mobile devices; hence they provide more variety apart from providing more features for the developers. But as it is fragmented, the development of usage of application becomes slightly complex.

There are various open-source libraries provided by Apple and Google to support image processing and analysis in smartphones. Some of them are Open Source Computer Vision (OpenCV), Open Source Graphics Library for Embedded Systems (OpenGL ES), Core Image, GPU Image, and Accelerate. There are a variety of mobile devices available in the market today, and developing separate applications for different platforms such as iPhone and Android would be very difficult. Hence, there is a need to develop cross-platform-based smartphone applications. These applications can run on different platforms with the same look and feel of the native applications. There are many solutions that help us in developing cross-platform mobile applications. Some of them are PhoneGap, Titanium, and Rhodes. These libraries and tools are summarized in Table 12.3.

12.4.1 Open-Source Libraries for Image Analysis in Smartphones

OpenCV is a library for computer vision techniques developed by Intel. OpenCV provides various functionalities to support image processing, feature detection, object detection, machine learning, motion tracking, and camera

Table 12.3 Libraries and tools useful for smartphone-based image analysis.

Library/tool	Website
OpenCV	http://www.opencv.org
OpenGL ES	http://www.khronos.org/opengles
Core Image	http://www.developer.apple.com/documentation/coreimage
Accelerate	http://www.developer.apple.com/accelerate
GPU Image	http://www.github.com/BradLarson/GPUImage
PhoneGap	http://www.phonegap.com
Titanium	http://www.appcelerator.com
Rhodes	http://www.github.com/rhomobile/rhodes

calibration. It is supported in both Android and iOS platforms. It is distributed under Berkeley Software Distribution (BSD) license and is completely open source. In order to use OpenCV in Android, OpenCV library Android Package Kit (APK) has to be first installed from Google Play. Then the OpenCV SDK should be included as an Android library project. OpenCV can also be used in iOS platform as it provides a great support for C and C++. In iOS, the OpenCV provides many functionalities including removing the differences in OpenCV's C++ types and iOS SDK's Objective-C types. The OpenCV library can be easily integrated with iOS.

OpenGL is a cross-platform graphics application programming interface (API) that specifies the interface for 3-dimensional (3D) graphics processing software. OpenGL ES is specifically meant for embedded devices. Android supports OpenGL through its framework API and the Native Development Kit (NDK). Before installing OpenGL ES on iOS or Android, Visual C++ for cross-platform mobile development option is required apart from the third-party tools. OpenGL ES utilizes the power of the graphics processor. The graphical processor unit (GPU) on iOS devices has the ability to execute complex 2-dimensional and 3D drawings as well as complex shading calculations on every pixel in the image.

High performance graphics is also supported by iOS using Core Image framework. Core Image framework provides near-real-time processing for still images and video. It provides an easy-to-use API; hence the complexity of low level graphics programming is hidden by this framework. Core Image framework supports many functionalities including access to built-in image processing filters, feature detection, image enhancement, ability to chain multiple filters, and support for creating custom filters for GPU. Core Image is mainly used for applying filters and other effects on images. It abstracts the pixel-level details during filtering; hence it is easy to learn and use.

iOS also supports Accelerate framework for making large-scale mathematical calculations and image processing optimized for high performance. Accelerate framework contains C APIs for vector and matrix operations, digital image processing, and a large number of numerical operations. Its functionalities specific to image processing include conversion of images from one format to another, convolution, filtering, geometric operations, histogram operations, transformation operations, and morphological operations.

The GPU Image framework is a BSD-licensed iOS library. It supports filters and other effects on images and live camera video that can be accelerated by the GPU. GPU Image is different from Core Image in two aspects. Firstly, it allows developers to write their own functions. Secondly, it provides a simpler interface. But certain features of Core Image such as face detection is not supported by GPU Image. This framework uses OpenGL ES. Hence, it hides the complexity of working with the OpenGL ES API with the help of a simplified interface.

12.4.2 Tools for Cross-Platform Smartphone Application Development

PhoneGap is an open-source development framework, which helps developers to create cross-platform mobile application using Hypertext Markup Language (HTML), Cascading Style Sheet (CSS), and JavaScript. It acts like a wrapper that converts the commands of native mobile to a JavaScript file that is linked to an HTML 5 file. This file is then executed from the smartphone application. It has a number of APIs, which makes it easy to be used.

Titanium is another commercially supported open-source framework used for creating cross-platform mobile applications using web technologies. The Titanium Mobile Software Development Kit (SDK) provides the necessary compilers and API for building an application suitable for the target platform. The Titanium Mobile API uses native user interface and platform APIs to access user interface components and functionalities of native device.

Rhodes is an open-source cross-platform smartphone application framework provided by Rhomobile. It uses HTML, CSS, JavaScript, and Ruby programming language to make the mobile application platform independent. It provides access to device, system, and framework through its Rhodes and RhoElements API libraries. It follows the model-view-controller approach.

12.5 Challenges and Future Perspectives

The advantages of using smartphones for medical applications are many. However, there have been some criticism over the usage of smartphones for medical application due to privacy issues and their accuracy (Buijink et al., 2012). Firstly, the images obtained from the smartphone camera depend on the resolution of the camera, lighting conditions, and camera linearity. In addition to this, the conditions under which the images are captured also play a vital role in providing the diagnosis results accurately. Hence, researchers have to consider all these conditions while designing their applications, and a proper training should be given to the users. Another aspect is that during the design and development of the smartphone applications, the opinion of medical experts or physicians is not taken into consideration (Visvanathan et al., 2012). This is one of the reasons why smartphone applications lack reliability. The expertise of medical experts/physicians can be used in the development of smartphone-based medical applications so that the applications are more reliable. This will be helpful if smartphones are used for preliminary and regular monitoring of various physiological parameters of an individual. In case of diagnosis and decision making, the individuals can consult with medical experts. The health-related information of individuals can be uploaded to a remote system or device, which can be accessed by physicians or medical experts. In cases of emergency or when individuals are not in a situation to travel and meet the physician, remote diagnosis would be very useful. Another aspect that has to be considered critically is the privacy related to the health information stored in the smartphones. As smartphones are connected to other devices or the Internet, the health-related information available in the smartphones are susceptible to ethical and privacy-related issues. Care must be taken to provide an additional layer of security when other devices are trying to access such information from the smartphones. Personal data, particularly health information of an individual, should not be transmitted without the knowledge of the individual. The developers and the smartphone companies should take this into consideration while providing security to the health information. Users have to protect their smartphones from malicious software attacks so that their health information is secure. They can also update the operating system and other software on smartphones regularly. The smartphones have some limitations such as limited battery capacity, storage, and display. The developers of smartphone-based healthcare applications should consider all these factors while designing the applications. Every day, many smartphone devices running on various platforms are coming up. The smartphone applications should be designed in such a way that they are able to run on all platforms and provide accurate results. This issue can be resolved by developing cross-platform-independent smartphone applications. Moreover, the researchers should design and develop intelligent and complex diagnosis algorithms, which are able to work accurately on various platforms and which have the capability to run on smartphones that come in the future. Smartphone-based diagnosis should be easily accessible by elderly, people with poor literacy, and people with disabilities. The smartphone applications should be designed so that they are user-friendly and can be easily learnt to be used. Variations of image-based smartphone applications can be developed, which can be easily used by elderly people and people with disabilities. These smartphone applications can be developed in regional languages so that people in rural areas can also access them. Although a number of commercial smartphone-based applications are available, the researchers have to yet investigate the working of these applications. The researchers have to investigate the available smartphone-based medical applications from an in-depth perspective (Lupton, 2012). Most of the smartphone applications available today are based on traditional image processing algorithms. But if they are adapted to be more complex by utilizing machine learning algorithms, then they will have the capability to solve computer vision problems more efficiently. Utilizing the features of machine learning in image processing algorithms will help in better understanding and analysis of images. The capabilities of smartphone camera can be improved by incorporating additional hardware and/or software technologies. Some such technologies that can improve the sensing capabilities of smartphone's camera are Google's Tango (Dent, 2014) and Intel's RealSense SDK (Miao, 2016). Google's augmented reality computing platform, Tango, allows the developers to incorporate indoor navigation, 3D mapping, environmental recognition, and augmented reality in their smartphone applications. Similarly Intel's RealSense SDK, an Android device with embedded Intel RealSense camera, supports many operations such as face and hand gesture recognition, background removal, and 3D scanning.

12.6 Conclusion

Smartphone-based medical image diagnosis using built-in or additional sensors/devices can provide various healthcare operations such as monitoring vital physiological parameters and diagnosis of diseases at an early stage. There are some limitations of the results provided by the smartphones, such as reliability and security. But these devices can be used for preliminary examinations based on which the individuals can consult the medical experts/physicians for further diagnosis/treatment. Currently, a lot of work is being carried out in smartphone-based medical image diagnosis. This chapter provided a review of the recent work that uses smartphones to provide health information based on captured images. The categorization of the work was based on whether or not smartphones use additional hardware to provide the diagnosis. The chapter also described some libraries and tools that are helpful in developing image-based smartphone applications. It also provided some insights on the challenges and future perspectives involved in smartphone-based medical image diagnosis.

Bibliography

Buijink, A.W., Visser, B.J., and Marshall, L. (2012). Medical apps for smartphones: lack of evidence undermines quality and safety. *Evidence-Based Medicine* **18**: 90–92. https://doi.org/10.1136/eb-2012-100885.

Dent, S. (2014). The next mobile imaging war won't be waged over megapixels. www.engadget.com/2014/02/27/smartphone-camera-competition (accessed 2 June 2017).

Do, T.-T., Zhou, Y., Zheng, H. et al. (2014). Early melanoma diagnosis with mobile imaging. In: Proceedings of Annual International Conference IEEE Engineering in Medicine and Biology Society, 6752–6757.

Jutel, A. (2011). *Putting a Name to It: Diagnosis in Contemporary Society*. Baltimore, MD: Johns Jopkins University Press.

Khan, W.Z., Xiang, Y., Aalsalem, M.Y., and Arshad, Q. (2013). Mobile phone sensing systems: a survey. *IEEE Communications Surveys and Tutorials* **15**: 420–427. https://doi.org/10.1109/SURV.2012.031412.00077.

Kim, T. and Youn, J. (2013). Development of a smartphone-based pupillometer. *Journal of the Optical Society of Korea* **17**: 249–254.

Kratzke, C. and Cox, C. (2012). Smartphone technology and apps: rapidly changing health promotion. *International Journal of Electronic Healthcare* **15**: 72–82.

Kurylyak, Y., Lamonaca, D., and Grimaldi, D. (2011). A neural network-based method for continuous blood pressure estimation from a PPG signal. In: Proceedings of IEEE International Conference IDAACS'2011, 488–491.

Lee, S., Oncescu, V., Mancuso, M. et al. (2014). A smartphone platform for the quantification of vitamin D levels. *Lab on a Chip* **14**: 1437–1442.

Lin, S., Yang, C., Yeh, P., and Ho, T. (2014). Smartphone fundoscopy for retinopathy of prematurity. *Taiwan Journal of Ophthalmology* **4**: 82–85.

Lupton, D. (2012). Critical perspectives on digital health technologies. *Sociology Compass* **8**: 1344–1359.

Miao, W. (2016). Introducing intel realsense smartphone developer kit. www .software.intel.com/en-us/blogs/2016/02/22/introducing-intel-realsense-smartphone-developer-kit (accessed 25 July 2017).

Oncescu, V., O'Dell, D., and Erickson, D. (2013). Smartphone based health accessory for colorimetric detection of biomarkers in sweat and saliva. *Lab on a Chip* **13**: 3232–3238.

Peleki, A. and Silva, A. (2016). Novel use of smartphone-based infrared imaging in the detection of acute limb ischaemia. *EJVES Short Reports* **32**: 1–3.

Poh, M.Z., McDuff, D.J., and Picard, R.W. (2010). Non-contact, automated cardiac pulse measurements using video imaging and blind source separation. *Optics Express* **18**: 10762–10774.

Prasanna, P., Jain, S., Bhagat, N., and Madabhushi, A. (2013). Decision support system for detection of diabetic retinopathy using smartphones. In: Proceedings of International Conference on Pervasive Computing Technologies for Healthcare and Workshops, 176–179.

Scully, C.G., Lee, J., Meyer, J. et al. (2012). Physiological parameter monitoring from optical recordings with a mobile phone. *IEEE Transactions on Biomedical Engineering* **59**: 303–306.

Seoho, L., Dakota, D., Jess, H. et al. (2014). NutriPhone: a mobile platform for low-cost point-of-care quantification of vitamin B12 concentrations. *Scientific Reports* **6**: 1–8.

Stopczynski, A., Stahlhut, C., Petersen, M.K. et al. (2014). Smartphones as pocketable labs: visions for mobile brain imaging and neurofeedback. *International Journal of Psychophysiology* **91**: 54–66.

Sukaphat, S., Nanthachaiporn, K., Uppaccha, K., and Tantipatrakul, P. (2016). Heart rate measurement on android platform. In: Proceedings of the International Conference on Electrical Engineering/ Electronics, Computers, Telecommunication and Information Technology, 1–5.

Vasudevan, L., John, Z., and Annette, M. (2015). Smartphone science in eyecare and medicine. *Optics & Photonics News*. **26** (1): 46–51.

Visvanathan, A., Hamilton, A., and Brady, R.R.W. (2012). Smartphone apps in microbiology - is better regulation required? *Epidemiology* **18**: E218–E220.

Wiseman, J.T., Fernandes-Taylor, S., Gunter, R. et al. (2016). Inter-rater agreement and checklist validation for postoperative wound assessment using smartphone images in vascular surgery. *Journal of Vascular Surgery Venous and Lymphatic Disorders* **4**: 320–328.

Zaman, R., Cho, C.H., Konrad, H. et al. (2017). Novel fingertip image based heart rate detection methods for a smartphone. *Sensors*. https://doi.org/10,3390/317020338.

Zhang, G. (2017). Smartphones Now Account for Hald the World's Mobile Connections. GSMA Intelligence Report. GSMA. https://www.gsmaintelligence.com/research/2017/02/smartphones-now-account-for-half-the-worlds-mobile-connections%20%20/600/ (accessed 22 July 2017).

Zhang, Q., Shang, J., Zhu, H. et al. (2013). A newtongue diagnosis application on android platform. In: Proceedings of IEEE International Conference on Bioinformatics and Biomedicine, 324–327.

Zhu, H., Sencan, I., Wong, J. et al. (2013). Cost-effective and rapid blood analysis on a cell phone. *Lab on a Chip* **13**: 1282–1288.

13

Bounds of Spreading Rate of Virus for a Network Through an Intuitionistic Fuzzy Graph

Deepa Ganesan[1], Praba Bashyam[2], Chandrasekaran Vellankoil Marappan[1], Rajakumar Krishnan[3], and Krishnamoorthy Venkatesan[4]

[1] School of Advanced Sciences, VIT University, Vellore, India
[2] Department of Mathematics, SSN College of Engineering, Affiliated to Anna university, Chennai, India
[3] School of Computer Science and Engineering, VIT, Vellore, India
[4] Department of Mathematics, College of Natural Sciences, Arba Minch University, Arba Minch, Ethiopia

In computer networks, we frequently come across the link structure of a website that can be demonstrated by the directed graph in terms of their links and the way interfacing between the links. In many situations, the complete topology for the alive network may not have been constantly accessible to the communication system in a state of time because of the reason that a few or many of its links (edges or arcs) may be incidentally disabled owing to harm or attack or blockage upon them. Obviously they are under repair by then of time. These cases are so frequent nowadays and it is rigorous and good consideration of the researchers, especially the individuals who are worried about great quality of service while in a network. Indeed, even in most of the cases, the parameters relating to its links are not crisp numbers, rather intuitionistic fuzzy numbers or fuzzy numbers. Many of the real-life environments can be represented by graph. However, when the system or network is large and complex, it is difficult to extract the exact information about the system using the classical graph theory. In such cases, the fuzzy graph or intuitionistic fuzzy graph is used to analyze the system.

Gutman (1978) introduced the concept of "graph energy" as the sum of the absolute of the eigen values of the adjacency matrix of a graph. Gutman and Polansky (1986) proposed the chemical applications on energy of a graph. Koolen et al. (2000) discussed the maximal energy of a graph. Gutman (2001) originated the mathematical properties on energy of a graph. Brankov et al. (2004) described the equal energy of a graph. An expertise and interpretation of an intuitionistic fuzzy set by Atanassov (1999) become more meaningful, applicable, and resourceful since it incorporate the degree of belongingness, degree of non-belongingness, and the hesitation degree.

Intelligent Pervasive Computing Systems for Smarter Healthcare, First Edition.
Arun Kumar Sangaiah, S.P. Shantharajah, and Padma Theagarajan.
© 2019 John Wiley & Sons, Inc. Published 2019 by John Wiley & Sons, Inc.

Computer virus remains a significant threat to networks in today's life. Several approaches have been proposed to model and simulate the virus spread in complex networks with different topologies. But epidemiological model is the suitable model to analyze the virus spread in random graph that is presented by Kephart and White (1991). Wang et al. (2003) proposed a model for virus propagation in arbitrary topology and an epidemic threshold of virus infection, and they proved that, under reasonable approximations, the epidemic threshold for a network is closely related to the largest eigenvalue of its adjacency matrix.

Susceptible-infected-susceptible (SIS) disease model can be regarded as one of the simplest virus infection models, in which persons or nodes in a network are either in two states: "healthy, but susceptible to infection" or "infected by the disease or virus and, thus, infectious to neighbors." Each node in the network is either infected or healthy. An infected node can infect its neighbors with an infection rate β, and it is cured with curing rate δ. The ratio $\tau = \frac{\beta}{\delta}$ is called the effective spreading rate of virus. Wang et al. (2003) discussed the epidemic threshold $\tau_c = \frac{1}{\lambda_{\max}A}$ where $\lambda_{\max}A$ is the largest eigenvalue of the adjacency matrix A of the network. If the effective spreading rate of virus $\tau = \left(\frac{\beta}{\delta}\right) > \tau_c$, then virus continue and a nonzero fraction of the nodes are infected, whereas if $\tau \leq \tau_c$, the epidemic dies out.

In this chapter we analyze the spreading rate of virus between incoming and outgoing links of a website through an intuitionistic fuzzy graph. We have taken the website http://www.pantechsolutions.net/. This website is modeled as an intuitionistic fuzzy graph $G = (V, E, \mu, \gamma)$ by considering the navigation of the customers. In this intuitionistic fuzzy graph, the links are considered as vertices and the path between the links is considered as edges. The weightage of each edge is considered as number of visitors getting the link from one link to another link (membership value); number of visitors not getting the link, i.e. under traffic from one link to another link (non-membership value); and drop-off case (intuitionistic fuzzy index). In four different time periods, the four links, namely, (i) /microcontroller-boards, (ii) /log-in, (iii) /html, and (iv) /project kits of the given website, are taken for our calculation. In this intuitionistic fuzzy graph, we constructed two intuitionistic fuzzy matrices using incoming and outgoing links of G. The energy of these matrices along with its lower and upper bounds is discussed. The spreading rate of virus of the given graph in terms of their energies is also discussed.

13.1 Intuitionistic Fuzzy Matrices Using Incoming and Outgoing Links

The energy of graph is extended to energy of fuzzy graph by Anjali and Mathew (2013). Praba et al. (2014) extended the concept of the energy of fuzzy graph to the energy of an intuitionistic fuzzy graph. There are no exact methods to analyze the virus spread in the user flow of the website. Hence we made an attempt to find the virus spread in a network in terms of energy of an intuitionistic fuzzy graph. In this section, intuitionistic fuzzy matrices using incoming and outgoing links and their energies are defined in the following definitions.

Definition 13.1 Let $G = (V, E, \mu, \gamma)$ be an intuitionistic fuzzy graph, for every vertex i, define $\alpha_j = \max\limits_i \mu_{ij}$ and $\sigma_j = \min\limits_i \gamma_{ij}$.

Theorem 13.1 Let $G = (V, E, \mu, \gamma)$ be an intuitionistic fuzzy graph. If $\alpha_j = \max\limits_i \mu_{ij}$ and $\sigma_j = \min\limits_i \gamma_{ij}$, then (α_j, σ_j) is an intuitionistic fuzzy set on V.

Proof: If $\alpha_j = \max\limits_i \mu_{ij}$, then $\alpha_j = \mu_{sj}$ for some $s \in V$. Similarly, if $\sigma_j = \min\limits_i \gamma_{ij}$, then $\sigma_j = \gamma_{tj}$ for some $t \in V$. Here, we have

$$\gamma_{tj} \leq \gamma_{sj}$$
that is $\qquad -\gamma_{tj} \geq -\gamma_{sj}$
Now $\qquad \alpha_j = \mu_{sj} \leq 1 - \gamma_{sj} \leq 1 - \gamma_{tj}$
which gives $\qquad \mu_{sj} + \gamma_{tj} \leq 1$
that is $\qquad \alpha_j + \sigma_j \leq 1$
Therefore, we get $\quad 0 \leq \alpha_j + \sigma_j \leq 1.$

Hence (α_j, σ_j) is an intuitionistic fuzzy set on V. $\qquad\square$

Definition 13.2 Let $G = (V, E, \mu, \gamma)$ be an intuitionistic fuzzy graph. An four l of an intuitionistic fuzzy graph is defined as $M_1(G) = [(r_{ij}, s_{ij})]$. We denote $R = [r_{ij}]$ as an In-Min intuitionistic fuzzy matrix of membership value, where $r_{ij} = \min(\alpha_i, \alpha_j)$, and $S = [s_{ij}]$ as an In-Min intuitionistic fuzzy matrix of non-membership value, where $s_{ij} = \min(\sigma_i, \sigma_j)$.

Lemma 13.1 $M_1(G)$ *is a symmetric matrix.*

Proof: $M_1(G) = [(r_{ij}, s_{ij})]$ where $r_{ij} = \min(\alpha_i, \alpha_j) = \min(\alpha_j, \alpha_i) = r_{ji}$ and $s_{ij} = \min(\sigma_i, \sigma_j) = \min(\sigma_j, \sigma_i) = s_{ji}$. Hence $M_1(G)$ is a symmetric matrix. $\qquad\square$

Theorem 13.2 Let $G = (V, E, \mu, \gamma)$ be an intuitionistic fuzzy graph and α_i, σ_j are as defined above. Let $M_1(G) = [(r_{ij}, s_{ij})]$, and if $r_{ij} = \min(\alpha_i, \alpha_j)$ and $s_{ij} = \min(\sigma_i, \sigma_j)$, then (r_{ij}, s_{ij}) is an intuitionistic fuzzy set.

Proof: Let $r_{ij} = \min(\alpha_i, \alpha_j)$ and $s_{ij} = \min(\sigma_i, \sigma_j)$. If $r_{ij} = \alpha_i$ and $s_{ij} = \sigma_i$, then $0 \leq r_{ij} + s_{ij} \leq 1$. Now, if $r_{ij} = \alpha_i$ and $s_{ij} = \sigma_j$, then $\alpha_i \leq \alpha_j \leq 1 - \sigma_j \Rightarrow \alpha_i + \alpha_j \leq 1$. Therefore $0 \leq \alpha_i + \alpha_j \leq 1$. Hence (α_i, σ_i) is an intuitionistic fuzzy set. Similarly we can prove the other cases also (if like $r_{ij} = \alpha_j$, $s_{ij} = \sigma_i$ and $r_{ij} = \alpha_j$, $s_{ij} = \sigma_j$). $\square$

Definition 13.3 The energy of an In-Min intuitionistic fuzzy matrix of an intuitionistic fuzzy graph G is defined as $E(M_1(G)) = (E(R), E(S))$, where $E(R)$ is the sum of the absolute eigenvalues of the matrix R and $E(S)$ is the sum of the absolute eigenvalues of the matrix S.

Definition 13.4 Let $G = (V, E, \mu, \gamma)$ be an intuitionistic fuzzy graph, for every vertex i, define $\theta_i = \max_j \mu_{ij}$ and $\phi_i = \min_j \gamma_{ij}$.

By Theorem 13.1, it can be proved that (θ_i, ϕ_i) is an intuitionistic fuzzy set on V.

Definition 13.5 Let $G = (V, E, \mu, \gamma)$ be an intuitionistic fuzzy graph. The Out-Min intuitionistic fuzzy matrix of an intuitionistic fuzzy graph is defined as $M_O(G) = [(u_{ij}, v_{ij})]$. We denote $U = [u_{ij}]$ as an Out-Min intuitionistic fuzzy matrix of membership value, where $u_{ij} = \min(\theta_i, \theta_j)$, and $V = [v_{ij}]$ as an Out-Min intuitionistic fuzzy matrix of non-membership value, where $v_{ij} = \min(\phi_i, \phi_j)$.

By Theorem 13.2, it can be proved that (u_{ij}, v_{ij}) is an intuitionistic fuzzy set, and by Lemma 13.1, it can proved that $M_O(G)$ is a symmetric matrix.

Definition 13.6 The energy of the Out-Min intuitionistic fuzzy matrix of an intuitionistic fuzzy graph is defined as $E(M_O(G)) = (E(U), E(V))$ where $E(U)$ is the sum of the absolute eigenvalues of the matrix U and $E(V)$ is the sum of the absolute eigenvalues of the matrix V.

Theorem 13.3 and Remark 13.1 give the relation between the eigenvalues (either real or complex) and the membership values (non-membership values) in both incoming and outgoing links.

Theorem 13.3 *Let $G = (V, E, \mu, \gamma)$ be an intuitionistic fuzzy graph, and if $r_1, r_2, \ldots, r_n$ are the real or complex eigenvalues of the matrix R, then*

$$\sum_{i=1}^{n} (r_i)^2 = \sum_{i=1}^{n} (r_{ii})^2 + 2 \sum_{1 \leq i < j \leq n} (r_{ij})^2$$

Proof: The sum of the square of the eigenvalues of R is equal to the trace of R^2, that is,

$$\sum_{i=1}^{n} (r_i)^2 = \text{trace}(R^2)$$

That is,

$$\sum_{i=1}^{n} (r_i)^2 = r_{11}r_{11} + r_{12}r_{21} + \cdots + r_{1n}r_{n1}$$

$$+ r_{21}r_{12} + r_{22}r_{22} + \cdots + r_{2n}r_{n2}$$

$$+ \cdots +$$

$$r_{n1}r_{1n} + r_{n2}r_{2n} + \cdots + r_{nn}r_{nn}$$

$$\Rightarrow \sum_{i=1}^{n} (r_i)^2 = \sum_{i=1}^{n} (r_{ii})^2 + 2 \sum_{1 \leq i < j \leq n} (r_{ij})^2.$$

Hence the proof ☐

Remark 13.1 Similarly we can prove that if $s_1, s_2, \ldots, s_n$ are the real or complex eigenvalues of the matrix S, then

$$\sum_{i=1}^{n} (s_i)^2 = \sum_{i=1}^{n} (s_{ii})^2 + 2 \sum_{1 \leq i < j \leq n} (s_{ij})^2$$

If $u_1, u_2, \ldots, u_n$ are the real or complex eigenvalues of the matrix U, then

$$\sum_{i=1}^{n} (u_i)^2 = \sum_{i=1}^{n} (u_{ii})^2 + 2 \sum_{1 \leq i < j \leq n} (u_{ij})^2$$

If $v_1, v_2, \ldots, v_n$ are the real or complex eigenvalues of the matrix V, then

$$\sum_{i=1}^{n} (v_i)^2 = \sum_{i=1}^{n} (v_{ii})^2 + 2 \sum_{1 \leq i < j \leq n} (v_{ij})^2$$

The upper and lower bounds of the energy of membership and non-membership values are derived for the case of real eigenvalues in both incoming and outgoing links by Theorem 13.4 and Remark 13.2.

Theorem 13.4 Let $G = (V, E, \mu, \gamma)$ be an intuitionistic fuzzy graph with n vertices, and if $r_1, r_2, \ldots, r_n$ are the real eigenvalues of the matrix R, then

$$\sqrt{\sum_{i=1}^{n} (r_{ii})^2 + 2 \sum_{1 \leq i < j \leq n} (r_{ij})^2 + n(n-1)|A|^{\frac{2}{n}}} \leq E(R)$$

$$\leq \sqrt{n \left(\sum_{i=1}^{n} (r_{ii})^2 + 2 \sum_{1 \leq i < j \leq n} (r_{ij})^2 \right)}$$

where $|A|$ is the determinant of R.

Proof: Upper bound: In Cauchy–Schwarz inequality

$$\left(\sum_{i=1}^{n} a_i b_i \right)^2 \leq \left(\sum_{i=1}^{n} a_i^2 \right) \left(\sum_{i=1}^{n} b_i^2 \right)$$

putting $a_i = 1$ and $b_i = |r_i|$, we get

$$\left(\sum_{i=1}^{n} |r_i| \right)^2 \leq \left(\sum_{i=1}^{n} 1 \right) \left(\sum_{i=1}^{n} (r_i)^2 \right)$$

By Theorem 13.3, we get

$$(E(R))^2 \leq n \left(\sum_{i=1}^{n} (r_{ii})^2 + 2 \sum_{1 \leq i < j \leq n} (r_{ij})^2 \right)$$

$$\Rightarrow E(R) \leq \sqrt{ n \left(\sum_{i=1}^{n} (r_{ii})^2 + 2 \sum_{1 \leq i < j \leq n} (r_{ij})^2 \right) } \qquad (13.1)$$

Lower bound: We know that

$$(E(R))^2 = \left(\sum_{i=1}^{n} |r_i| \right)^2$$

$$= \sum_{i=1}^{n} |r_i|^2 + 2 \sum_{1 \leq i < j \leq n} |r_i||r_j|$$

$$= \left[\sum_{i=1}^{n} (r_{ii})^2 + 2 \sum_{1 \leq i < j \leq n} (r_{ij})^2 \right] + 2 \frac{n(n-1)}{2} AM\{|r_i||r_j|\}$$

Since

$$AM\{|r_i||r_j|\} \geq GM\{|r_i||r_j|\}, 1 \leq i < j \leq n$$

we get

$$E(R) \geq \sqrt{ \sum_{i=1}^{n} (r_{ij})^2 + 2 \sum_{1 \leq i < j \leq n} (r_{ij})^2 + n(n-1) GM\{|r_i||r_j|\} }$$

But

$$GM\{|r_i||r_j|\} = \left(\prod_{i=1}^{n} |r_i| \right)^{\frac{2}{n}} = |A|^{\frac{2}{n}}$$

Hence, we have

$$E(R) \geq \sqrt{ \sum_{i=1}^{n} (r_{ii})^2 + 2 \sum_{1 \leq i < j \leq n} (r_{ij})^2 + n(n-1)|A|^{\frac{2}{n}} } \qquad (13.2)$$

From Eqs. (13.1) and (13.2), we get

$$
\sqrt{\sum_{i=1}^{n}(r_{ii})^2 + 2\sum_{1\le i<j\le n}(r_{ij})^2 + n(n-1)|A|^{\frac{2}{n}}} \le E(R)
$$

$$
\le \sqrt{n\left(\sum_{i=1}^{n}(r_{ii})^2 + 2\sum_{1\le i<j\le n}(r_{ij})^2\right)}
$$

Hence the proof. □

Remark 13.2 Similarly we can prove that if $s_1, s_2, \dots, s_n$ are the real eigenvalues of the matrix S, then

$$
\sqrt{\sum_{i=1}^{n}(s_{ii})^2 + 2\sum_{1\le i<j\le n}(s_{ij})^2 + n(n-1)|B|^{\frac{2}{n}}} \le E(S)
$$

$$
\le \sqrt{n\left(\sum_{i=1}^{n}(s_{ii})^2 + 2\sum_{1\le i<j\le n}(s_{ij})^2\right)}
$$

where $|B|$ is the determinant of S.

If $u_1, u_2, \dots, u_n$ are the real eigenvalues of the matrix U, then

$$
\sqrt{\sum_{i=1}^{n}(u_{ii})^2 + 2\sum_{1\le i<j\le n}(u_{ij})^2 + n(n-1)|C|^{\frac{2}{n}}} \le E(U)
$$

$$
\le \sqrt{n\left(\sum_{i=1}^{n}(u_{ii})^2 + 2\sum_{1\le i<j\le n}(u_{ij})^2\right)}
$$

where $|C|$ is the determinant of U.

If $v_1, v_2, \dots, v_n$ are the real eigenvalues of the matrix V, then

$$
\sqrt{\sum_{i=1}^{n}(v_{ii})^2 + 2\sum_{1\le i<j\le n}(v_{ij})^2 + n(n-1)|D|^{\frac{2}{n}}} \le E(V)
$$

$$
\le \sqrt{n\left(\sum_{i=1}^{n}(v_{ii})^2 + 2\sum_{1\le i<j\le n}(v_{ij})^2\right)}
$$

where $|D|$ is the determinant of V.

Corollary 13.1 shows the relation between the upper bound of the energy of membership values and the lower bound of the energy of non-membership values for the case of real eigenvalues in both incoming and outgoing links.

Corollary 13.1   *If* $r_1, r_2, \ldots, r_n$ *are the real eigenvalues of R and* $s_1, s_2, \ldots, s_n$ *are the real eigenvalues of S and if* $E(R) \geq E(S)$, *then*

$$n\left(\sum_{i=1}^{n}(r_{ii})^2 + 2\sum_{1\leq i<j\leq n}(r_{ij})^2\right) \geq \sum_{i=1}^{n}(s_{ii})^2 + 2\sum_{1\leq i<j\leq n}(s_{ij})^2 + n(n-1)|B|^{\frac{2}{n}}$$

Proof: From Theorem 13.4, we have

$$\sqrt{n\left(\sum_{i=1}^{n}(r_{ii})^2 + 2\sum_{1\leq i<j\leq n}(r_{ij})^2\right)} \geq E(R)$$

$$\sqrt{n\left(\sum_{i=1}^{n}(r_{ii})^2 + 2\sum_{1\leq i<j\leq n}(r_{ij})^2\right)} \geq E(S)$$

Again, by Theorem 13.4, we have

$$E(S) \geq \sqrt{\sum_{i=1}^{n}(s_{ii})^2 + 2\sum_{1\leq i<j\leq n}(s_{ij})^2 + n(n-1)|B|^{\frac{2}{n}}}$$

Therefore, we get

$$\sqrt{n\left(\sum_{i=1}^{n}(r_{ii})^2 + 2\sum_{1\leq i<j\leq n}(r_{ij})^2\right)} \geq \sqrt{\sum_{i=1}^{n}(s_{ii})^2 + 2\sum_{1\leq i<j\leq n}(s_{ij})^2 + n(n-1)|B|^{\frac{2}{n}}}$$

$$\Rightarrow n\left(\sum_{i=1}^{n}(r_{ii})^2 + 2\sum_{1\leq i<j\leq n}(r_{ij})^2\right) \geq \sum_{i=1}^{n}(s_{ii})^2 + 2\sum_{1\leq i<j\leq n}(s_{ij})^2 + n(n-1)|B|^{\frac{2}{n}}$$

Hence the proof.   □

Remark 13.3 shows the relation between the upper bound of the energy of non-membership values and the lower bound of the energy of membership values for the case of real eigenvalues in both incoming and outgoing links.

Remark 13.3   Similarly we can prove that if $E(S) \geq E(R)$, then

$$n\left(\sum_{i=1}^{n}(s_{ii})^2 + 2\sum_{1\leq i<j\leq n}(s_{ij})^2\right) \geq \sum_{i=1}^{n}(r_{ii})^2 + 2\sum_{1\leq i<j\leq n}(r_{ij})^2 + n(n-1)|A|^{\frac{2}{n}}$$

If $u_1, u_2, \ldots, u_n$ are the real eigenvalues of U and $v_1, v_2, \ldots, v_n$ are the real eigenvalues of V and if $E(U) \geq E(V)$, then

$$n\left(\sum_{i=1}^{n}(u_{ii})^2 + 2\sum_{1\leq i<j\leq n}(u_{ij})^2\right) \geq \sum_{i=1}^{n}(v_{ii})^2 + 2\sum_{1\leq i<j\leq n}(v_{ij})^2 + n(n-1)|D|^{\frac{2}{n}}$$

If $E(V) \geq E(U)$, then

$$n \left(\sum_{i=1}^{n} (v_{ii})^2 + 2 \sum_{1 \leq i < j \leq n} (v_{ij})^2 \right) \geq \sum_{i=1}^{n} (u_{ii})^2 + 2 \sum_{1 \leq i < j \leq n} (u_{ij})^2 + n(n-1)|C|^{\frac{2}{n}}$$

In real-life environment, we cannot expect the roots are always real, but it has complex roots also. Because of that, the upper and lower bounds of the energy of membership and non-membership values for the case of complex eigenvalues in both incoming and outgoing links are derived in Theorem 13.5 and Remark 13.4.

Theorem 13.5   *Let $G = (V, E, \mu, \gamma)$ be an intuitionistic fuzzy graph with n vertices, and if $r_1, r_2, \ldots, r_n$ are the complex eigenvalues of the matrix R, then*

$$\sqrt{\sum_{i=1}^{n} |r_i|^2 + n(n-1)|A|^{\frac{2}{n}}} \leq E(R) \leq \sqrt{n \sum_{i=1}^{n} |r_i|^2}$$

where $|A|$ is the determinant of R.

Proof: Upper bound: Applying Cauchy–Schwarz inequality to the n numbers $1, 1, \ldots, 1$ and $|r_1|, |r_2|, \ldots, |r_n|$, we get

$$\sum_{i=1}^{n} |r_i| \leq \sqrt{n} \sqrt{\sum_{i=1}^{n} |r_i|^2}$$

That is,

$$E(R) \leq \sqrt{n \sum_{i=1}^{n} |r_i|^2} \tag{13.3}$$

Lower bound: We know that

$$(E(R))^2 = \left(\sum_{i=1}^{n} |r_i| \right)^2$$

$$= \sum_{i=1}^{n} |r_i|^2 + 2 \sum_{1 \leq i < j \leq n} |r_i||r_j|$$

$$= \sum_{i=1}^{n} |r_i|^2 + 2 \frac{n(n-1)}{2} AM\{|r_i||r_j|\}$$

Since

$$AM\{|r_i||r_j|\} \geq GM\{|r_i||r_j|\}, 1 \leq i < j \leq n,$$

we get

$$E(R) \geq \sqrt{\sum_{i=1}^{n} |r_i|^2 + n(n-1)GM\{|r_i||r_j|\}}$$

But

$$GM\{|r_i||r_j|\} = \left(\prod_{i=1}^{n} |r_i|\right)^{\frac{2}{n}} = |A|^{\frac{2}{n}}$$

Hence, we have

$$E(R) \geq \sqrt{\sum_{i=1}^{n} |r_i|^2 + n(n-1)|A|^{\frac{2}{n}}} \tag{13.4}$$

From Eqs. (13.3) and (13.4), we have

$$\sqrt{\sum_{i=1}^{n} |r_i|^2 + n(n-1)|A|^{\frac{2}{n}}} \leq E(R) \leq \sqrt{n \sum_{i=1}^{n} |r_i|^2}$$

Hence the proof. □

Remark 13.4 Similarly, we can prove that if $s_1, s_2, \ldots, s_n$ are the complex eigenvalues of the matrix S, then

$$\sqrt{\sum_{i=1}^{n} |s_i|^2 + n(n-1)|B|^{\frac{2}{n}}} \leq E(S) \leq \sqrt{n \sum_{i=1}^{n} |s_i|^2}$$

If $u_1, u_2, \ldots, u_n$ are the complex eigenvalues of the matrix U, then

$$\sqrt{\sum_{i=1}^{n} |u_i|^2 + n(n-1)|C|^{\frac{2}{n}}} \leq E(U) \leq \sqrt{n \sum_{i=1}^{n} |u_i|^2}$$

If $v_1, v_2, \ldots, v_n$ are the complex eigenvalues of the matrix V, then

$$\sqrt{\sum_{i=1}^{n} |v_i|^2 + n(n-1)|D|^{\frac{2}{n}}} \leq E(V) \leq \sqrt{n \sum_{i=1}^{n} |v_i|^2}$$

Corollary 13.2 shows the relation between the upper bound of the energy of membership values and the lower bound of the energy of non-membership values for the case of complex eigenvalues in both incoming and outgoing links.

Corollary 13.2 *If $r_1, r_2, \ldots, r_n$ are the complex eigenvalues of R and $s_1, s_2, \ldots, s_n$ are the complex eigenvalues of S and if $E(R) \geq E(S)$, then*

$$n \sum_{i=1}^{n} |r_i|^2 \geq \sum_{i=1}^{n} |s_i|^2 + n(n-1)|B|^{\frac{2}{n}}$$

Proof: From Theorem 13.5, we have

$$\sqrt{n \sum_{i=1}^{n} |r_i|^2} \geq E(R)$$

$$\sqrt{n \sum_{i=1}^{n} |r_i|^2} \geq E(S)$$

Again, by Theorem 1.5, we have

$$E(S) \geq \sqrt{\sum_{i=1}^{n} |s_i|^2 + n(n-1)|B|^{\frac{2}{n}}}$$

Therefore, we get

$$\sqrt{n \sum_{i=1}^{n} |r_i|^2} \geq \sqrt{\sum_{i=1}^{n} |s_i|^2 + n(n-1)|B|^{\frac{2}{n}}}$$

$$\Rightarrow n \sum_{i=1}^{n} |r_i|^2 \geq \sum_{i=1}^{n} |s_i|^2 + n(n-1)|B|^{\frac{2}{n}}$$

Hence the proof. $\qquad\qquad\square$

Remark 13.5 shows the relation between the upper bound of the energy of non-membership values and the lower bound of the energy of membership values for the case of complex eigenvalues in both incoming and outgoing links.

Remark 13.5 Similarly we can prove that if $E(S) \geq E(R)$, then

$$n \sum_{i=1}^{n} |s_i|^2 \geq \sum_{i=1}^{n} |r_i|^2 + n(n-1)|A|^{\frac{2}{n}}$$

If $u_1, u_2, \ldots, u_n$ are the complex eigenvalues of U and $v_1, v_2, \ldots, v_n$ are the complex eigenvalues of V and if $E(U) \geq E(V)$, then

$$n \sum_{i=1}^{n} |u_i|^2 \geq \sum_{i=1}^{n} |v_i|^2 + n(n-1)|D|^{\frac{2}{n}}$$

If $E(V) \geq E(U)$, then

$$n \sum_{i=1}^{n} |v_i|^2 \geq \sum_{i=1}^{n} |u_i|^2 + n(n-1)|C|^{\frac{2}{n}}$$

Theorem 13.6 provides that the sum of the energy of membership and non-membership values is less than or equal to twice the square of the number of vertices.

Theorem 13.6 *Let $G = (V, E, \mu, \gamma)$ be an intuitionistic fuzzy graph with n vertices, and if*

$$E(R) \leq 2 \sum_{i=1}^{n} \sum_{i=1}^{n} r_{ij}, \quad E(S) \leq 2 \sum_{i=1}^{n} \sum_{i=1}^{n} s_{ij},$$

then $E(R) + E(S) \leq 2n^2$.

Proof: By the assumption

$$E(R) \leq 2 \sum_{i=1}^{n} \sum_{i=1}^{n} r_{ij}$$

$$\leq 2 \sum_{i=1}^{n} \sum_{i=1}^{n} (1 - s_{ij})$$

$$= 2 \sum_{i=1}^{n} \sum_{i=1}^{n} 1 - 2 \sum_{i=1}^{n} \sum_{i=1}^{n} s_{ij}$$

$$\leq 2n^2 - E(S)$$

$$E(R) + E(S) \leq 2n^2$$

Hence the proof. □

13.2 Virus Spreading Rate Between Outgoing and Incoming Links

In this section we analyze the spreading rate of virus between incoming and outgoing links of a website through an intuitionistic fuzzy graph. Spreading of virus in a network was considered by Wang et al. (2003) and Ganesh et al. (2005). Epidemic threshold is defined in Definitions 13.7–13.10 in terms of the energy of membership and non-membership values.

Definition 13.7 If $E(R) > E(S)$, then the infection rate of an intuitionistic fuzzy graph is defined as $\beta = \max_{i,j} r_{ij}$, and the curing rate of an intuitionistic fuzzy graph is defined as $\delta = \min_{i,j} s_{ij}$. The ratio $\tau = \frac{\beta}{\delta}$, $(\delta \neq 0)$ is the effective spreading rate and $\tau_c = \frac{1}{\lambda_{max} R}$ where $\lambda_{max} R$ is the largest eigenvalue of R of an intuitionistic fuzzy graph.

Definition 13.8 If $E(R) < E(S)$, then the infection rate of an intuitionistic fuzzy graph is defined as $\beta = \min_{i,j} r_{ij}$, and the curing rate of an intuitionistic fuzzy graph is defined as $\delta = \max_{i,j} s_{ij}$. The ratio $\tau = \frac{\beta}{\delta}$ is the effective spreading rate and $\tau_c = \frac{1}{\lambda_{max} S}$ where $\lambda_{max} S$ is the largest eigenvalue of S of an intuitionistic fuzzy graph.

Definition 13.9 If $E(U) > E(V)$, then the infection rate of an intuitionistic fuzzy graph is defined as $\beta = \max_{i,j} u_{ij}$, and the curing rate of an intuitionistic fuzzy graph is defined as $\delta = \min_{i,j} v_{ij}$. The ratio $\tau = \frac{\beta}{\delta}$, $(\delta \neq 0)$ is the effective spreading rate and $\tau_c = \frac{1}{\lambda_{max} U}$ where $\lambda_{max} U$ is the largest eigenvalue of U of an intuitionistic fuzzy graph.

Definition 13.10 If $E(U) < E(V)$, then the infection rate of an intuitionistic fuzzy graph is defined as $\beta = \min_{i,j} u_{ij}$, and the curing rate of an intuitionistic fuzzy graph is defined as $\delta = \max_{i,j} v_{ij}$. The ratio $\tau = \frac{\beta}{\delta}$ is the effective spreading rate and $\tau_c = \frac{1}{\lambda_{max} V}$ where $\lambda_{max} V$ is the largest eigenvalue of V of an intuitionistic fuzzy graph.

Let us illustrate the above concepts in the following. Let us analyze the spreading rate of virus in terms of incoming and outgoing links. For the intuitionistic fuzzy graph in Figure 13.1, the In-Min intuitionistic fuzzy matrix is given by

$$M_1(G) = \begin{pmatrix} (0.9, 0.1) & (0.8, 0.1) & (0.5, 0.1) & (0.6, 0.1) \\ (0.8, 0.1) & (0.8, 0.1) & (0.5, 0.1) & (0.6, 0.1) \\ (0.5, 0.1) & (0.5, 0.1) & (0.5, 0.1) & (0.5, 0.1) \\ (0.6, 0.1) & (0.6, 0.1) & (0.5, 0.1) & (0.6, 0.3) \end{pmatrix}$$

where

$$R = \begin{pmatrix} 0.9 & 0.8 & 0.5 & 0.6 \\ 0.8 & 0.8 & 0.5 & 0.6 \\ 0.5 & 0.5 & 0.5 & 0.5 \\ 0.6 & 0.6 & 0.5 & 0.6 \end{pmatrix} \text{ and } S = \begin{pmatrix} 0.1 & 0.1 & 0.1 & 0.1 \\ 0.1 & 0.1 & 0.1 & 0.1 \\ 0.1 & 0.1 & 0.1 & 0.1 \\ 0.1 & 0.1 & 0.1 & 0.3 \end{pmatrix}$$

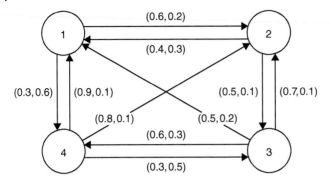

Figure 13.1 Intuitionistic fuzzy graph.

The energy of the In-Min intuitionistic fuzzy matrix of an intuitionistic fuzzy graph is

$$E(M_1(G)) = (2.8000, 0.6000)$$

Here we note that

$$E(R) > E(S)$$

so the infection rate and curing rate are given by

$$\beta = \max_{i,j} r_{ij} = 0.9, \quad \delta = \min_{i,j} s_{ij} = 0.1$$

and the spreading rate of virus and sharp epidemic threshold are given by

$$\tau = \frac{\beta}{\delta} = 9, \quad \tau_c = \frac{1}{\lambda_{\max} R} = \frac{1}{2.4958} = 0.4007$$

For the intuitionistic fuzzy graph in Figure 13.1, the Out-Min intuitionistic fuzzy matrix is given by

$$M_O(G) = \begin{pmatrix} (0.6, 0.2) & (0.5, 0.1) & (0.6, 0.1) & (0.6, 0.1) \\ (0.5, 0.1) & (0.5, 0.1) & (0.5, 0.1) & (0.5, 0.1) \\ (0.6, 0.1) & (0.5, 0.1) & (0.7, 0.1) & (0.7, 0.1) \\ (0.6, 0.1) & (0.5, 0.1) & (0.7, 0.1) & (0.9, 0.1) \end{pmatrix}$$

where

$$U = \begin{pmatrix} 0.6 & 0.5 & 0.6 & 0.6 \\ 0.5 & 0.5 & 0.5 & 0.5 \\ 0.6 & 0.5 & 0.7 & 0.7 \\ 0.6 & 0.5 & 0.7 & 0.9 \end{pmatrix} \quad \text{and} \quad V = \begin{pmatrix} 0.2 & 0.1 & 0.1 & 0.1 \\ 0.1 & 0.1 & 0.1 & 0.1 \\ 0.1 & 0.1 & 0.1 & 0.1 \\ 0.1 & 0.1 & 0.1 & 0.1 \end{pmatrix}$$

The energy of the Out-Min intuitionistic fuzzy matrix of an intuitionistic fuzzy graph is

$$E(M_O(G)) = (2.7000, 0.5000)$$

Here we note that

$$E(U) > E(V)$$

so the infection rate and curing rate are given by

$$\beta = \max_{i,j} u_{ij} = 0.9, \quad \delta = \min_{i,j} v_{ij} = 0.1$$

and the spreading rate of virus and sharp epidemic threshold are given by

$$\tau = \frac{\beta}{\delta} = 9, \quad \tau_c = \frac{1}{\lambda_{\max} U} = \frac{1}{2.4054} = 0.4157$$

13.3 Numerical Examples

In this section, we illustrate the abovementioned concepts through real-time example. Here the "user flow of the website" is represented by a directed intuitionistic fuzzy graph. The spreading rate of virus of the "user flow of the website" is discussed for the four different time periods between incoming and outgoing links in the following examples.

Example 13.1 In the website http://www.pantechsolutions.net/ we considered the same four links – namely, 1./microcontroller-boards, 2./log-in html, 3. /, and 4./project kits – for 16 July 2013 to 15 August 2013 (period I). For the intuitionistic fuzzy graph in Figure 13.2, the energy of the In-Min intuitionistic fuzzy matrix of an intuitionistic fuzzy graph is

$$E(M_1(G) = (0.6000, 1.4000)$$

Here note that $E(R) < E(S)$ so the infection rate and curing rate are given by

$$\beta = \min_{i,j} r_{ij} = 0.1, \quad \delta = \max_{i,j} s_{ij} = 0.6$$

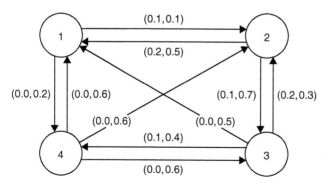

Figure 13.2 Intuitionistic fuzzy graph for period I.

and the spreading rate of virus and sharp epidemic threshold are given by

$$\tau = \frac{\beta}{\delta} = 0.1667, \quad \tau_c = \frac{1}{\lambda_{max}S} = \frac{1}{1.1630} = 0.8598$$

For the intuitionistic fuzzy graph in Figure 13.2, the energy of the Out-Min intuitionistic fuzzy matrix of an intuitionistic fuzzy graph is

$$E(M_O(G) = (0.5000, 1.5000)$$

Here note that $E(U) < E(V)$ so the infection rate and curing rate are given by

$$\beta = \min_{i,j} u_{ij} = 0, \quad \delta = \max_{i,j} v_{ij} = 0.6$$

and the spreading rate of virus and sharp epidemic threshold are given by

$$\tau = \frac{\beta}{\delta} = 0, \quad \tau_c = \frac{1}{\lambda_{max}V} = \frac{1}{1.2677} = 0.7888$$

Example 13.2   In the same website we consider the same four links for 16 August 2013 to 15 September 2013 (period II). For the intuitionistic fuzzy graph in Figure 13.3, the energy of the In-Min intuitionistic fuzzy matrix of an intuitionistic fuzzy graph is

$$E(M_I(G) = (0.5000, 1.3000)$$

Here note that $E(R) < E(S)$ so the infection rate and curing rate are given by

$$\beta = \min_{i,j} r_{ij} = 0, \quad \delta = \max_{i,j} s_{ij} = 0.6$$

and the spreading rate of virus and sharp epidemic threshold are given by

$$\tau = \frac{\beta}{\delta} = 0, \tau_c = \frac{1}{\lambda_{max}S} = \frac{1}{1.0391} = 0.9624$$

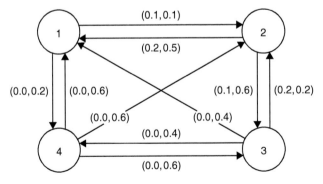

Figure 13.3 Intuitionistic fuzzy graph for period II.

For the intuitionistic fuzzy graph in Figure 13.3, the energy of the Out-Min intuitionistic fuzzy matrix of an intuitionistic fuzzy graph is

$$E(M_O(G)) = (0.5000, 1.4000)$$

Here note that $E(U) < E(V)$ so the infection rate and curing rate are given by

$$\beta = \min_{i,j} u_{ij} = 0, \quad \delta = \max_{i,j} v_{ij} = 0.6$$

and the spreading rate of virus and sharp epidemic threshold are given by

$$\tau = \frac{\beta}{\delta} = 0, \quad \tau_c = \frac{1}{\lambda_{\max} V} = \frac{1}{1.1630} = 0.8598$$

Example 13.3 In the same website, we consider the same four links for 16 September 2013 to 15 October 2013 (period III). For the intuitionistic fuzzy graph in Figure 13.4, the energy of the In-Min intuitionistic fuzzy matrix of an intuitionistic fuzzy graph is

$$E(M_I(G)) = (0.5000, 1.3000)$$

Here note that $E(R) < E(S)$ so the infection rate and curing rate are given by

$$\beta = \min_{i,j} r_{ij} = 0.1, \quad \delta = \max_{i,j} s_{ij} = 0.5$$

and the spreading rate of virus and sharp epidemic threshold are given by

$$\tau = \frac{\beta}{\delta} = 0.2, \quad \tau_c = \frac{1}{\lambda_{\max} S} = \frac{1}{1.1168} = 0.8954$$

For the intuitionistic fuzzy graph in Figure 13.4, the energy of the Out-Min intuitionistic fuzzy matrix of an intuitionistic fuzzy graph is

$$E(M_O(G)) = (0.4000, 1.5000)$$

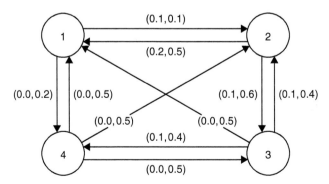

Figure 13.4 Intuitionistic fuzzy graph for period III.

Here note that

$$E(U) < E(V)$$

so the infection rate and curing rate are given by

$$\beta = \min_{i,j} u_{ij} = 0, \quad \delta = \max_{i,j} v_{ij} = 0.5$$

and the spreading rate of virus and sharp epidemic threshold are given by

$$\tau = \frac{\beta}{\delta} = 0, \quad \tau_c = \frac{1}{\lambda_{\max} V} = \frac{1}{1.3639} = 0.7332$$

Example 13.4   In the same website, we consider the same four links for 16 October 2013 to 15 November 2013 (period IV). For the intuitionistic fuzzy graph in Figure 13.5, the energy of the In-Min intuitionistic fuzzy matrix of an intuitionistic fuzzy graph is

$$E(M_1(G) = (0.4000, 1.3000)$$

Here note that $E(R) < E(S)$ so the infection rate and curing rate are given by

$$\beta = \min_{i,j} r_{ij} = 0, \quad \delta = \max_{i,j} s_{ij} = 0.1$$

and the spreading rate of virus and sharp epidemic threshold are given by

$$\tau = \frac{\beta}{\delta} = 0, \quad \tau_c = \frac{1}{\lambda_{\max} S} = \frac{1}{1.0391} = 0.9624$$

For the intuitionistic fuzzy graph in Figure 13.5, the energy of the Out-Min intuitionistic fuzzy matrix of an intuitionistic fuzzy graph is

$$E(M_O(G)) = (0.5000, 1.5000).$$

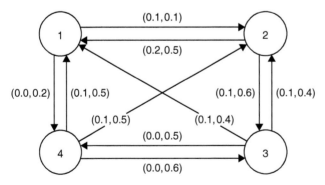

Figure 13.5 Intuitionistic fuzzy graph for period IV.

Here note that

$$E(U) < E(V)$$

so the infection rate and curing rate are given by

$$\beta = \min_{i,j} u_{ij} = 0.1, \quad \delta = \max_{i,j} v_{ij} = 0.5$$

and the spreading rate of virus and sharp epidemic threshold are given by

$$\tau = \frac{\beta}{\delta} = 0.2, \quad \tau_c = \frac{1}{\lambda_{max} V} = \frac{1}{1.3639} = 0.7332$$

Table 13.1 represents the comparison of energy of $M_1(G)$ and the energy of $M_O(G)$. Table 13.2 represents the comparison of spreading rate of virus and sharp epidemic threshold of $M_1(G)$ and $M_O(G)$.

Figure 13.6 represents the spreading rate of virus between incoming and outgoing links of the website http://www.pantechsolutions.net/ for four different time periods.

From Examples 13.1 to 13.4, we observe that the spreading rate of virus differs between incoming and outgoing links in terms of their energies. Also we conclude that the spreading rate of virus is maximum through incoming links and minimum through outgoing links.

Table 13.1 Comparison of energy $M_1(G)$ and $M_O(G)$.

Period	Energy of A(G)	Energy of $M_1(G)$	Energy of $M_O(G)$
July–Aug	(0.4, 2.1078)	(0.6000, 1.4000)	(0.5000, 1.5000)
Aug–Sep	(0.4, 2.0068)	(0.5000, 1.3000)	(0.5000, 1.4000)
Sep–Oct	(0.3464, 1.9129)	(0.5000, 1.3000)	(0.4000, 1.5000)
Oct–Nov	(0.3758, 1.9879)	(0.4000, 1.3000)	(0.5000, 1.5000)

Table 13.2 Spreading rate of virus and epidemic threshold of $M_1(G)$ and $M_O(G)$.

Period	τ on $M_1(G)$	τ on $M_O(G)$
July–Aug	0.1667	0
Aug–Sep	0	0
Sep–Oct	0.2	0
Oct–Nov	0	0.2

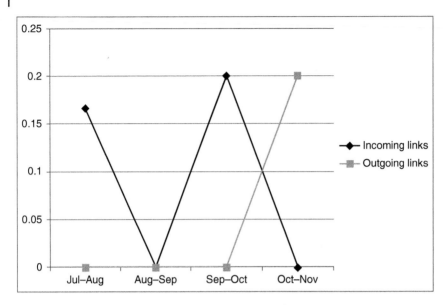

Figure 13.6 Spreading rate of virus between incoming and outgoing links.

In this chapter we analyzed the spreading rate of virus between incoming and outgoing links of a website through the intuitionistic fuzzy graph. In this intuitionistic fuzzy graph, we constructed two intuitionistic fuzzy matrices using incoming and outgoing links of G. The energy of these matrices along with its lower and upper bounds is discussed. The spreading rate of virus of the given graph in terms of these two matrices is discussed. These concepts are illustrated with real-time examples.

Bibliography

Anjali, N. and Mathew, S. (2013). Energy of a fuzzy graph. *Annals of Fuzzy Mathematics and Informatics* **6**: 455–465.

Atanassov, K. (1999). *Intuitionistic Fuzzy Sets: Theory and Applications*. Heidelberg, New York: Physica-Verlag.

Brankov, V., Stevanovic, D., and Gutman, I. (2004). Equienergetic chemical trees. *Journal of the Serbian Chemical Society* **69**: 549–553.

Ganesh, A., Massoulie, L., and Towsley, D. (2005). The effect of network topology on the spread of epidemics. Proceedings of IEEE INFOCOM 2005, Miami, FL, Volume 2, 1455–1466.

Gutman, I. (1978). The energy of a graph. *Ber. Math. Statist. Sekt. Forschungszentram Graz.* **103**: 1–22.

Gutman, I. (2001). The energy of graph: old and new results. In: *Algebraic Combinatorics and Applications* (ed. A. Betten, A. Kohnert, R. Laue, and A. Wassermann), 196–211. Berlin: Springer-Verlag.

Gutman, I. and Polansky, O.E. (1986). *Mathematical Concepts in Organic Chemistry*. Berlin: Springer-Verlag.

Kephart, J.O. and White, S.R. (1991). Directed-graph epidemiological models of computer viruses. In: Proceedings of IEEE Computer Society Symposium on Research in Security and Privacy, 343–359.

Koolen, J.H., Moulton, V., and Gutman, I. (2000). Improving the McClelland inequality for total π-electron energy. *Chemical Physics Letters* **320**: 213–216.

Praba, B., Chandrasekaran, V.M., and Deepa, G. (2014). Energy of an Intuitionistic fuzzy graph. *Italian Journal of Pure and Applied Mathematics* **32**: 431–444.

Wang, Y., Chakrabarti, D., Wang, C., and Faloutsos, C. (2003). Epidemic spreading in real networks: an eigenvalue viewpoint. In: Proceedings of the 22nd International Symposium Reliable Distributed Systems (SRDS'03), 25–34.

14

Data Mining Techniques for the Detection of the Risk in Cardiovascular Diseases

Dinakaran Karunakaran[1], Vishnu Priya[2], and Valarmathie Palanisamy[3]

[1] *Department of Information Technology, Saveetha Engineering College, Anna University, Chennai, India*
[2] *Department of Computer Science and Engineering, P.M.R. Engineering College, Anna University, Chennai, India*
[3] *Department of Computer Science and Engineering, Saveetha Engineering College, Anna University, Chennai, India*

14.1 Introduction

A photoplethysmograph (PPG) is an optically obtained plethysmograph, a volumetric measurement of an organ. A pulse oximeter is used to obtain PPG, which illuminates the skin and measures changes in light absorption. To monitor the perfusion of blood to the dermis and subcutaneous tissue of the skin, pulse oximeter is used (Allen 2003). The pressure pulse is somewhat wet by the time it reaches the skin; it is enough to expand the arteries and arterioles in the subcutaneous tissue. If the pulse oximeter is attached without reducing the skin, a pressure pulse can also be seen from the venous plexus as a small secondary peak.

The change in volume caused by the pressure pulse is identified by illuminating the skin with the light from a light-emitting diode (LED) and then assessing the amount of light either transmitted or reflected to a photodiode. Because blood flow to the skin can be modulated by multiple other physiological systems, the PPG can also be used to monitor breathing, hypovolemia, and other circulatory conditions (Kadhim et al. 2007). Additionally, the shape of the PPG waveform varies from person to person with the location and manner in which the pulse oximeter is attached.

PPG is a noninvasive, electro-optical method that provides information about the blood flowing volume in a test region close to the skin of the body. PPG is obtained by lighting up the region of interest of the body using reflected or transmitted light. The wavelength λ of a light source on one side is placed in a projection, for example, a finger and a photodetector (PD) are placed to another side of the source to capture the transmitted light. A typical PPG

Intelligent Pervasive Computing Systems for Smarter Healthcare, First Edition.
Arun Kumar Sangaiah, S.P. Shantharajah, and Padma Theagarajan.
© 2019 John Wiley & Sons, Inc. Published 2019 by John Wiley & Sons, Inc.

signal consists of the large DC component by skin, muscle, and bone not involving blood vessels; a small AC component occurred into the blood vessels leaving from the skin, muscle, and bone; and heartbeat frequency components occurred from passing light into arterial blood vessels (Kadhim et al. 2007). PPG is commonly used in biomedical applications such as pulse oximetry, detection of varicose veins, muscle pump test, etc.

Wavelet analysis has characteristics of multi-resolution; it is a time–frequency domain analysis method that adapts to process the nonstationary signal. It is superior to the traditional Fourier transform in the analysis of the signal details. The soft and hard threshold functions are the most common functions; however, due to the discontinuity of the hard threshold function, the reconstructed signal contains residual noise and thus leads to serious distortion, but the soft threshold function is a continuing one.

PPG describes the use of a reflection mode system to measure blood quantity changes in the fingers induced by the Valsalva maneuver or exercise and with contact to cold. Their input to the field demonstrated the potential clinical utility of this method. In 1938, Hertzman undertook a validation of the PPG technique by contrasting blood volume changes with those measured simultaneously by mechanical plethysmography.

Hertzman and Dillon in 1940 separated the AC and DC components of PPG with filters and electronic amplifiers and monitored vasomotor activity. The potential sources of error with the procedure have been identified by Hertzman, who emphasized that good contact with skin was needed, but without excessive pressure that would result in lightening, and advised that movement of the measurement probe against the skin should be avoided.

These observations led to the development of elaborate positioning devices. This PPG method was based on the idea that if an externally applied pressure in the cuff is equal to the arterial pressure instantaneously, the arterial walls will be unloaded (zero transmural pressure), and the arteries will not change in size. In this condition, the blood volume will not change. This PPG method was an attempt to realize for the first time by Penaz in the year 1973 using photoelectric technique of detecting blood flow, equipped with a transparent inflatable cuff controlled by a servocontrol system in the human finger.

In recent decades, the desire for small, reliable, low-cost, and simple-to-use noninvasive cardiovascular assessment techniques is key factor that has helped in the progress of PPG technique. Advances in optoelectronics and clinical instrumentation have also significantly contributed to its advancement. The developments in semiconductor technology, i.e. LEDs, photodiodes, and phototransistors, have made considerable improvements in the size, sensitivity, portability, reliability, and reproducibility of PPG probe design.

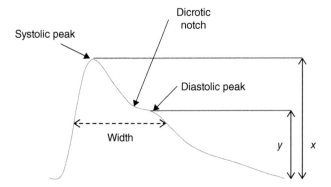

Figure 14.1 A typical waveform of the PPG and its characteristic parameters, where the amplitude of the systolic peaks is *x* and *y* is the amplitude of the diastolic peak.

14.2 PPG Signal Analysis

The form of the PPG pulse is commonly divided into two phases: the anacrotic phase is the rising edge of the pulse, whereas the catacrotic phase is the falling edge of the pulse as shown in Figure 14.1. The first phase is primarily concerned with systole, and the second phase to diastole and wave reflections from the periphery. A dicrotic notch, shown in Figure 14.1, is typically seen in the catacrotic phase of subjects with healthy compliant arteries.

14.2.1 Pulse Width

The pulse width in the PPG wave is shown in Figure 14.1. Awad et al. (2007) used the pulse width as the half height of the systolic peak. They have suggested that the pulse width correlates with the systemic vascular resistance better than the systolic amplitude.

14.2.2 Pulse Area

It is calculated as the total area under the PPG curve. Seitsonen et al. (2005) found the PPG area response to skin incision to vary between movers and non-movers. Wang et al. (2009) have divided the pulse area into two areas at the dicrotic notch as shown in Figure 14.2. It can be used as an indicator of total peripheral resistance. This ratio is called the inflection point area (IPA) ratio and is defined as IPA=A2/A1.

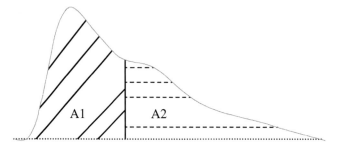

Figure 14.2 Original fingertip photoplethysmograph. A1 and A2 are the areas under the whole PPG wave separated at the point of inflection. Thus, the inflection point area ratio can be calculated as the division of A2 by A1.

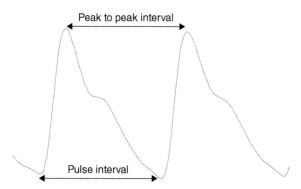

Figure 14.3 Two consecutive PPG waves represent pulse interval and peak-to-peak interval.

14.2.3 Peak-to-Peak Interval

The distance between two successive systolic peaks will be referred to as peak-to-peak interval, as shown in Figure 14.3.

A complete heart cycle represents both R-R intervals in the ECG signal comparing closely with the peak-to-peak interval PPG signal. The peak-to-peak interval has been used to detect the heart in PPG signals (Jubadi and Sahak 2009).

14.2.4 Pulse Interval

The distance between the beginning and the end of the PPG waveform is shown in Figure 14.1. The pulse interval is usually used when the diastolic peaks are more clear and easier to identify compared with the systolic peak. Fu et al. (2008) advised that ratio of pulse interval to its systolic amplitude is used for recognizing the properties of a person's cardiovascular system. In 2006, Linder et al. the heart rate variability (HRV) using the pulse interval in PPG signals with the HRV using R-R intervals in ECG signals are compared. The results demonstrated that HRV in PPG and ECG signals are highly correlated. They strongly suggested that PPG signals could be used as an alternative measurement of HRV.

14.2.5 Augmentation Index

The augmentation pressure (AG) measures the contribution that the wave reflection makes to the systolic arterial pressure, and it is obtained by measuring the reflected wave coming from the periphery to the center. Decreased compliance of the elastic arteries causes an earlier return of the "reflected wave," which arrives in systole rather than in diastole, causing a disproportionate rise in systolic pressure and an increase in pulse pressure, with a consequent increase in left ventricular afterload and a decrease in diastolic blood pressure and impaired coronary perfusion.

Takazawa et al. defined the augmentation index (AI) as the ratio of y to x as follows: $AI = y/x$ where y is the height of the late systolic peak and x is the early systolic peak in the pulse. The RI is used as a reflection index as follows: $RI = y/x$. The alternative AI is as follows: $AI = x - y/x$.

14.2.6 Large Artery Stiffness Index

The systolic component of the waveform occurs from a forward-going pressure wave transmitted along a direct path from the left ventricle to the finger. The diastolic component arises from pressure waves transmitted along the aorta to small arteries in the lower body, from where they are then reflected back along the aorta as a reflected wave that then travels to the finger. The upper limb provides a common channel for both the directly transmitted pressure wave and the reflected wave and, therefore, has little influence on their relative timing. As shown in Figure 14.4, the time delay between the systolic and diastolic peaks (or, in the absence of a second peak, the point of inflection) is related to the

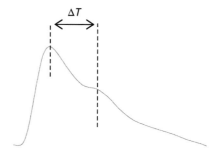

Figure 14.4 Typical waveform of the PPG and its ΔT feature.

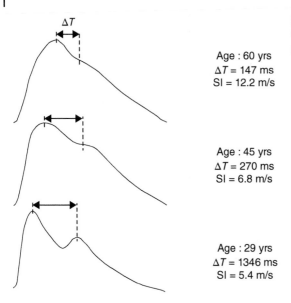

Figure 14.5 Typical PPG waveforms show the parameters change with age.

Age : 60 yrs
ΔT = 147 ms
SI = 12.2 m/s

Age : 45 yrs
ΔT = 270 ms
SI = 6.8 m/s

Age : 29 yrs
ΔT = 1346 ms
SI = 5.4 m/s

transit time of pressure waves from the root of the subclavian artery to the visible site of reflection and back to the subclavian artery. This path length can be assumed to be proportional to subject height (h).

Therefore, Millasseau et al. formulated an index of the contour of the PPG (SI) that relates to large artery stiffness: $SI = h/\Delta T$.

They have examined the timing of discrete components of the PPG to formulate an index of the contour of the PPG expected to relate to large artery stiffness SI. As shown in Figure 14.5, the time delay between the systolic and diastolic peaks decreases with age as a consequence of increased large artery stiffness and increased pulse wave velocity of pressure waves in the aorta and large arteries. Therefore, Lu et al. (2008) proved that the SI increases with age.

PPG is an instrument mainly used to identify and register variations in blood volume or blood flow in the body that occur with each heartbeat. PPG is an optical measurement technique that can be used to identify blood volume changes in the microvascular bed of tissue. The basic form of PPG technology requires only a few optoelectronic components: for illumination a light source (e.g. skin) and a photodetector to measure the small variation in light intensity associated with changes in perfusion in the catchment volume. PPG is most frequently employed noninvasively and operates at a red or near-infrared (IR) wavelength (Padilla et al. 2006).

In order to facilitate the interpretation of the original PPG waves, Ozawa differentiated the PPG signals to be able to evaluate the PPG wave contour (Takazawa et al. 1998).

14.2.7   Types of Photoplethysmography

1. Reflectance PPG – It detects the reflected light at tissue levels. The amount of reflected light is very small in comparison with the transmitted type. The weak signals detected on the PPG cannot be transmitted.
2. Transmission PPG – In opposite side of the emitter, the detector is positioned. So, the benefit of this kind is we get a clear signal.

14.3   Related Works

Many studies have shown an increasing trend in arterial stiffness in type 2 diabetes (Rubins et al. 2008). The main contributor to the increased arterial stiffness in type 2 diabetes is age. Other possible contributors are impaired glycemic control (Benetos et al. 2002) and the formation of advanced glycation end products (AGEs). Arterial stiffness has been assessed using brachial–ankle pulse wave velocity (ba-PWV), which is a noninvasive technique. Several works have applied noninvasively PPG as a substitute method for assessing arterial stiffness (Salih et al. 2012).

PPG is an optical noninvasive measuring technique that can be used to identify blood volume changes in the peripheral vessels at different body parts (fingers, earlobes, toes, etc.) and used in clinical research (Rubins et al. 2008). The blood volume pulsations produced by the heart circulate through the arterial tree. These pulsations are affected by reflected waves from the arterial branching sites. The fingertip PPG denotes change in the volume of blood in the fingertip as the pulse waves. This provides information on beats of aortic origin, characteristics of the vascular system, properties of peripheral vessels, and the state of blood flow (Benetos et al. 2002). The blood pressure pulse is similar to the PPG blood volume pulse, with related changes occurring in vascular diseases, such as damping and loss of pulsatility. The damping has been associated with a reduction in vessel compliance and increased peripheral resistance, although these variations have yet to be fully explained. PPG is the most often noninvasively employed and operates at a red or near-IR wavelength (Rubins et al. 2008).

PPG signals are taken from individual's persons using bio kit at a sample rate of 1000 samples/seconds. Wearable pulse rate sensors based on PPG have become increasingly popular, with more than ten companies producing these sensors commercially. The principle behind PPG sensors is the optical identification of blood volume variation in the microvascular bed of tissue. The sensor system consists of a light source and a detector, with red and IR LEDs, which are commonly used as the light source. The PPG sensor examines changes in the light intensity via reflection as of transmission through the tissue. The changes in light intensity are associated with small variations in blood perfusion of the tissue and provide information on the cardiovascular system, specially the pulse rate (Huotari et al. 2011). Due to simplicity, the wearable PPG pulse rate sensors have been developed.

Light wavelength: The interaction of light with biological tissue can be quite difficult and may involve scattering, absorption, and/or reflection. Anderson and Parrish examined the optical characteristics and penetration depth of light in human skin; within the visible region, the dominant absorption peak matched to the blue region of the spectrum, followed by the green-yellow region (between 500 and 600 nm) corresponding to red blood cells. The shorter wavelengths of light are strongly absorbed by melanin. Water absorbs light in the ultraviolet and longer IR regime; however, red and near-IR light overtake easily. As a result, IR wavelengths have been used as a light resource in PPG sensors. Blood absorbs more light than the surrounding tissue. Therefore, a reduction in the amount of blood is identified as an increase in the intensity of the detected light.

To determine the penetration depth, the wavelength and distance between the light source and PD are calculated for the light. The green light is suitable for the measurement of superficial blood flow in the skin. Light with wavelengths between 500 and 600 nm (the green-yellow region of the visible spectrum) exhibits the largest modulation power with pulsatile blood absorption. IR or near-IR wavelengths are better for measurement of deep-tissue blood flow (e.g. blood flow in muscles). Thus, IR light has been used in PPG devices for a few times.

However, green-wavelength PPG devices are becoming more popular due to the large intensity variations in modulation observed during the cardiac cycle for these wavelengths (Rhee et al. 2008). A green LED has much better absorptivity for both oxyhemoglobin and deoxyhemoglobin compared with IR light. Therefore, the change in reflected green light is larger than that in reflected IR light when blood pulses through the skin, resulting in a better signal-to-noise ratio for the green light source. Several green-light-based PPGs are available commercially. For example, MIO Global has developed the MIO ALPHA in cooperation with Philips; this measures the electrocardiogram (ECG) with 99% accuracy, even while cycling at speeds of up to 24 kmph. The use of video cameras using the signal based on the red-green-blue (RGB) color space has been considered.

The green signal was found to produce the strongest plethysmographic signal among camera RGB signals. Hemoglobin absorbs green light enhanced than red, and green light penetrates tissue to a deeper level than blue light. Therefore, the green signal contains the strongest plethysmographic signal. The reflected and transmitted signals in which the wearable PPG has two modes − transmission and reflectance. In the transmission mode, the light transmitted through the medium is detected by a PD opposite the LED source, while in the reflectance mode, the PD detects light that is backscattered or reflected from tissue, bone, and/or blood vessels (Nitzan et al. 2002).

The transmission mode is capable of obtaining a relatively good signal, but the measurement site may be controlled. To be effective, the sensor must be placed on the body at a site where transmitted light can be readily detected, such as the fingertip, nasal septum, cheek, tongue, or earlobe. Under anesthesia, sensor placement on the nasal septum, cheek, or tongue is effective. The fingertip and earlobe are the preferred monitoring positions; however, these sites have limited blood perfusion. In addition, the fingertip and earlobe are more susceptible to environmental extremes, such as low ambient temperatures (e.g. for military personnel or athletes in training). The greatest disadvantage is that the fingertip sensor interferes with daily activities. Reflectance mode eliminates the problems associated with sensor placement, and a variety of sizes can be used. However, reflection mode PPG is affected by motion artifacts and pressure disturbances (Laulkar and Daimiwal 2009).

Any movement, such as physical activity, may lead to motion artifacts that collapse the PPG signal and limit the measurement accuracy of physiological parameters. Pressure disturbances acting on the probe, such as the contact force between the PPG sensor and measurement area, can deform the arterial geometry by compression (Usman et al. 2002). Thus, in the reflected PPG signal, the AC amplitude may be controlled by the pressure exerted on the skin.

Adaptive filtering, when combined with an improved mechanical design and probe configuration, increased the precision of the receiving PPG signal. Motion robustness can be gained using accurate motion reference signals using three-dimensional (3D) low-noise accelerometers with dual-channel IR sensing. Nonlinear modeling and the spatial diversity of the sensor can be used to eliminate the motion contributions in optical signals and the reciprocal contributions in the two channels, respectively. Spatiotemporal principal component analysis (PCA) takes gain of both the spatial and temporal correlations between and within observed noise signals (Shaija et al. 2007). The basic concept of PCA-based noise reduction is to monitor the noisy data in a large m-dimensional space of delayed coordinates.

The noise is assumed to be random; it extends in an approximately uniform manner in all directions in this space. In distinction, the dynamics of deterministic systems underlying the data confine the trajectories of useful signals to a lower-dimensional subspace of dimension $p < m$. Consequently, the eigenspace of the observed noisy mixtures is divided into a noise and a signal-plus-noise subspace. In this case, noise reduction is performed by projecting the noisy mixtures onto the signal and noise subspace. Multi-scale principal component analysis (MSPCA) (Woodman and Watts 2003) combines the ability of PCA to decorrelate the uneven with wavelet analysis for motion artifact reduction from recorded PPG data. MSPCA performs PCA of the wavelet coefficients for each scale and then combines the results at relevant scales. Objective assessment of vascular aging is very significant since arterial stiffness is associated with hypertension, a risk factor for stroke and heart disease. In experimental studies, MSPCA outperformed the basic wavelet-based processing techniques for motion artifact reduction of PPG signals and was shown to be best suitable for pulse oximetry applications.

14.4 Methodology

14.4.1 PPG Design and Recording Setup

PPG signal is obtained from the patient using IR led and phototransistor. The acquired signal is sent to the amplifier for enhancing the signal information and removing the noise. Figure 14.6 shows a block diagram of signal detection.

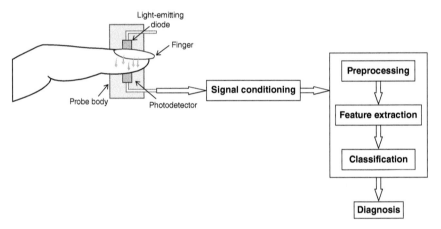

Figure 14.6 PPG signal detection block diagram.

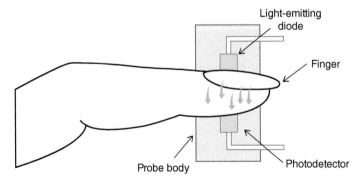

Figure 14.7 Sensor placements for transmittance mode.

In PPG, there are two modes of operation. They are transmissive mode for fingers/toes/earlobe and reflective mode for forehead/cheek. The received signal is assumed to be a measure of volume changes due to localized blood flow. Figure 14.7 shows the mode of measurement and placement of the sensor on fingertip.

14.5 Preprocessing in PPG Signal

The quality of the PPG signal depends on the location and the characteristics of the subject's skin at measurement, including the individual skin structure, the blood oxygen saturation, blood flow rate, skin temperatures, and the measuring environment. These factors generate several types of the additive object, which may be contained within the PPG signals. This may affect the extraction of features and hence the overall diagnosis, especially when the PPG signal and its derivatives will be evaluated in an algorithmic fashion. The main challenges in processing the PPG signals are described as follows:

- *Powerline interference:* This artifact could be suitable to the instrumentation amplifiers, the recording system picking up the ambient electromagnetic signals and another artifact. Moreover, a high-frequency artifact caused by mains power sources interference is induced onto the PPG recording cable. This artifact introduces a sinusoidal component into the recording. In Australia, this component is at a frequency of 50 Hz. The periodic interference is clearly displayed as a point not only its fundamental frequency of 50 Hz but also as points at 100 Hz and its higher harmonics.
- *Motion artifact:* It may be on the basis of poor contact to the fingertip photosensor. Variations in temperature and unfairness in the instrumentation amplifiers can sometimes cause baseline drift. The body movement was constrained due to the short time of measurement (20 seconds) and the fixed position of the arm during the fingertip PPG signal collection. It is difficult to arrange a procedure to measure PPG signal without low-frequency artifact, a noisy PPG signal with a power line, and motion artifacts. The low-frequency artifact can be eradicated using a high-pass filter or vice versa. Usually, the cause of motion artifacts is due to vibrations or movement of the subject. The shape of the baseline disturbance due to motion artifacts can be assumed to be a biphasic signal resembling one cycle of a sine wave.
- *Low amplitude PPG signal:* In general, the PPG waveform is subject to sudden amplitude changes due to the automatic gain controller that alters the gain of the amplifier automatically based on the amplitude of the input signal. This may cause amplitude saturation in the amplitude of the PPG waveform at a maximum or minimum value or rest at some fixed random value. A low amplitude PPG signal is generated by the automatic gain controller. However, the reduction of PPG amplitude can be directly attributable either to

loss of central blood pressure or to narrowing of the arterioles perfusing the skin.

- *Premature ventricular contraction:* The premature ventricular contractions (PVCs) causes an irregular beat interrupting the normal heart rhythm. This is called as a "missed beat" or a "flip-flop" in the chest. PVCs are often harmless, but when they occur repetitively, they can lead to more serious rhythm disturbances. This type of arrhythmia will affect the main events sensing accuracy in PPG signals. In PVC it is clear that detection of heartbeats in PPG signals will be challenging with the existence of PVCs. PPG sample contains different tests in analyzing PPG signals: motion artifacts, muscle artifact, arrhythmia, high-frequency artifact, and low amplitude.
- The PPG signal is composite and sensitive to artifacts, and because of these reasons, the PPG signal has not been widely investigated beyond its use in oximetry (Yong et al. 2011).

The parameters that can be determined by analyzing the morphology of the PPG signal are as follows:

(a) *Systolic peak:* Pulsatile changes in blood volume.
(b) *Delay time (ΔT):* Time between systolic peak and diastolic peak.
(c) *Pulse interval:* Time between beginning and end of the PPG waveform.
(d) *Heart rate (HR):* Heart rate is calculated as follows: HR = 60/pulse interval.
(e) *Stiffness index:* The stiffness index can be determined by using the formula (Asada et al. 2003) $SI = h/\Delta T$, where h is the height of the subject.

The heart pumps the blood into the arterial system in a series of strong bursts. The arterial walls have to withstand the pressure caused by the injected blood from the left ventricle causing distension and contraction for a proper functioning of all the cardiovascular system. Arterial stiffness measures the lack of elasticity of the arterial wall, providing important information about the properties of the wall material independent of the geometry (Chua and Heneghan 2006). Nowadays, arterial stiffness has been strongly related to the development of cardiovascular disease (CVD) (Murray and Foster 1996). Arterial stiffness increases the velocity at which the pulse wave travels through the vessels. It causes a premature return of the reflected waves in late systole, increasing the systolic blood pressure (SBP) and subsequently the central pulse pressure (PP). Thus, the load on the ventricle is raised, reducing the ejection fraction, which increases the myocardial oxygen demand (Dorlas and Nijboer 1985). Another reason for the increase of the SBP is due to the lack of distensibility and elasticity of stiffer arteries. Stiffer arteries cannot accommodate the ejected blood by the left ventricle, and for the same stroke volume, this results in an increase of the SBP and central PP (Chua et al. 2010). Support vector machine (SVM) classify the signals based on the four data segment selection policies: best fit, three best fit, ten best fit, and average best fit.

14.6   Results and Discussion

The data that we have analyzed for two groups of diabetic patients with H1bAc are 8% and 10%. Each group consists of 100 persons in total for 200 persons being analyzed. The data consists of age, systole, diastole, triglycerides, Hdl, Ldl, and total cholesterol values. The Weka tool is used to identify the signal and its accuracy of early detection of diseases. The artificial neural network (ANN) is used to optimize the signal for better results. The systolic and diastolic rate of signal is used for classification.

Using the Ranker method InfoGainAttributeEval, we evaluated the important criteria in the arterial stiffness determination (in reference to the subjects from the group I). The parameters are ranked according to their predictive value that measures the degree of correlation within the class. This method individually assesses the predictive ability of each attribute and the degree of redundancy among them. Higher values are obtained for the ones that are highly correlated with class 1, but with low inter-parameter correlations. The Pit and systolic time (SPt) time positions were revealed as the best predictors. This task was essential in discriminating the most interesting features to include in the classification model. The parameters with low merit (it was considered a threshold of 0.1) were discarded.

In this stage, the classifiers were evaluated using the accuracy (the percentage of correctly classified instances in a dataset) and the area under the ROC curve. The classification results, presented in Table 14.1, demonstrate the superior performance achieved by random forest. Classifiers within the 90–95% accuracy gap are regarded as solid rules (Lantelme et al. 2002), which in this case represent three out of the four evaluated classifiers, the last one remaining very close to 90%.

Naturally, SPt also appears as one of the key attributes in this dataset. Its importance is easily understood by the known relation with Pi. This effect is evident in where, for hypertensive subjects, the higher SPt is visibly affected by the overlap of early reflected waves, that coming before SPt. Other indices, R1, R2, and R3, still have considerable merit, but not as high as those of Pi and SP. However, they are quite important, because being Pi-independent parameters, they can turn robust the class prediction, whenever Pi is hidden in the APW and its parameterization is not achieved.

Table 14.1 The accuracy of different classifiers.

Classifier	Random forest	J48	JRIP	BayesNet
Accuracy(%)	96	95	94	88

The final results clearly indicate that random forest performs better than others, reaching an accuracy of 96%. Nevertheless, all the other algorithms have shown high classification results, especially in the case of J48 and JRIP, where the results were high above 90.00% (95% and 94%, respectively). The less accurate was the BayesNet with 88%.

Dicrotic wave values (both DWt and DWa) changed less than expected, due to the absence of known cardiac valve complications in this dataset. Related to this fact, the low predictive value of the R4 ratio in the dataset was verified. Through this study, we come to the conclusion that the combination of various classifiers should be used for the interpretation of APW data to avoid the specific limitations of the single-parameter analysis. One of the limitations of this analysis was the absence of studies for maximum accuracy levels. As the accuracy increases with the number of training samples, we are not aware if the maximum value has been achieved for each one of the classifiers. However, the levels of accuracy are high enough to assume that the maximum value was achieved during the training procedures.

It includes ANN and SVM that can improve the accuracy due to their capability in dealing with non-categorical features. We also consider that the inclusion of data from biochemical analysis and from cardiac equipment setups can provide a more helpful tool, able to correlate the information retrieved from APW with other cardiac disorders.

APW contains important physiological information easily identifiable by pulse wave analysis. The nature of arterial wave propagation of incident and of reflected waves plays a major role in the determination of important parameter indicators, which can serve as health status predictors of the cardiovascular system.

Results from the ROC curves, information about true positive rate (TPR) against false positive rate confirm the good accuracy of the values. A very high TPR was achieved for random forest, J48, and JRIP contrasting with the BayesNet performance. These differences are clear in the zoom view where the x-axis is plotted on a logarithmic scale. In the validation group, the subjects belonging to group III are young (24 years old, average) but also present positive AIx values, out of the normal range for this age (Takazawa et al. 1998), varying from 3:33% to 19:05%.

With the application of the previous model, we have intended to discriminate patterns and relationships in the pulse morphology and the identification of risk value labels (Stratton et al., 2000; Choi et al. 2011). These values were validated by the AIx, where it was verified a positive correlation between risk (class A in our dataset) and AIx positive values (Shriram et al. 2017). The knowledge gained from this study provides more information than the one provided by typical pulse wave analysis techniques (Figure 14.8).

The range of normal resting heart is 60–100 bpm theoretically. If the heart rate is below 60 bpm, it is known as bradycardia. If the heart rate is above 100

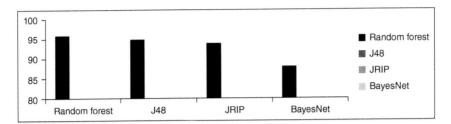

Figure 14.8 Accuracy of classifiers using data mining techniques.

bpm, it is known as tachycardia. Clinically, if the heart rate is above 90, it is considered as tachycardia, and that subject may require special attention. The heart rate above 90 may be a sign of hyperthyroidism or anemia.

The normal range for stiffness index is $5\,m/s \leq SI < 15\,m/s$. Higher arterial stiffness index means the arteries are getting hardened. Arterial stiffness slowly increases with an increment of age in healthy subjects.

However, in diabetic subjects, it increases rapidly. In our result, we have found that the person who is diabetic has higher stiffness index value. So, after few years, the diabetic persons may exceed the normal range for stiffness index. Hence, the diabetic patient with higher stiffness value requires special attention.

If the device is wearable, then the device will transmit the signal data through Bluetooth to smartphones, and for this communication we need pervasive computing through Android smartphones. Then the phone will communicate through Wi-Fi to the Internet. Based on the information the patients can easily identify the high risk of arterial stiffness. The pervasive computing is used to communicate data to the doctors periodically, and in the case of emergencies, it alerts the nearest hospital or critical care unit.

14.7 Conclusion

The earliest detection of diseases are necessary for preventing the cardiovascular diseases using PPG signal to prevent the diseases. The PPG device will be placed on forefinger based on the signal by the PPG; the arterial stiffness is calculated. A PPG signal is a device that is placed on the finger, used to detect the arterial stiffness at the earliest stage. It is used in critical care areas to easily identify and alert the cardiovascular disease and alleviate the pain of the patient. Using data mining classification technique, the accuracy of results has been improved considerably, i.e. 96% of accuracy is obtained. In the future, wearable device is proposed to be in use in order to communicate with the doctor and hospital automatically in case of emergencies. The healthcare public and private system faces the challenge of an increasingly aging population and the escalation of medical costs.

Bibliography

Allen, J. (2003). Photoplethysmography and its application in clinical physiological measurement. *Physiological Measurement* **28**: R1–R39.

Asada, H.H., Shaltis, P., Reisner, A. et al. (2003). Mobile monitoring with wearable photoplethysmographic biosensors. *IEEE Engineering in Medicine and Biology Magazine* **22** (3): 28–40.

Awad, A., Haddadin, A., Tantawy, H. et al. (2007). The relationship between the photoplethysmographic waveform and systemic vascular resistance. *Journal of Clinical Monitoring and Computing* **21** (6): 365–372.

Benetos, A., Waeber, B., Izzo, J. et al. (2002). Influence of age, risk factors, and cardiovascular and renal disease on arterial stiffness: clinical applications. *American Journal of Hypertension* **15** (12): 1101–1108.

Choi, S.W., Shin, M.H., Yun, W.J. et al. (2011). Association between hemoglobin A1c, carotid atherosclerosis, arterial stiffness, and peripheral arterial disease in Korean type 2 diabetic patients. *Journal of Diabetes and its Complications* **25** (1): 7–13.

Chua, C.P. and Heneghan, C. (2006). Continuous blood pressure monitoring using ECG and finger photoplethysmogram. The 28th Annual International Conference of the IEEE Engineering in Medicine and Biology Society.

Chua, E., Redmond, S., McDarby, G., and Heneghan, C. (2010). Towards using photo-plethysmogram amplitude to measure blood pressure during sleep. *Annals of Biomedical Engineering* **38** (3): 945–954.

Dorlas, J. and Nijboer, J. (1985). Photo-electric plethysmography as a monitoring device in anesthesia. Application and interpretation. *British Journal of Anaesthesia* **57**: 524–530.

Fu, T.-H., Liu, S.-H., and Tang, K.-T. (2008). Heart rate extraction from photoplethysmogram waveform using wavelet multi-resolution analysis. *Journal of Medical and Biological Engineering* **28** (4): 229–232.

Gil, E., Orini, M., Bailón, R. et al. (2010). Photoplethysmography pulse rate variability as a surrogate measurement of heart rate variability during non-stationary conditions. *Physiological Measurement* **31** (9): 127–1290.

Huotari, M., Vehkaoja, A., Määttä, K., and Kostamovaara, J. (2011). Photoplethysmography and its detailed pulse waveform analysis for arterial stiffness. *Rakenteiden Mekaniikka (Journal of Structural Mechanics)* **44** (4): 345–362.

Jubadi, W.M. and Sahak, S.F.A.M. (2009). Heartbeat monitoring alert via SMS. IEEE Symposium on Industrial Electronics & Applications.

Kadhim, A.Y., Ali, M.A.M., and Zahedi, E. (2007). Sensor module for multi-channel wireless photoplethysmography system. The 5th Student Conference on Research and Development - SCOReD, Malaysia (11 December 2007).

Lantelme, P., Mestre, C., Lievre, M. et al. (2002). Heart rate: an important confounder of pulse wave velocity assessment. *Hypertension* **39**: 1083–1087.

Laulkar, R. and Daimiwal, N. (2009). Acquisition of PPG signal for diagnosis of parameters related to heart. *International Journal of Electronics Engineering Research* **1**: 287–298.

Linder, S., Wendelken, S., Wei, E., and McGrath, S. (2006). Using the morphology of photoplethysmogram peaks to detect changes in posture. *Journal of Clinical Monitoring and Computing* **20**: 151–158.

Lu, S., Zaho, H., Ju, K. et al. (2008). Can photoplethysmography variability serve as an alternative approach to obtain heart rate variability information? *Journal Clinical Monitoring and Computing* **22** (1): 23–29.

Murray, W. and Foster, P. (1996). The peripheral pulse wave: information overlooked. *Journal of Clinical Monitoring and Computing* **12**: 365–377.

Nitzan, M., Khanokh, B., and Solvik, Y. (2002). The difference in pulse transit time to the toe and finger measured by photoplethysmography. *Physiological Measurement* **23**: 88–93.

Padilla, J.M., Berjano, E.J., Saiz, J. et al. (2006). Assessment of relationships between blood pressure, pulse wave velocity and digital volume pulse. *Computers in Cardiology* **33**: 893–896.

Poon, C.C.Y., Teng, X.F., Wong, Y.M. et al. (2004). Changes in the photoplethysmogram waveform after exercise. 2003 IEEE International Workshop on Computer Architectures for Machine Perception.

Rhee, M.-Y., Lee, H.-Y., and Park, J.B. (2008). Measurements of arterial stiffness: methodological aspects. *The Korean Society of Cardiology Korean Circ J* **38**: 343–350.

Rubins, U., Grabovskis, A., Grube, J., and Kukulis, I. (2008). *Photoplethysmography Analysis of Artery Properties in Patients with Cardiovascular Diseases*. Berlin, Heidelberg: Springer-Verlag.

Salih, F., Luban Hameed, A.K., and Bolz, A. (2012). Arterial stiffness detection depending on neural network classification of the multi- input parameters. *World Academy of Science, Engineering and Technology* **6** (10): 1221–1224.

Seitsonen, E., Korhonen, I., van Gils, M. et al. (2005). EEG spectral entropy, heart rate, photoplethysmography and motor responses to skin incision during sevoflurane anaesthesia. *Acta Anasthesiologica Scandinavica* **49** (3): 284–292.

Shaija, P.J., Jayasree, V.K., and Radhakrishnan, P. (2007). Blood Volume pulse sensor using peripheral pulse detected in the finger tips with photoplethysmography and assessment of bilateral symmetry. SENNET'07: Proceedings of International Conference on Sensors and Related Networks (12–14 December 2007).

Shriram, R., Martin, B., and Sundhararajan, M. (2017). Future of CPPG-EEG concurrent modality. *International Journal On Intelligent Electronics Systems* **11** (1): 19–26, 8p.

Stratton, I.M., Adler, A.I., Neil, H.A.W. et al. (2000). Association of glycemia with macrovascular and microvascular complications of type 2 diabetes (UKPDS 35): prospective observational study. *BMJ* **321** (7258): 405–412.

Takazawa, K., Tanaka, N., Fujita, M. et al. (1998). Assessment of vasoactive agents and vascular aging by the second derivative of photoplethysmogram waveform. *Hypertension* **32**: 365–370.

Usman, S., Reaz, M.I., and Ali, M.A.M (2002). Measuring Arterial Stiffness Using Photoplethysmogram, Ministry of Science, Technology and Innovation (MOSTI), Malaysia (No.SF0703 03- 01-02).

Wang, L., Pickwell-MacPherson, E., Liang, Y.P., and Zhang, Y.T. (2009). Noninvasive cardiac output estimation using a novel photoplethysmogram index. Annual International Conference of the IEEE Engineering in Medicine and Biology Society.

Woodman, R.J. and Watts, G.F. (2003). Measurement and application of arterial stiffness in clinical research: focus on new methodologies and diabetes mellitus. *Medical Science Monitor: International Medical Journal of Experimental and Clinical Research* **9** (5): RA81–RA89.

Yong, K.L.. Shin, H.S., Jo, J., and Lee, Y.K. (2011). Development of a wristwatch-type PPG array sensor module. In: IEEE International Conference on Consumer Electronics Berlin (ICCE-Berlin), 189.

15

Smart Sensing System for Cardio Pulmonary Sound Signals

Nersisson Ruban[1] and A. Mary Mekala[2]

[1] *School of Electrical Engineering, VIT University, Vellore, India*
[2] *School of Information Technology and Engineering, VIT University, Vellore, India*

15.1 Introduction

Cardio pulmonary sound signals are the bio acoustic signals generated by the contraction and relaxation of heart muscles, opening and closure of heart valves, turbulent blood flow, air in and out flow during breathing cycles and lung muscle activities (Khan and Vijayakumar, 2010). In healthy adults there are two heart sounds often described as *lub* (first heart sound S1) and *dub* (second heart sound S2). *heart murmurs*, S3 and S4 are the other sounds present with the normal heart sounds (Yoshida et al., 1997, Santos and Souza, 2001). Breath sounds are classified into inspiratory breath sounds and expiratory breath sounds. Both the sounds differ in amplitude and frequency components. These cardio pulmonary sounds are generally very weak and have low frequency signals. The frequency range of these signals is normally 20 Hz to 600 Hz (Zhang et al., 2016). In addition to these signals, heart murmurs generated due to various clinical conditions are also present in the thoracic region. The frequency range of those heart murmurs are 30 Hz to 700 Hz.

The common acoustic system for capturing the cardio pulmonary sound signal and other bioacoustics signal is stethoscope with microphone. There are different types of stethoscopes available. The classification is mostly based on the senor used. Contact type microphone and Air coupled microphones are commonly used as sound sensing module in stethoscopes. The sensitivity of microphone based stethoscope for the cardiopulmonary sound detection is very less and the Signal to Noise ratio (SNR) of this system is very low. The noises present in the detected signal will overlap with the actual signal of interest, because of the poor sensitivity. So for weak signal like cardio pulmonary

Intelligent Pervasive Computing Systems for Smarter Healthcare, First Edition.
Arun Kumar Sangaiah, S.P. Shantharajah, and Padma Theagarajan.
© 2019 John Wiley & Sons, Inc. Published 2019 by John Wiley & Sons, Inc.

acoustic signals, a high sensitive smart sensing system is essential for the accurate cardio pulmonary diagnostic needs (Nersisson and Noel, 2017b).

A polyvinylidene fluoride (PVDF) (Lee et al., 2012, Rajala and Lekkala, 2012) based smart stethoscope is proposed for the detection of cardio pulmonary sound signal. PVDF is a piezo electric material with very high sensitivity. **The sensitivity of the PVDF is approximately 10 times higher** than any other ceramic material. PVDF sensor will convert the mechanical pressure or strain or stress into electrical energy. This is a film like substance with very thin size. It is very flexible, light weight. It is also very tough material with plastic properties. The frequency spectrum is very high; the acoustic impedance is very low. It can be attached with any structure with normal adhesives. It is having a high moisture resistance. The output voltage generated by the PVDF sensor will be proportional to the mechanical pressure produced by the heart activity in the case of heart sound detection or the air inflow and outflow sounds in case of breath sound recording. The PVDF is a charge device. The charge generated will be captured by a charge amplifier and with suitable filter design, and the noise free high sensitive signal is detected. The captured signal is segmented using a LabVIEW based segmentation algorithm. The S1 and S2 components of the heart sound have lot of clinical significance.

15.2 Background Theory

Many hospitals and health clinics use diagnostic and monitoring devices to ensure that patients are receiving the necessary treatment and care. Electronic medical devices provide a vast array of medical information while allowing the patient to have a user-friendly interface. The sound signals from the heart are fed into a system that implements both hardware and software to display. The signal is amplified and filtered, and the clear version of the signal will be displayed to give pertinent information related to heart sound. Heart sounds are the noises generated by the turbulence created when the heart valves open and close (Kumar et al., 2007). In people with healthy cardiac conditions, there are different heart sounds described as lub (S1) and dub (S2) (these two are the major sounds). Heart murmurs S3 and S4 are the other sounds from heart present with the normal heart sounds. Third heart sound is generally present in infants and adults above 40. A polyvinylidene fluoride (PVDF)-based sensor can be used for detection of the heart sounds. PVDF material works on the basis of the piezoelectric effect, which gives charge output. So, the sensor gives charge that is proportional to the vibrations of the heart. This charge is converted to voltage using charge amplifier. The voltage signal is interfaced with the data acquisition (DAQ) board and connected to the computer with LabVIEW software where signal processing is done to reduce the noise present and separate the sounds (Guo et al., 1998; Topal et al., 2008).

15.2.1   Human Heart

The human heart is a main part of the body made by strong muscle structures. It provides blood continuously to the body parts through cardiac cycle (Reed et al., 2004). It is really nothing more than a pump, composed of muscle that pumps blood throughout the body, beating approximately 72 beats per minute (BPM). The heart pumps the blood, which carries all the vital materials that help our bodies function and removes the waste products. The heart is divided into four chambers: the two upper chambers are called the left and right atrium, and two lower chambers are called the right and left ventricle. There is a thick wall of muscle called septum, which will separate the right side and the left side of the heart. Normally with each beat, the right ventricle pumps the same amount of blood into the pulmonary circuit that the left ventricle pumps out into the body. Physicians commonly refer to the right atrium and right ventricle together as the **right heart** and to the left atrium and ventricle as the **left heart**. The pathways of blood through the human heart are part of the pulmonary and systemic circuits. These pathways include different one-way valves known as tricuspid, mitral, aortic, and pulmonary valves. The mitral and tricuspid valves are classified as the atrioventricular (AV) valves. This is because they are found between the atria and ventricles. The aortic and pulmonary semilunar valves separate the left and right ventricle from the pulmonary artery and the aorta, respectively. These valves are attached to a stringlike structure known as chordae tendineae, which connects the valves to the papillary muscles of the heart. Blood flows through the heart in single direction. Blood is prevented from flowing backward by the tricuspid, bicuspid, aortic, and pulmonary valves (Figure 15.1).

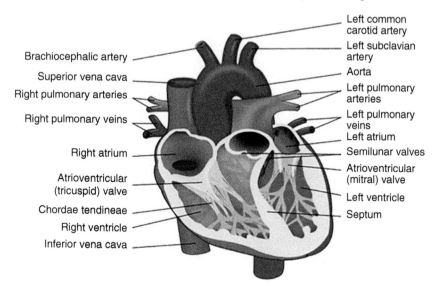

Figure 15.1 Human heart.

Table 15.1 Characteristic of heart sounds.

Sound	Origin	Frequency	Domain
S1	Closure of valve between the upper and lower chambers of heart	30–100 Hz	50–100 ms
S2	1. Slight backflow blood 2. Closure of valves in arteries leading out of the ventricles	Above 100 Hz	25–50 ms
S3	Inflow of blood to the ventricle		
S4	Contraction of atria		

15.2.2 Heart Sounds

In normal adult with healthy heart conditions, the various heart sounds, the generation of those sounds, and the specifications are given in Table 15.1.

15.2.3 Origin of Sounds

S1: The first heart sound is caused by the sudden block of reverse blood flow due to closure of the AV valves (tricuspid and mitral valves) at the beginning of ventricular contraction. When the ventricles begin to contract, so do the papillary muscles in each ventricle.

S2: The second heart sound is generated because of sudden block of reversing blood flow due to closure of the semilunar valves (aortic and pulmonary valves) at the end of ventricular systole.

S3: It is a rare sound that is also known as **protodiastolic gallop** or **ventricular gallop**. It occurs at the beginning of diastole after S2 and is lower in pitch than S1 or S2 as it is not of valvular origin (Kumar et al., 2006; Wang et al., 2006). S3 is generated by the oscillatory blood flow between the walls of the ventricles back and forth. This is initiated by blood speeding from the atria.

15.2.4 Significance of Detection

Analyzing heart sounds helps to get useful information about the cardiovascular system and also about the valves with heart and their functioning. Applications based on heart sound signals include detection of pulmonary hypertension, ventricular dysfunction, coronary artery disease, and cardiomyopathies. Phonocardiography is a noninvasive, low-cost, but accurate monitoring method based on sound detecting sensors for the detection of heart sounds. It is mainly used for valves abnormality diagnosis; it is non-risk and user-friendly method. The procedure can be repeated for *n* number of times without any risk to the patients. But the other side of the story is that the auscultation procedures require high manual expertise in listening to the sounds captured by the sensors and getting informations from the sounds. Thus automatic sound detection and diagnosing of the abnormalities of heart sounds plays a very important role. In automatic diagnosis of phonocardiograms, smart sensing systems are unavoidable (Dan et al., 2008; Debbal and Bereksi-Reguig, 2008).

15.3 Heart Sound Detection

Precise auscultation or listening to heart sounds provides important information related to the health condition of the heart to the doctors (Padmanabhan et al., 1993; Gill et al., 2005). Unfortunately, due to manual intervention in auscultation, this type of detection can be highly subjective and labor intensive. As a result, doctors have become more reliant on expensive but useful automated metrics of determining cardiovascular health. The common device used for detection of the heart sounds are:

- Stethoscope
  - Piezoelectric crystal
  - Microphone
- PVDF

15.3.1 Stethoscope

A stethoscope is mainly used for the detection and study of heart, lung, stomach, and other bioacoustic signals in human and animals. Using the stethoscope, the user can listen to normal and abnormal respiratory, heart, venous, arterial, fetal, uterine, and intestinal sounds. When stethoscope is used to hear the heart sounds, one should keep the sensor to the left side of the chest, where the heart is located (exactly, it is between the fourth and sixth ribs). The user should move the stethoscope all around the surface of the thoracic region to capture the cardiopulmonary sounds. The bell-shaped part of the instrument captures the sounds of low pitch, and then there is a diaphragm element that is used to move and hear the sounds at different areas of the heart.

When the AV valves are closing, the user can hear *lub*. If the user hears *dub*, then the cardiac event is pulmonic and aortic valves. Heart murmurs are heard if there is any turbulent blood flow. These are common sounds heard with many of the normal adult human being.

Drawbacks

- Since stethoscope magnifies the sounds, any noise accidently heard through the instrument can damage the ears of user.
- The cleaning and reusing of the instrument is the major issue when it is used with critically ill people.

Another advanced variant of stethoscope is electronic stethoscope, which also suffers from various issues, which are associated with the equipments used:

- Power sources are the major technical problem with electronic stethoscopes, in which most of them use batteries, and maintenance of batteries creates issues to the medical person.
- The interference from other devices like mobile phones and laptops is another major problem in the case of electronic stethoscopes.

15.4 Polyvinylidene Fluoride (PVDF)

Polyvinylidene fluoride or polyvinylidene difluoride (**PVDF**) is produced due to the polymerization of vinylidene difluoride. This fluoropolymer is thermoplastic in nature, and it is nonreactive. It is mostly used for high sensitivity applications and high accuracy. Since it is nonreactive, this material can be used for applications that require resistance to acids and bases. The density of the material is low and it is given as 1.78. The melting point of this PVDF material is 177 °C. It is available in different shapes and structures like piping products, sheet, films, plate, and an insulator. The major application fields are medical, defense, chemical, and battery industries. The glass transition temperature (T_g) of PVDF is about −35 °C and is typically 50–60% crystalline, which is responsible for the strong piezoelectric properties. It is mechanically stretched to orient the molecular chains and then poled under tension. PVDF are available in different chemical structures – alpha (TGTG'), beta (TTTT), and gamma (TTTGTTTG') phases – depending on the chain conformations as trans (T) or gauche (G) linkages. The advantages and disadvantages of PVDF are given in Table 15.2.

Table 15.2 Advantages and disadvantages of PVDF.

Advantages	Disadvantages
• It is weightless, so it can be easily attached with skin • Mechanical strength is very good • Different shapes and designs are possible with it • The operating frequency spectrum is large; it is 0.001–109 Hz • Very high sensitivity (216×10^{-3} Vm/N) compared with other piezo materials	• Sensitive to movements

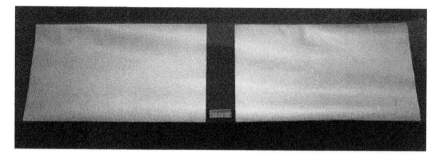

Figure 15.2 Poly-1,1-difluoroethene.

Figure 15.3 Structure of the PVDF material.

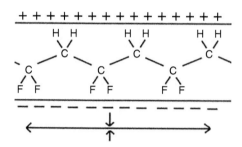

15.4.1 Properties of PVDF

- It is a polymer material with piezoelectric property.
- Like another piezo material, it produces electrical charge when subjected to mechanical force or stress and vice versa.
- This is due to atoms being displaced from normal positions in the lattice.
- The amount of produced electrical charge is directly proportional to the applied force.

Complete gold over platinum metallization over the two sides is shown in Figure 15.2.

- *Other names*: Polyvinylidene difluoride
- *Appearance*: Whitish or translucent solid
- *Molecular representation of PVDF*: $(CH_2CF_2)_n$-

The molecular structure is shown in Figure 15.3.

15.4.2 PVDF as Thin Film Piezoelectric Sensor

Piezoelectric materials convert mechanical stress or strain into proportionate electrical energy (McLaughlin et al., 2003). Piezo film has relatively high output voltage, about ten times greater than ceramic materials. It is a thin, flexible, lightweight, mechanically tough plastic film. It has a wide frequency range (0.001–109 Hz), low acoustical impedance, and moisture resistance and can be glued with commercial adhesives. The low acoustic impedance when close to human tissue permits more efficient transduction of acoustic signals in tissue. The PVDF material is a thin plastic polymer that has a thin electrically conductive nickel copper alloy deposited on each side. Wire connections are made to the piezo film sensor. Two important parameters of these films are:

- Piezoelectric strain constant $= 23 \times 10^{-12}$ mV^{-1}
- Piezoelectric voltage constant $= 216 \times 10^{-3}$ mN^{-1}

Key Benefits

- Low weight.
- Low thermal conductivity.
- High chemical corrosion resistance.
- Heat resistance.
- Mechanical strength and toughness.
- High abrasion resistance.
- Resistant to most chemicals and solvents.
- Low permeability to most gases and liquids.
- Withstands exposure to harsh thermal and chemical conditions.
- Unaffected by long-term exposure to ultraviolet radiation.

15.4.3 Placement of the Sensor

- Auscultation is an essential part of cardiac exam. Listening to the heart gathers information about:
  - Rate and rhythm.
  - Value functioning (e.g. stenosis, regurgitation/insufficiency).
  - Anatomical defects.
- Correct auscultation of heart sounds provides doctors with vital information related to the well-being of the heart and heart valves.
- The surface of human heart can be imagined as a square with four corners. The acoustic sensor can be put on any of these corners to capture the sound signals shown in Figure 15.4). For example, if the sensor/stethoscope is put over aortic valve corner, the sound captured will have a major contribution from the sound produced by the aortic valve in addition to the other sounds. But the aortic valve sound will be louder and clearer than other sounds, so the listener can focus toward the particular sound and do the necessary diagnostic steps. Similarly each spot in the heart surface focuses a particular heart sound produced by a specific part of the heart.

Figure 15.4 Location of heart sounds and valves.

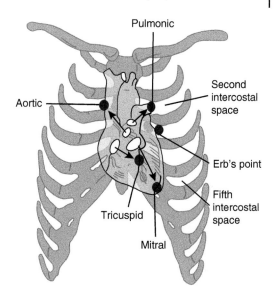

- The four spots are divided into four individual locations:
  - *Top right*: At costal cartilage where ribs connects to the sternum of the right third rib and the sternum.
  - *Bottom right*: At right sixth rib where ribs connect to the sternum.
  - *Top left*: At left second rib where ribs connect to the sternum.
  - *Bottom left*: It lies in the fifth rib that is in fifth intercostal space at the midclavicular line.
- For S1 the sensor should be placed in between tricuspid and mitral valve positions. For S2 the sensor should be placed in between aortic and pulmonary valve positions.
- S3 and S4 are mostly heard in the left lateral decubitus position and at the apex of the heart.

15.4.4 Development of PVDF Sensor

PVDF sensor shows strong piezoelectric behavior and has high sensitivity. It gives charge output that is then converted to voltage by charge amplifier. PVDF material of size 1 cm x 1 cm is taken to sense the vibrations caused by the heart. This material is kept upon compressed thermocol piece, which is again kept upon the hard surface like a rubber stamp. This hard surface and compressed thermocol helps in minimizing static pressure. The sensor may be spoiled if the wires are connected using hot solder because this thin film cannot withstand high temperature and can be burnt; therefore the wires are connected

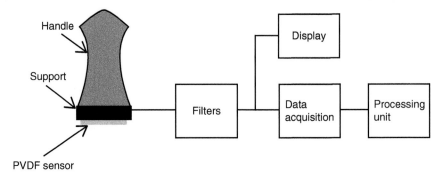

Figure 15.5 Block diagram of the PVDF-based smart sensing system.

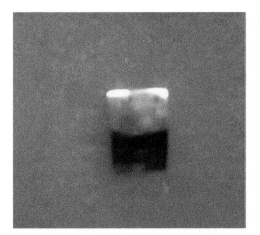

Figure 15.6 PVDF material.

using cold solder or by paste made by mixing Araldite with silver powder (this mixture becomes conductive) (Figure 15.5).

15.4.4.1 Steps Involved in the Development of Sensor
- 1 cm × 1 cm PVDF material is taken (Figure 15.6).
- Wires are connected on each side, which gives positive and negative signal.
- Wires are connected using Araldite mixed with silver powder, which makes it conductive.
- Sensor is pasted on a compressed thermocol, which is further mounted on hard surface like a stamp, which helps in reducing the static pressure as shown in Figure 15.7.
- Hence the sensor is developed and can be used for detection of the heart sounds.

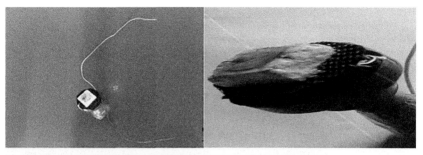

Figure 15.7 The PVDF-based sensing system.

15.5 Hardware Implementation

The electric dipole is the key factor for the piezoelectricity. At rest no electric field is generated, because at the molecular level, the piezoelectric material is an ionic bonded crystal. So the dipoles formed by positive and negative ions get cancel due to symmetry at rest. This symmetry is distributed when the material is stressed. Dipole moment is created due to the deformation of the crystal structure. Thus the electric charge is produced because of the dipole moment, which will be directly proportional to the applied force or stress or pressure. This sensor is not suitable for static applications because of its dynamic behavior.

15.5.1 Charge Amplifier

Since the dipole moment generates electric charge, to convert this electric charge into potential, a charge amplifier is used. Basically the charge amplifier is constructed by two methods, which is shown in Figure 15.8. The first one is considered the piezo element as charge source with parallel capacitor and resistor, and the second is piezo as voltage source and a series of resistor and capacitor combination.

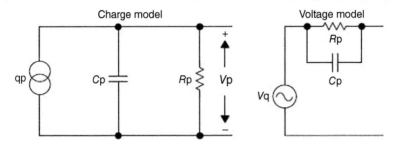

Figure 15.8 Charge and voltage circuits for the device.

15.5.2 Signal Conditioning Circuits for PVDF Sensor

Normally output potential from piezoelectric sensors ranges from micro-volts to few volts. Since the signal is very weak and noisy, the role of signal conditioning circuit is essential. The major element of the signal condition-ing part is amplifier. The features considered while designing an amplifier are frequency spectrum, the strength of the input signal, the expected strength of output signal, the input impedance of the amplifier, and the gain requirements.

Consider the desired signal levels are in the 3–5 V range for full scale. JFET or CMOS input op-amps, like the OPA111, satisfy most of the requirements for an amplifier.

For piezo material-based sensor, normally two types of electric circuits are used for signal conditioning. One is voltage mode amplifier circuit (which is used when the amplifier is very close to the sensor), and other one is charge mode amplifier circuit (which is used when the amplifier is remote to the sensor).

Charge mode amplifier: The charge mode amplifier is designed with a feedback capacitor C_f and a feedback resistor R_f. The value of R_f and C_f are set based on the required cutoff frequency of the amplifier. The biasing of the amplifier will make the output voltage 0.5 V_{cc} with no input. The output will swing around this DC level.

The high-pass filter with cutoff frequency f_c is given by:

$$f_c = \frac{1}{(2\pi C_f R_f)} = 0.34 \text{ Hz} \tag{15.1}$$

- $C_s = (213\text{–}1237 \text{ pF})$

$$\text{Gain} = \frac{C_s}{C_f} \tag{15.2}$$

- Gain = (0.05–0.26)

Signal amplifier: To amplify the weak voltage obtained from the sensor by the charge amplifier,

$$\text{Gain} = \frac{R_2}{R_1} \tag{15.3}$$

- Gain = 220

15.5.3 Hardware Circuits

The hardware design for this sensing system consisted of building a charge amplifier circuit. The PVDF sensor induces charge signals due to the heart vibrations, and the charge amplifier circuit converts it into voltage signal (Figure 15.9).

15.5.3.1 Design of Charge Amplifier

Assuming the patient's heart beat as 90 BPM. Therefore, time period, T, is

$$T = \frac{60}{\text{BPM}} \tag{15.4}$$

- T = 0.667 seconds

Frequency, f, is

$$f = \frac{1}{T} \tag{15.5}$$

- $f = 1.5$ Hz

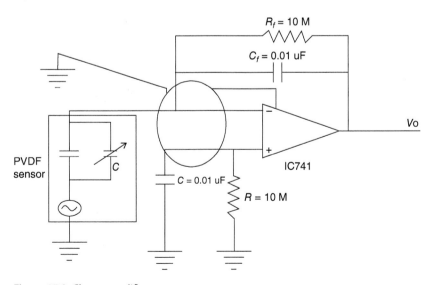

Figure 15.9 Charge amplifier.

Also, frequency f is

$$f = \frac{1}{2\pi RC} \tag{15.6}$$

$$C = \frac{1}{2\pi Rf} \tag{15.7}$$

When $R = 10$ MΩ,

$$C = \frac{1}{2\pi \times 10 \times 10^6 \times 1.5} = 0.01 \text{ μF} \tag{15.8}$$

15.5.3.2 Filter Design

The signal of interest is very weak and mixed with different types of noises. When the signal is tested on CRO, the frequency of noise is around 50 Hz. Narrow band-stop filter of cutoff frequency 50Hz is placed at the output of the charge amplifier, which helps in removing the noise present in the signal to some extent. And also a low-pass filter (LPF) is included in the circuit (cutoff frequency of 500 Hz) for further noise reduction.

Narrow Band-Stop Filter **Design of Band-Stop Filter**

$$f = \frac{1}{2\pi RC} \tag{15.9}$$

As the filter is designed for 50 Hz, $f = 50$ Hz (Figures 15.10 and 15.11).

- Assume $C = 0.01$ μF.
- Therefore, $R = 3.3$ kΩ (approx.).

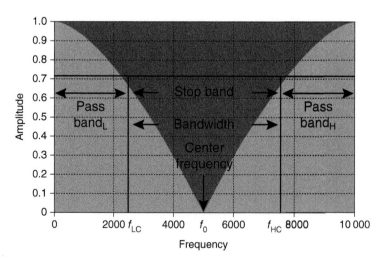

Figure 15.10 Frequency response of the band-rejection filter.

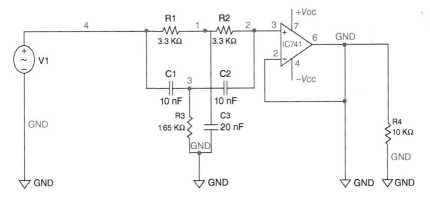

Figure 15.11 Band-stop filter circuit diagram.

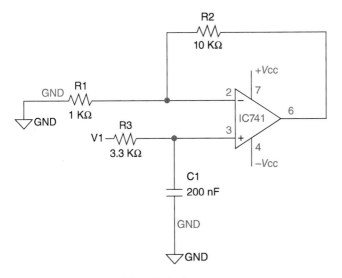

Figure 15.12 Low-pass filter circuit diagram.

Low-Pass Filter The meanings of "low" and "high" – that is, the cutoff – depend on the characteristics of the filter. The term "low-pass filter" merely refers to the shape of the filter's response; a high-pass filter could be built that cuts off at a lower frequency than any LPF – it is their responses that set them apart. Electronic circuits can be devised for any desired frequency range, right up through microwave frequencies (above 1 GHz) and higher. The circuit for LPF is shown in Figure 15.12.

Design of Low-Pass Filter

$$f = \frac{1}{2\pi RC} \tag{15.10}$$

As the filter is designed for 300 Hz, $f = 300$ Hz.

- Assume $R = 3.3$ kΩ.
- Therefore, $C = 0.2$ μF (approx.).

15.6 LabVIEW Design

Charge amplifier is interfaced with the PC using National Instruments (NI) DAQ USB-6221 and LabVIEW software. Output of the charge amplifier is given to the channel AI 0 of the DAQ. To reduce noise, similar circuit has been designed, and at the same time, output of the new circuit is given to the channel AI 1. Both the signals are captured in which one has the desired signal and the other has only noise. This helps in reducing the noise by directly subtracting the noise from the signal, and hence the desired signal can be captured in the PC.

Stage 1: Input signal from PVDF sensor: PVDF Sensor shows strong piezoelectric behavior and has high sensitivity. PVDF material of size 1 cm × 1 cm is taken to sense the vibrations caused by the heart. This material is kept upon compressed thermocol piece, which is again mounted upon the hard surface like a stamp. Then the sensor is kept on the chest, and due to the heart vibrations, PVDF sensor produces charge output that is proportional to the vibrations. This output is fed into charge amplifier for conversion of charge into voltage.

Stage 2: Charge amplifier: Amplifier is designed on the breadboard using op-amp IC 741 with sensor output as its input and resistance and capacitance of 10 M? and 0.01 μF, which is chosen according to the patient's heart rate. This amplifier gives voltage that is proportional to the charge input.

Stage 3: NI DAQ interface: NI USB-6221 device is used for interfacing the hardware circuit to the PC having LabVIEW installed in it. NI USB-6221 works with Measurement and Automation, which is a DAQ module from NI. The sensing system can be configured with the required settings using that module (Figure 15.13).

Stage 4: LabVIEW software: For capturing the signal, DAQ Assistant block is taken, and the required setup is made. The real-time signal captured is saved into .lvm file so that it can be used further. Then further processing is done for smoothening the signal and getting the signal of interest.

15.6.1 Signal Acquisition

With recent bandwidth improvements and new innovations from NI, USB has evolved into a core bus of choice for measurement and automation application. NI M series USB-based devices deliver high performance DAQ

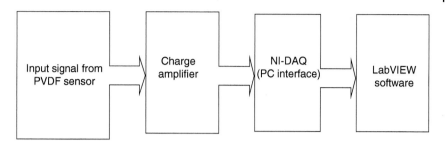

Figure 15.13 Block diagram of data acquisition.

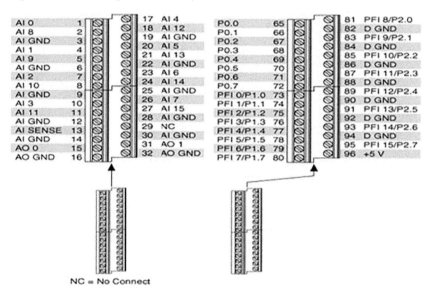

NC = No Connect

Figure 15.14 USB-6221 DAQ device pin layout.

in an easy-to-use and portable form factor through USB ports on laptop computers and other portable computing platforms. M series multifunction DAQ modules for USB are optimized for superior accuracy at fast sampling rates. They ensure 16-bit accuracy even when measuring all available channels at maximum speed. All externally powered M series devices have a minimum of 16 analog inputs, 24 digital I/O lines, digital triggering, and two counters/timers. Figure 15.14 shows the pin configuration of USB-6221 DAQ, and Figure 15.15 shows the DAQ setup.

15.6.1.1 Data Acquisition with LabVIEW

In LabVIEW, DAQ VIs are available in the DAQ palette. The VIs are organized so that the most common operations can be performed using the VIs. The DAQ Assistant Express VI is an easy method to configure the DAQ device.

Figure 15.15 USB-6221 DAQ setup.

Procedure

- Connect the sensor assembly to AI 0 and AI 1.
- Place the DAQ Assistant Express VI on the block diagram – a dialogue box appears.
- Select:
  - The channel for which input from LPF is given.
  - The type of input given.
  - Sampling rate.
  - Type of sampling.
- Reconfigure the DAQ Assistant Express VI by double-clicking the VI and creating a new task.
- As two channels are used, the split signal block is used to separate the signal. First channel is the signal with the noise and second channel is purely noise.
- Both the signals are fed into band-stop filter with cutoff frequency of 50 Hz.
- This can be done for controlling external hardware like motor, actuator, etc.
- The output of the filter is given to an LPF (third-order Butterworth filter). The cutoff frequency is 300 Hz.
- The outputs of both filters are displayed using a graph, and also both signals are subtracted to minimize the noise.
- The subtracted signal is displayed, and at the same time the signal is saved into .lvm file for future reference.

15.6.2 Fixing of the Threshold Value
Steps Involved

- The .lvm file that was saved while capturing the signal is now read using Read from Measurement File block to get back the captured signal for processing.

- Simulate Arbitrary Signal generates a DC signal of the threshold value. The threshold value is set by considering the overall signal strength and the input signal. In arbitrary signal generated as a threshold, signal is generated with the specific amplitude value.
- These both signals are then merged using Merge Signals block, and the result is displayed on the graph indicator.
- Comparison block is configured for greater than or equal to function of the required threshold value, and then it is applied to the signal from .lvm file.
- This helps in detecting only those values that are above the threshold.
- The result is displayed in the graph indicator.

15.6.3 Fixing the Threshold for Real-Time Signal
Steps Involved

- As shown in Figure 15.16, the real-time signal is captured, and it is saved in .lvm file for future references. But the environmental and other factors are different every day, so real-time signal processing is much better.
- The same concept of threshold as in Figure 15.17 is used for real-time detection. The acquired signal is compared with the arbitrary signal generated as a threshold signal, and the difference signal is displayed.
- The subtracted signal obtained is directly given to Greater than or Equal to block, and threshold is applied rather than saving it into .lvm file.
- With the help of this algorithm, threshold can be applied real time.

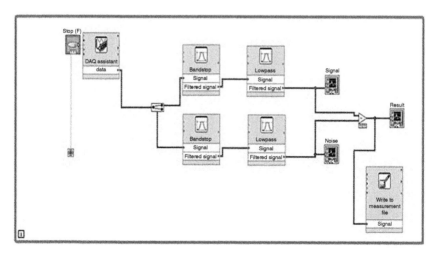

Figure 15.16 Signal acquisition.

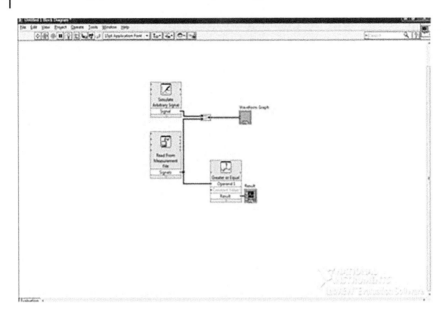

Figure 15.17 Fixing of threshold value.

15.6.4 Fixing the Threshold in Time Scale

Steps Involved

- Desired signal that was saved in .lvm file is retrieved and stored in an array name output array 2 of size 700 using Build Array block.
- The elements of array are fed to a FOR loop of 700 iterations.
- Within the FOR loop, a case structure is created having two cases, namely, True and False. The case selection is done with the help of logic derived from x-threshold coefficients (Figure 15.18).

Logic of Determining the Case from x-Threshold Coefficient

- A range of x-axis is selected using Greater Than or Equal to and Less Than or Equal to blocks.
- Comparison is done with the help of iteration number of the FOR loop.
- The range is set according to the limits within which the heart sounds (S1 and S2) lie.
- The comparison is ORed and the result is fed to the case structure.
  - Inside the case structure, when the condition is True, i.e. iteration is in the selected range, then the elements from output array 2 are retrieved using Index Array block and are stored in a new array. The shift registers are added in the FOR loop so that the element is stored in the previous stored array.

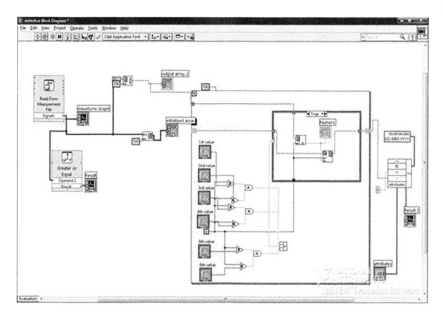

Figure 15.18 Threshold on *x*-axis.

- If the condition is False, i.e. iteration is not in the selected range, then the element "0" is added in the stored array.
- The result of the entire loop is an array of *y* values of output array 2 within the desired *x* range and no values outside the range.
- This array is converted into Waveform Graph using Array to Waveform Conversion block.
- The waveform is displayed in the Result 2 Graph.

15.6.5 Separation of Peaks from Resultant Signal (Sample 1)

From Figure 15.19, the subtracted signal is further processed. On watching closely to the graph, the threshold has been set to be 0.0667. On the below waveform, it can be seen clearly that the peaks has been separated.

15.6.6 Separation of Peaks from Resultant Signal (Sample 2)

This waveform has been captured by the same technique on some other day. This sample also has some peaks at some intervals. In this sample threshold, value is set as 0.0567. In the below graph, there are peaks that represent S1 and S2. This signal is captured for about 2 seconds, and around 700 sample data are stored in .lvm file.

In this result the threshold is set on *x*-axis because the third heart sound is just after the second one. So the original signal is taken, and by setting the

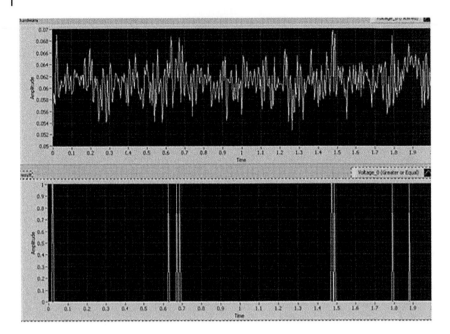

Figure 15.19 Separations of peaks.

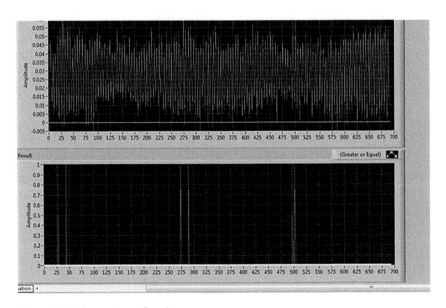

Figure 15.20 Separations of peaks.

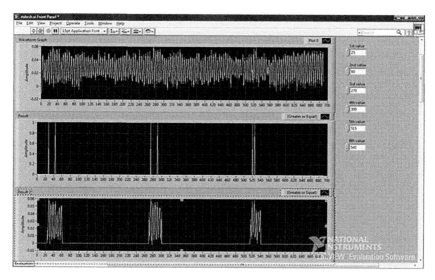

Figure 15.21 Results of keeping threshold on x-axis.

signal on x-axis, only the part that contains the three sounds can be separated, and the rest of the signal is set to zero. The width of the x-axis threshold value (also known as x-threshold coefficient) can be varied according to the peaks (Figures 15.20 and 15.21).

15.7 Heart Sound Segmentation

The most obvious of the heart sounds are the first and second sounds, or S1 and S2, which demarcate systole from diastole. Although S1 and S2 are considered to be discrete sounds, each of them is created by the near-instantaneous closing of two separate valves. For the most part, it is enough to consider that these sounds are single and instantaneous (Nersisson and Noel, 2017a). When listening to a patient's heart, the cadence of the beat will usually distinguish S1 from S2. Because diastole takes about twice as long as systole, there is a longer pause between S2 and S1 than there is between S1 and S2. However, rapid heart rates can shorten diastole to the point where it is difficult to discern which is S1 and which is S2. The heart sound you hear when you first feel the pulse is S1, and when the pulse disappears is S2.

Both S1 and S2 are composed of different subcomponents. In case of S1, it is M1 followed by T1. Right bundle branch block (RBBB) can be diagnosed if M1 slightly succeeds T1. In case of second sound S2, it is A2 followed by P2. Different cardiac abnormalities like RBBB and pulmonary stenosis are normally diagnosed by the wide split between A2 and P2. Thus individual analysis of heart sounds carries important diagnostic information. So segmenting S1 and S2 plays a significant role in heart abnormalities detection (Ruban et al., 2012).

15.7.1 Algorithm for Signal Separation

A flat sequence is used and it is split into two frames. Each frame contains a FOR loop and a case structure. The input values are divided into two sets of values and stored in an array. These values are fed into the individual frames of the flat sequence. The operation executed in order. The case structure compares the values with the separation coefficient y and $y\prime$, which are set differently for different signals with few iterations. The data leave the frame and the flat sequence after comparison and get stored in an array. The separation coefficients y and y' for normal heart sound signal are given in Table 15.3.

The input values are manipulated with separation coefficient. The values are further divided by a constant value 2 to check for even or odd cases (TRUE/FALSE cases). By the identified case, the signal is segmented into required component.

15.7.1.1 Case Structure Algorithm

The resultant of the above operation set the case selection value as 1, and then TRUE case is considered. All the input values that come within this case are stored in a 2D array using "Insert into Array" function. The index of the array is set as 0 to read only column 0. If the resultant operation is set as FALSE case (selective value is 0), then 0 is written in the same array by the same way. The final array that emerges from stage 1 is the input array for the second frame and the second case structure. The overall output is used to form the final segmented waveform, which is shown in Figures 15.23 and 15.24.

The input is read using a wav read sub VI. The file path is given in the input handling VI. For every different input signal, the path and separation coefficients need to be assigned individually (Figure 15.22).

15.7.2 Segmented S1 and S2 Sounds

Following are the outputs of normal heart sound signals. Figures 15.23 and 15.24 show an ON/OFF switch, which is used to select the heart sound

Table 15.3 Separation coefficients for normal heart sounds.

Signal	Separation coefficient (y)	Separation coefficient (y')
Normal heart sound signal (S1, S2)	3800	4200

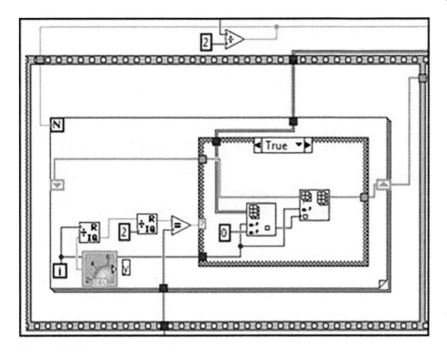

Figure 15.22 Flat sequence used for separation.

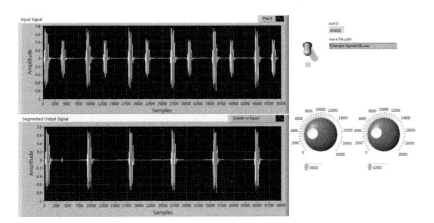

Figure 15.23 Segmented S1 from normal heart sound.

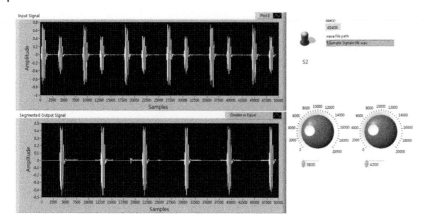

Figure 15.24 Segmented S2 from normal heart sound.

component. In this work only S1 and S2 are segmented. So ON position is allotted for S1, and OFF position for S2. The upper section shows the sample signal, i.e. normal heart sound containing first heart sound (S1) and second heart sound (S2), and the lower section shows separated heart sound. In this case, it is the first heart sound separated from the above waveform. Presently the knob located in the right side of the figure is in OFF position. If it is set to ON position, the lower section of the figure would show the other part of the waveform, i.e. second heart sound. The right side of the figure shows two knobs that signifies separation coefficients y and $y\prime$. In this case, their values are 3800 and 4200, respectively. Depending upon the values of these separation coefficients, the heart sounds get separated. Figures 15.23 and 15.24 also show the value of array size of the sample, which is 49 408, and the file path section, in which the address of the sample signal is fed.

15.8 Conclusion

The PVDF sensor-based bioacoustic signal detecting system is developed. The charge amplifier circuit was able to amplify and convert the charge into voltage signal to make it suitable for display on LabVIEW while protecting the patient from macroshock. The signal of interest is very weak, and also there is a lot of noise in the circuit. To reduce the noise, filters are made in the hardware. This helps in reducing noise due to charge amplifier, but the components of the filters were adding extra noises. Thus it is decided to design the filter in the LabVIEW software itself. Thus the signal from the charge amplifier is directly taken into LabVIEW for processing. Interface between the hardware and the LabVIEW software was successfully achieved by a NI USB-6221 DAQ card.

Filter has been designed for the acquired signal, and the noise has been reduced to a great extent. For determining the peaks, threshold concept is used, and various peaks of S1 and S2 are separated at some intervals that depend from person to person. S3 heart sound indicates rapid filling of ventricle due to decrease in flexibility in mitral valve. If S3 is present, then it is just after S2 with very low value. To detect the third sound, threshold has been put on the x-axis. This PVDF sensor cannot withstand high temperature; therefore, hot solder is not used for connecting the wires. Hardware filters are not accurate, and also they add a lot of noise to the desired signal. Charge amplifier itself produces a lot of noise. The threshold is set by hit and trial method, so it may be not that accurate. On detecting the sound peaks, the interval between S1 and S2 are not same, and also due to noise, it is difficult to detect S3. A LabVIEW-based heart sound segmentation algorithms are applied, and the separated S1 and S2 signals are given. It is difficult to detect the third sound with the help of stethoscope; therefore the designed sensor can be used for detecting third sound as well.

Bibliography

Dan, C., He, W., Zhou, J., and Li, X. (2008). Playing and acquiring heart sounds and electrocardiogram simultaneously based on lab view. In: Automation Congress, 2008. WAC 2008. World, 1–4. IEEE.

Debbal, S.M. and Bereksi-Reguig, F. (2008). Computerized heart sounds analysis. *Computers in Biology and Medicine* **38** (2): 263–280.

Gill, D., Gavrieli, N., and Intrator, N. (2005). Detection and identification of heart sounds using homomorphic envelogram and self-organizing probabilistic model. In: Computers in Cardiology, 2005, 957–960. IEEE.

Guo, Z., Moulder, C., Durand, L.-G., and Loew, M. (1998). Development of a virtual instrument for data acquisition and analysis of the phonocardiogram. In: Proceedings of the 20th Annual International Conference of the IEEE Engineering in Medicine and Biology Society, 436–439. IEEE.

Khan, T.E.A. and Vijayakumar, P. (2010). Separating heart sound from lung sound using labview. *International Journal of Computer and Electrical Engineering* **2** (3): 524.

Kumar, D., Carvalho, P., Antunes, M. et al. (2006). Detection of S1 and S2 heart sounds by high frequency signatures. In: 28th Annual International Conference of the IEEE Engineering in Medicine and Biology Society, 2006. EMBS'06, 1410–1416. IEEE.

Kumar, D., Carvalho, P., Antunes, M. et al. (2007). Near real time noise detection during heart sound acquisition. In: 2007 15th European Signal Processing Conference, 1387–1391. IEEE.

Lee, W.K., Chung, G.S., Baek, H.J., and Park, K.S. (2012). Heart sounds measurement using PVDF film sensor and their comparison with RR intervals of ECG signals. In: 2012 IEEE-EMBS International Conference on Biomedical and Health Informatics (BHI), 864–866. IEEE.

McLaughlin, J., McNeill, M., Braun, B., and McCormack, P.D. (2003). Piezoelectric sensor determination of arterial pulse wave velocity. *Physiological Measurement* **24** (3): 693.

Nersisson, R. and Noel, M.M. (2017a). Hybrid nelder-mead search based optimal least mean square algorithms for heart and lung sound separation. *Engineering science and Technology, An International Journal* **20** (3): 1054–1065.

Nersisson, R. and Noel, M.M. (2017b). Heart sound and lung sound separation algorithms: a review. *Journal of Medical Engineering & Technology* **41** (1): 13–21.

Padmanabhan, V., Semmlow, J.L., and Welkowitz, W. (1993). Accelerometer type cardiac transducer for detection of low-level heart sounds. *IEEE Transactions on Biomedical Engineering* **40** (1): 21–28.

Rajala, S. and Lekkala, J. (2012). Film-type sensor materials PVDF and EMFI in measurement of cardiorespiratory signals–a review. *IEEE Sensors Journal* **12** (3): 439–446.

Reed, T.R., Reed, N.E., and Fritzson, P. (2004). Heart sound analysis for symptom detection and computer-aided diagnosis. *Simulation Modelling Practice and Theory* **12** (2): 129–146.

Ruban, N., Arneja, G.P.S, Bansal, K., and Noel, M.M. (2012). Heart sound analysis using labview. *Journal of Theoretical & Applied Information Technology* **46** (2): 1029–1033.

Santos, M.A.R. and Souza, M.N. (2001). Detection of first and second cardiac sounds based on time frequency analysis. In: Proceedings of the 23rd Annual International Conference of the IEEE Engineering in Medicine and Biology Society, Volume **2**, 1915–1918. IEEE.

Topal, T., Polat, H., and Güler, I. (2008). Software development for the analysis of heartbeat sounds with labview in diagnosis of cardiovascular disease. *Journal of Medical Systems* **32** (5): 409–421.

Wang, P., Kim, Y., Ling, L.H., and Soh, C.B. (2006). First heart sound detection for phonocardiogram segmentation. In: 27th Annual International Conference of the Engineering in Medicine and Biology Society, 2005. IEEE-EMBS 2005, 5519–5522. IEEE.

Yoshida, H., Shino, H., and Yana, K. (1997). Instantaneous frequency analysis of systolic murmur for phonocardiogram. In: Proceedings of the 19th Annual International Conference of the IEEE Engineering in Medicine and Biology Society, 1997, Volume **4**, 1645–1647. IEEE.

Zhang, G., Liu, M., Guo, N., and Zhang, W. (2016). Design of the MEMS piezoresistive electronic heart sound sensor. *Sensors* **16** (11): 1728.

16

Anomaly Detection and Pattern Matching Algorithm for Healthcare Application: Identifying Ambulance Siren in Traffic

Gowthambabu Karthikeyan, Sasikala Ramasamy, and Suresh Kumar Nagarajan

School of Computer Science and Engineering, VIT University, Vellore, India

16.1 Introduction

Motivation: Letting an ambulance reach its destination via Indian roads is very difficult nowadays due to increase in number of vehicles day by day. One good thing is that people are ready to allow or make a path once they hear an ambulance sound behind them. But that does not work with a traffic signal. When you hear an ambulance sound, you cannot move forward or give way to the ambulance because the other side of the traffic will be free to go.

Ambulance sound should be detected by the sensor before vehicle reaches the signal and then all adjacent signals are blocked immediately. This helps the ambulance to cross the traffic signal with ease.

Also when the traffic is very high and can't let the ambulance to move forward then we have to notify before 500 m so that the signals can be properly managed and let the ambulance reach the hospital. Most of the times when ambulance cannot cross any traffic signal, the traffic cops try to remove the divider placed in the centre of the roads and leave the ambulance to go. But our projects a view of how can an ambulance leave the traffic signal without any trouble.

Advantages: One of the main advantages of our proposed idea is that it helps the ambulance reach the hospital by passing all the traffic signal with ease. It helps the doctors to save a patient's life faster. It also saves lot of time and helps the drivers to cross the traffic without panicking and maintain the same speed level in the traffic signals.

Restrictions: When implementing this project, we need to be careful with the signals that are not working. Nowadays not all the signals are working properly, only few are working with traffic cops and many are unmanned. This project works only with the signals that are working. That is the drawback of our project.

Intelligent Pervasive Computing Systems for Smarter Healthcare, First Edition.
Arun Kumar Sangaiah, S.P. Shantharajah, and Padma Theagarajan.

Also this does not need any traffic cops to operate. Mostly the traffic signal does not work during the night till early morning. In that case our project will not work, and probably there will not be any traffic during that time. So this is the core of our project, and basically it helps the ambulance to cross the traffic signal and reach the hospital faster than before. This works with the ambulance sound and traffic signals using sensor.

Traffic signals are unmanned in many places around the country, and rarely we can see a traffic enforcer. Usually when there is a traffic cop operating any traffic signals and if they find an ambulance approaching the traffic signal, they push the red signal to green signal and let the vehicles to move forward so that the ambulance can cross the traffic signal without any trouble. But what will happen if these traffic cops are not operating and the traffic signals are left unmanned? In that case, sensors fixed in the traffic signal gets triggered when Ambulance siren is received as input. So this functions with the help of pattern matching algorithm and makes it easy for the ambulance to reach the hospital faster than before.

Expected output in proposed system: With an assumption that traffic signals have sensors already. Now when the ambulance sound is heard in the traffic signal, the color of the signal changes from red to green. So that the traffic can be cleared before the ambulance reaches the signal. When the ambulance approaches, the traffic signal is turned from red to green, and all the other traffic signals will be turned to red. Now that the rest of the traffic signals are blocked, the ambulance can cross the traffic signal faster than before.

The sensors kept inside the traffic signal works when it hears the ambulance sound within 500 m. And the sensor acts on the direction in which it is placed. So that it works on the direction in which the ambulance sound strikes the signal. Also when the traffic signal changes from red to green, it helps the other sensors fixed nearby in the same traffic signal to change to red by blocking the traffic. This way the sensor helps the nearby traffic signals.

So now let us see in what way these sensors could detect the ambulance sound. There are many types of algorithm used to detect a unique sound from the source. We have used the pattern matching algorithm to detect the ambulance sound in a heavy traffic. Here, ambulance siren sound is taken as source point and sound sensor fixed inside the traffic signal is the destination point. Once the destination receives the ambulance sound, it changes the traffic signal, and other processes take place.

Algorithm: Pattern matching algorithm is used here to detect the ambulance sound in the traffic signal. Pattern matching algorithm helps us to find the unique pattern in a collection of patterns. Patterns referred here are the sounds produced in the traffic signals. We all know that when there is a heavy traffic, we usually hear the noises from vehicles standing in the signal. These are the collection of sounds, and we need to take only the ambulance sound from these noises. So we use pattern matching algorithm to identify the ambulance sound and send it to the sensor device where the input is received. When ambulance siren sound is received in the sound sensor as input, pattern matching algorithm compares it with the default sound. Here the ambulance default sound contains all the collections of the ambulance sound because there are many types of siren fixed in an ambulance. When the default ambulance sound matches with the received ambulance siren, then it changes the red signal to green signal. Meanwhile the nearby signals will be blocked and the ambulance can reach the hospital without any delay.

Once the ambulance crosses the traffic signal, then the signals will be back to normal with same traffic signals. It pauses when the ambulance reaches the traffic signal and resumes when the ambulance leaves the traffic signal. This does not affect the vehicles in that traffic signal but when the ambulance is approaching a specific traffic signal, then the vehicles can move ahead to avoid further traffic. As illustrated in Figure 16.1, the private and public vehicles standing in

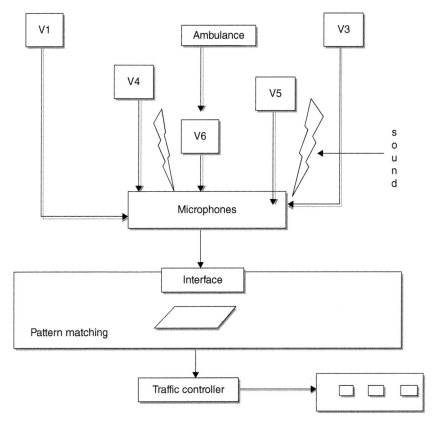

Figure 16.1 The general structure of integrated traffic system for ambulance sound detection.

that area has to move forward and provide some space for the ambulance to leave the traffic signal with ease.

Each and every traffic signal has to get the sensor because once the ambulance crosses the traffic signal, it has to respond to other traffic signals and block the traffic. For seamless flow, sensors should be present in all traffic signals. Also these sensors are kept inside the traffic signal and are connected with the traffic signals directly. It has the control to change the traffic signal anytime.

During night time these traffic signals starts to blink, and the sensors will work only when the traffic signals are stable. When traffic is less and it is night-time, the system stops its process. So in night time it stops working and the traffic is pretty less. When the traffic signals look stable, the sensors are then connected with the traffic signals and checks for the ambulance sound. This way it works during the night time.

The objective of our proposed system and literature survey: The details of the pattern matching algorithm, the working diagrams, and data are recorded, and result analysis is in subsequent chapters.

16.2   Related Work

The recent developments in the design of vehicles have constituted noise insulation within the vehicles that can detach the interaction of the driver from the external environment. The air conditioners and sound systems are the two main causes of noise insulation within the vehicles. Due to these factors, the drivers find difficulty in the recognition of emergency horns from high priority vehicles like ambulances. Patel and Shekokar (2015) highlight the need for a noise recognition system to schedule the high priority vehicles in a heavy traffic environment. Palecek and Cerny (2016) mark the emergency horn detection system as a hot topic of research to tackle the present traffic scenario. Ambulance visibility groups states that a vehicle that has no interruption from ventilators and sound systems is able to recognize the emergency horns initiated within 100 m of distance, whereas the modern vehicles equipped with artificial ventilators and music systems with noise production capacity of more than 90 dB reduce the range of recognition of the drivers to 2 m.

The reduction in the capacity of recognition of emergency horns by the drivers in the traffic environment has resulted in traffic congestion and deadlocks on roads. Hence there rises a requirement for the development of alert systems in vehicles, providing the capacity to interpret the horns and alert the driver for maintaining smooth traffic conditions. The chapter reviews the existing research that sheds light on the importance of emergency noise detection systems, existing techniques to estimate and sound detection applications in real world.

As modern vehicles are loaded with many retrofits, the drivers are becoming less aware/less interactive with the external environment to distinguish the emergency horns Palecek and Cerny (2016). Hence this work has proposed an emergency horn detection system for cars in myRIO platform using FPGA. The work has made a case study on the traffic environment of Czech Republic where three types of nonreflective white sirens, namely, Wail, YELP, and Hi-Lo, are used. This chapter has taken a dataset of 11 samples of filtered Wail siren with four emergency horns. The hamming window function is used to segment the audio samples, processed with a band-pass filter and converted with Fourier transformation. The spike algorithm captures the peaks in the test audio signal on the condition that peak number should be greater than 2 and signal height greater than 0, 15. A decision-making AND gate function is programmed to detect the hooters out of the tested signals. The algorithm has detected the emergency wail signals with an accuracy of 90%. Patel and Shekokar (2015) proposed an urban traffic management system with wireless sensor networks and vehicular ad hoc networks. The system has implemented a distance-based emergency vehicle dispatching (DBEVD) algorithm.

A Priority for Emergency Traffic-Based MAC (PE-MAC) protocol is proposed. The distance between the source vehicle and the sensor is measured using the time taken by the signals. This chapter compares three different distance measures - Euclidean, Manhattan, and Canberra. The Euclidean distance outperforms other methods with an accuracy rate of 98.60%. Friedland et al. (2010) have attempted to estimate the location of the multimedia signals with leverage cues extracted from the acoustic and visual information with metadata. The work has tried to locate the city of the ambulance in a video dataset extracted from 200 YouTube video clips from 11 cities. The MFCC technique is combined with machine learning models such as GMM, HMM, and SVM. The video location of the dataset is defined by parameters such as visual landmarks, landscape, and written text and signs. The acoustic information is estimated by the acoustic landmarks, noise, speech, and environmental sounds.

The metadata-based estimation exploits the information such as the words used, language of the words, situation, location, and GPS information. Combining the data obtained from these three estimation methods, the location of the ambulance is mapped. An MFCC-based machine learning method of 70% training and 30% testing is carried out with the acoustic files of ambulance horns from the video data with algorithms such as Gaussian mixture model and support vector machine. The experimental results show that the GMM SVM method on audio files outperforms all other combinations with an accuracy of 47.72%. Agarwal et al. (2016) have performed a semi-supervised computational auditory scene analysis with MFCC vectors of acoustic data in back propagation neural networks for classification of emergency horns. This paper classifies the sound data as a cocktail party problem where extraction of a required band of noise has to be done from a group of unclassified noise recorded through one single source. This paper has used urban sound dataset along with a synthetic and natural noise dataset. The MFCC features from the dataset are extracted with openSMILE with a Hamming window of size 10s. The generated MFCC is learned with a back propagation neural network with 70% training and 30% testing. Later the audio separation from the polyphonic dataset is carried out by principal component analysis-based feature selection along with NMF, implemented using the FASST toolbox. The highest accuracy obtained on synthetic and natural noise data is 85% on (engine idling + unknown sound 1) and 82% on (siren + unknown sound 2), respectively.

Number	Title	Parameters	Discussion
1	Traffic management for emergency vehicle priority-based on visual sensing	Distance between the emergency horn propagator and the sensor	An urban traffic management system with a DBEVD algorithm. Euclidean distance achieves 98.60% accuracy
2	Emergency horn detection using embedded systems	Accuracy of detection of emergency horn	Emergency sound identification in 11 wail sirens dataset. The algorithms classifies the emergency horns with an accuracy of 90%
3	Multimodal location estimation	Acoustic, visual, and metadata	MFCC machine learning-based detection of the location of the emergency vehicle from the 200 YouTube videos dataset containing ambulance episodes
4	Minimally supervised sound event detection using a neural network	Accuracy detection	Audio dataset of MFCC features with GMM and SVM and features are extracted with PCA and NMF. Accuracy of detection 85% of synth data 82% of Nat data

16.2.1 Role of Sound Detection in Existing Systems

Recent sound detection algorithms are used only for commercial purposes like few household items stop after hearing a sound in its device, air conditions stops after keeping the timer when there is a sound which makes the machine stop. These sound and conditions applied inside these machines will work because they are interconnected to each other. But this is not going to help people in many situations. A sound recognition device should sense the sound and act accordingly. It should react based on the volume of the sound and type of sound received and start feeding the appropriate output data to the public. Hence the the public can identify what is going to happen in few hours. These are not used in the existing machines as they only concentrate on a particular products like microwave oven, air conditioners, etc.

16.2.2 Input and Output Parameters

1) *Input Parameters:* (i) Traffic sounds: Many types of vehicle noises are received by the microphone kept in the sensors. These sounds are checked, and if these do not match the ambulance sound, then these will be ignored by the device. (ii) Ambulance sound: Once this ambulance sound enters the microphone, it will be checked, and if it matches the default sound fixed in the sensor device, then the condition is satisfied.
2) *Output Parameters:* (i) *Signals:* If the condition is satisfied, then the signal that received the ambulance sound turns green and sends the message to nearby signals. All the other signals will turn red to avoid traffic jam.

16.2.3 Features of Pattern Matching

- Patterns can be combined, leaving dispatch over trees that have arbitrary depth. Method dispatch is constrained for non-nested case.
- Patterns make way for subpatterns to be shared. Method dispatch allows sharing when methods are from classes that happen to share the same base class. Or else you should manually factor out the common things in a separate member with a separate name and then insert calls manually from all places to this superfluous function.
- Pattern matching algorithm gives exhaustiveness and redundancy checking that holds a large number of errors, and it is useful only when different types evolve during development. Object orientation gives exhaustiveness checking only and not redundancy checking.
- Nontrivial parallel pattern matches are optimized for the user by the F# compiler. Method dispatch will not tell the user enough details to the compiler's optimizer, so comparable performance is achieved only in other mainstream languages by painstakingly optimizing the decision tree by hand, which results in unmaintainable code.
- Active patterns allow the user to insert custom dispatch semantics.

16.3   Pattern Matching Algorithm for Ambulance Siren Detection

16.3.1   Sensors

There are different types of sensors available in the market. But here we are concentrating only on sound-detecting sensors. It transforms the physical parameters like temperature, pulse rate, blood pressure, humidity, speed, etc. into a signal data in the form of electrical signal. Sensor groups are classified into many divisions (Patel and Shekokar, 2015).

1) *Accelerometers:* Accelerometers are based on the technology of microelectromechanical sensor, which is used for patient monitoring in hospitals that includes pacemakers for heart patients and vehicle dynamic systems.
2) *Biosensors:* The Biosensors are based on the technology of electrochemical, which are used for agriculture, fisheries, biogas plant, food testing, medical care device, water testing, and biological warfare agent detection.
3) *Image sensors:* Image sensors are using CMOS technology, which are used for consumer electronics, biometrics, traffic and security surveillance, airports, railways, hospitals, and PC imaging.
4) *Motion detectors:* Motion detectors are a type of sensor that accepts infrared in military, ultrasonic in hospitals and disaster management, and microwave or radar technology in underwater research. Motion detectors are mainly used in playing videogames and simulations tools, light activation, and security detection applications.

16.3.2   Sensor Deviations

1) Noise is a random deviation of the signal from other signals that changes with respect to time.
2) The sensor is to be sensitive to all the properties but not with the property being measured, and most sensors are triggered by the temperature of the surrounding (TSDS,).
3) If the sensor contains the output in digital format, the output obtained is always an approximation of the measured property, and this error is known as quantization error.
4) If the signal received in the output slowly changes, independent of the measured property, this is known as drift, and long-term drift can take months or years which is created by physical changes in the sensor.
5) Deviation created by quick changes of the measured property over time is known as dynamic error, and often, this situation is created with a bode plot

showing sensitivity error and phase shift as a function of the frequency of a periodic signal as output.

6) Nonlinearity is a change of a transfer function in the sensor from a straight line transfer function. Most of the time this is calculated by the amount of the resulted output that differs from ideal stage over the sensor's complete range.

16.3.3 Traffic Signal

The normal traffic signal contains green light below the red light, with yellow signal between them. When all the traffic signals are arranged in a horizontal manner or sideways, the arrangement depends on the traffic rules of the respective road. The countries that follow the right lane, the sequence (left to right) is red, yellow, and green light, and countries that follow the left lane, the sequence is green, yellow, and red light. Also more traffic signals are included for adding control, for the public vehicles and left or right side turns allowed when the green signal is displayed or specifically not allowed if the red light is displayed.

Green signals are displayed generally in at least one direction of traffic at junctions at any place in the given cycle. Sometimes, for a small period, all traffic signals at the junction display red signal parallely to avoid traffic jam in the junction. Traffic jam are usually due to conditions of the road, physical structure, weekends, office hours and legal requirements and also new age traffic signals which are built everywhere to make way for all the red signal in a junction, even if this function is not used.

Many traffic signals do not have "all red signal" mode: the signal may changeg to green for cross traffic, and at the same time the other traffic signals are changed to red. Another change in the locations is the pedestrian scramble, where the signals for cars and four wheelers change to red light, and pedestrians can easily walk on the road to cross the junction. As transportation engineers say, traffic signals have both good and bad effects on road safety and flow, but the division of various streams of traffic depending on time can decrease the incidence of right-angle collision between vehicles. If we check the frequency for back-end crashes, then it is always high by the increase in number of traffic signals. They create chaos for the bicycle riders and pedestrians and also they increase the amount of traffic capacity at all the junctions, but it could result in very high traffic delay.

16.3.3.1 How Do Traffic Signals Work?

Traffic signals are working with simple principle, but there are many questions revolving it. A traffic signal contains a controller, traffic signal heads, and detection. The important materials is "brains," which is working behind this formation and it includes the functions needed to change the lights for all the sequences. Traffic signals are dependent on location and time.

In the given time, green and red signals will get same interval and each cycle is independent of condition of the traffic. However this is not applicable in crowded areas but a lightly trafficked pathway is considered in a given time which is not useful and in many cycles there will not be any vehicles standing so the time cane be given to busy roads.

It is the most used function in traffic signals, and as the name says it is important that all the vehicle demands on different ways and changes the green signal accordingly.

The detectors fixed with the traffic signal indicate the traffic load and changes the green signal accordingly. Green lights are displayed in minimum and maximum times by the controller, and it cannot be violated.

If a vehicle tries to cross a detector then it asks for a particular phase and if the given phase is green light then all upcoming vehicles which is crossing the detector tries to extend more and traffic will go beyond the green light until either the traffic demand ceases and next approach gets green signal, or continuous demand gives more number of green signal timer to begin the count down.

When a pedestrian tries to cross the road in a junction, the traffic is stopped until the road is free to use. This VA phase is regular than constant time; it is still not efficient if there contains huge lines formed on conflicting approaches, and attaching more timers is very tough due to the increase of changes in patterns formed in traffic because junctions over time form effective operation and the timings should be displayed in regular intervals. If the local highway authority does not take care of it due to the lack of labor, then the traffic signals become ineffective.

16.3.3.2 Traffic Signal

This is how the traffic signal looks inside as shown in Figure 16.2 (Snider). Here we need to insert the sensor that is connected to all the three lights in common. But we can exclude yellow because we do not need yellow light in this process. Red light and green light can be connected with the sound-detecting sensor.

A sound-detecting sensor senses the ambulance sound using pattern matching algorithm. Here the pattern matching algorithm helps the sensor to detect the ambulance sound from the traffic sound and then sensor device absorbs the traffic sound and sends the input to traffic signals, which then converts from red light to green light.

Now, all the adjacent traffic signals are switched to red making way for the ambulance to cross the signal without any vehicle intervention.

16.3.3.3 Sound-Detecting Sensor

Figure 16.3 depicts the inside view of a sound-detecting sensor (Henry's Bench). This sensor works under the pattern matching algorithm. Microphone, which is

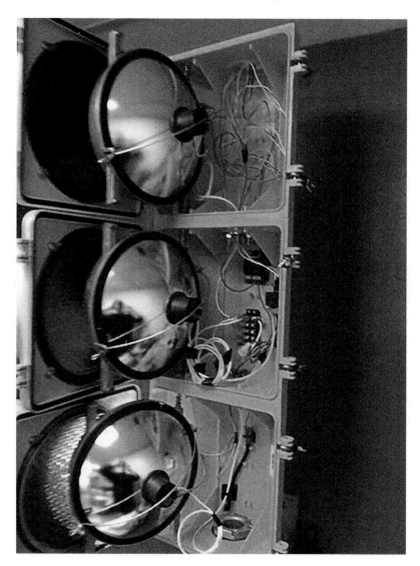

Figure 16.2 Traffic signal.

fixed at the front side, is the input area. All the sound heard from the traffic will be received in the input area. Sound-detecting LED will start blinking once the correct sound is received, and then the signal is sent through the output device.

After the signal is sent through the output device, it will automatically change the red color to green color, and also it passes the signal to nearby traffic signals. The traffic signals that are situated nearby will change the signal

Figure 16.3 Sound detecting sensor.

from green light to red light. Now the ambulance can cross the signal without any confusion.

The sound-detecting sensor also contains sound set point, amplifier, power led, VCC, and ground connected to the device.

16.3.4 Pattern Matching Algorithm: Anomaly Detection

All characteristics and categories of pattern matching algorithms have been checked by Sunday, Hume, and Pirklbauer, among others, but significant understanding of conceptual frameworks and estimation of space and time complexity is provided to understand the behavior of these algorithms in the worst cases or using randomly generated string patterns and targets.

Therefore, there is a lack of data about the behavior of all these algorithms present when used with the original text called corpora, which does not have normal distributed symbols that are used in the medical sublanguage, and when neither preprocessing nor indexing is supported for the target, and only less number of preprocessing in time and space is used for the pattern.

Now the comparison step can be obtained by the use of a hashing table. Also, hash functions provide multiple ways to compare other strings. This is completely based on the comparison of other string hash values however character comparison needs the text to be preprocessed. Hashing is a simple method for accessing information, but again powerful. Each key is changed into a number, and later those numbers are used and input the index into a table. But in typical applications, it is always required for a number of strings to map to the same index.

Hash function obtains values in a key of the characters with the binary codes, and the r position of the record in the table is measured on the key value by itself, and not how many elements are present in the table, but this is the reason why hash table does delete, insert, and search rated constant time.

Skip table is used if there is any failure, and it allows to jump from one character to another. Thus it can display the slide step, and to know the heuristic skip tables, we need to accept the fact that the result is obtained in a window. Therefore this window does not include a part of the target and contains length of the pattern and that window moves along with the output from one to another and is shifted according to rules only for each algorithm. Windows's position is fixed on a target; the algorithm checks if the pattern occurs or not by checking every symbol given in the window with the aligned symbols, and if it is correctly matched, then the pattern's position is informed, and during the scan, the algorithm obtains all the details from the output that is used to provide the distance of the successive shift of the window. Therefore the operation is repeated until the final pattern goes beyond or it clicks the end of the output and it is an effective procedure to increase time cost in the scanning time that can be used in right-to-left or left-to-right search engines.

Naive or brute force algorithm is the important function to the pattern matching for a string problem and matches with the correct pattern in the output at every position from left to right. But if that does not work, then it converts the comparison window from every character.

In the worst case complexity, this method functions in O(mn) time, but, the expected overall performance is near O(n + m) and also the theoretic bad performance of this algorithm, output is obtained in such a way that the naïve algorithm works when there is a less sequence of words.

The Knuth–Morris–Pratt method gives an algorithm with the two-way deterministic automata that acts, in the worst case, in O(m + n) time for some random works, and the idea behind this algorithm is to avoid backtracking the output string in the mismatch time and take advantage of all the notifications provided by the type of mismatch.

The output is made in a horizontal manner from left to right, and if a substring matches or if it fails, the before symbols are used to confirm if the pattern can be moved from left to right for another attempt.

Moore and Boyer introduced an algorithm during 1974, and the growth of the algorithm is obtained by excluding portions of the output that are not participated in a successful match.

16.3.4.1 Algorithm and Implementation

Fast Fourier transform: A sensor device is fixed in the traffic signal. The sensor device receives all the sounds encountered in the traffic signal. Each sound is received in the form of wave patterns, and each wave pattern contains different frequencies. Each digital signal will be converted into numbers, and when the frequency matches with the frequency of an ambulance sound, then the signal is sent to the traffic signals. Comparing and detecting the ambulance sound will be done by the pattern matching algorithm that checks the different sounds being received. In this way the ambulance sound is detected in the sensor and sent to the traffic signal.

We use the pattern matching algorithm to find the ambulance sound found in the sound detecting software. Here, all the sounds from the traffic enter the sound-detecting sensor, and inside the sensor the pattern matching algorithm finds the unique ambulance sound. If the sound received is matching with the ambulance sound, then the signal is sent to the traffic signal, and then it changes the color from red signal to green signal. Also it conveys the message to nearby signals in the same traffic signal, and other signal changes from green light to red light. This way except the ambulance approaching the road, all the other traffic signal changes to red and blocks the traffic. Now the ambulance can cross the traffic signal without any confusion and reach the hospital faster than before (Miyazakia et al., 2013; Carmel et al., 2017).

Aho-Corasick Pattern Matching Algorithm (Patel and Shekokar, 2015)

Step 1: Different types of sound enters the sensor device.

Step 2: FFT assists the system to convert into frequency pattern. After separating each sound, it will be compared with the ambulance sound.

Step 3: Pattern matching algorithm is used to compare one sound with another sound.
   a) Assign a number as element and take input parameter as first sound.
   b) Calculate percentage of match, if not equal move to next level.
   c) Iterate (b) for all the children and check match percentage.

Step 4: After identifying the ambulance sound, the sensor device sends the message to the traffic signal.

Step 5: Once the process reaches the traffic signal, it turns the red to green and blocks the nearby signals.

16.3.4.2 Sound Detection Module

```
int soundDetectionPin = 10; int soundDetectedVal = HIGH; boolean boAlarm
    = false;
unsigned long lastSoundDetectionTime; int soundAlarmTime = 500;
void setup ()
Serial.start(9600);
pinMode (soundDetectionPin, INPUT) ;
void loop ()
soundDetectedVal = digitalRead (soundDetectionPin) ;
if (soundDetectedVal == LOW) //
lastSoundDetectionTime = millis(); if (!boAlarm){ Serial.println("LOUD,
    LOUD"); boAlarm = true;
else
if( (millis()-lastSoundDetectionTime) > soundAlarmTime && boAlarm)
Serial.println("quiet");
boAlarm = false;
```

16.4 Results and Conclusion

An ambulance can reach its destination faster. People are ready to allow or make a path once they hear an ambulance sound behind them. But they do not have any idea on how to clear the path when they hear an ambulance sound in a heavy traffic jam or traffic signal. In a traffic signal, when an ambulance siren sound is heard, the vehicles cannot move forward or sideward to give way for the ambulance. So this ideology can be applied.

So when you try to move forward and give way to the ambulance, it creates more traffic in that signal. So the only way to clear the ambulance in a traffic signal is to block all the other signals and let the ambulance to go. But that is not possible when the ambulance had already reached the signal and is waiting for the vehicles to clear the way. In that case we need to know the ambulance sound before it approaches the signal and block all the other signals and let the ambulance leave the signal immediately. So to receive the ambulance sound and start the process, we need a sensor to be kept in the traffic signal.

As mentioned earlier, in the case of heavy traffic, vehicles cannot move forward or sideward to give way for the ambulance. In that situation, ambulance siren should be identified before a particular range to alert the vehicles waiting at the signal. According to our data, the sensor fixed inside the traffic signal received the ambulance siren sound before some particular distance and changes the traffic signal lights accordingly.

One of the main processes in our project is that it makes the ambulance reach the hospital by passing all the traffic signal with ease. It helps the doctors to save a patient's life faster than before. It also saves a lot of time and helps the drivers to cross the traffic without panicking and maintain the same speed level in the traffic signals.

When implementing this project, we need to be careful with the signals that are not working. So this project depicts an easy way to cross the traffic signal without any trouble.

Traffic pattern	Searching speed (ms) – without pattern matching algorithm	Searching speed (ms) – with pattern matching algorithm
Low	70.0	66.2
Medium	64.2	62.1
High	63.7	60.4

When we use pattern matching algorithm, the time taken to detect the ambulance sound is very less. The process completes faster, and ambulance can cross the traffic signal without stopping. But when we do not use pattern matching algorithm, it is very difficult for the detector to find the ambulance sound, and the ambulance has to stop in the traffic signal. The results are shown in Table. In the future, these types of sensors can be fixed in many important places to be aware of the consequences of the disaster before it occurs. For example, when we fix this sensor in boats, in ships, and in the beaches, then these sensors will register the volume of water waves. When this volume crosses the limit, it can be concluded that the speed of the waves are increased, and there might be some disaster occurring in few minutes. In same way these sensors can be used where sounds are playing an important role.

Bibliography

Agarwal, A., Quadri, S.M., Murthy, S., and Sitaram, D. (2016). Minimally supervised sound event detection using a neural network. In: 2016 International Conference on Advances in Computing, Communications and Informatics (ICACCI), 2495–2500.

Carmel, D., Yeshurun, A., and Moshe, Y. (2017). Detection of alarm sounds in noisy environments. In: 2017 25th European Signal Processing Conference (EUSIPCO), 1839–1843.

Friedland, G., Vinyals, O., and Darrell, T. (2010). Multimodal location estimation. In: Proceedings of the international conference on Multimedia - MM '10, 1245–1252.

Henry's Bench. Sound detecting sensor: tutorial and user manual. http://
henrysbench.capnfatz.com/henrys-bench/arduino-sensors-and-input/
arduino-sound-detection-sensor-tutorial-and-user-manual/.

Miyazakia, T., Kitazonoa, Y., and Shimakawab, M. (2013). Ambulance siren
detector using FFT on DSPIC. Proceedings of the 1st IEEE/IIAE International
Conference on Intelligent Systems and Image Processing 2013.

Palecek, J. and Cerny, M. (2016). Emergency horn detection using embedded
systems. In: 2016 IEEE 14th International Symposium on Applied Machine
Intelligence and Informatics (SAMI), 257–261.

Patel, N. and Shekokar, N. (2015). Implementation of pattern matching algorithm
to defend SQLIA. *Procedia Computer Science* **45**: 453–459.

Snider, M. Traffic light hardware. http://mattsnider.com/continuous-deployment-
traffic-light-hardware/ (accessed 08 March 2019).

Traffic Signal Design Services. http://traffic-signal-design.com/ (accessed
08 March 2019).

17

Detecting Diabetic Retinopathy from Retinal Images Using CUDA Deep Neural Network

Ricky Parmar[1], Ramanathan Lakshmanan[2], Swarnalatha Purushotham[2], and Rajkumar Soundrapandiyan[2]

[1] *Dell EMC, Bangaluru, India*
[2] *School of Computer Science and Engineering, Vellore Institute of Technology, Vellore, India*

17.1 Introduction

In this populace of working age, diabetic retinopathy (DR) is considered as the main source of visual deficiency. It has been assessed that this has affected more than 93 M (million) individuals living in this developed world. The number of individuals in 2013, all over the globe, suffering from diabetes, has increased up to 382 M, and by the year 2035, it has been predicted to reach around 592 M (Guariguata et al. 2014). DR in its early phase can be described by its symptoms, for example, inconsistencies and defectiveness of veins; however if this condition becomes serious, this may lead to blindness. Recognizing DR, as of now, is a manual and tedious process that requires analysis and assessment of computerized color fundus retinal images by a qualified clinician by observing association of lesions with vascular anomalies. Because of the method's effectiveness, the demand for resources is high. Frequently resources, such as medical expertise and equipment, are not available in regions where the percentage of the population having diabetes is high, thus needing DR detection. With time, the number of individuals with diabetes keeps on growing, and with this growing number of patient's, infrastructure to avoid blindness caused by DR will be even more inadequate. A non-painful disease, visual defect is not observed till the late stages, when it becomes very difficult to treat. Treatment at this stage is mostly ineffective. To make sure that patient is treated on time by proper diagnosis of DR at an initial stage, multiple screening of the patient must be done at that stage (Bresnick et al. 2000; Patton et al. 2006), where retinal picture analysis is a noteworthy part. As all the essential resources for this process are not available in all the regions around the world, the need for automated screening of DR is recognized. Our

Intelligent Pervasive Computing Systems for Smarter Healthcare, First Edition.
Arun Kumar Sangaiah, S.P. Shantharajah, and Padma Theagarajan.

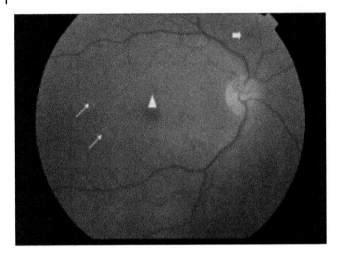

Figure 17.1 Non-proliferative diabetic retinopathy.

evaluating procedure includes micro-aneurysms which are minor details as well as exudates which is a major feature. There are many occasions where the relative position of microaneurysms to exudates is also considered as a feature.

In Figure 17.1, hard exudates are indicated by thin arrows, internal retinal hemorrhage is depicted by thick arrow, whereas microaneurysms are shown by thick arrow. Per (Philip et al. 2007; Abrámoff et al. 2008), improvement in computerized classifications to recognize DR has become of an incredible significance for the research communal. Harangi et al. (2012) have recognized the locales containing exudates in retinal pictures by utilizing grayscale morphology, and afterward dynamic form-based technique was utilized to extricate the exact fringes of the hopefuls.

Research works such as Hinton and Salakhutdinov (2006) have called attention to that the profound structures, for example, multilayer neural systems, demonstrated better execution when the customary back-propagation calculation was gone before by an unsupervised pretraining. This brought back the enthusiasm of the scholarly club into multilayer neural systems once more, and profound learning techniques (Deng and Yu 2014) have since surpassed expectations in being the top entertainer in numerous applications, for example, question identification and acknowledgment, speaker identification (Hinton et al. 2012), content mining, and handwriting recognition (Wan et al. 2013). Although a solid numerical thinking of the achievement behind these systems is yet hazy, a few natural reasons have been explained in Bengio et al. (2013a,b). Walter et al. (2002) has proposed another system, in which certain chosen elements, for example, microaneurysms alone, are improved. Cree et al. (1999) have connected a picture reclamation method for pictures of exceptionally low quality. Image restoration technique where images are considered as trial functions of stochastic procedure was used by Peli and Peli (1989).

Using intensity properties for dynamic clustering, Hsu et al. (2001) could find normal and abnormal areas in images. Exact contours were found using morphological reconstruction and high gray-level variation, and in this manner exudates were detected by Walter et al. (2002). A new method using fuzzy c-means to detect abnormal region was proposed by Xiaohui and Chutatape (2004). Another method for exudate detection with statistical classification by applying brightness adjustment was proposed by Wang et al. (2000).

In Welikala et al. (2014), authors have used a dataset of merely 60 images and used support vector machine (SVM) algorithm for classification and have only done dual classification. While in Zhang et al. (2014), they only focus on exudates and use basic algorithm such as random forest so DR caused by microaneurysms are not detected. Meanwhile in Akram et al. (2013), the authors only focus on microaneurysms for the early detection of DR. Also, all classify images into two classes. While in comparison with (Akram et al. 2013; Welikala et al. 2014; Zhang et al. 2014), our model uses the latest state-of-the-art algorithm such as convolutional neural network and takes advantage of the very powerful GPU by using NVIDIA CUDA deep neural network (cuDNN). Also, we use a huge dataset of 53 576 images for testing our model (validation) and train on 35 100 images. Data used is around 85 GB in size. Our model focuses on both exudates and microaneurysms for early detection of DR. For microaneurysm detection we use digital artifact effect explained in Section 17.2. Unlike any other previous methods that do only dual classification, our model does multiclass classification and classify images into five categories (i.e. normal, mild NPDR, moderate NPDR, severe NPDR, PDR) with weighted mean sensitivity of 0.85 and specificity of 0.81. Also, to predict the class of 53 576 pictures, it took only 21 minutes for our algorithm (dimension reduced to 512×512), and for a huge size image (dimension 4752×3186), it takes only four hours to predict the class of all 53 576 images.

This chapter is organized as follows: Section 17.2 provides an overview of our model. Such as preprocessing, describing architecture of the convolutional neural network in our model, techniques we used in our model. In Section 17.3 we discuss the results of our model as well as other various analyses such as accuracy of the model and statistics such as specificity and sensitivity of the model. Section 17.4 has conclusion.

17.2 Proposed Method

We use around 35 100 pictures (of retina) as training set in our examination, where each image is marked by patient id and whether it is an image of the left or

Table 17.1 Class distribution.

Name	Class#	#Images	%Distribution
Normal	0	25 810	73.48
Mild NPDR	1	2 443	6.96
Moderate NPDR	2	5 292	15.07
Severe NPDR	3	873	2.48
PDR	4	708	2.01

right eye (e.g. 234_left.jpg). Images are per eye, not per patient. Therefore, each patient has two images. These pictures are distributed into five classes which one can state are equally unhinged. The following is the image distribution in training set per class (Table 17.1).

We have about 53 576 pictures as a test case, and we classify these images into the abovementioned five classes. Data for retinal images is provided by Eye-PACS. The most predominant, soonest indication of diabetic macular edema relates to the nearness of exudates inside the macular district. Henceforth, the assignment of identifying exudates by utilizing computer-based examination assumes an indispensable part in the conclusion of DR (Faust et al. 2012). These exudates have high-dark-level variety from its encompassing foundation; furthermore, consequently they are much obvious as splendid examples in shading fundus pictures (Tariq et al. 2013). In our proposed work, we identify these exudates, microaneurysms, and internal retinal hemorrhage from our retinal images.

17.2.1 Preprocessing

Our initial phase of preprocessing these images would be to downscale them, as original images are quite huge in their dimension, i.e. around 4752×3186 pixels. We have decided to downscale these images about five times of their actual size, which would be around 512×512 pixels, without interpolation. Below is an example before initial preprocessing of the image. It is evident from Figure 17.2 that each image varies in size and there is a black border around it, which we intend to remove. Figure 17.3 depicts the same image after processing it through the first phase. Enhancing these images computationally was made easier with these new set of images. The next phase of preprocessing will now involve various enhancement of images such as resizing, cropping (with certain probability), zooming, flipping images, rotation, color balance, contrast, brightness, etc.

While training, arbitrary specimens are selected from the training set and are then transformed beforehand, then are queued for input to the network.

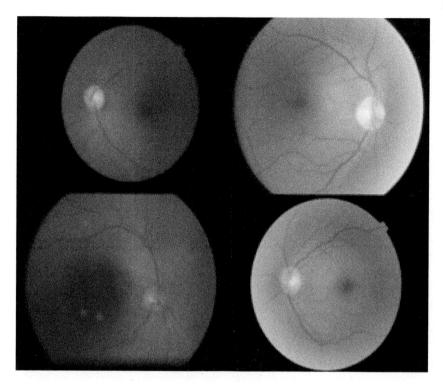

Figure 17.2 Before initial preprocessing.

The enhancements were done dynamically during training on images by spawning a thread whenever needed from the CPU; it was ensured that no delay is observed, in waiting, for samples to process. Resizing of the images had to be taken care of before any other enhancements, and before resizing, images should be cropped. If it were not done, the computation would be too intensive. This resizing altered the original aspect ratio of the image by using normal bilinear rescaling. To normalize our input, we subtract total mean from it and after that we divide it with standard deviation, which is estimated on few hundred of samples before training, this normalization is done during training.

17.2.2 Architecture

In our input, we have two retinal images for every patient, which is each per eye (left and right).

We use both the images to classify individual image by coalescing them before the last two dense layers, out of the two-dense layer at the end one of them is SoftMax layer. Below is the architecture for 512×512 input.

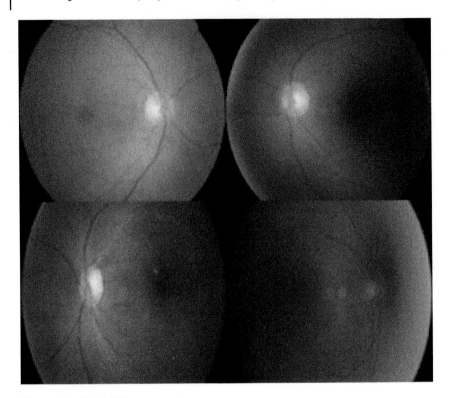

Figure 17.3 After initial preprocessing.

First layer in our neural net (i.e. Layer 0) is the input layer, which is mentioned as "Input" in Table 17.2. Our input to the neural net is (3 × 512 × 512), which is a raw pixel value of the retinal image with 512 as width and 512 as height, in a three color channel, i.e. RGB.

The next layer is ConvNet (i.e. Layer 1) where we perform a 2D convolution on our input data with 32 filters, resulting in a 32 × 256 × 256 layer. We also add bias and element-wise nonlinearity. This layer will process the outputs of the locally connected neurons in the input. After this is the MaxPool layer (i.e. Layer 2), where we perform a downsampling operation on the previous layer, which results in volume such as (32 × 127 × 127). Now, till "Layer 18" in our neural net, we make combination of a convolution and MaxPooling layers for optimization of our model.

Now we have a dropout layer (i.e. Layer 19, 24, and 27); we use this layer randomly between some layers to reduce the overfitting. This layer acts as a regularizer that randomly sets the input to 0, which in turn takes care of overfitting. Next, we have the dense layer (i.e. Layer 20). These are the fully linked layers of our neural network. After the dense layer, we have the feature pooling

Table 17.2 Architecture.

Layer #	Layer name	Batch size	Channels	Width	Height
0	Input	64	3	512	512
1	ConvNet	64	32	256	256
2	MaxPooling	64	32	127	127
3	ConvNet	64	32	127	127
4	ConvNet	64	32	127	127
5	MaxPooling	64	32	63	63
6	ConvNet	64	64	63	63
7	ConvNet	64	64	63	63
8	MaxPooling	64	64	31	31
9	ConvNet	64	128	31	31
10	ConvNet	64	128	31	31
11	ConvNet	64	128	31	31
12	ConvNet	64	128	31	31
13	MaxPooling	64	128	15	15
14	ConvNet	64	128	15	15
15	ConvNet	64	128	15	15
16	ConvNet	64	128	15	15
17	ConvNet	64	128	15	15
18	MaxPooling	64	256	7	7
19	Dropout	64	256	7	7
20	DenseLayer	64	1024		
21	FeaturePoolLayer	64	517		
22	ConcatLayer	64	514		
23	ReshapeLayer	32	1028		
24	Dropout	32	1028		
25	DenseLayer	32	1024		
26	FeaturePoolLayer	32	512		
27	Dropout	32	512		
28	DenseLayer	32	10		
29	ReshapeLayer	64	5		
30	Apply nonlinearity	64	5		
31	SoftMax	64	5		

layer, which we use for 2D maxout; it is simply a layer where the activation function is max of the inputs. Here the dropout only occurs in the linear part of our network, so we use maxout to approximate our activation function. It can also pool across a given axis of input.

After the feature pool layer, we use the concat layer, which as the name suggests concatenates multiple inputs along the axis we specify. This layer is used to merge two images (i.e. two eyes per patient, so we can detect patterns created by digital artifact). Following concat layer is the reshape layer, which reshapes its input tensor to another tensor of the similar overall numeral of elements. Then again, we optimize our neural network with different layer combinations. The next layer is nonlinearity layer (Layer 30), which simply applies nonlinearity. Our last layer is SoftMax layer (Layer 31), which is a fully linked layer that computes class scores, resulting in a channel of 5, i.e. five classes in which we classify our images. The most crucial effect on performance of the model was by using leaky rectify units with comparatively higher leakiness. Initially, alpha value remained 0.3, but after few runs it was changed to 0.5 to get higher accuracy. Accuracy will be even increased more if we do not downscale the images to five times, which we did in the initial preprocessing stage. Even downscaling the image to two times of the original will have a lot of effects on accuracy. But the hardware used was not powerful enough to carry out that intensive computation, so images downscaled up to five times were used. Overfitting of rather subsequent uniform distribution of smaller classes was done. Reshape layer in our architecture is the place where images for each patient are merged to one in first reshape layer, while in second they are split to two again.

17.2.3 Digital Artifacts

When we take a look at two pictures of a certain patient, side by side, there is something noticeable (digital artifact) that can be seen, compared to when looking at just one picture. Figure 17.4 shows an example of digital artifact, dark spots and stripes on the external right side and small dark dabs on the external left side. They resemble microaneurysms, and in some cases, they are, while in others it's just tiny black dots, so to figure out when it is microaneurysms, we need both the images of patient. So, it is very unlikely that the model can distinguish with just single image and detect microaneurysms. A lot of spatial information is gotten rid of when layers are fully linked. But merging two images (with dense representation) means it has a very high level of representation. Also, enhancement on each image were done separately, independent of patient. Because paired enhancement will not lead to any improvement.

Here outputs "x" and "y" from the output of some layer (one output for each eye of the patient) are taken, exchanged with "xy" and "yx", and stacked on the channel, which brings about nets having entry to lower representation and not losing any input space. If we merged the outputs of the first convolution layer

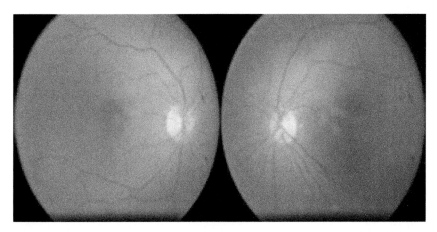

Figure 17.4 Digital artifact.

for each of two eyes, then theoretically our model would be able to recognize similar patterns for each eye of patient. However, input space was reduced way too much with this approach. Thus, the before mentioned method (stacking) was carried out, because merging had to be done in the first few layers of the network.

17.2.4 Pseudo-classification

This strategy utilizes the predictions from different ensembles of the model on the test set to help manage or normalize a new model. While training some set of images from the test set that were added to the batches in training set, roughly around 25% of the batch contained pictures from the test set that were predicted with SoftMax from ensemble.

17.3 Experimental Results

The experimental results of the proposed method is briefly discussed in this section.

17.3.1 Dataset

Dataset consists of high resolution retina images taken under different imaging conditions. An image of the left and right eye is provided for each subject. The name of the image consists of patient id and which eye is photographed (e.g. 2_right.jpeg is the right eye of patient id 2). DR on each image is rated from 0 to 4 by a clinician, according to the following scale: 0, no DR; 1, mild;

2, moderate; 3, severe; and 4, proliferative DR. Different models and types of cameras were used to take images in our dataset, which can affect the pictorial appearance of left vs. right. Some images are shown as one would see the retina structurally (macula on the left and optic nerve on the right for the right eye). Others are shown as one would see through a microscope shrinking lens (i.e. inverted, as one sees in a typical live eye exam). There are generally two ways to tell if an image is inverted: (i) It is inverted if the macula (the little dim focal territory) is somewhat higher than the midline through the optic nerve. On the off chance that the macula is lower than the midline of the optic nerve, it is not transformed. (ii) On the off chance that there is an indent in favor of the picture (square, triangle, or circle), at that point it is not altered. In the event that there is no notch, it is inverted. Like any real-world dataset, noise was encountered in both the images and labels. Images may contain artifacts, be out of focus, overexposed, or underexposed. So an algorithm was developed in such a way that it takes care of all scenarios, as our major aim was to develop an algorithm that can be easily used in real life.

17.3.2 Performance Evaluation Measures

For evaluating the performance of the proposed method, sensitivity, specificity, accuracy, and F1 score metrics (Soundrapandiyan and Chandra Mouli 2016, 2017a) are used, and it is defined in Eqs. (17.1)–(17.4).

$$\text{Sensitivity} = \frac{\text{TP}}{\text{TP+FN}} \tag{17.1}$$

$$\text{Specificity} = \frac{\text{TP}}{\text{TP+FP}} \tag{17.2}$$

$$\text{Accuracy} = \frac{\text{TP+FN}}{\text{TP+FP+FN+TN}} \tag{17.3}$$

$$\text{F-score} = 2 \times \frac{\text{precision} \times \text{recall}}{\text{precision} + \text{recall}} \tag{17.4}$$

where, TP, TN, FP, and FN indicate true positives, true negatives, false positives, and false negatives, respectively (Soundrapandiyan and Chandra Mouli 2017b; Pillai et al. 2018).

17.3.3 Validation of Datasets Using Exponential Power Distribution

Few things that emerged were how different models varied on the different validation sets. Discrete metric is the reason behind this. While evaluating our model on quadratic kappa metric, it is calculated by

$$K = 1 - \frac{\sum_{i,j} W_{i,j} C_{i,j}}{\sum_{i,j} W_{i,j} Er_{i,j}} \tag{17.5}$$

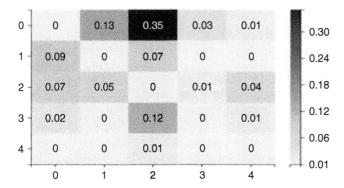

Figure 17.5 Normalized "nomi," for (a, b), for actual label b, predicted a.

In Eq. (17.5), *Er* is *m* by *m* matrix of expected rating and *W* is *m* by *m* matrix of weights, whereas $C_{i,j}$ corresponds to images that received rating "*i*" by "x" and rating "*j*" by "y." Loss from quadratic kappa is calculated by two important metrics; let us call it "nomi" and "denomi." 1 - $\sum$(nomi)/ $\sum$(denomi) is how kappa evaluation score is given. Therefore, we would like to minimize "nomi" as much as possible and look to maximize "denomi" as much as possible. "Denomi" being stable encapsulates distributions of forecasts and the targets. However we base most of insights of our model on "nomi." Following is the look at "nomi" and "denomi" for a model with 0.83 score on kappa metric, where the frameworks are standardized and demonstrate the rate of the aggregate total situated in that position. The mistakes of foreseeing class practically rule the error "0," while it was truly class "2" (which means moderate NPR is predicted as normal eye). The issue with this, and overall, was that the ground truth did not know by any stretch of the imagination. In Figures 17.5 and 17.6, *x*-axis represents predicted

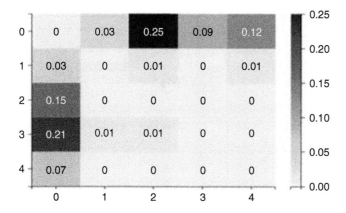

Figure 17.6 Normalized "denomi," for (a, b), for actual label b, predicted a.

class and *y*-axis indicates actual class. Both figures indicate the distribution of error, where Figure 17.6 is the normalized version.

17.3.4 Ensemble

Ensembling multiple models brought about a decent change by utilizing the log probabilities for every class by averaging them, then again bringing them back to their typical original probabilistic state of [0, 1], and utilizing the positioning unraveling technique from one of the past sections to relegate names to the pictures. Best kappa score generated by our model would be of +0.84.

17.3.5 Accuracy and Stats

Our model has overall accuracy of 0.8496 (85% approx.) and following are the statistics per class. Figure 17.7 shows the graph for the confusion matrix, where *x*-axis represents the predicted class and *y*-axis denotes actual class (where 0, 1, 2, 3, and 4 are class names). We trained our model on 35 100 retinal images, where images were preprocessed and the dimension of the image was reduced to 512 × 512. This model was trained on GPU with 4 GB of memory; we used NVIDIA GPU, namely, GeForce GTX 980, which has 2048 CUDA cores; it takes about less than one day for training the model on this device. If we train the model on low configuration GPU for, e.g. GTX 960 or 970, the model takes three to four days to train. One can simply use parallel or multiple graphics card to speed up the process, then it may take even less than 24 hours.

We ran our model on about 53 576 images. Table 17.4 describes confusion matrix for our model. Table 17.3 describes the statistics of the model, like specificity and sensitivity for each class. Model has weighted mean sensitivity of 0.85 and specificity of 0.81.

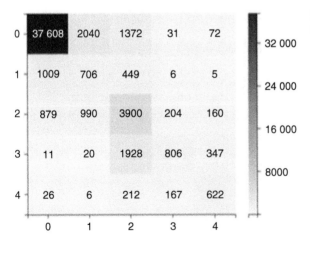

Figure 17.7 Graph for confusion matrix.

Table 17.3 Classification stats.

Classes	0	1	2	3	4
Sensitivity	0.95	0.27	0.58	0.69	0.93
Specificity	0.91	0.97	0.96	0.97	0.99
Accuracy	0.89	0.92	0.90	0.97	0.99
F1 Score	0.93	0.333	0.641	0.545	0.882

Table 17.4 Confusion matrix.

Predicted actual	0	1	2	3	4	All
0	37 608	1 009	879	11	26	39 533
1	2 040	706	990	20	6	3 762
2	1 372	449	3 900	1 928	212	7 861
3	31	6	204	806	167	1 214
4	72	5	160	347	622	1 206
All	41 123	2 175	6 133	3 112	1 033	53 576

Once we train the model, we can store the model dumps into a pickle file, so we can make quick predictions on our image using those dumps. To on all the images in test set i.e. 53 576 images.

For testing, images are loaded into GPU in batches of 256. So, GPU with more memory and speed means faster predictions and training. Performance of the proposed method is measured by specificity and sensitivity of the model. Table 17.5 shows comparison with various methods for specificity and sensitivity. All the present method does the classification of the images in two class (binary classification), our proposed method classifies image into five classes (multiclass classification), which gives more clarification on how alert patient should be so that it can be detected at earlier stage whereas other methods fail to do that. Hence, in comparison with other methods, we considered only class 0 and class 4 (i.e. normal and PDR). Our method took 21 minutes to classify 53 576 images, which means 42 images per second when images are at 512 × 512. When we use high dimension images (i.e. 4752 × 3186), it takes four hours to classify, at four images per second. Hence, our model is more accurate and much faster than any other previous method. Also, our model focuses on both exudates and microaneurysms unlike (Fleming et al. 2006; Akram et al. 2013; Welikala et al. 2014; Zhang et al. 2014).

Table 17.5 Comparison with existing models.

Method	Sensitivity	Specificity
SVM and voting classifier (Welikala et al. 2014)	0.86	0.94
Random forest classification (Zhang et al. 2014)	0.83	0.76
Watershed transform technique (Fleming et al. 2006)	0.85	0.83
Proposed method	0.94	0.95

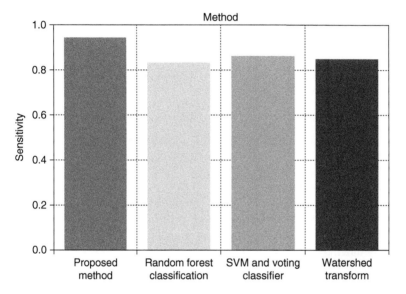

Figure 17.8 Comparison of sensitivity values of the proposed method with the other methods.

In Table 17.5 we show comparison of our proposed model with the current existing model. We have compared the following methods: SVM and voting classifier in Welikala et al. (2014), random forest classifier in Zhang et al. (2014), and watershed transform technique in Fleming et al. (2006). Figures 17.8 and 17.9 show the bar chart for each sensitivity and specificity against each method, where y-axis is sensitivity in Figure 17.8 and specificity in Figure 17.9, whereas x-axis shows various methods against which we compared our proposed method in Figures 17.8 and 17.9. Bar charts in Figures 17.8 and 17.9 are graphical representation of Table 17.5.

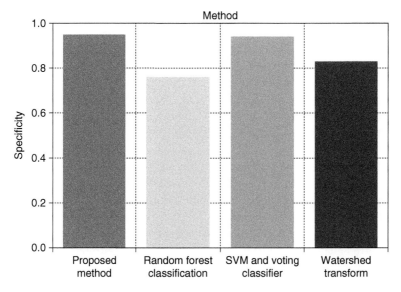

Figure 17.9 Comparison of specificity values of the proposed method with the other methods.

17.4 Conclusion and Future Work

An effective technique for the identification and division of the exudates as well as microaneurysms from the retinal pictures, which plays a critical part in the finding of DR, has been exhibited in this chapter. In this chapter, we have examined and exhibited a novel method that consequently distinguishes the exudates and microaneurysms from the DR patient's retinal pictures.

Shading data was utilized as part of the preprocessing phase of our calculation, and in this way better execution was accomplished in the picture division arrange. It is thought to be an essential highlight to recognize distinctive scores introduced in the shading fundus pictures. Training stage in this work demands intense computational work to identify microaneurysms and exudates from retinal images, using convolutional neural network and powerful GPU (like NVIDIA GTX 980). Training takes around 80 hours when it is run on this hardware. There are many other methods to detect DR from retinal images, but most of those approaches are manual where we construct several filters and use pipelines to extract features from images. But ConvNets can do all that on its own, in a way this solution is more accurate and elegant than other previous solutions. Huge variance from extremely small classes, noisy labels, and discrete metrics that heavily affect misclassification were big issues during the process. Enhancing learning on the extraordinary kappa metric appeared to be of a great deal more imperative than improving the design.

Our approach achieved around 85% of accuracy, with good mean sensitivity as well as specificity, and it was tested on very huge amount of data, i.e. 53 576 high resolution images. This screening framework is reasonably very less demanding; we only need high-end GPU and high configuration device while training the network; once training is done, its dumps can be stored and using that one can easily make predictions and it can run on device with very low configuration easily. This model can be used in developing countries and rural areas or wherever a scarcity of ophthalmologists is observed or at places with less resources. Other use of this tool can be as preliminary diagnosis tool for detecting DR. This will help in earlier detection and faster treatment of DR as it can only be treated in earlier stage. Our model shows that detecting DR at an earlier stage becomes quite easy using this computer-dependent tool.

In future works, this network is trained on images of resolution 512×512 because of lack of hardware, but one can test it using higher resolution images. Another future enhancement can be training the network with unsupervised learning instead of pseudo-classification technique used in this model.

Bibliography

Abrámoff, M.D., Niemeijer, M., Suttorp-Schulten, M.S.A. et al. (2008). Evaluation of a system for automatic detection of diabetic retinopathy from color fundus photographs in a large population of patients with diabetes. *Diabetes Care* **31** (2): 193–198.

Akram, M.U., Khalid, S., and Khan, S.A. (2013). Identification and classification of microaneurysms for early detection of diabetic retinopathy. *Pattern Recognition* **46** (1): 107–116.

Bengio, Y., Courville, A., and Vincent, P. (2013a). Representation learning: a review and new perspectives. *IEEE Transactions on Pattern Analysis and Machine Intelligence* **35** (8): 1798–1828.

Bengio, Y., Mesnil, G., Dauphin, Y., and Rifai, S. (2013b). Better mixing via deep representations. In: Proceedings of the 30th International Conference on Machine Learning (ICML-13), 552–560.

Bresnick, G.H., Mukamel, D.B., Dickinson, J.C., and Cole, D.R. (2000). A screening approach to the surveillance of patients with diabetes for the presence of vision-threatening retinopathy. *Ophthalmology* **107** (1): 19–24.

Cree, M.J., Olson, J.A., McHardy, K.C. et al. (1999). The preprocessing of retinal images for the detection of fluorescein leakage. *Physics in Medicine and Biology* **44** (1): 293.

Deng, L. and Yu, D. (2014). Deep learning: methods and applications. *Foundations and Trends ® in Signal Processing* **7** (3–4): 197–387.

Faust, O., Acharya, R., Ng, Y.-K. et al. (2012). Algorithms for the automated detection of diabetic retinopathy using digital fundus images: a review. *Journal of Medical Systems* **36** (1): 145–157.

Fleming, A.D., Philip, S., Goatman, K.A. et al. (2006). Automated microaneurysm detection using local contrast normalization and local vessel detection. *IEEE Transactions on Medical Imaging* **25** (9): 1223–1232.

Guariguata, L., Whiting, D.R., Hambleton, I. et al. (2014). Global estimates of diabetes prevalence for 2013 and projections for 2035. *Diabetes Research and Clinical Practice* **103** (2): 137–149.

Harangi, B., Lazar, I., and Hajdu, A. (2012). Automatic exudate detection using active contour model and regionwise classification. In: 2012 Annual International Conference of the IEEE Engineering in Medicine and Biology Society (EMBC), 5951–5954. IEEE.

Hinton, G.E. and Salakhutdinov, R.R. (2006). Reducing the dimensionality of data with neural networks. *Science* **313** (5786): 504–507.

Hinton, G., Deng, L., Yu, D. et al. (2012). Deep neural networks for acoustic modeling in speech recognition: the shared views of four research groups. *IEEE Signal Processing Magazine* **29** (6): 82–97.

Hsu, W., Pallawala, P.M.D.S., Lee, M.L., and Eong, K.-G.A. (2001). The role of domain knowledge in the detection of retinal hard exudates. In: Proceedings of the 2001 IEEE Computer Society Conference on Computer Vision and Pattern Recognition, 2001. CVPR 2001, Volume **2**, II. IEEE.

Patton, N., Aslam, T.M., MacGillivray, T. et al. (2006). Retinal image analysis: concepts, applications and potential. *Progress in Retinal and Eye Research* **25** (1): 99–127.

Peli, E. and Peli, T. (1989). Restoration of retinal images obtained through cataracts. *IEEE Transactions on Medical Imaging* **8** (4): 401–406.

Philip, S., Fleming, A.D., Goatman, K.A. et al. (2007). The efficacy of automated "disease/no disease" grading for diabetic retinopathy in a systematic screening programme. *British Journal of Ophthalmology* **91** (11): 1512–1517.

Pillai, A., Soundrapandiyan, R., Satapathy, S. et al. (2018). Local diagonal extrema number pattern: a new feature descriptor for face recognition. *Future Generation Computer Systems* **81**, 297–306.

Soundrapandiyan, R. and Chandra Mouli, P.V.S.S.R. (2016). A novel and robust rotation and scale invariant structuring elements based descriptor for pedestrian classification in infrared images. *Infrared Physics and Technology* **78**: 13–23.

Soundrapandiyan, R. and Chandra Mouli, P.V.S.S.R. (2017a). An approach to adaptive pedestrian detection and classification in infrared images based on human visual mechanism and support vector machine. *Arabian Journal for Science and Engineering* **43** (8): 3951–3963.

Soundrapandiyan, R. and Chandra Mouli, P.V.S.S.R. (2017b). Robust pedestrian detection in infrared images using rotation and scale invariant-based structure element descriptor. *International Journal of Signal and Imaging Systems Engineering* **10** (3): 157–167.

Tariq, A., Akram, M.U., Shaukat, A., and Khan, S.A. (2013). Automated detection and grading of diabetic maculopathy in digital retinal images. *Journal of Digital Imaging* **26** (4): 803–812.

Walter, T., Klein, J.-C., Massin, P., and Erginay, A. (2002). A contribution of image processing to the diagnosis of diabetic retinopathy-detection of exudates in color fundus images of the human retina. *IEEE Transactions on Medical Imaging* **21** (10): 1236–1243.

Wan, L., Zeiler, M., Zhang, S. et al. (2013). Regularization of neural networks using dropconnect. In: Proceedings of the 30th International Conference on Machine Learning (ICML-13), 1058–1066.

Wang, H., Hsu, W., Goh, K.G., and Lee, M.L. (2000). An effective approach to detect lesions in color retinal images. In: Proceedings IEEE Conference on Computer Vision and Pattern Recognition, 2000, Volume 2, 181–186. IEEE.

Welikala, R.A., Dehmeshki, J., Hoppe, A. et al. (2014). Automated detection of proliferative diabetic retinopathy using a modified line operator and dual classification. *Computer Methods and Programs in Biomedicine* **114** (3): 247–261.

Xiaohui, Z. and Chutatape, A. (2004). Detection and classification of bright lesions in color fundus images. In: 2004 International Conference on Image Processing, 2004. ICIP'04, Volume 1, 139–142. IEEE.

Zhang, X., Thibault, G., Decenciére, E. et al. (2014). Exudate detection in color retinal images for mass screening of diabetic retinopathy. *Medical Image Analysis* **18** (7): 1026–1043.

18

An Energy-Efficient Wireless Body Area Network Design in Health Monitoring Scenarios

Kannan Shanmugam[1] and Karthik Subburathinam[2]

[1] *Department of Computer Science and Engineering, Malla Reddy Engineering College, Hyderabad, India*
[2] *Department of Computer Science and Engineering, SNS College of Technology, Coimbatore, India*

18.1   Wireless Body Area Network

18.1.1   Overview

In concern with medical environment, a wireless body area network (WBAN) is a group of energy-constrained, persistent or nonpersistent, and lightweight wireless sensor nodes that are used to monitor the patient's health condition and the medical environment. As per the description given in IEEE 802.15.6 standard, medical environment is one of the crucial applications of WBAN (Jovanov et al. 2000). The applications of WBAN in medical and healthcare environment can be classified into three categories: wearable, implant and remote-controlled WBANs. The wearable WBAN is used in scenarios like monitoring the sleeping disorder, monitoring sport training, etc. Medical field functions like diabetic monitoring, cardio function monitoring, etc. can be fulfilled by wearable WBANs and these types of sensor devices are either implanted in a patient's body or transmitted in the bloodstream (Malan et al. 2004; Otto et al. 2005; Hanson et al. 2009). The remote-controlled WBANs are used for exchange of the patient medical information from one place to another for assisting back-end medical network. This will enable the speedy exchange of medical data on a particular patient from one to another to give speedy treatment.

The sensor nodes in the WBAN can be classified into three types based on their nature of work in the network, namely, coordinator, end nodes, and relay nodes. The communication between the two or more sensor nodes and the communication with other outside networks are coordinated and monitored by the coordinator nodes. Upon monitoring and controlling the sensor nodes,

Intelligent Pervasive Computing Systems for Smarter Healthcare, First Edition.
Arun Kumar Sangaiah, S.P. Shantharajah, and Padma Theagarajan.
© 2019 John Wiley & Sons, Inc. Published 2019 by John Wiley & Sons, Inc.

the coordinator receives or collects medical information from them. Later the collected information is transferred to medical care center or central server for further processing. In general the coordinator could be a personal digital assistant and they may transmit necessary information and notifications to users directly. Due to various limitations like small size, short transmission range, and less battery power, the end nodes are limited to collecting and transferring the sensing data to the nearby coordinator or the relay nodes. The end nodes and relay nodes are normally small-sized sensor devices that consist of sensing unit, power unit, communication, storage, and processing units. Sometimes the relay nodes can act as coordinator node when the actual coordinator is far away from the end nodes. In few cases, the WBAN may have special node called actuator. These nodes are meant for performing some small specific task when they are receiving the signals from the on-patient end nodes (Gyselinckx et al. 2007; Golmie et al. 2005).

18.1.2 Architectures of Wireless Body Area Network

In general, the healthcare monitoring system based on WBANs has been broadly composed of the following three-tier communication:

- Tier 1: Intra-WBAN communication
- Tier 2: Inter-WBAN communication
- Tier 3: Beyond-WBAN communication

Figure 18.1 gives an illustration on the working process of these three components.

18.1.2.1 Tier 1: Intra-WBAN Communication

In the intra-WBAN communication level, the communication between the sensor nodes and the coordinator nodes is considered. This level also includes the communication among the sensor end nodes. Here, the data transmission is limited to 2 m around the human body. Basically the star topology is utilized in the WBAN environment due to the limited size of the network. This also leads to crucial design of WBAN design. However, due to limited transmission range and irregular human body movement, the WBAN has great challenges to attain reliable communication. In WBAN, though the multi-hop communication causes higher transmission delays, at the same time it consumes lower power for transmissions (Cavalcanti et al. 2007).

18.1.2.2 Tier 2: Inter-WBAN Communication

This layer aims to connect the WBAN to broader network to improve or enhance the availability of the WBAN by connecting with the Internet and mobile networks. The entry point to the any mobile network is an access point (AP). Hence, WBAN's coordinator nodes establish a direct connection to these

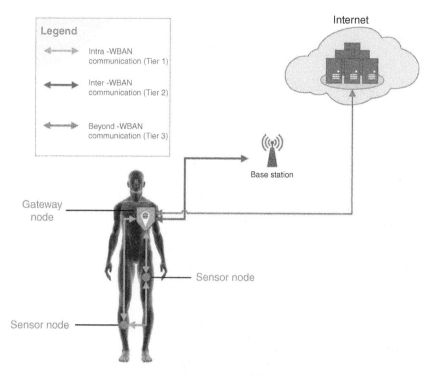

Figure 18.1 WBAN-based healthcare monitoring architecture.

APs, which will enable inter-WBAN communication in a limited space, for example, some conference room in a hospital (Figure 18.2).

18.1.2.3   Tier 3: Beyond-WBAN Communication

The major advantage of the WBAN system is to enable the doctors to perform remote diagnosis and give the formal instructions for treating the patient by the doctors in site. This could be achieved by establishing the communication medium between the AP and the outside work with the help of Internet resources. This kind of environment for the doctors as well as the patient for accessing the treatment database remotely allows the patients to get the automatic notifications about the series of treatments and follow-up of the given treatment (Figure 18.3).

18.1.3   Challenges Faced in System Design

In WBAN, reliability is most concern among anything since the treatments are given based on the values received by the communication. The following

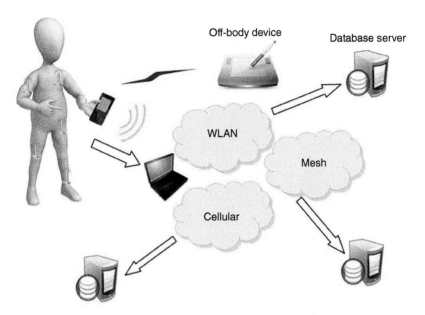

Figure 18.2 Inter-WBAN communication: infrastructure-based architecture.

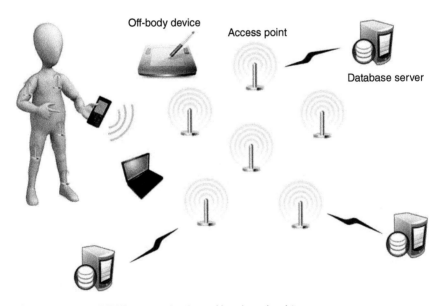

Figure 18.3 Inter-WBAN communication: ad hoc-based architecture.

are some of the most concerned challenges that need to be addressed in the WBANs (Ullah et al. 2008; Lo and Yang 2005; Ye et al. 2004).

18.1.3.1 Energy Constraint

Unlike wireless sensor networks, the WBANs are needed to be more energy-efficient. This is because the WBAN sensor nodes are likely to be implanted on or inside the human body. Large-sized sensors on or inside the human body will strongly persuade patient's day to day life activities and, hence, should not be larger in size than the WSN nodes.

On the other hand, by aiming the reduction in the size, it should not reduce the lifetime of the sensor devices. Because the nodes heavily depend on the energy of the batteries, these tiny sensors are expected to work for long durations, since replacement or charging is not an easy one. Hence, the transmission will be an effective one and might result in less consumption of energy.

18.1.3.2 Interference in Communication

All on-body and in-body sensor nodes in the human body could be controlled by the centralized coordinator node. This strategy will be the effective one unless there is a movement of the sensor node. For example, consider a case where there are number of patient coming together by wearing number of sensor nodes on them. In this case, the strategy designed for maintaining the coordination among the sensor nodes to their respective coordinator node may fail. This will lead to collision on data transmission to the coordinators. Hence, it is mandatory to have a good network design such that to have effective interference mitigation system to handle the topology changes in a very fast manner.

18.1.3.3 Security

The WBAN handles the personal and private data of the individual patient, that should not be known to anyone. Hence, the primary objective of WBAN system is to maintain such a private data with the highest security. The valuable patient's data stored and handled in the data center cannot be accessed by the public and it should be made available to the doctors irrespective of denial of service (DoS) attacks. Any attack to the data center of WBAN will lead to severe damage and worst results. However, it is very difficult to implement an encryption key mechanism in body area network since it has more limitations on battery, processing capability, storage, and transmission power.

18.1.4 Research Problems

Considering the various challenges in WBANs, this chapter aims to achieve reliable and energy-constrained communication among the sensor nodes and among the coordinator nodes. This chapter also considers some important aspects of network design such as scheduling scheme, fixing the transmission power to the nodes, usage of relay nodes, and number of sensor nodes for any coordinator.

The static scheduling schemes do the scheduling without considering the variation in the wireless channel on the MAC layer. Generally this kind of scheduling produces poor performances due to not avoiding bad channels completely and not demoralizing all good channels. In this chapter, we focus the effectiveness of opportunistic scheduling in less overhead WBAN environment, in which the current status of the wireless channel is considered to adjust the scheduling of the transmission and super-frame length. Also an outage rate is significantly reduced by effective scheduling in the data transmission, and it is illustrated in the following simulation study.

18.2 Proposed Opportunistic Scheduling

18.2.1 Introduction

This simulation study addresses the problem currently faced by the WBAN with fixed scheduling, which failed to react to the channel fluctuations: an opportunistic scheduling approach is proposed and executed. This scheduling utilizes a two-state Markov model and beacon-based time division multiple access (TDMA). Here, the two-state Markov models are used to count the state transition samples, which will be useful when estimating the probability distribution and channel dynamics in which the fixed scheduling failed. We use ρ as a factor to discounting by considering the highly dynamic characteristics of network for coordinating the coordinator nodes. From the studies in the literature, it is shown that the Markov model delivers much better estimations on state values since this method produces more perfect transition probability values for modeling the wireless channel (Patel et al. 2012).

We also propose and prove that the heuristic scheduling method is performing comparatively good and optimal under some insignificant assumptions. Based on the literature study and observation, we further extend the proposed method to dynamic adjustment in length of the super frame according to the status of the channel.

The designed system follows the principle based on super-frame length. Within the super-frame range, the dynamic scheduling does not have much control on it when the length of the frame is small. On the other hand, the current condition of the channel is unreliable or the frame length could not be large.

The simulation results show that the proposed dynamic heuristic scheduling with super-frame adjustment methods results in better performance than the fixed scheduling and any other opportunistic scheduling approaches considered in the study. In particular, the dynamic scheduling avoids at least 8% of outage when compared with static or fixed scheduling. Also the dynamic heuristic frame length adjustment scheme gains 25% more of the overall system's throughput when compared with the flipping method and 30% than the random method.

18.2.2 System Model and Problem Formulation

18.2.2.1 System Model

This proposed system model adopts star topology with one-hop routing. It is due to the scenario that is considered here in health monitoring environment, where the communication of signals between the sensor nodes and the coordinator node is more frequent. Hence, one-hop communication between the sensor nodes and the coordinator node may result in better throughput. It is recommended to use beacon-enabled TDMA mode of process by IEEE 201.15.4 for WBANs, since the coordinator nodes are mobile devices. At the beginning of every super frame, the beacon frame is broadcasted to all the coordinator nodes in the network for resource allocation and synchronization among the coordinator nodes. Because of this super frame, synchronized process in every node will be activated in the allocated time slots and can go for transmission (Darkins et al. 2008; Akkaya et al. 2005).

Each time slot is defined by two channel states and they are named as good and bad state; also they are represented by 1 and 0, respectively. Based on the literature studies, the Gilbert model is chosen since it is very effective on dynamic behavior of on-body sensor network environment and also the probing of the wireless channel is not feasible. The current status of the coordinator node is monitored only during the node's transmission of signals to the coordinator. On the other hand, during the idle time slots, the system uses the state belief information instead of current channel status to calculate the current status or condition of the channel. For the node i, the state transition matrix at super-frame time slot $P^i(K)$ is represented as follows:

$$P^i(K) == \begin{pmatrix} P_{00}^i(k) & P_{01}^i(k) \\ P_{10}^i(k) & P_{11}^i(k) \end{pmatrix} \tag{18.1}$$

At this state of transition for the ith node, the initial state belief is represented as

$$\begin{bmatrix} P_0^i(k) \\ P_1^i(k) \end{bmatrix} \tag{18.2}$$

Hence, the state belief of the ith node at super-frame time slot n can be premeditated as

$$\begin{bmatrix} P_0^i(n) \\ P_1^i(n) \end{bmatrix}^T = \begin{bmatrix} P_0^i(0) \\ P_1^i(0) \end{bmatrix}^T \prod_{k=1}^{n} \begin{pmatrix} P_{00}^i(k) & P_{01}^i(k) \\ P_{10}^i(k) & P_{11}^i(k) \end{pmatrix} \tag{18.3}$$

where

$P_0^i(0)$ – Probability value of channel to be a bad channel.

$P_1^i(0)$ – Probability value to have good channel during the transition.

18.2.2.2 Problem Formulation

By considering the objective as maximizing the successful attempts in a number of packet transmissions from the sensor nodes to the coordinator for attaining higher throughput in the systems, assume that the quality belief of the channel is represented by $h_i^r(\tau)$, which represents the probability values for the ith sensor node to have a good channel at time slot τ in round r. Thus the problem is expressed as follows:

$$\text{Maximize} \sum_{1\leq i\leq M,1\leq\tau\leq T,1\leq r<\alpha} h_i^r(\tau)L_i^r(\tau) \tag{18.4}$$

Subject to $\sum_{1\leq i\leq M}L_i^r(\tau) \leq 1$

$\sum_{1\leq\tau\leq T}L_i^r(\tau) \leq x_i$

where

$L_i^r(\tau)$: Scheduling of the node i at slot τ in round r.

x_i: Number of packets to be transmitted by the node i in one round.

M : Number of nodes.

T : Number of slots in a round.

As mentioned previously, the calculation of $h_i^r(\tau)$ is done in each round in an independent manner. These independent local solutions in the attempt of increasing the network throughput by maximizing the successful transmissions at individual rounds will make up the optimal global solution.

18.2.3 Heuristic Scheduling

Based on the study, a greedy method that has low complexity than the other methods is considered to guarantee the tolerable complexity during the scheduling. To accomplish this during the scheduling, the sensor nodes are formed as two different groups. On the one hand, one group will contain the set of sensor nodes whose transmission was successful during the last round. However, on the other hand, the other group combine the set of sensor nodes whose transmission failed or was unsuccessful during the last round (Otto et al. 2006). When a sensor node goes for forwarding more than one packet, then the node's last transmission of packet in that specific round is considered to find which group the node belongs. However, the successful node's transmission must be scheduled before the failed node's transmission. Due to this advantage, a node with the good channel will have the advantage to access the channel before it becomes worse; at the same time the nodes with the bad channel may have sufficient time to recover from the failed state to success state to have good channel.

In addition, by using the success rates of the transmission and transition matrix estimation values during the last round, we can calculate state belief in any random time slot of the considered current round. By the same way, the future time slot for the future round also can be estimated. Based on the literature study, almost all the WBAN has the coherence time of 400 ms and it is longer than the length of the super-frame, which is considered in this system design. Hence, the estimated channel belief will be reliable.

The calculation of P_1^i to approximate h_i^r is in the objective function, where the last communication in the previous round is the early state belief of P_1^i. It is proved that P_1^i progress as an exponential function. Here, we skip the round number r and use εi to symbolize the probability value of transiting to good channel from bad channel $P_{01}^i(r)$ and δi is considered to represent the probability value of transiting to bad channel from good channel $P_{10}^i(r)$. This is taken by the basis of dynamic channel properties during the scheduling.

The calculation of channel state belief to have good channel at given time t can be represented in the following formula;

$$P_1^i(t) = \begin{cases} \left[1 + \dfrac{\delta_i}{\varepsilon_i}(1 - \varepsilon_i - \delta_i)^t\right] \dfrac{\varepsilon_i}{\varepsilon_i + \delta_i}, & \text{Successful node} \\ [1 + (1 - \varepsilon_i - \delta_i)^t] \dfrac{\varepsilon_i}{\varepsilon_i + \delta_i}, & \text{Failed node} \end{cases} \tag{18.5}$$

where t is the number of time slots away from the initial state, which is the result of the previous transmission.

Here we considered that fluctuation range of the current channel belief could be the heuristic function. In specific, to all successive sensor nodes, we are determining the difference of channel belief of each node between the start and end of the round for all successful node's transmission. Let us assume N_i is a cumulative number of time slots that happened between previous transmission of ith node and commencement of the next round. Also assume every successful transmission is assigned with N_{Good} number of time slots.

Hence, the utility function for successive nodes is calculated as per the given formula (18.6):

$$U_i = P_1^i(N_i) - P_1^i(N_i + N_{\text{good}}) \tag{18.6}$$

Figure 18.4 shows the design of scheduling the node at front that has the larger utility function. Let us assume five sensor nodes, in that one among five nodes failed while transmitting the packet.

Similarly, the failed node's utility function is calculated as per the given formula (18.7):

$$U_i = P_1^i(N_i + T - N_{\text{bad}}) - P_1^i(N_i + T) \tag{18.7}$$

where N_{bad} represents the failed node's time slot and T is the total number of time slots in a single round.

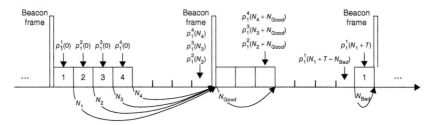

Figure 18.4 Illustration of utility function calculation.

Algorithm 1: Heuristic scheduling

Initialize: $r = 1$, $W^i_{s1,s2}(r) = 0$, random schedule for 1st round.
   While $r \geq 1$ *do*
  Transmission as per the schedule;
  for $i = 1,2; \ldots,M$ do
    if S_1 is observed at one slot and S_2 at the next then

$$W^i_{s1,s2}(r) = W^i_{s1,s2}(r) + 1;$$

    end if
  End for
  for $i = 1,2,\ldots,M$ do

$$P^i_{s1,s2}(r) = \frac{W^i_{s1,s2}(r)}{\sum_s W^i_{s1,s2}(r)}$$

  End for
  To schedule successive nodes at front and failed nodes at last;
  Calculate Utility function U_i and sort each group in
  decreasing order;
  $r = r+1;$
End while

This utility function works in such a way that the scheduling process must be fast enough to schedule the node, which has the successive transmission in the previous round, which depreciates fast. Also the scheduling must be completed as early as possible so that the successive node can complete the transmission before the transmission channel becomes bad. Similarly, when a channel state improves from bad state to good state for a node, previous transmission failed. Then this node should be scheduled as soon as possible in its own group. The below pseudo code shows this approach in Algorithm 1.

The complexity of the proposed dynamic scheduling approach is represented as $O(M \times N_p + M \log M)$ by assuming that at every round of packet transmission, each sensor node transmits an average of N_p packets. However, this complexity is insignificant for the coordinator nodes whose load is low and has limited number of sensor nodes. In practical, the mere requirement of sharing the same $\varepsilon + \delta$ value by all sensor nodes is true and the proposed dynamic heuristic approach achieved this.

18.2.4 Dynamic Super-Frame Length Adjustment

Based on the literature study, the effectiveness of time slot scheduling within some assured round is relatively limited due to an improper length of the super frame. The reason behind this is that the channel property does not change too much in certain rounds where the length of the super frame is short. In this scenario the process of time slot scheduling will become unimportant. On the other hand, the state belief of a channel converges to steady state and hardly has any details for scheduling when the system has lengthy super frame. Moreover, the length of the super frame changes dynamically when the objective gesture changes (Venkatasubramanian et al. 2005).

Hence, we propose a dynamic Super-Frame length adjustment approach based on temporal difference (TD) error. By this approach, the performance of the proposed dynamic system improves further.

18.2.4.1 Problem Formulation

In the processes of determining the length of the super frame, the coordinator node will act as an agent and it is responsible to make decisions based on "states" and "rewards." The terms states, rewards, and action are defined as follows:

1) *State:* Packet delivery rate (PDR) at the last round.
2) *Action:* Determining length of the super frame T and choosing a packet by its number to deliver in x_ith round.
3) Reward: Reward (rw) = $(1 - \text{PDR}) + \text{PDR}$ at state.

During the dynamic computation and adjustment of the super frame while data is being transmitted, to maintain the constant rate of data, the length will be calculated by multiple of minutes length T_0. And the total number of packets to be transmitted x_i will be dynamically calculated and adjusted proportionally to T. We use the function $Q(s, a)$, which represents value of performing action a in state s. In every state the approach chooses the action with the highest Q value. The following equation shows the dynamic calculation of action value function:

$$Q(s, a) = \sum_{s'} P(s' \mid s, a)[rw(s, a, s') + \gamma \max_{a'} Q(s', a')] \tag{18.8}$$

Algorithm 2: Dynamic super frame length adjustment

Initialize Q(s,a) at random, default length of super frame: T_0, default packet no.: x_{i0} in single super frame, r = 1;

while r $\geq$ 1, do

Step 1 : decide action as per Q(s,a) values being ε-greedy. T=a X T_0, x_i=a X x_{i0};

Step 2 : do heuristic forecast and send out with length T and packet no x_i;

Step 3 : scrutinize transmission result and calculate rw and the new state s';

Step 4 : revise Q(s, a) belief using

$Q(s, a) \leftarrow Q(s, a) + \alpha[rw + \gamma^{max}_{a'} Q(s', a') - Q(s, a)]$

Step 5 : s $\leftarrow$ $s', r - r + 1$.

end while

Here we use Q learning method to calculate the Q value in action value function. This is because of considering the difficulties on obtaining the value of transition probability.

$$Q(s, a) \leftarrow Q(s, a) + \alpha[rw + \gamma^{max}_{a'} Q(s', a') - Q(s, a)] \tag{18.9}$$

Algorithm 2 gives the pseudo code for this above approach.

18.3 Performance Analysis Environment and Metrics

The experiment is conducted by using five sensor nodes and one coordinator node on human body. The time slot is fixed as 5 ms. The number of packets transmitted by every sensor node is assumed as identical (Vijendra 2011). The channel samples are used as datasets. For any subject, five channels are allocated as gain channels. This experiment collects the data from the five sensor nodes that are placed in different locations on the body of an adult object. When the gain at the channel is less than the fixed outage threshold value, outage is starting to occur and results in failed transmission. The final value of the result is arrived by averaging the considered all eight datasets. In the comparison study two other scheduling schemes are also considered to assess the performance of the proposed dynamic scheduling. The first one is random scheduling method, in which the sensor nodes are grouped into successive group and failed group. The second method is flipping method. Here, the performance of the fixed scheduling method is considered as baseline to evaluate the performance of the proposed dynamic scheme. The experiment and the simulations are performed on MATLAB environment.

18.3.1 Heuristic Scheduling with Fixed Super-Frame Length

This section presents the performance of heuristic scheduling over fixed and flipping approaches. Figure 18.5 shows the impact of the number of delivered packets for each sensor nodes in each round of transmission. In this evaluation all the nodes are allowed to have 80 rounds of transmission of packets in order to have a wide range of results with respect to packet delivery ratio. So this simulation will take 400 ms long, which is close to on-body channel's coherence value. The results show that the design of placing the successive nodes at the front and the failed nodes at the last in every individual round gains better packet delivery ratio when compared with fixed scheduling at the outage value of 80 dB. This also shows that the heuristic scheduling approach results with better value than the flipping method.

Figure 18.6 shows the performance of different length of super frames with respect to outage rate reduction. When the length is 20 slots, each sensor node is allowed to transmit two packets. Further, the number of packets to be transmitted increases proportionally, and the length is maintained as constant rate. The figure reveals that the proposed scheduling scheme performs better than the other two considered approaches. The curve presented in the figure has the consistency throughout the simulation. It depicts that a medium length of the super frame has a good balance between the accuracy level of estimated channel state and scheduling outcomes.

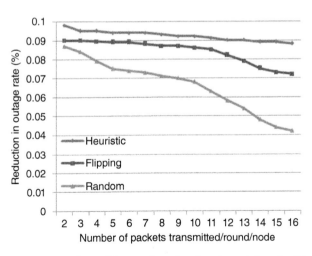

Figure 18.5 Effects of the number of packets in static length of the frame.

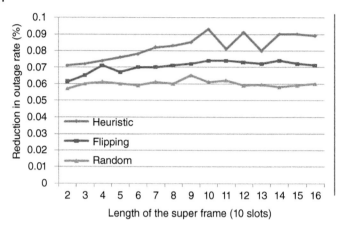

Figure 18.6 Effects of the length of the super frame.

18.3.2 Heuristic Scheduling with Dynamic Super-Frame Length

In this section, we discuss the performance and its comparison of dynamic adjustment of length of the super-frame approach with the proposed heuristic scheduling method. As per the literature study it is observed that the length of the super frame should not be growing large in unreasonable manner. This will effect in worst performance of channel belief estimation of unreliable channel. So it is necessary to restrict the growing of super frame unnecessarily. To achieve this, here we set T_0 as default initial value, which is more over equal value adopted in other models. Figure 18.7 shows the performance of proposed dynamic method. The number of packets to be transmitted per round is fixed in a range of 2–7 for the other fixed length methods. The dynamic method is fixed with the initial value of X_{i0}. The figure depicts that the proposed heuristic scheduling and the variable length schemes are showing better performance than any other static methods.

18.4 Summary

The communication between the coordinator and sensor nodes in WBAN are crucial part to improve the performance of the network. The dynamic and heuristic super-frame length adjustment methods are introduced for measuring and controlling the super-frame length to improve the performance in packet transmissions between the sensor nodes and the coordinator nodes. The heuristic scheme is used to estimate the length of the super frame to regulate the packet transmission, which is based on the utility function. The dynamic adjustment method is also used to estimate the length of the super

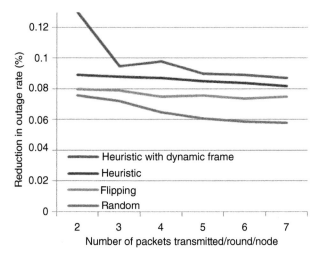

Figure 18.7 Effects of the number of packets in dynamic length.

frame and to improve the efficiency in the packet transmission rate. The performances of the above approaches are compared against two other static methods, namely, flipping and random methods. The simulation results are showing that the heuristic and dynamic frame length adjustment methods are performing better against the static methods in all the considered conditions.

Bibliography

Akkaya, K., Younis, M. and Youssef, M. (2005). Efficient aggregation of delay-constrained data in wireless sensor networks. *Proceeding of ACS/IEEE International Conference on Computer Systems and Applications.*

Cavalcanti, D., Schmitt, R., and Soomro, A. (2007). Performance analysis of 802.15.4 and 802.11e for body sensor network applications. *4th International Workshop on Wearable and Implantable Body Sensor Networks, BSN.*

Darkins, A., Ryan, P., Kobb, R. et al. (2008). *Telemedicine and e-Health* **14** (10): 1118–1126. https://doi.org/10.1089/tmj.2008.0021.

Golmie, N., Cypher, D., and Rebala, O. (2005). Performance analysis of low rate wireless technologies for medical applications. *Computer Communications* **28** (10): 1255–1275.

Gyselinckx, B., Penders, J., and Vullers, R. (2007). Potential and challenges of body area networks for cardiac monitoring. *Journal of Electrocardiolog,* **40** (6): S165–S168.

Hanson, M.A., Powell, H.C. Jr., Barth, A.T. et al. (2009). Body area sensor networks challenges and opportunities. *IEEE Computer Society* **42** (1): 58–65.

Jovanov, E., Price, J., Raskovic, D. et al. (2000). Wireless personal area networks in telemedical environment. *Proceedings of the Third International Conference on Information technology in Biomedicine (ITAB-ITIS2000).* Arlington, VA, pp. 22–27.

Lo, B. and Yang, G.Z. (2005). Key technical challenges and current implementations of body sensor networks. *IEEE Proceedings of the 2nd International Workshop on Body Sensor Networks (BSN'05)* (April), pp. 1–5.

Malan, D., Fulford-Jones, T.R.F. Welsh, M., and Moulton, S. (2004). CodeBlue: an ad hoc sensor network infrastructure for emergency medical care. *Proceedings of the MobiSys 2004 Workshop on Applications of Mobile Embedded Systems (WAMES 2004).* Boston, MA, (June), pp. 12–14.

Otto, C., Gober, J.P., McMurtrey, R.W. et al. (2005). An implementation of hierarchical signal processing on a wireless sensor in TinyOS environment. *Proceedings of the 43rd ACM Southeastern Conference,* Kennesaw, GA (March), Vol. 2, pp. 49–53.

Otto, C., Milenkovic, A., and Sanders, C. (2006, 2006). System architecture of a wireless body area sensor network for ubiquitous health monitoring. *Journal of Mobile Multimedia* **1** (4): 307–326.

Patel, S., Park, H., Bonato, P. et al. (2012). A review of wearable sensors and systems with application in rehabilitation. *Journal of NeuroEngineering and Rehabilitation* **9**: 21. https://doi.org/10.1186/1743-0003-9-21.

Ullah, S., Higgins, H., Cho, Y.W. et al. (2008). Towards RF communication and multiple access protocols in a body sensor network. *JDCTA: International Journal of Digital Content Technology and Its Applications* **2** (3): 9–16.

Venkatasubramanian, K., Deng, G., Mukherjee, T. et al. (2005). Ayushman A wireless sensor network based health monitoring infrastructure and testbed. *Springer Lecture Notes in Computer Science* **3560**: 406–407.

Vijendra, S. (2011). Efficient clustering for high dimensional data: subspace based clustering and density based clustering. *Information Technology Journal* **10** (6): 1092–1105.

Ye, W., Heidemann, J., and Estrin, D. (2004). Medium access control with coordinated adaptive sleeping for wireless sensor networks. *IEEE Communications Letters* **12** (3): 493–506.

Index

Intelligent Pervasive Computing Systems for Smarter Healthcare, First Edition.
Arun Kumar Sangaiah, S.P. Shantharajah, and Padma Theagarajan.
© 2019 John Wiley & Sons, Inc. Published 2019 by John Wiley & Sons, Inc.